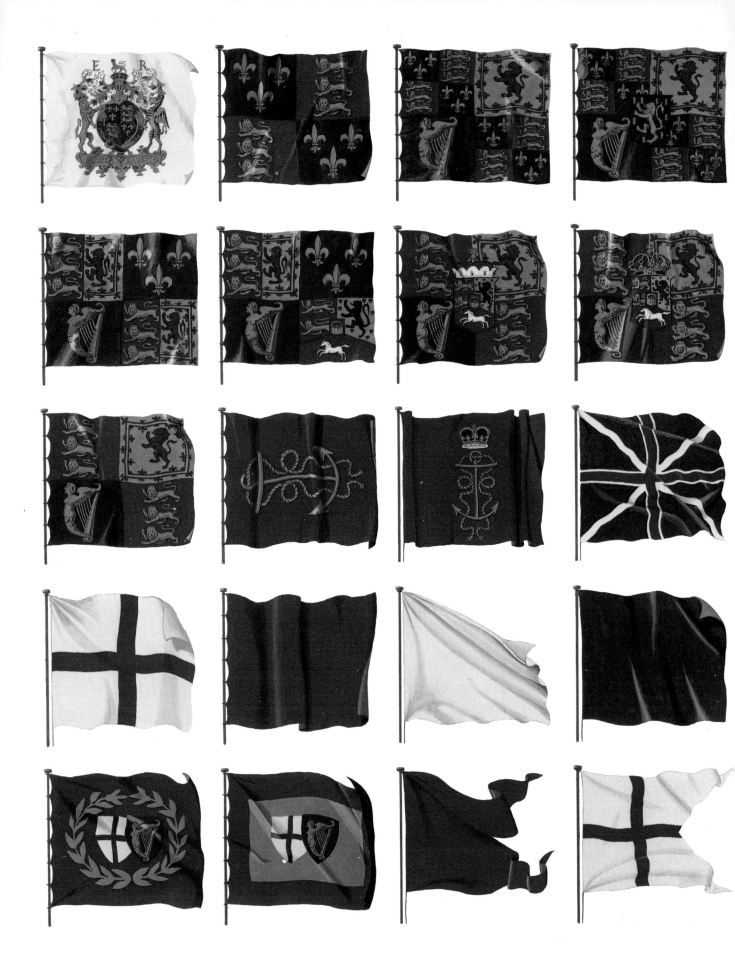

The Best
of
Antique Collecting

The articles in this book first appeared in
Antique Collecting,
the journal of the Antique Collectors' Club,
between September, 1979, and September, 1981.

Antique Collectors' Club

Published for the Antique Collectors' Club by the
Antique Collectors' Club Ltd.

Printed in England by Baron Publishing, Woodbridge, Suffolk

Frontispiece:
Flags from England and Britain illustrated in the Dictionary of Sea Painters *by E.H.H. Archibald,
published by the Antique Collectors' Club. Left to right, top to bottom: Lord Admiral, late 16th-
early 17th century; standard of the Tudors; standard of the Stuarts, 1603-1689, and Lord High
Admiral from c.1618 and 1702-07; standard of William III and Lord High Admiral; standard of
Queen Anne and Lord High Admiral to 1709; royal standard 1714-1801; standard of George III
from 1801-16; royal standard 1816-37; royal standard 1837 to present; admiralty flag from c.1620
and Lord High Admiral since 1709; admiralty flag of James II; Union flag 1603-1801; flag of Saint
George used by Elizabethan and Jacobean flag officers, flag officers of the white 1700-1864, full
admiral 1864-present; flag of command of vice and rear admirals of the red, 1660-1864, admirals of
the red 1805-64; flag of command of admirals (including vice and rear) of the white 1660 to the
1690s; flag of command of admirals (including vice and rear) of the blue, 1660-1864; flag of generals
at sea, c.1650-58; other flag officers during the Commonwealth; commodores' broad pendant
1674-1864; commodores' broad pendant from 1864.*

Introduction

Fifteen years ago the Antique Collectors' Club came into existence. The idea of formalising a series of social contacts based on a mutual passion for antiques into a club had been mooted for some time, but it was not until a three line classified advertisement appeared in the *Sunday Times* and resulted in some 150 replies that the idea took off. The object of the Club was, and is, the dissemination of practical knowledge about collectable antiques among collectors; so it became a first essential to establish a means of communication.

The first issues of the Club magazine were modest. Typed and duplicated, they lacked illustrations simply because, using an office duplicator, pictures were not technically possible. The standard of the first articles must have been on a par, for a piece expounding the quality of cabriole legs resulted in an enthusiastic but puzzled letter, asking what a cabriole leg was! Enthusiasm and encouragement have always been strongly sustaining features of the Club with the result that the membership has grown and continues to do so.

But growth stemmed also from the fact that the magazine provided two elements lacking in contemporary conventional magazines. Firstly, trying to learn about antiques ourselves, we were acutely conscious of the lack of information for collectors to enable them to make an informed judgement on the genuineness or quality of the piece being offered, let alone the value for money that their prospective purchase represented. Cynically we noted the bulk of dealers advertising in the commercial advertising magazines and reasoned that any discussion of authenticity or comments on values would be excluded from magazines which relied heavily on advertising income. So the Club journal became the first antiques magazine to discuss prices, comment on quality and value for money and to be run without the help of advertising revenue. Secondly we offered collectors social contacts based on a mutual interest in antique collecting. Regional clubs formed; now their activity extends well outside Britain and they are autonomous.

The "For Sales" columns, based on the principle that the seller is the person to woo, not the buyer (a point taken up by the major London auction houses a decade later when they introduced the buyer's premium), have always attracted long lists of antiques (or near antiques) for sale privately. The nominal charge to the potential buyer for the contact has never paid for the space the feature occupies in the magazine, but the interest it has caused and the specialist collecting contacts that have been made more than justify its existence.

The lack of illustrations in the early issues imposed restrictions that taught the lesson that a picture (or, more correctly, the right photograph) is worth a hundred words. So, as soon as funds could be raised (and here we would like to say "thank you" to Barclays Bank who, despite some hairy moments, not least of which was the prolonged postal strike of 1971, have never refused a request for money), a small bankrupt local printing works was purchased. Not only could we illustrate the magazine but now the door was opened to the publishing of books.

Books on antiques in the 1960s suffered from the same faults as the magazines: lack of practical help for collectors. The few illustrations in most of the books were of museum quality pieces which we, the small private collectors, had no hope of ever owning, while the subjects of fakes, forgeries and improvements, with one or two isolated and honourable exceptions, such as Symonds' excellent works, were entirely ignored.

So, based on auctions and amateur photographs, the first edition of *The Price Guide to Antique Furniture* appeared. It was the first book on antique furniture to discuss prices to be published in England for nearly half a century. For present-day collectors surrounded by a plethora of imitations and derivations on the theme it is hard to visualise the impact that John Andrews' first book made when it appeared at Christmas 1968. We were in the classic position of selling more than we could print or, in those days, hand-bind ourselves. Over the next decade the Club published some sixteen specialist price guides. Of course, as readers who know them will appreciate, the Price Guide contains a great deal more than just prices; indeed many of them contain more practical help on collecting than most textbooks.

The 1960s and the 1970s were the decades of prosperity generally and antique collecting flourished. The media found "the treasure in your attic" magic irresistible while the ever expanding great auction houses could always bring forward examples to show that the football pools were by no means the only way to riches. Gradually commercial antiques magazines started to quote prices and books appeared devoted solely to fakes and forgeries. The world of commercial publishing climbed on the bandwagon and one can now buy books stuffed with illustrations which seem to imply that between one set of covers is to be found the key to valuing antiques. This trend has clearly gone too far: one doesn't need to be a collector to realise that a specialist subject calls for a specialist book which is perhaps why *The Price Guide to Antique Furniture* has probably sold more copies than any other book on the subject.

Spurred on by the requirements of members frustrated by the lack of good books on their subject, the book publishing expanded to areas of interest unconnected with values. A series of books on individual types of clocks has no rivals while the books on British art of various periods (18th century, Victorian, 1880-1940) are the standard works on the subject and are to be found in reference libraries throughout the world. This success has greatly benefited the magazine for authors are more often than not collectors themselves and their comments on current price trends and individual sales attract a knowledgeable audience. Whatever the reasons, the fact is that *Antique Collecting*, the Club magazine, from which the extracts that follow are taken, has steadily increased its circulation since it was formed, as opposed to two of its commercial rivals whose circulation has now almost halved from their peak figures.

We hope that you will find a good proportion of the articles of interest and that, having had a glimpse of what we publish, you will be tempted to join the Club.

Membership costs £8.95 for the U.K., £10 for overseas and $22.50 for the U.S.A. and Canada, and the eleven monthly issues of ANTIQUE COLLECTING *(none in August) are sent free of charge to members. Copies sent by airmail, however, cost extra.*

For Collectors — By Collectors — About Collecting
The Antique Collectors' Club, 5 Church Street, Woodbridge, Suffolk

Contents

The Articles

The articles in this book
first appeared over the last two years in
ANTIQUE COLLECTING

the monthly journal of the Antique Collectors' Club.
They represent only a selection of those that are published.
The various editorial comments on current trends, dates
for forthcoming antiques fairs and auctions, details of club

meetings, etc., have all been
omitted, as have the long lists
of antiques for sale privately.

Fakes in 19th Century British Pottery

Figure 1. Value as fake £10-£15.

taken from *The Price Guide to 19th and 20th Century British Pottery* by David Battie and Michael Turner *recently published* by the *Antique Collectors' Club*

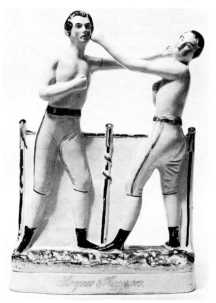

Figure 2. Staffordshire c.1860. Height 13ins. No mark. An extremely rare group of the boxers, John Carmel Heenan and Tom Sayers, of which only a handful of examples is known. Smaller examples of a slightly later date are more readily available, £80-£150, as are quantities of modern reproductions (figure 1), which are good enough to fool the unwary. £250-£300.

The collector of 19th century British pottery is still quite secure when it comes to fakes. There has been little, up until the last few years, to warrant the serious attention of the faker with the exception of the continuation of the production of a few Staffordshire models, particularly dogs, mostly from the original moulds. With some original figures now fetching in the upper hundreds and reproductions being cheap to produce from easily obtained clay and glazes and fired at a low temperature, it is inevitable that more and more dubious figures will come on the market.

The boxers (figure 1) are a fair example of a recast from the original Heenan and Sayers group (figure 2). They display many of the faults found with copies, such as the too smooth and black hair and boots, and poorly drawn features, the ill considered gilding and the flat pink of the bodies. These superficial characteristics are, however, nothing like as condemning as the inherent faults in the production such as

the difference in size caused by the shrinkage in the clay during the firing process, in this case from the original 13ins. to 8⅝ins. (22cm). The Price Guide can be used to establish the size of the original figures and anything smaller should be looked at with care, but remember that many figures were made in different sizes. If in doubt check with P.D. Gordon-Pugh's *Staffordshire Portrait Figures and Allied Subjects of the Victorian Era.*

Perhaps the best guide to modern reproductions is the glaze crackle, wrong in figure 3 and right in figure 4. In the former the glaze is tight to the body and, where it forms pools, is glassy and clear and the crazing very uniform and the cracks brown. On the original the glaze varies in thickness, often forming blobs at the base and pools where it is a distinctly blue colour, the crazing being clear or black.

The Staffordshire cottage (figure 5) is a far more sophisticated fake than Heenan and Sayers; the glaze is only slightly too shiny and with a far more convincing crackle, but the base has the same wiped-clean look as the former. The colours do not have the same density of shade as the originals and they are too heavily potted. These houses are appearing with different names and places in country sales rooms. Compare with the original in figure 6.

Another form of fake which appears fairly regularly is the spirit flask or jug, reproducing in earthenware what should be stoneware. The jug in figure 7 apparently commemorates the death of Wellington in 1852 but the lettering is the best give-away of the reproduction. On the originals it was impressed from bookbinders' or printers' type and is crisp and clear; on the copies it forms part of the mould and the definition is

lost. Here the jug is under a brown glaze that is far too shiny and consistent. The spirit flask in figure 8 is under a more mottled glaze on a greyish body, both have the curious thinning of the glaze round the bottom of the piece. Compare with an original in figure 9.

I have recently seen, and they are apparently turning up in country salerooms in fair numbers, porcelain jugs and vases with black photo-lithographic copies of the Victoria and other coronation prints. It is hard to believe that they would fool anyone with any knowledge, but the marks on the piece I saw had been ground off the base, and an attempt is being made at deception.

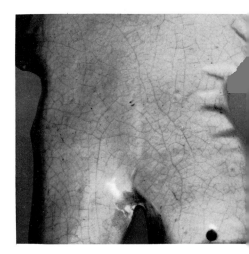

Left: Figure 3. Glaze crackle on a modern reproduction.

Right: Figure 4. Glaze crackle on an original.

Right: Figure 6. F. & L. Pratt c.1800. Height 4½ins. No mark. A small money box in the form of a house and typically glazed in browns, green and ochre. These money boxes and pastille burners are generally considered as late 18th century but some would appear to be considerably later, probably cast from the same moulds. £70-£100.

Figure 5. Value as fake £15-£20.

Figure 10 illustrates an awful warning to the unwary, the dish appearing as a perfectly respectable piece of George Jones majolica moulded with leaves, cherries and twigs under the usual bright, clear glazes. The close up detail in figure 11 just discloses the deception; the squirrel which originally sat on the twigs has been broken off and the remains ground down leaving only traces of the feet, the stumps having been restored. A complete nut dish is illustrated in figure 12.

Sunderland lustre is a great problem as the jugs and mugs with famous bridges have been in almost continuous production since 1800 and it is impossible to decide whether one made in 1820, 1850, 1900, 1930 or a brand new one is a fake. The earlier the piece, generally speaking, the finer and lighter the body and the better the pink splashing.

Figure 7. Value as fake £10-£15.

Figure 9. Probably Lambeth c.1825. Height 8ins. No mark. A stoneware spirit flask as the Duke of York and titled. Unusually well detailed and glazed an attractive honey brown on the upper half stopping smartly at his waist. The reverse is impressed with a retailer's name and address. This is a good example of a rare flask. £120-£180. Less well cast £60-£100.

Figure 11. Close up of "repair" to nut dish in figure 10.

Figure 8. Value as fake £8-£12.

Figure 10. Value as fake 50p-£2.

Figure 12. Possibly George Jones c.1870. Width 10ins. Impressed registration mark. £60-£80.

DINING ROOM FURNITURE
1730 - 1830

by Jerome Phillips

Until the later 17th century dining took place in the hall, there being no separate dining room, and of course this earlier custom continued for many decades afterwards. Yet by 1803 Thomas Sheraton could write that "the dining room is one of the principal apartments of a house and ought always to be of bold and accommodating proportions. The large sideboard, inclosed or surrounded with Ionic pillars; the handsome and extensive dining table; the respectable and substantial looking chairs; the large face glass; the family portraits; the marble fire places; and the Wilton carpets; are the furniture that should supply the dining room". The main pieces of dining furniture are of course dining tables, dining chairs, side tables or sideboards.

By the late 17th century there were two main types of dining tables, both oak (or at least nearly always so); the so-called "refectory" dining table and the oval gate-leg table with turned legs and stretchers. The virtual absence of walnut dining tables in the early 18th century, when walnut was clearly the fashionable wood for nearly all other types of furniture, can only lead one to the conclusion that these oak tables continued to be used well into the early 18th century.

The earliest mahogany dining tables, dating from the 1730s, were the so-called drop leaf type (figures 1 and 2), in many ways an extension of the oak gate-leg tables. Occasionally these tables had ends, leaves being inserted between them. From about 1750 to about 1790 the dining tables consisted of two circular ends with a gate-leg centre section, all the legs being straight. Thomas Chippendale supplied a table of this type for Sir Rowland Winn in 1766. That dining tables seem to have been made in this conservative taste for a

Figure 1. A mahogany drop leaf dining table with pad feet, of early Georgian period, c.1730. Most such tables consist of only one section with a flap on each side.

Figure 2. The same table split into two separate parts as side tables. A similar table is at Hampton Court Palace.

Figure 3. A mahogany two pillar dining table of the Sheraton period, c.1790. This table has boldly curved legs on the pillars, whereas in the early 19th century this form was replaced by the less attractive "hump" leg in the pillar.

period of forty years is somewhat surprising. The highly sophisticated styles of the time, such as rococo, Chinese, Gothic and neo-classical, might as well never have been, as far as the dining table was concerned.

It was only in the very late 18th century that significant changes occurred, with the introduction of the "pillar" dining table and the various forms of "patent" tables. In 1791 Thomas Sheraton mentions the "large range of dining tables, standing on pillars with four claws each, which is now the fashionable way of making these tables". The late 18th century pillar tables (figure 3) were marked by bold curved legs and simple box castors, whereas in the Regency period such tables tended to be less attractive, with "humps" in the pillars, which rather spoilt the design. Most of these tables had two ends, each supported by a pillar, and a centre leaf, hence being known as two pillar dining tables. There

were, however, three and even four pillar tables, presumably made for larger dining rooms.

The other change was the introduction of various "patent" dining tables, which attracted the attention of some ingenious inventors around this time. Gillows of Lancaster received a patent in 1800 for the "telescopic dining table". This table still had legs, not pillars, although usually reeded, but the legs could be moved, thus enlarging or reducing the length of the table as required (figures 4, 5 and 6). A particular advantage over the pillar table was that the legs were set well in from the end of the table, not interfering with the people using the table. The basic

Figure 4. This mahogany dining table, c.1800, has the "telescopic" action patented by Gillows of Lancaster in 1800. It consists of two ends and three centre leaves. When the leaves are removed the two ends slide together, thus making it a small centre table. An unusual feature is that two inner legs unscrew.

Figure 5. The continuation of Gillows' "telescopic" action in the post-Georgian period, c.1840. The table is richly veneered with burr yew tree. This huge table has nine leaves supported by only eight legs, thanks to the "telescopic" action. Indications of its relatively late date are the gilded collars and the winding handle action.

Figure 6. The extra leaves from this table in its own box. Such boxes appear to have been supplied for large tables from about 1800 onwards. Note also the winding handle.

Figure 7. Left: A mahogany dining table with the same pillar legs, but of a very unusual design. The centre leaf is here buried, but when the outer leaves are pulled out the centre leaf comes up, thus forming a larger table (see figure 8). This type of table was patented by William Pocock in 1805 as the "Patent Sympathetic Self-Acting Dining Table". In view of the date of Pocock's patent this must be dated c.1805-10, which shows how the purity of the Sheraton style (normally dated around 1790) continued for some time afterwards. Figure 8. Right: The table fully extended.

Figure 9. A set of ten mahogany shield back side chairs of the Hepplewhite period, c.1780, perhaps the most popular form of dining chair.

Figure 10. A set of six and two mahogany dining chairs of the Sheraton period, c.1790, as evidenced by the square tapering legs and neo-classical urn motif in the uprights of the armchairs. An unusual feature is the maple inlay.

and could even be regarded as a kind of single pillar dining table.

Although Sheraton distinguishd fairly clearly between "parlour" chairs for the dining room and "drawing room" chairs, the former being of mahogany and the latter being painted or gilded, it is not always possible to determine whether chairs were used in the dining room or some other room. It is clear, however, that at least a very large proportion of chairs made in the Georgian period were intended for a dining room. The design of these dining room chairs reflected the general evolution of furniture design, that is from the early Chippendale style through the Hepplewhite (figure 9), Sheraton (figure 10) and Regency influences. Continuation of stretchers on chairs may well have been to strengthen chairs, particularly when they were used in a dining room.

An important piece of dining room furniture was the side table or its successor, the sideboard. About 1730-80 the main serving table was the side table. The early ones were of walnut or mahogany, generally upon cabriole legs, and with either a marble or wooden top. In the 1750s, such tables were nearly always made of mahogany and usually upon straight legs. Chippendale in his *Director* illustrated a few examples, describing them as "sideboard tables". These tables were not made with drawers, but used as serving tables. From about 1750 onwards, these might be flanked on either side by a pair of pedestal cupboards (figure 11).

The great change came in the Hepplewhite period around 1780, with the introduction of the sideboard (figure 12). In these pieces, the pedestal cupboards were in effect replaced by drawers in the sideboard itself. Sideboards thus had the storage space of the old pedestal cupboards and also the

design was continued by other makers, such as Morgan and Sanders, who advertised an "Imperial Dining Table", and George Remington, who in 1807 patented an extending table with "lazy tongs" action.

A particularly ingenious form of extending dining table was the "Patent, Sympathetic Self-Acting Dining Table" for which William Pocock received a

patent in 1805. In this surprisingly modern design (figures 7 and 8) the centre leaf can be buried, without being taken out, so that the table combines the advantages of a small table with the extra capacity of a larger one.

Mention should also be made of the "breakfast" table. These pieces, if not technically made for the dining room, followed the basic design of pillar tables,

Figure 11. The dining room before the sideboard. A mahogany side table acts as a serving board, and Thomas Chippendale described this type of piece as "sideboard tables". The table would have no drawers, but instead storage was provided by the pair of pedestal cupboards on either side.

Figure 12. The side table and pedestal cupboards have now become a sideboard, with storage space in the central drawer and the two side drawers or cupboards. This is a classical example of the Hepplewhite sideboard, c.1780. In the Sheraton period, c.1790, the bow front shape replaced the serpentine front.

Figure 13. A mahogany table with wine bucket, very similar indeed to the "Gentleman's Social Table" shown in The London Cabinet-Maker's Book of Prices *of 1793, plate 22. Loudon in 1833 explained that such tables were used for the gentlemen to sit round and drink after the ladies had withdrawn.*

Figure 14. A mahogany three pillar semi-circular dining table of very unusual design. Thomas Sheraton in his "Cabinet Dictionary" illustrates a more elaborate table of this type as "A Grecian Dining Table" with the chairs placed round the outer edge.

serving surface of the old side tables. They were also of course useful for smaller dining rooms which could not accommodate both side table and a pair of pedestals. A typical arrangement was to have a drawer in the centre and a cellarette drawer (looking rather like a double drawer) in each of the two ends or wings. The Hepplewhite sideboards of the 1780s were usually serpentine fronted and on square tapering legs, whereas the Sheraton ones of the 1790s were bow front. This bow front design continued into the Regency period, but normally with heavier reeded legs, typical of the period. The Regency also saw a sideboard with extremely deep pedestals almost reaching to the ground, which in a sense was a reversion to the old idea of the side table and pair of pedestal cupboards.

While dining chairs, dining tables and sideboards were clearly the essential pieces in a dining room, there are also a number of interesting and unusual accessories, such as wine coolers and knife boxes. Wine coolers (figure 15) could vary from the very simple to the highly sophisticated. Robert Adam, in some of his dining rooms, such as that at Harewood House, designed oval wine coolers to fit underneath side tables, and to be *en suite* with them as well as the pair of pedestals. Knife boxes were made to go above pedestal cupboards. By the end of the Georgian period furniture for dining had clearly moved from the hall to the dining room, which was one of the principal rooms in the house.

Figures 1, 2, 4, 5, 6, 7, 8, 9 and 10 may be seen in an exhibition of "Dining Room Furniture 1730-1830", being held by Phillips of Hitchin (Antiques) Ltd., The Manor House, Hitchin, Herts., from 1st to 30th June 1981

Figure 15. A pair of mahogany brass bound wine buckets or cellarettes, the stands having fluted legs and "C"-scroll brackets, c.1765.

Figure 1. T.B. Hardy, Katwijk, watercolour, signed, inscribed and dated 1890, 18ins. x 28ins. Over £4,000. Courtesy Sotheby's Belgravia.

Watercolours

by

Chris Beetles

It is curiously true that the English watercolour market has been hardly ravaged by the recession at all, perhaps just nibbled a bit at the lower end where the goods tend to be shop soiled and undesirable anyway. The trend I described in the October 1980 issue has accelerated faster than anyone might have anticipated — "....inferior or flawed works by even good artists are not moving.....the main feature that emerges from the boom of recent years is a huge widening of the range through which an artist's work can be valued ....the good examples despite economic stringency are still rising in popularity and money while the second rate and indifferent are relatively still going down".

Happily at last perfect condition is being demanded by those with money to spend and this has helped to overcome that ageing prejudice of oil over watercolour and canvas over paper. Watercolours have caught up and at the moment the right type are surging past with an inflationary smile and lots more running in them.

The pressure on the best works by the best artists will I am sure continue for many years before even levelling off, and though nothing is simple in a market there are many reasons why the watercolour is the leader of the domestic fine art and antiques market. It is firstly a collectors' market and not so sensitive to wider economic strategies and budgeting. Collectors are growing in number, becoming better informed,

more demanding of the standards offered and are not afraid to talk of pleasure and investment in the same breath. Rich and impecunious alike can pursue "a hobby with responsibility", especially now that over the last ten years watercolours have shown up consistently better than traditional forms of investment. Finally, the old economic forces of supply and demand are fuelling the fire. The drop in supply from private sources, within the trade and from auction is noticeable not over years but six month to six month period, while the demand is more than able to take it up, even in harder times. Just at the moment, though, for most of the range the quantity and variation in a very complex changing market is such that there still has never been a better time to try to buy, whether for stock or for that expanding collection. It is obvious too that many collections are expanding at an enormous rate. The age of the large private collection is returning and it will be a further age before we see these latter day "Nettlefolds" and "Newalls" put back on the market.

A few examples from recent auctions may clarify the trends. Sotheby's Belgravia in March offered eight Thomas Bush Hardys from a private collection. This prolific and popular watercolourist's tendency to fade, to be forged and to be sniffed at by superior "dealers in art" has kept him always well below £1,000. This collection was in mint condition, had never seen the fading light of day and was quite simply the best all round group I had ever seen.

Figure 2. Arthur Rackham, watercolour, signed, 15ins. x 10½ins. Over £7,000. Courtesy Christie's.

Figure 1 shows T.B. Hardy at his very best and made, with premium, over £4,000.

Christie's in December put up the delicate and delightful Ratty and Moley looking for Badger's den in the snow, an illustration by Arthur Rackham from *Wind in the Willows* (figure 2). Was the doyen of illustrators ever better? The price of over £7,000 said no. Another snow scene by that rare and rising star, William Fraser Garden, came up at Sotheby's Belgravia in May (figure 3). It had all the right ingredients with that exquisite draughtsmanship and unique weird quality. It fetched another record, bought by a Garden enthusiast with his collector's hat on, at £1,700.

At present Albert Goodwin is the fastest riser in the market and with a major exhibition, starting in August (see News and Views), to enhance his reputation further, he is likely to fetch even more in future than the £4,400 for the view of Eton sold at Christie's in April (figure 4).

Figure 3. W.F. Garden, watercolour, signed and dated '88, 7¼ins. x 14½ins. £1,700. Courtesy Sotheby's Belgravia.

Figure 4. Albert Goodwin, Eton, signed, inscribed and dated 1923, 9½ins. x 14½ins. £4,400. Courtesy Christie's.

Antique Watches

by
Terence
Camerer Cuss

Cameret Cuss & Co.

Figure 1. *A really large early 18th century silver pair cased alarm watch by William Cartwright, diameter 79mm.*

Figure 2. *View of movement of figure 1 showing pierced and engraved alarm barrel and bell inside case. The index plate, cock and pillars are of silver, the wheels and plates of gilt brass and the steel parts either polished or blued.*

Figure 3. *A further view of figures 1 and 2. This, as they say, I would like for Christmas! Difficult to value, but it could leave your bank balance about £5,000 lighter.*

As a major centre for the antiques market the London auction rooms put in a very poor showing during the last twelve months. A few pieces, some commanding some very respectable prices for what they were, appeared thinly spread through the very run of the mill sales. However, the tendency for some of the very best pieces to by-pass the rooms has increased and they have been handled by dealers who have successfully disposed of them either in this country or abroad, in the latter case quite frequently directly through foreign auction houses each of whom have enough loyal clients for them to obtain excellent prices. The overall impression is that the trade has fared better than the through-put of watches in the English auction rooms suggests.

The lower end of the market (say up to £2,000) with the occasional exception as, for instance, of an excellent example in pristine condition, is in poor shape, both here and, to a lesser extent, on the Continent. The middle ranges (say £2,000-£6,000) have not altered very much in value over the last twelve months, although those for which the demand is largely in this country have fallen back a bit (typically English minute repeaters). Higher up the market exceptionally good enamels from any period have increased significantly, most typically Huaut from the late 17th century and those large gold "Chinese Duplex" watches of the early 19th century, particularly if they are, for instance, signed Dupont. Highly complicated watches from the late 19th century and early 20th century have once again put in a very good performance. A large number of minute repeating perpetual calendars with chronograph mechanisms have been auctioned abroad where the prices were in the £10,000-£15,000 bracket and higher where there were additional complications or a name to conjure with. Indeed, sums in excess of £20,000 are not exceptional for these,

and there have been enamels and, of course, Tourbillons and some very good Breguets which have also broken this barrier. A splendid Tourbillon watch by S. Smith and Sons, also having a minute repeating and grande sonnerie, made about £60,000 in New York this February. A Karrusel (considered a poor relation of a Tourbillon) signed by the same maker made a hammer price of £7,000 in London quite recently although Karrusels are still more sensibly quoted at around £3,500 to £4,500. Even this, however, is a significant increase over the last year and compares with English free sprung fusee keyless levers with up and down for which the urgent interest current a year ago seems to have waned. Subjectively the market must be illogical to allow a collector to have maybe three really good examples of the latter to only one of the former.

Figure 4. *The repoussé back of a gold pair cased watch by Thomas Grignion hallmarked 1765, diameter 49mm. The scene depicts Odysseus returning to Penelope. Beside Odysseus' left foot the letters G.M.M.F. appear. George Michael Moser is probably the most sought after repoussé artist of the 18th century. Even though it is in fairly rubbed condition, the current market value must be in the region of £3,500.*

The gap between the top and bottom ends of the market has widened very significantly and it is increasingly difficult to a collector to swap his way up the market. Increasingly there are dealers who are not at all keen to lose a really good piece (there are not that many about) and to be left with maybe four much more ordinary watches even if a somewhat better profit might possibly be realised at the end of the day. Significantly, he is finding (more than usually!) that the evaluation of lesser items by the collector is really too high and that he can go to the rooms and, given his mix of talent and luck, buy similar articles at lower prices. In turn the London rooms have been bleating a little as they have seen the trade buying the lower and middle ranges more cheaply than a little while ago and at the same time having rather too many lots unsold. Quite often faced with the same over optimistic vendors the reserve prices are too high, although, to be fair to the auctioneers, some lots are so dull that maybe whatever the reserve no reasonable bid would be forthcoming. For instance, some gold watches have now fallen back to their value as scrap — in other words the interest or lack of it is where it was before we all got the gold bug.

To summarise, it is certainly not that there are unusually large quantities of watches for sale, but simply that, at any rate at the price levels established during the last few years, supply at the lower end of the market to some extent exceeds demand.

Maybe a shake out was overdue anyway and a period of more stable prices would be welcomed by many. We can only wait and see whether the top of the market will maintain the dramatic increases achieved in the recent past. Quite as interesting, perhaps, is what watches will attract the most attention from collectors and speculators alike during the next twelve months.

Fans — The Lesser Examples
by Maril Murchie

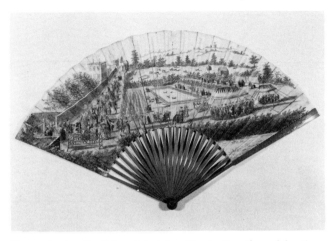

Figure 1. An English printed fan illustrating the celebrations organised by Mr. Thomas Osborne in 1754. The sticks are of wood.

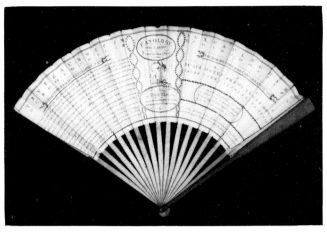

Figure 2. Another illustration of an 18th century printed fan, inscribed "Fanology, or the Ladies Conversation Fan", dated 1797, mounted on plain wooden sticks. An identical fan mount is recorded in the Schreiber Collection.

Throughout the course of its long history the fan has been employed in a number of divers ways. Essentially by displacing the air and creating a refreshing draught its main function has been to cool. However, apart from this purely functional purpose, its use has also been both decorative and symbolic, and by some societies it has been regarded as an essential part of ceremonial. This was particularly the case in the East, where in Chinese Court circles there was at one time a strict code of etiquette governing the use of the fan, whereby each rank of official was required to use a certain type of fan according to his position. In the West, where the rigid fan is believed to have been introduced from the Orient via Portugal in the early 16th century, its use has been both functional and decorative, and the folding fan came to

be considered an essential requisite for the elegant lady of fashion in the late 17th century, continuing to be so throughout the 18th and 19th centuries, before finally sinking into comparative obscurity during the early years of the 20th century with the onset of the frenetic way of life in which we now find ourselves caught up.

When it first appeared in the West the hand fan was a rarity, generally made from expensive and often exotic materials, and so was only to be found in the possession of the rich and mighty. Trade between Portugal, Spain and Italy promoted its use amongst the elite of these countries, and it was only when Catherine de Medici married Henry II of France in 1533, taking her Italian retinue with her to Paris, that French interest in the fan was aroused. By the end of the

17th century the fan had become an object of high fashion in Europe, a prized possession of the wealthy and the grand who frequented the magnificent courts of Europe. Without doubt the 18th century may be regarded as the "Great Age of the Fan", with superbly decorated ivory, tortoiseshell or mother-of-pearl sticks and delicately painted mounts, France leading the rest of Europe in both quality of workmanship and output.

However, the history of the fan is not only a story which concerns a world of opulence and magnificence. Over the years many lesser examples have been produced and in the 18th century, both in France and England, the printed fan also enjoyed wide popularity. Although known in the late 17th century, it reached the zenith of its popularity in

Figure 3. A typical example of a mid-19th century lithographed fan, the mother-of-pearl sticks and guards pierced and foiled. The lithographed paper mount was often hand-coloured.

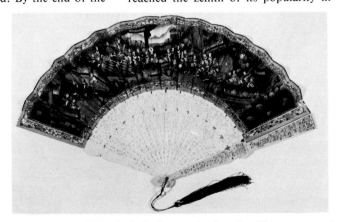

Figure 4. A "Mandarin" fan made for the Chinese export market in the mid-19th century, with carved ivory sticks and guards. The mount is brilliantly painted, the face of each figure being made of ivory. A rumour once circulated that the ivory faces were made from finger nails but this is quite without foundation.

Colour plate 1. Three 20th century advertising fans, the two on either side of the attractive Cherry Blossom fan unfolding to form a circular cockade.

Colour plate 2. A Chinese ivory and feather brisé fan made specifically for export, c.1840. The white goose feathers are brightly painted and trimmed with peacocks' feathers.

Colour plate 3. A late 19th century ostrich feather fan.

Colour plate 4. Two humming-bird fans, c.1870.

Figure 5. Three brisé fans, one of bone, another of ivory, the third made from horn, all first half of the 19th century.

the 18th century, before falling from favour in the early years of the 19th century when the lithographed fan came very much into vogue. An English Act of 1735 required publishers to mark their work with the date of issue and the publisher's name which facilitates dating these fans, although it is by no means a guarantee as the date and name were often trimmed off in fitting the mount to the sticks.

The main appeal of the printed fan lay in its cheapness and variety. Production was prolific, and it could be replaced at very little cost. The prints covered a wide range of subjects recording a passing moment in history, a quirk of fashion, or some amusing but not particularly significant event which may otherwise have passed unrecorded. The French publishers showed a particular leaning towards political subjects — the birth of the Dauphin in 1781 is well recorded, as are events of the French Revolution, and

in a light-hearted mood the first experiments in ballooning by the Montgolfier brothers with their hot air balloon in 1772.

Fans of every type were produced — fans giving directions for new dances, rules for card games, words for songs, a seating plan for the theatre or opera, fortune telling fans, fans celebrating the return to health of George III — and so it continued limitlessly. One of the most famous of English printed fans is entitled "Mr. Thomas Osborne's Duck Hunting 1754" (figure 1), printed to commemorate a party given by that gentleman when he became a resident of Hampstead in September 1754, each lady who attended the gathering being presented with one of these fans. Outstandingly the most notable and illuminating collection of printed fans, mounted and unmounted, forms the Schreiber Collection housed at the British Museum (figure 2).

Although intrinsically and artistically of little value, the printed fan, initially produced at such low cost, can now command increasingly high prices on the fan market. For example, a printed fan inscribed with rules for card games sold at auction at Sotheby's last November for £190, a fan on Fanology fetching £160 earlier in the year. In May 1978 a hand-coloured printed fan of Jeu de Piquet des Differentes Nations de l'Europe with pierced ivory sticks, part of the Baldwin Collection, realised £490 at Christie's South Kensington, while a printed Oracle fan with plain wooden sticks fetched £60 at auction recently.

Following the same theme, mention should be made of the advertising fan, first in circulation during the last years of the 19th century, and increasingly so during the early years of the 20th century (see colour plate 1). These fans were produced at absolutely minimum cost and were distributed by hotels, restaurants and manufacturers in the promotion of new products. Usually eye-catching and vibrant, they were certainly varied and can be both attractive and amusing. Due to the fact that they were produced in such quantity, in fact mass produced, they can easily be found in antique markets and on bric-a-brac stalls and can be a source of inexpensive amusement to the not so affluent fan collector. A French fan advertising perfume was sold at Phillips last December for £9.

Lithography, surface printing from stone, was invented at the end of the 18th century, and by the 1840s was in frequent use as a means of decorating fan mounts. In many cases the lithographed fan mount was also hand-coloured (figure 3). The design was often a pastiche of an earlier 18th century French model, but the borders were usually excessively ornate with heavy gilt scrollwork and foliate decoration. Quality varied. The best examples can be very attractive, and in some instances the sticks show obvious

Figure 6. A horn brisé puzzle fan. This is a fan where sticks and ribbon are so designed as to open as well from left to right as right to left, thus allowing the fan to be decorated with four illustrations instead of the usual two, one on either side. These hidden scenes may be of a somewhat risqué *nature. This example is dated c.1820.*

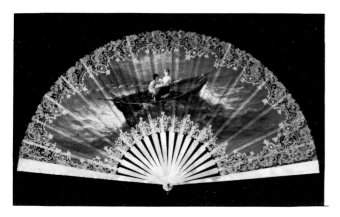

Figure 7. This French lace trimmed gauze fan, delicately painted with a young couple in a fishing boat far out to sea, is a fine example of a type of fan fashionable in the late 1870s and 1880s. The overall length of the fan should be noted, this particular example measuring 37cm long.

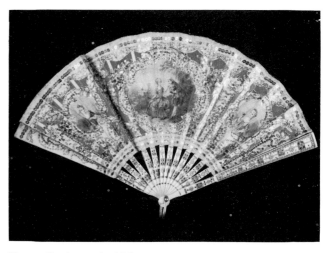

Figure 8. An early 20th century painted gauze fan showing excessively ornate spangled decoration.

craftsmanship. However, on the whole, this type of fan was inexpensively produced and, although decorative, the design of the sticks can be unimaginative and the mount perhaps somewhat over-sentimentalised. These lithographed fans can range in price from anything in the region of £20 to £200.

Throughout the 18th century and into the 19th century trade between China and the West developed and flourished, the main centres of trade being Canton and Macao. The West appeared to have an insatiable appetite for Oriental merchandise of a wide range, including fans and fancy goods. Fans from China were made specifically for export and tended to be of inferior quality to those made for the home market. Neither were they regarded as the smartest of accoutrements by Western society ladies, often tending to be gaudy and excessively detailed.

The "Mandarin" fan, which became very popular in the mid-19th century is a good example of this (figure 4). The paper mount is brightly painted with scenes from Chinese ceremonial and active daily life, crammed full of figures with applied ivory faces and silk robes. The sticks were made from carved tortoiseshell, ivory or sandalwood, or painted lacquer, and the fan was often sold in an attractive fitted lacquer case. Here again quality varied a great deal and although many show a high standard of workmanship, these were but few in comparison to those of inferior quality which flooded the market. They have now become popular with both fan collectors and dealers for their decorative merit and can bring anything from £30 to £200 in the saleroom today. Feathers, enamel, silver and gold filigree were all used by the Chinese in the manufacture of fans and in the 19th

century embroidery was employed as a means of decoration. It is fascinating to see the strange union of East and West which can be found on a Chinese fan mount made for export where the Chinese have tried to emulate Western styles in an effort to please their European clients.

Amongst the earliest type of fan to be exported from the East was the brisé fan. This is a fan without a mount comprised solely of sticks and guards held together by means of a rivet and a ribbon. In the late 17th century and early years of the 18th century fine painted examples were exported to the West, and to acquire such a fan at auction today one would expect to pay in the region of at least £200-£300 if it were in reasonable condition. However, the Chinese excelled at carving and towards the end of the 18th century and throughout the 19th century this talent

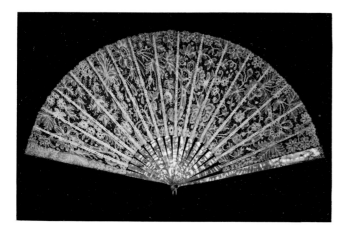

Above: Figure 9. A mother-of-pearl fan, c.1880, with a very attractive Brussels lace mount.

Right: Figure 10. At a fancy dress ball at Marlborough House in 1874 the Princess of Wales, dressed as Marie Stuart, carried a feather fan very similar to the fan illustrated here, with a small bird resting in the centre of the feathers.

Above: Figure 11. An early 20th century autographed fan commemorative of an event which took place in 1903, each guest having been asked to inscribe the fan which was then kept as a souvenir.

Right: Figure 12. An unusual late 19th century fan guard carved from wood in the form of a long thin musician with ivory hands and face.

was employed to advantage as they used pierced and carved ornament, rather than painted, to decorate the ivory, tortoiseshell and sandalwood sticks. Late 18th century carving tended to be comparatively restrained, the ground being pierced *en mosaique* to give a finely ribbed effect, but as the 19th century progressed the carving became increasingly elaborate and detailed depicting scenes from Chinese life with figures packed tightly together, frequently entwined amid trailing foliage and architectural landscapes.

Today prices for such fans vary enormously, governed, of course, by the quality of the carving, but on the whole prices range between £20 to £180. The quality of these fans deteriorated in the 19th century, the carving becoming more crude, and sometimes the design would only appear on one side of the fan. They were regarded as tourist items and were exported in large numbers at low cost. So prolific was the output that they are far from scarce today and can very often still be purchased at reasonably low prices (colour plate 2).

Brisé fans were also manufactured in Europe. For those who could not afford the more extravagant examples made from exotic materials such as ivory and tortoiseshell, brisé fans were also made from hollywood, satinwood and laburnum at even lower cost. During the Regency period horn brisé fans with pierced and/or painted decoration were also being produced in large quantity to cater for this lesser end of the market (figures 5 and 6). A collector may find an attractive example of a horn brisé fan, either with brightly painted flower ornament or pierced to give a fine lace

effect, for as little as £15. Prices range up to £100 which is what one can expect to pay for a fine pierced cockade fan made from horn.

Another type of fan in use during the 18th and 19th centuries was the gimmick fan, an example of which is the lorgnette fan of which there were two types. The first type of lorgnette fan was in fashion during the Regency period and bears witness to the affectation of that time. In this instance a "peep hole" would be cut in silk or skin mount so that a young lady, while pretending to avert her eyes by hiding behind her fan, could still ensure that she had a good view of whatever was going on. The other type of lorgnette fan, with more serious purpose in mind, was intended as a vision aid, the mount being pierced with a series of circular apertures overlying each other when folded and covered by a guard fitted with a spy glass. The glass might alternatively be set into the rivet.

Other varieties of gimmick fan include the telescopic, puzzle (figure 6) and dagger fans to name but a few. Obviously an 18th century lorgnette fan would be a rarer find than an ordinary fan of the same date, and the price is correspondingly higher. It is difficult to say exactly how much one would have to pay for a lorgnette fan, or any gimmick fan, as so much depends on the condition of the fan itself. A late 18th century fan with articulated guards, if in good condition, can easily fetch several hundred pounds.

The 19th century witnessed a general deterioration in standards of workmanship where the fan was concerned. Towards the end of the century a wide variety of textiles was used for fan

mounts, such as silk, satin, gauze (figure 7) and net with embroidered, painted or spangled decoration. Spangled ornament was particularly favoured (figure 8). On the fan market today it is the condition and decorative quality of these later fans which determines the price rather than the actual material from which the fan mount is made. Originally they were usually produced at low cost and at speed. Sometimes ladies even embroidered their own fan mounts at home.

During the second half of the 19th century the lace fan (figure 9) became extremely fashionable and was often carried by a young bride as one of her most treasured accoutrements. At auction a lace fan can bring anything from as little as £10 for a rather poor example in bad condition to in the region of £1,300 which was the price paid for a cream Brussels lace fan, c.1890, included in a jewel sale at Sotheby's last year. The mother-of-pearl guards were most beautifully applied with gold and enamel ornament in the manner of Giuliano.

Feathers too were in common use in the later years of the 19th century ranging from ostrich feather fans (colour plate 3) with luxuriant plumage (which entered a period of renewed popularity as presentation Court fans around the 1920s) to smaller neater examples particularly favoured during the late Victorian and Edwardian era (figure 10 and colour plate 4).

Mourning fans should also be mentioned and are easily identifiable by the joyless black or purple colouring of the usually unremarkable mount. There was obviously no cause for ostentation, heavy ornament or excessive expenditure on production where these fans were concerned and they are rarely of any great artistic merit. However, as with any rule, there are always exceptions and although prices for these fans are generally low, a very attractive mourning fan was sold at auction at the end of last year for £70.

With the onset of the 20th century, bringing with it the turmoil and upheaval resultant from the First World War, with the rapid advance in technology and consequent hastening of the pace at which we pursue our lives, for most women the struggle to remain feminine and elegant has been a hard one. Speed seems to be the essence of the 20th century and sadly a world has been created in which there is little use or room for the folding fan, except as a source of constant enjoyment, excitement and amusement to the collector. The fan fulfils this role most amply giving, by virtue of its own extensive variety, great pleasure to all collectors, including both those who are affluent and those who are not quite so fortunate.

"CANDLESTICKS"

(An appreciation of a type of postal scale
that is both unusual and decorative)

by Brian Brass

*Figure 1. Five "candlestick" postal scales, ranging from 4½ins.
to 7ins. in height; all date from about 1840 to 1865.*

The "candlestick" was one of the most interesting of the early type of postal scales. It was introduced almost immediately after the inauguration of the penny post, prior to which mail had been charged by distance rather than by weight. It was during this period that the inventiveness that provided the inspiration for the industrial revolution merged so spectacularly with the genius for artistry and design that typified the early Victorian society.

Seldom is this partnership better exemplified than in the candlestick type of postal scale. A quick look at the small group in figure 1 will show why they acquired this description. The first examples date from early 1840 and the design here in England is thought to have lasted about twenty-five years.

Production over such an extended period provides some indication of their popularity, and is also partly responsible for a reasonable supply being still available. Curiously, despite their abundance, there are only three known makers.

The vast majority of candlestick postal scales were manufactured by Robert Winfield and the brothers Joseph and Edmund Ratcliff. Robert Walker Winfield operated in the Birmingham area from 1829 to 1860 and had a factory on the Baskerville Estate. He manufactured all types of scales, including sovereign "rockers". The Ratcliffs also had a factory in Birmingham, at 59/60 St. Paul's Square, and featured in trade directories from 1839 to 1864. They too manufactured all types of scales. Joseph died in 1862 and Edmund continued on his own until 1881.

With one or two exceptions, these two firms made not only items which bore their own names, but are also thought to have manufactured a vast number of un-labelled scales for sale by wholesalers and retailers of specialist office supplies. One or the other almost certainly made the items which appeared in the American Fairbanks catalogues in the 1850s with that company's label firmly embossed. (Was this perhaps the earliest example of the "own label" technique of merchandising?)

The third known maker was the American firm of Chatillon. Their individualistic design appears in the catalogue of that firm dated 1894 — some thirty years after production in this country had given way to the more precise robervals (equal pan) and later Salter spring balances with dial faces.

In terms of construction, as can be seen from the drawing in figure 2, they are all based on a spring compressed within the confines of a slender tube. (Certain extremely rare varieties use a spring in similar manner but in tension

form.) The spring is attached to a rod housed within the centre of the tube which carries the letter plate above.

Some candlesticks bear a date but this is not, as may be thought, the day of manufacture but the date on which the design was first registered. For example, an early Winfield bears the inscription "JANUARY 13 1840" and figure 3 shows the actual design registered by Winfield at the Office of Registry of

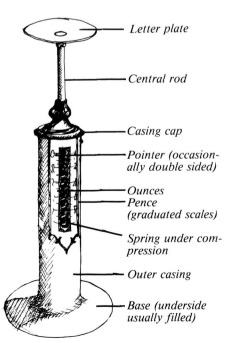

Figure 2. Drawing of a typical candlestick postal scale capable of weighing up to 4oz.

- Letter plate
- Central rod
- Casing cap
- Pointer (occasionally double sided)
- Ounces
- Pence (graduated scales)
- Spring under compression
- Outer casing
- Base (underside usually filled)

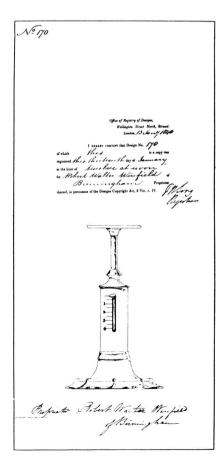

Figure 3. The registration certificate for Winfield's "candlestick" postal scale, No. 170, dated 13th January 1840. Courtesy Public Record Office, Kew.

Figure 4

Figure 5

Figure 6

Figure 7

Figure 8

Figure 4. An early Winfield, in bronze, 6½ins. high.

Figure 5. Another Winfield with an unusually decorated letter plate bearing a rose and a thistle, also in bronze, 5ins. high.

Figure 6. An unusually tall candlestick by an unknown maker, brass, 8ins. high (tension spring variety).

Figure 7. A superb example in brass, showing scenes from the industrial revolution. The letter plate is particularly beautiful.

Figure 8. An example in Bristol milk glass, 7ins. high.

Designs on 13th January 1840. (The issue of the *London Gazette* dated 28th December 1839 carried the announcement that the penny post would begin on 10th January 1840 — from which it can be seen how keen Mr. Winfield was to profit from this new field of endeavour that had suddenly been opened up.)

What makes them so delightful as collectables is the fact that each specimen seems to differ slightly from the next. Some bear outstandingly beautiful design work (figures 4, 5 and 6), many have a pastoral motif, while others, such as figure 7, depict scenes from the industrial revolution itself. Some of the English examples, like the one in Bristol milk glass (figure 8), and all of the Chatillons have the tube and base made in one piece, but the majority have a sturdy base as a separate part.

The materials from which these scales were constructed also varied, and examples have been noted in brass, bronze, ivory (figure 9), silver and glass. They are mostly self-standing, but a few have been set in elaborate bases such as wood and marble (see figure 11, page 38, December 1977 *Antique Collecting*). One example seen has a thermometer attached to the stem (one wonders what purpose was served by combining these two measuring devices) and another (figure 10) has a handbell set into the base. The letter scales usually weigh up to 4oz., although the petite example in figure 11 weighs only up to 1oz.

They also vary considerably in height. They can be as small as 3½ins. (one example seen of this height being in solid silver, by an unknown American manufacturer) and as tall as 15ins., the latter being in the form of a parcel scale.

As with antiques the world over, prices vary with condition and age. As a general guide, the candlesticks in brass and bronze (both with and without the name of the manufacturer) sell for between £30 and £40. The more elaborate items, particularly those in glass or silver, will command about double. Rare and highly unusual items will bring in excess of £200.

Where to Buy

Gerald Sattin (of Burlington Arcade, Piccadilly, London W.1) has the occasional item in silver. Others who deal primarily in scientific instruments but frequently stock these scales are

Arthur Middleton of 12 New Row, W.C.2

"Mark" of Stand A/10 Chenil Galleries, New King's Road, London S.W.3

Graham Forsdyke of 158 Hampton Road, London E.4

but by far the greatest opportunities lie in the usual foraging in antique shops and fairs where it is still possible to pick up these delightfully pretty pieces quite cheaply.

Bibliography

M.A. Crawforth: *A Brief Guide to Weighing Instruments* (ISASC — International Society of Antique Scale Collectors — 1978)
Bob Stein: *Collecting Letter and Parcel Scales* (*Antique Finder* and *Antique Collecting* magazines, December 1977)
Harry Green: *Profile on R.W. Winfield* (*Equilibrium* magazine — organ of ISASC — Inaugural Issue Spring 1978)
Howard Robinson: *(History of) Britain's Post Office*

Acknowledgements

My thanks to Michael Crawforth, Morton Wormser and Bob Stein for information and assistance, to Paul Balen for the black and white photography, and to Clare Brass for the drawing (figure 2).

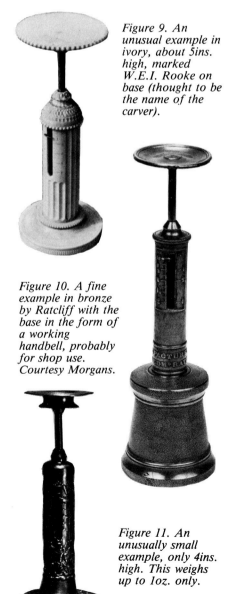

Figure 9. An unusual example in ivory, about 5ins. high, marked W.E.I. Rooke on base (thought to be the name of the carver).

Figure 10. A fine example in bronze by Ratcliff with the base in the form of a working handbell, probably for shop use. Courtesy Morgans.

Figure 11. An unusually small example, only 4ins. high. This weighs up to 1oz. only.

IN SEARCH OF CATS

Part I

by
M.I.N. Evans

Some authorities say that the cat existed millions of years before man, so it is not surprising that this animal, more than any other, has played its part in legend and mythology. It has been a symbol of both good and evil and was worshipped and revered by the Ancient Egyptians by whom, it is thought, it was first domesticated — in fact it was revered to such an extent that it was forbidden to export one, and the penalty for killing one was death.

Inevitably a profitable smuggling business started up, and eventually the cat arrived in Europe — it is not known exactly when, but the Phoenicians are credited with carrying Egyptian cats on their ships to foreign ports, and probably introduced them into Britain when they visited tin mines in Cornwall.

Many mummified bodies of cats have been found in Egypt, testifying to their ancient importance, and Herodotus, the Greek historian who travelled in Egypt in the year 450 B.C., described the shrine of Bast, the Ancient Egyptian cat-headed goddess, as "standing on an island completely surrounded by water except for the entrance passage. It was built of finest red granite, the vestibule 60ft. high, and ornamented with handsome figures of cats 6 cubits in height". (A cubit is about 17ins. to 22ins.) The building of such a shrine shows yet again the importance attached to the cat.

Probably the veneration for this animal arose from its usefulness to the national economy, by keeping down rats and mice etc. and thus protecting stores of grain — and in Japan stories tell of how cats were kept in temples to protect sacred manuscripts. This worship of cats continued for many centuries until Christianity took over.

Fortunately there are relics of those days still to be seen. Talismans, which were worn in the same way as lucky charms are worn today, were made from all types of materials, and can be seen in some museums, and there are also models of cats — a particularly fine example of a bronze cat from Egypt c.30 B.C. is in the British Museum.

The collecting of models of cats was bound to follow, and this can be a rewarding and fascinating hobby and one to suit all pockets as there is a wide price range from very expensive pieces to objects of modest price.

To set the scene, therefore, an example of the former is the aristocratic 6th century B.C. Egyptian bronze cat shown in figure 1. It has a very good green and red patina, and is on a slate stand. Its ears are pierced for ear rings, and its eyes and the top of its head are recessed for the inlay of a jewel. Originally in the collection of Nessim Bey of Egypt, this cat came up for auction in 1977. Since £26,000 was the price paid it would hardly come within

the scope of the average collector. However, someone bought it, and there must have been an underbidder — and because of its sheer beauty it must be included in this article.

The production of cat figures would seem to be world wide and in many materials — but from now on this article will be restricted to British pottery and porcelain cats.

Many centuries pass to bring us now to c.1675 A.D. and a very rare cat (figure 2). This is a London Delft cat, standing 6½ins. high and is in the shape of a vase. It is beautifully coloured with a pale blue and manganese striped coat, and the tail and toes are also enriched in manganese. This would be a most amusing animal to possess, as it does look so suspicious of the world around it — or could it be a smug look as it sold in 1979 for £3,600, despite the crack from the ear to the tip of the tail?

Only four other London Delft cats of this type are known. They are all in the

Figure 1. 6th century B.C. Egyptian bronze cat, 10¾ins. Courtesy Christie's.

Figure 2. London Delft cat in the shape of a vase, 6½ins. Courtesy Christie's.

shape of a jug, are 6ins. high, and all dated, having a medallion on their front bearing initials and a date. One of these cats is in the Manchester City Art Gallery, where it has joined the Greg collection of five cats. It is dated 1671 and bears the initials M.B. The other three are dated 1672 (Brighton Museum), 1674 (British Museum) and 1676 (in the Schreiber Collection at the Victoria and Albert Museum).

Probably more attractive to the eye is a smaller and more realistic London Delft cat (figure 3). This little blue and white seated cat c.1680 is only 4¼ins. high and sold last year for £4,000. A

similar one, but with rather more elaborate decoration, is in a private collection, while yet another, a small recumbent cat, is in the Cecil Higgins Museum, Bedford.

So much for the really expensive end of a collection.

Figure 4 shows a delightful group of creamware, Whieldon, solid agate and saltglaze cats, all of which come up for auction from time to time, although the Whieldon variety do not appear quite as often as the others.

The prices of these cats ranged from £100 (back centre) to £280 for the Whieldon (far right). Alas, that was in 1970 — and prices have risen dramatically since then. The solid agate (lower centre) animal was £135 whereas a similar one today would be nearer £500.

However, they are highly collectable and very colourful, the agate cats in particular, being produced by mingling variegated clays so as to resemble a veined stone or agate, and in many cases they are splashed with blue on the body, whereas others also have their ears enriched with blue.

A particularly fine example (figure 5) of a solid agate mouser is in a private collection. It has a body of chocolate brown striations, again splashed in blue, and its face also has a blue splash. It has brown eyes and the mouse is also brown.

Well worth seeing are the cats in the collections of the Leeds Art Galleries at Temple Newsam House; these include Pratt type, pearlware and stoneware, as

Figure 4. A collection of agate, saltglaze and Whieldon cats. Courtesy Christie's.

Figure 5. Solid agate mouser, 5ins. Courtesy Miss J.L. Hopkins.

Figure 6. Chelsea scent bottle, gold anchor period, 3¼ins. Courtesy Sotheby's.

Figure 3. London Delft seated cat, 4¼ins. Courtesy Christie's.

well as an agate mouser.

Figure 6 brings us to what is thought to be England's first porcelain factory — Chelsea. Many small scent bottles were made there, and this little gem of only 3¼ins. in height has several little cats climbing up it, as well as one perched on the top to form the stopper. It bears a factory mark of a small gold anchor which dates it between 1756-69.

Another porcelain factory was in the fishing village of Lowestoft where a small but very successful business was started in 1757 and continued till 1799. This produced soft paste porcelain which included some animals, all of which are rare. Of the four cats known,

three are in private collections and one is in the Castle Museum, Norwich. They are 2¼ins. high and seated on a pale green mound. One is a tortoiseshell cat and the others are tabbies, in each case with a white front.

There is a fine collection of cats in the Castle Museum — the Langton Collection, donated in 1972 — which includes some ninety-five models dating from the Roman period to the present day, and is interesting because of the number of factories represented.

In 1770 a factory was opened by Maurice Thursfield in the small Shropshire town of Jackfield and this name was applied to wares made there.

Left: Figure 7. Jackfield type cat, 7ins. Courtesy Miss J.L. Hopkins.

Right: Figure 8. Possibly from one of the Yorkshire potteries, c.1810.

Below: Figure 9. Cream, yellow and brown striped cat from the Portobello factory, 7¼ins. Courtesy The Royal Scottish Museum, Edinburgh.

Figure 7 shows a typical example in red earthenware, covered with a very shiny, almost glasslike, black glaze, with gilt decoration, in this case around the base, and the features outlined in gilt. Whether it is Jackfield or Jackfield type, it is still a nice animal to have, especially if a collection is to have a representative from as many factories as possible.

Apart from the Rockingham animals which will appear in another article, there appear to be very few cats from the Yorkshire potteries. However, on good authority the seated cat (figure 8) has been attributed an origin in a Yorkshire pottery — possibly even Leeds.

It is very light in texture and colour, having a hollow cream body with greyish blue mottled markings, which are carried out on the mound on which it is seated. The figure is 7½ins. high and was probably made c.1810. It was bought as a Staffordshire cat for a modest £7.

Moving over the border, there are quite a number of very attractive cats from Scottish factories. A pair of agate ware (banded brown and white clays) are in the Royal Scottish Museum, Edinburgh, and although attributed to Portobello it is thought that they might have been produced at the Seaton Pottery at Aberdeen.

The Portobello Pottery (1810-1850) near Edinburgh produced animals and figures which were in great demand and figure 9 shows a fine example from that pottery — a cat 7¼ins. high coloured in cream, yellow and brown.

This, too, is at the Royal Scottish Museum.

Also in Edinburgh, at the Huntley House Museum, is a penny bank in the form of a seated cat. It is made from cream earthenware, covered with a brown glaze, which in places is very thinly applied, and is on a square base. It is quite small and is attributed to Prestonpans, mid-19th century. Also in this museum is a large brown cat on an oval base, which may have been made to sit by the fire and is thought to be of Prestonpans manufacture c.1820, together with a pair of life size pottery cats which are facing in opposite directions and were used as mantelpiece ornaments. They are pure white with pink tipped noses and yellowish eyes. A pale blue ribbon is tied round their necks. They are attributed to John McNay of the West Lothian Pottery, Bo'ness.

This survey of older and rather rare cats ends with one by Charles Bourne (figure 10). He is recorded as a pottery manufacturer in Lane Delph as early as 1805 and in 1817 he moved to the Foley Pottery (Fenton, Staffs.) where he worked until 1830 when ill health forced him to retire.

His porcelain was of a very high quality and he marked his wares with the pattern number under his initials — this cat is CB over 209. It is of bone china with a clear glaze. It has a grey mottled coat with a white face and front, is wearing a red collar, and is seated on an orange, black tasselled cushion. It is also illustrated in Godden's *British Porcelain, An Illustrated Guide,* plate 32, in the chapter covering the Charles Bourne Factory, and the actual cat is in The City Museum and Art Gallery, Stoke-on-Trent.

Figure 10. Very rare model of a tabby cat from the Charles Bourne factory. Courtesy Geoffrey A. Godden, Esq.

FRENCH FURNITURE STYLES

Part 3   Rococo

Beginners' Page

by Pierre Le Marchand

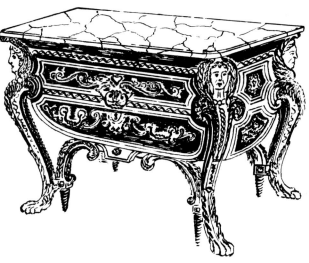

Figure 1. The commode was one of the principal prestige pieces in 18th century France. This example is of the type first made by Boulle for Louis XIV in 1708/9. Although still baroque in feeling, the curvilinear carcass and the early form of cabriole leg formed the basis on which the rococo designers developed their elegant serpentine curves.

Figure 2. Commode of the Régence period, 1715-23, showing the development of the bombé shape and the use of parquetry in association with gilded bronze (ormolu) mounts as both protection and decoration on the corners. The Régence commode was usually of three-drawer depth, and this style persisted in certain other countries, notably Holland and Sweden, after it had been displaced in France by a lighter style.

Figure 3. Commode of the Louis XV period, c.1750. It is of two-drawer depth and is raised on taller legs than those of the Régence type. The rail between the drawers is concealed so that the whole frontal area can be treated as one for purposes of decoration in floral marquetry, as here, or with chinoiseries in vernis Martin — a varnish invented by the Martin family (see figure 9). The ormolu mounts are more delicate than those of the Régence, and are noticeably asymmetrical in design.

Anyone wishing to learn what is really meant by *rococo* would be put off at the outset by some of the definitions in the Oxford English Dictionary: "Old-fashioned, antiquated. Of furniture and architecture: Having the characteristics of Louis Quatorze or Louis Quinze workmanship, such as conventional shell- and scroll-work and meaningless decoration; tastelessly florid or ornate. 1844."

Rococo was an early 19th century corruption of the French *rocaille,* a term which had been used to describe the rock-and-shell work of the artificial grottoes constructed in the gardens of Versailles. As now used, however, neither *rococo* nor *rocaille* describes the Louis XIV style, which was baroque, albeit with a strong flavour of classicism evident in some of the more stately examples. However, some elements which went to make up the rococo style were already apparent in late baroque furniture design, particularly shells and scrolls — the O.E.D. is right about that. It is therefore to the last years of the Louis XIV period that one must look for that rebellion against its "old-fashioned"

manner which resulted in the Louis XV style. Whether that result was "tastelessly florid or ornate", or elegant, whimsical and charming is a judgement to be made only after studying the best of the originals, not the worst of the later copies.

The Commode

One of the most characteristic pieces

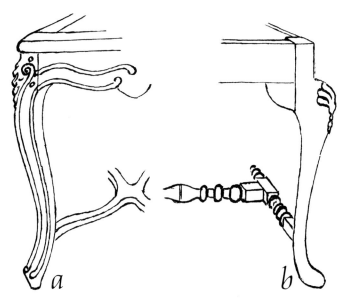

Figure 4a. French version of the cabriole leg — pied de biche — on a chair of the Régence period, when it was still a novelty and not entirely trusted by the makers, who therefore strengthened it with stretchers — often, as here, formed as a curved X-shape. Note that the leg joins the seat-rail in an upward curve, and that the heads of the pegs securing the tenon and mortise joint are visible; this last characteristic is usual on French seat furniture, but is not always very evident when the piece has been coated with gesso and painted or gilded. Many chairs and canapés *(settees of various kinds) were, however, made in oak, walnut or beech and left in their natural colour.*

Figure 4b. English version of the cabriole leg on a chair of the Queen Anne period. Note that the leg joins the seat-rail with a downward bulge under the rail, and that pegs are not generally visible. Stretchers, when used, are more often turned than sawn as in the French type (4a). There are exceptions to these usual practices, but it is seldom one sees an English chair conforming to 4a, or a French one closely resembling 4b.

Left:Figure 5. Armchair of the Régence period, exhibiting the features noted in figure 4a. It has a cartouche-shaped back which, like the seat, is caned. English 18th century caned chairs are often described as ''bergère'', but this does not apply to French furniture. For a true French bergère, *see figure 6. The correct name for a chair with open arms is a fauteuil. Chairs and settees were made by the* menuisier, *not the* ébéniste, *who normally confined himself to veneered furniture.*

Right: Figure 6. Fully upholstered armchair, early Louis XV period, c.1740 — properly called a bergère, *as it has enclosed arms and is designed for comfort. (The word also means ''lover, lass, nymph, shepherdesss, nightcap'' — all implying a degree of comfort, in one way or another). The back of a bergère is always well-padded, but not necessarily stuffed over the frame.*

of 18th century French furniture, extensively imitated (but with interesting variations) in many other countries, was the commode or decorative chest-of-drawers. Its inventor may well have been André-Charles Boulle, who supplied a pair of commodes for the bedroom of Louis XIV at the Trianon in 1708/9 (figure 1). The shape is curvilinear and is derived from a classical tomb; the type is therefore known as a *commode en tombeau*. It is supported by legs following an S-shaped curve.

Louis XIV had only a few years to enjoy this pair of prototype commodes, as he died in 1715, having occupied the throne since 1643 — the longest recorded reign in European history — and outlived his eldest son, his eldest grandson and one of his great-grandsons. And so another of them became Louis XV. Like his great-grandfather before him, he was a child of five when he became, nominally, King of France. The Duke of Orleans

was therefore appointed Regent.

During the Régence period (1715-23), the commode became a fashionable item for the salon, where it replaced in popularity the tall cabinets on stands which had been obligatory in the later 17th century. The typical Régence commode has a serpentine front, sometimes shaped vertically as well as laterally, resulting in the curvaceous form known as *bombé* (blown up). It has two drawers side by side in the top tier, and two long

Figure 7. A fauteuil, *or open-armed chair, in the fully developed Louis XV style, with no straight line apparent in its entire composition and typical of the rococo manner c.1750. The shaping of the carved frame is bold and confident in its assembly of curves, and the true rococo spirit is further manifested in the asymmetrical design of the tapestry cover. In the grandest houses, different suites of seat furniture were available, with upholstery fabrics suited to the season of the year.*

Figure 8. Writing table (bureau-plat) in the more restrained Louis XV style, mounted in ormolu and veneered in figured woods with their grains diagonally opposed, but without marquetry decoration. Such desks were made in varying sizes, but the larger ones were, in spite of their rather delicate appearance, intended for male use. The top is leathered.

drawers below, with a shaped apron reaching almost to floor level (figure 2). The top, as with virtually all French commodes, was of marble. The front and ends were veneered with parquetry in walnut and *palisandre* (a variety of rosewood) on a foundation of oak or, sometimes, pine. In general, it may be noted that the veneers on bombé surfaces are often thinner than on flat surfaces, due to the problems of making a thick layer of wood adhere over curves and to the extra rubbing down required to achieve a smooth finish.

Throughout the Régence period there was a growing trend towards a lighter style. It was probably Cressent, cabinet-maker to the Regent, who perfected the typical Louis XV commode, of clearly defined bombé shape, only two drawers in depth and raised on higher legs. The earlier examples still exposed the rail between the drawers, but the cabinet-makers soon found ways of concealing this with overlapping drawer-fronts — or even dispensing with it entirely — to produce the commode *sans traverse*. The front could thus be treated as one area for decoration in marquetry (figure 3). Floral subjects were the most popular, being executed in a wide variety of woods, of which tulipwood, kingwood, citrus, walnut, satinwood, rosewood of various kinds, ebony and mahogany played their part. Mahogany, however, was not widely used in France until the later 18th century.

Bronze mounts

Commodes and, indeed, most cabinet furniture (as opposed to seat furniture) of the Régence and Louis XV periods were almost invariably mounted in gilded bronze — known in England as ormolu. The process was long and costly, involving casting, chiselling and gilding with an amalgam of pure gold and mercury. The workers in this field had their own guild.

The Guilds

The cabinetmakers and joiners were organised into a guild which, from 1743 until its disbandment in 1791, insisted on high standards and required its members to stamp their products with their name, often followed by the letters "JME" *(Juré des Menuisiers et Ebénistes)*. This became a legal requirement in 1751. Some makers, especially those working for the Crown, and certain privileged immigrants, were excused from marking their products in this way, but signed pieces usually command higher prices than unsigned ones. Forgeries are not unknown. A fairly complete list of known furniture-makers is provided in *L'art des Maîtres Ebénistes Français* by J. Nicolay (1959).

However, if the rococo style can be credited to any particular names, rather than to the general spirit of the times, it was the architect-designers Juste-Aurèle Meissonier (c.1693-1750) and Nicolas Pineau (1684-1754) who were chiefly responsible for introducing the light-hearted, feminine flavour, the rejection of the straight line in favour of subtle curves, and the asymmetrical composition that characterise it. Almost every type of furniture employed the *pied chantourné* or *pied de biche* — known in English by the 19th century term "cabriole leg". (In French, furniture has "feet", not "legs".) The French form differs from the more usual English type (figure 4), although English makers adopted the French form for certain sophisticated pieces later in the century, e.g. the "French Hepplewhite" style, employing it when it was no longer fashionable in France.

The Louis XV style was notable for elegance and comfort in seat furniture, of which there was a wide variety (figures 5, 6 and 7) and which in the 18th century was almost never veneered, but sometimes left natural, sometimes painted or gilded. Among the many pieces produced, writing tables or bureaux were important items in a society which was, at least in some ways, highly civilised (figures 8 and 9) and, the O.E.D. notwithstanding, seldom "tastelessly florid".

Figure 9. Bureau-de-dame *or lady's bureau, Louis XV, c.1750-60, with veneered frame and borders around drawer-fronts and panels decorated with chinoiseries in* vernis Martin. *This substitute for Oriental lacquer was invented c.1730 by four brothers by the name of Martin. It was also used for other decorative styles involving trellis-work, flowers, scenes in the manner of Boucher, Fragonard and Watteau, and for cleverly matching plaques of Sèvres porcelain incorporated in the overall design. Note also the almost manic use of curves in the construction. The furniture of the Louis XV period is the most feminine that has ever been created.*

Silver Buying: Apologetic Notes on Choice

by John Webster

Apologetic because I refuse to dictate taste, for choice is precious in all things. But, that said, none of us fails to observe changes in our buying habits and tastes, and below is a humble glimpse of my own.

The four object comparisons briefly discussed here all have something in common; the desirable items to the left and their less desirable companions to the right are worth roughly the same, an indication that when purchasing relatively common forms of domestic silver quality does not always mean more expensive.

The mugs are by John Lias, 1784, and John Payne, 1754, and each worth around £150-£250. Yet the first is preferable. Its barrel shape and broad bands of reeded decoration are distinctive of the last three decades of the 18th century. Furthermore, it has the more unusual strap form of handle and contemporary initials in a delicate rayed bright-cut surround. The other mug, whilst of traditional baluster form, has been later chased with heavy Victorian foliage and later initialled. Originally it was completely plain. Whilst both are pretty mugs, the first is a stylistically pure piece which has a specific and immediately identifiable position in English silver. The other is a hybrid confused by two periods of work a century apart. In summary, one is individual, stylistically precise, typical of a short period of manufacture, representative of contemporary taste and a good buy. The other lacks all these qualities and reflects only a variety of English silverwork and taste unfortunately all compounded into one.

The casters tell a similar tale but of slightly different purpose. Both are the same period and type, 1727 and 1724 respectively. Both are worth £80-£120 because they have been later worked. But whereas one, like the baluster mug, is smothered with more blooming scrolls while originally it too would have been plain, the other, unaltered except for some script initials, is for me a more pleasing object, particularly as the proportions are better, especially of the spreading foot, and the bun-top cover is more distinctively pierced. So even amongst altered pieces, choice can be exercised to advantage.

The salt cellars should achieve prices of around £40-£50 each and the comparison here is one of usual and unusual forms of the same type. To the right is a compressed circular example with waved gadroon rim and hoof supports, common throughout the 18th century and still in plentiful supply. This one is by Arthur Annesley, 1760. The other is a silver-mounted gourd or nut shell by Phipps and Robinson, c.1785. The shell is an attractive tan brown and not as dark as the photograph depicts. This salt is distinctive again of the late 18th century and of its particular makers, but also continues the tradition of mounting coconuts, shells and other natural forms which can easily be traced to pre-Elizabethan silver in this country. Many such coconut cups, bowls or salts still sell for comparatively low prices, perhaps because they seem in plentiful supply, but many such items will prove on examination to be Continental or South American, and good English examples, well hallmarked as here, are a little more unusual. Whether or not they possess investment qualities, they are certainly good value for money and colourful interesting pieces. The one here is from a set of four which should fetch around £200-£300.

Our last comparison is relevant to the ever popular field of small work whose card cases, snuffs, vinaigrettes, nutmegs, toothpick and lancet cases, wine labels and rattles seem to have a timeless appeal to collectors of all types and experience. It is not hard to understand this vertu approach to silver when one handles the best objects. The prices of our objects are not equal. The plain oval snuff box by George Cowdery, 1792, is a typical and sound example although just a little rubbed and tired; it should bring about £70-£110. The toothbrush and brush box by Joseph Taylor, Birmingham, 1797 will probably make £200-£300. The object lesson is twofold. In the first instance, as with the salts, it is the choice between common and less common objects, and in the second place it is a good example of the most valuable adage any collector can be given: "Always buy the best", no matter what your budget.

The toothbrush set is quite delightful. The case, with twin flush-hinged covers bright-cut and wriggleworked with formal borders and vacant shields, if separated from the brush might be taken for a toothpick case, but the twin compartments are specifically to hold the detachable ivory and bristle brush heads. All items fit into a contemporary red leather case with slip top not illustrated here. Many similar smallwork items of a more unusual type are to be found, like sugar crushers, invalid straws, calendars, eye baths and nipple shields, (many of a vague medicinal application), and are worth serious attention if only because of their often amusing personal nature which sets them aside from the majority of other silverwares both functional and decorative and therefore excellent gifts for Christmas or any other time.

Figure 2. *Rear view of settee, showing fabric design, and the outward-curving back uprights ending in acorn finials. Note how the design shows off the fabric to advantage. Courtesy Haslam and Whiteway.*

Figure 1. *William Morris and Co. settee of c.1890 with original covering. Based on the "Morris" design of armchair. Courtesy Haslam and Whiteway.*

A WILLIAM MORRIS SOFA
by John Andrews

For my Christmas present this year you can stroll down Kensington Church Street to Haslam and Whiteway's and buy me a William Morris sofa. It would fit beside a convivial fireplace at home where we have a very suitable space. With William Morris such a famous household name, such a landmark in domestic design and so famous for his opposition to shoddiness in manufacture, what better present could I have than a pretty, small settee of original William Morris and Co. manufacture, covered in an original William Morris fabric? It would be at once a charming, useful piece and a splendid investment.

The piece I would like — shown in figures 1 and 2 — is a mahogany-framed, small settee with a green and cream floral covering. Unfortunately, the seat covering has suffered, parting company in the undyed areas from the rest of the surface. But no doubt repairs could be effected, or a similar new fabric used for restoration. The settee itself is a variant on the famous "Morris" armchair design and, to show its origins, one of the "Morris" adjustable armchairs, in oak, is illustrated here as well (figure 3). This celebrated design was devised from a traditional prototype found by the Morris and Co. manager, Warington Taylor, at an old carpenter's, named Ephraim Colman, in Herstmonceux, Sussex, about fifteen miles from where

I now live. William Morris himself was not very closely involved with the firm's furniture manufacture and, after a few early attempts, left much of the design of furniture to the architect, Philip Webb, who was a close friend. Indeed, after the firm of Morris, Marshall, Faulkner and Co. was founded in 1861, its first product was a cabinet designed by Webb and painted by Morris which now rests in the Victoria and Albert Museum. It was exhibited in the International Exhibition in London in 1862. At that time the books of the firm were kept by C.J. Faulkner, a mathematics don from Oxford, while Morris himself, who put up much of the money, was elected manager by his friends, Rossetti, Burne-Jones, Webb, Ford Madox Brown, Marshall and Arthur Hughes — who all put their services at the disposal of the firm — because, in the words of Rossetti, "it was not that we ever dreamed that he would turn out to be a man of business, but because he was the only one of us who had both time and money to spare".

Morris in fact was very successful, especially in the early days of the firm. In 1865-9 Faulkner was replaced by the extraordinary Warington Taylor, responsible for this "Morris" armchair's origination. Taylor was an Old Etonian from the West Country and had known Swinburne at school. After

adopting Roman Catholicism he was disinherited by his father and sank rapidly in economic circumstances, being reduced to working as a check-taker at the opera. Despite this, he knew Godwin and Burges, the two celebrated architects, and was a keen musical enthusiast. The design for the "Morris" chair was sent, around 1866, to Webb by Taylor in the form of a sketch and description in a written note, and the model was adapted for production by the firm. It was widely copied, by Gustav Stickley in America and by Liberty and Co. in England.

Warington Taylor died in 1870, but the firm kept the design in their catalogues into the 1890s, by which time they were making reproduction 18th century furniture as well as the original designs. Indeed, the "Morris" oak chair here is covered with the "Squirrel" design wool tapestry, designed by John Henry Dearle, who joined the firm in 1878, and produced this pattern in the 1890s. By this time Philip Webb had been replaced by the furniture designer George Jack, who took over as chief designer around 1890. Jack and Dearle were· responsible for many of the best designs produced by Morris and Co. in the 1890s, Jack being particularly associated with the bold, spiky marquetry set into mahogany and other woods on the firm's top quality pieces.

The settee, dating also from the 1890s, uses the same front frame decoration as the chair, with its "bobbins" set into the square section and slightly tapering legs. The back, however, flares slightly outwards, ending in acorn finials at the corners, giving a more sophisticated approach and more comfort than the photograph implies. The proportion and colour are ideal for a modern or traditional room, so that the appeal of the piece is universal. Morris and Co. have inevitably been associated, particularly in their early days, with products that were far too expensive for anyone but the extremely rich. In the "Sussex" range of rush-seated chairs and the "Morris" upholstered chairs they demonstrated, however, that it was possible for the aesthetically-inclined to keep up with fashion without heavy expenditure and, at the same time, deeply influenced many of the Arts and Crafts Movement designers with their approach.

George Jack has gone on record as saying that Morris was "hardly interested in furniture at all" and that he was left to get on with things. This was probably just as true in the 1860s, when Morris was more interested in textiles and wall coverings, but by the 1890s his con-

Figure 3. Oak "Morris" armchair designed by Philip Webb from a sketch sent by Warington Taylor c.1866 of a traditional type found in Herstmonceux, Sussex. Covered with "Squirrel" wool tapestry designed by John Henry Dearle in the 1890s. Shown by the Fine Art Society, New Bond Street, in conjunction with Haslam and Whiteway in 1979.

cern with Socialism and printing, quite apart from his proficiency in poetry (he declined the laureateship in 1892), painting, prose, metalwork and Icelandic sagas, must have left little time for anything else. He died in 1896. He has left an enormous mark on attitudes to design. The price of the sofa? £800. Wrap carefully please, and send to. . .

Left: Attractive coach lamp with plated interior. £95.

Auction Feature — Vintage Lamps
J.M. Welch & Son   17th November

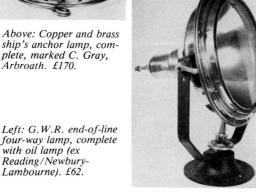

Miners' safety lamps, left to right. By The Lamp and Lighting Co. of Eccles, brass and plated finish. £60. "The Protector", by The Lamp and Lighting Co. of Eccles, with lock. £80. Early pattern, c.1818. £35. By Hailwood & Ackroyd (blue lens). £55. Copper and brass (later model), Prima, Birmingham. £57.50.

Above: Copper and brass ship's anchor lamp, complete, marked C. Gray, Arbroath. £170.

Left: G.W.R. end-of-line four-way lamp, complete with oil lamp (ex Reading/Newbury-Lambourne). £62.

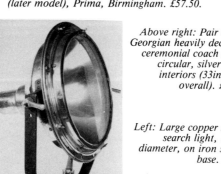

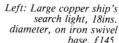

Above right: Pair of fine Georgian heavily decorated ceremonial coach lamps, circular, silver plated interiors (33ins. high overall). £1,200.

Left: Large copper ship's search light, 18ins. diameter, on iron swivel base. £145.

Right: One of a pair of brass Lucas car oil head lamps. £130 (the pair).

Figure 1.

White Dialled Longcase Clocks

by
G.K. Hadfield

Wherever I go these days, be it to auctions, fairs or other traders, and even overseas, I hear the same tale of stagnant sales.

Certainly the price of the run of the mill longcase clock is now lower since there are fewer buyers here at home and in traditional European markets. This real depression, which affects our trade as much as any other, has swept aside many of the shippers who arrogantly used to display "trade only" signs! There is good news, however, for those buying and selling good quality clocks as the value of these has not fallen at all. When I came into the trade I was given

two words of advice from a dealer who had been in the trade man and boy and is now nearer eighty than seventy. The first was that I should use every penny of my capital and the second that I should always, always buy quality. Certainly the latter advice is more relevant now than ever. The value of a worthwhile clock is as great now as ever and I can see no probability of a reduction in its price.

If you accept, as I do, that the long-

Figure 2.

Figure 3.

case is the king of clocks, what steps might the canny buyer take to acquire an example that will both constantly delight and hopefully prove a worthwhile investment? I suggest that he puts his shirt on a good white dialled example. For too long, despite valiant attempts principally by Brian Loomes, they remained the poor relation. Yet between 1775 and, say, 1810, hundreds of thousands of good, elegant longcase clocks were made.

A white dialled need not be ordinary — see figure 1, an eight day with place name apertures above the two subsidiary dials. Figure 2 shows a glimpse of the handsome movement. Figure 3 shows the dial and hood only of a Hunter of Burlington (today known as Bridlington as every Yorkshireman will tell you!) with manually set novel moon disc and calendar work. Automata abound in enamel dials, particularly in West Country clocks, and see-saws, rocking

Figure 4.

ships, rolling eyes and similar are not uncommon. I even know of an enamel dial longcase clock c.1800 showing equation of time!

My canny buy, therefore, will be an enamel dial longcase carefully selected from thousands on offer in the U.K. One of the noted Barwise family made the mahogany clock shown in figure 4. The case is restrained and of fine colour and the dial is exceptionally well decorated with the maker's name within a cartouche, roses in the corners, the moon's age shown in the arch and the date shown by a concentric brass hand.

Consider figure 5 which is another mahogany clock of Lancashire origin. The beautiful figured mahogany is enhanced with fluted columns to the hood and trunk and a rich royal blue glass panel decorated with gold scrolls above the square dial which shows moon phases rather than the usual seconds.

Smith of Pittenweem made the little oak cased clock in figure 6. This is obviously an early example, as you will notice that the clock has a date ring rather than the less desirable disc, and again is of good colour with a beautiful original dial which shows carnations, roses and strawberries. The frets to the swan neck pediments are, of course, a delightful Scottish feature.

Figure 7 shows a clock by a Bristol maker that has two early features. The first is a moon disc which does not have the traditional derelict cottage and storm tossed ship but two likenesses of the moon against a dark blue ground and gold stars. The second is that, as with the Smith of Pittenweem, this Bristol painted dial moonphase shows the date via a silvered ring rather than the normal small disc.

The next clock, by Bunyan of Lincoln (figure 8), is just a bit of a cheat as the strike silent is a dummy though the rest of the clock, with its original finials and asymmetrical steel hands, is doubtless elegant.

The last illustration, figure 9, shows a simple oak cased Samuel Deacon clock. This maker from Barton in the Beans is too well known for me to need to sing his praises.

I do not believe that the thoughtful and discerning need to spend thousands on marquetry, walnut or mahogany clocks by London makers in order to buy well.

All clocks shown, with the exception of the first two, have a number of things in common. They all have asymmetrical hands. They are all as original as one may reasonably hope to find in clocks 180 to 200 years old. All have long doors, roman hour numerals and full minute chapter rings. All have raised gesso work in the spandrels.

I admit to bias, but put off the car replacement for another twelve months and buy a good longcase clock!

Figure 5.   *Figure 6.*   *Figure 7.*   *Figure 8.*   *Figure 9.*

Further Notes on BROWN SALTGLAZED STONEWARE of the 19th Century

by Hugh Turner

Figure 1

Figure 2

Figure 3

Figure 4

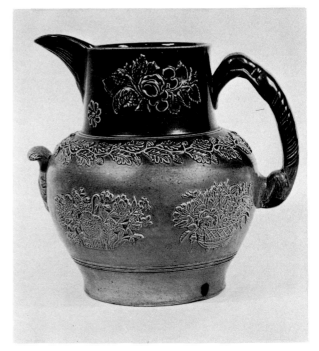

It is now two years since we first explored Brown Saltglazed Stoneware of the 19th century. In that time I have answered many letters from members who have things to say about their collections.

Mrs. Evans from Derbyshire takes me to task for perpetuating the widely used term "Nottingham" as group name for the potteries based on the Brampton area near Chesterfield. I agree that we should try to get this ware accepted as "Brampton".

Of the Brampton potters, we know that Matthew Knowles worked the Welshpool and Payne Potteries, one of which he had taken over from Luke Knowles in 1835. He was later joined by his son and the firm continued into this century. The Briddens, who started with three Williams, father, son and grandson, built and maintained the Walton Pottery for a century from 1790. Oldfield, in various partnerships from 1810, probably became the biggest firm in this area. He more than the others impressed his name on his "antique ware" which was originally only a minor part of the production of all these potteries.

These firms and many others produced that fine dark, whole coloured distinctive range of barrels, jugs and filters with which we are here concerned. Marks are seldom found on larger items, but Mrs. Evans has two charming pottery baskets marked S & H Briddon as well as flasks marked Oldfield & Co.

The inns liked the magnificent moulding of the Brampton spirit barrels and jugs with their patriotic motifs. One wonders if the fashion of having larger jugs stamped or incised with the name of the hostelry was pride of possession or to stop them "wandering". What of the taste for Prince of Wales Feathers and

Fine 7ins. jug, 1800, ribbed neck, overcrowded decoration, perfect texture, £55. Wine flask, 1820, a rather self-conscious attempt at classical elegance, £35. Very "smooth" little tobacco jar, 1830, good design, well worth £40.

Figure 5

had been the popular choice since Dwight's Bellarmines.

Saltglaze did of course survive into the 20th century. It had, however, become consciously "antique" and in the end only studio potters like the Martin Brothers retained it.

I believe that domestic ware was different in style from that required by the inn trade. It had less coats of arms and more classical scenes and silver mounts, as will be seen in the illustrations.

Lastly, water filters, so essential to house and cottage when water sources were so doubtful. Lipscombe of Manchester & London is a good name to be found on "Brampton" ware. George Robins of London has much more the look of the London potters. Anyway, buy them, they look very fine on the patio or in the hall planted with a

Figure 6

Figure 7

Figure 8

Georgian arms? Did this indicate support for the Prince Regent? Surely not!

While all this was so popular in the north, Kishere, Doulton & Watts and Stiff, all mentioned in my previous article, were continuing in their different style in the London area.

All these firms and many others from Bristol to Tenby were beginning to lose interest in saltglazing by about 1860. As early as 1835 Powell of Bristol had introduced a glazed stoneware which became known as Bristol Ware. This only needed one firing, as the glaze was produced at the same time as the ware itself.

Although this new ware was considered in every way superior to the earlier method, it was really the end of the long tradition of "saltglaze" which

Figure 9

Figure 10

Figure 11

geranium and are very nearly indestructible. I've a friend in the antiques trade at Bildeston who puts orchids in his and people come for miles to see them.

All barrels seem to come in two sizes. Figure 1 is 14ins. and figure 2 11ins. Both are probably Matthew Knowles and certainly Brampton. Note the Prince of Wales feathers on figure 1 and the fine knight on the other. They both have good Georgian arms and the lions have the typical "soapy" expression one expects to find around this period.

The beer jugs are both 10½ins. and have the same spouts, handles and neck decoration. In spite of the difference in colour and decoration on the body, they both appear to be Brampton. They bear out the remarks which I made earlier, figure 3 being an inn jug and figure 4 domestic.

Two very fine jugs for the home with classical scenes and domed lids appear in figure 5. (a), 9ins., is silver mounted, 1804, and (b) is Sheffield plate of the same period. Strangely, for all their sophistication, they still have rather ordinary hounds and huntsmen around the base. These are from one of the London potters. Figure 6 raises the question of who these puzzle jugs puzzle. The liquid is sucked up through the handle while the fingers close various holes in the rim and elsewhere.

The Silenus jug in figure 7 is 10ins. and of quite superlative quality. It is included because it is Doulton, a firm about whom I have not always been very complimentary.

The fine jug by Meigh, 7½ins., is not of course saltglaze. It is included in figure 8 to show how the same designs were so often used on very dissimilar

jugs. These dressed-up monkeys of Hogarth origin are only one of a number of designs copied by our potters from of designs copied by our potters from other more fashionable ware.

The sharp and intricate design on figure 9 is very uncommon on saltglaze stoneware. In fact this 9½ins. jug is something of a puzzle. If any members have any theories, they must write and let me know.

The filters mentioned above are illus-

trated in figure 10 (Robins) and figure 11 (Lipscombe). If they look a bit grubby, it's because I've just brought them in from the garden to be photographed. They are 16ins. high.

Prices have gone up a little since my last article. Anyway, these are larger items.

Figure 1. £50 with a good original tap.

Figure 2. Although smaller, no less than the other. The design is crisper.

Figure 3. £50. A fine jug sometimes found with the inn name stamped or incised, which adds another £5 to the value.

Figure 4. Rather rarer, so a little more valuable.

Figure 5a. Over £100, Georgian silver and quality together.

Figure 5b. £80/£100, old Sheffield plate and a slightly unsatisfactory tapering at the base.

Figure 6. £50. Americans love them.

Figure 7. £60. I think I prefer figures 3 and 4.

Figure 8. The saltglazed jug is rather rustic. About £30.

Figure 9. Very unusual, if a bit puzzling. £35.

Figures 10 and 11. £25, or with a lid and interior fittings, £40.

This is the end of what I originally set out to describe. There were, of course, hundreds of other items from jam jars to footwarmers, many of them exported to farflung outposts of the Empire as well as Holland and Imperial Russia.

There are still a lot of interesting things about at considerably less than the prices quoted above. Watch out for the unusual and don't forget the orange peel texture of this ware. It's saltglaze that you're collecting, not Bristol ware.

Fine 18th century pot board dresser base with original patination, or is it?

CAVEAT EMPTOR
by Derek Green B.A.D.A.

Over the last few years, the increasing popularity and therefore demand for oak furniture has created a scarcity of goods and an increase in their value. These factors have begat greed and, in turn, unscrupulous forgeries. Many of us have watched the progress of these fakes from the known sources to the salerooms. Lack of knowledge by the auctioneer's cataloguing staff or, less charitably, greed again, has resulted in the fakes being catalogued as genuine.

So far let us be quite clear that no crime has been committed. The manufacturer of the fake has no legal requirement to tell the auctioneer its true pedigree and, on the back of the auctioneer's catalogue — which I'm sure you all read — the small print absolves most salerooms from any responsibility.

From here the progress of our fake can lead in three directions, all of which are disastrous to the eventual owner. A private person can outbid the opposition at the auction, going away feeling cock-a-hoop that he has deprived those greedy dealers of their profit. An unknowledgeable dealer, keen to join the specialists, can purchase what on the surface appears to be a cheap lot, with plenty of profit left in it. A knowledgeable but unscrupulous dealer can buy it, knowing exactly what it is and fully aware of the profit he can see in the piece by continuing the deception. This latter course has, I believe, been perpetrated mainly by certain Continental dealers which, although fortunate for us, is still bad for trade in the long term.

Although over the last few years I have seen and been offered numerous fakes, I have never had the opportunity to document and photograph one. The low dresser base (figure 1) which is the star of this article was brought to me by an unfortunate and unsuspecting client who requested that it should be restored and repolished. Before examining this dresser in detail, let me summarise the possible profits to the parties concerned to illustrate the commercial reasoning behind these fakes.

The Faker. The dresser in my opinion would cost about £300 to construct. He

Figure 1.

mouldings have been cleverly distressed only where distress would be expected.

3. Sections of drawer linings and the back board have been deliberately broken away or left missing. (Figures 2 and 3.)

4. Two side mouldings have been made in pine and left to look like later replacements. (Right-hand side as viewed from front.)

5. A long, crude plank of painted pine has been affixed underneath the drawers to simulate a recent amateur strengthening repair.

sends it to auction where, duly catalogued as early 18th century, it could make from around £1,000 to over £2,000 if two bidders believed what they read in their catalogue. Assuming the former situation, however, the faker makes £1,000 minus 10% (auctioneer's commission) = £900 minus £300 (cost) = £600 or 100% on cost.

The Auctioneer makes 10% from seller = £100 plus 10% from buyer = £100 = £200.

After this there are several alternatives for the disposal of the piece which has cost £1,000 plus 10% = £1,100.

The Unknowledgeable Dealer. He doesn't know that the piece is wrong and sees the sense in undercutting the specialist dealer with this "lucky buy". He asks £1,400, so he makes £1,400 minus £1,100 = £300 or 27%.

The Unscrupulous Dealer. He may or may not know and certainly doesn't lose any sleep over the originality of the piece. He asks the full price that would be paid by an ethical specialist dealer. When it sells he makes £2,500 minus £1,100 = £1,400 or 127%.

The Unscrupulous Foreign Dealer. His customers won't be able to tell so unless he is very unlucky indeed, his economics are £4,000 minus £1,100 plus £100 shipping costs = £2,800 profit or 230%.

Having discussed the economics of faking and selling fakes in this case, let us now examine this piece in detail, so that we may be aware that it is unscrupulously constructed to deceive all but the very knowledgeable. First we will put ourselves in the shoes of the faker and see the features that he has built in to fool us, and then examine the points that an observant and knowledgeable eye will recognise as wrong.

Simulation of Age

1. The dresser base is made completely from old timbers and the original wear and tear has been carefully positioned so that it is where one would expect to find it. The back boards, back of the legs, feet and drawer linings show exactly the correct type of wear and rot. (Figure 2.)

2. The new turnings on the legs and all

Figure 2.

Figure 3.

Figure 4.

Figure 5.

6. The cock beading around the drawers has been chipped and broken away in places as would be expected. (Figure 4.)

7. Remnants of some period swan-neck handles and two old escutcheons were affixed to the drawers. Holes were made in the centre of the drawer fronts and plugged to simulate the position of the "original" knobs. Two old locks have been fitted and the drawers lined with newspaper. This of course is an easy way to camouflage new joints, and was genuinely done in the past to keep out dust. Our faker had used a Welsh newspaper and I discovered that a photograph depicted a local Member of Parliament who had only been in the House of Commons a year!

8. Old nails have been used throughout except on the "replacement" mouldings. (Figure 5.)

9. Wooden pegs have been carefully finished proud of the surface to simulate the correct shrinkage signs. (Figure 4.)

10. Before final construction the timbers were probably placed in a hen coop. The ammonia from the excrement rapidly darkens any new cuts and "evens-up" the colour of the timber throughout. This is a well-known faker's trick which can rapidly simulate age. After construction the whole carcase was probably again left for some time in a hen coop or stable to accrue further dirt in all the cracks and joints before a rudimentary wax polish for its journey to the auction house.

Evidence of Faking

Let us now examine the features that tell us the article is a fake. First I should make it clear that a knowledgeable dealer or collector has an initial "gut reaction" that says "FAKE". This is impossible to define; were it possible we should all be experts and there would be no market for the faker! The gut reaction is normally sufficient to resist further examination, but should we continue some of the following tell-tales are likely to be found.

1. Old timber with no previous evidence of use in another context is very hard to find. Oak floorboards provide the major source of supply for fakers (or for replacement tops for gateleg tables, etc.). However, floorboards were originally nailed to joists at approximately 15 inch centres. In this particular fake the perpetrator did not conceal these giveaway holes as well as he might have done. Figure 6 shows the underside of the pot board and I have marked the old holes with chalk. Figure 7 shows the top. The position of these old holes cannot, in this case, be confused with correct construction. Beware of the refined faker who provides strategically placed strengthening members to provide reasons for otherwise unaccount-

able holes. Figure 8 shows the underside of the top where the evidence of the joists is apparent. I was surprised to see that the faker had not made more effort to remove the evidence.

2. Having mentioned that wooden pegs have been carefully finished to stand proud of the surface, you will note in figure 9 that there is no peg joining the stretcher to the leg, as should have been the case. This factor would not have been apparent had we not removed a section of moulding. Nor would the evidence of recent staining be visible. You will also see only one new nail with no other evidence of a previous fixing for the moulding. The fact that the nail

Figure 6.

Figure 7.

Figure 8.

Figure 9.

has not even had time to discolour proves that the fake is very recent.

3. Even the most dedicated faker of furniture must be tempted by the advantages modern machinery provide in speeding up his task. Tell-tale marks of this machining would normally be removed by hand but, if you are lucky, somewhere will be a section he has missed. I found only one such piece about 6ins. long under the front garter moulding where the unmistakable evidence of a thicknesser/planer had been at work. (Figure 10.)

Conclusion

What can be learnt from this little example of the faker's art? We know that all forms of art have been faked from the year dot and that "con people" have been in existence since Eve. The title I have chosen does in fact apply to life in general and may I digress with a tale of an incident years ago in Naples when I was Officer in Charge of a Naval shore patrol? The aircraft carrier on which I was serving had made a two-day stop after returning from the Far East. I was called to the local police station to help sort out an incident that had occurred.

Some of our Chinese sailors had sold to a Neapolitan street trader several full cartons of two hundred cigarettes. The street trader had sold a packet to some innocent purchaser who discovered that on removing the cellophane and then the silver paper he was faced with a slice of bread!

Understandably, the nearest policeman was summoned, the street trader grabbed a Chinese sailor and we all ended up at the local station.

In this instance the customer got his money back, the street trader got fined for trading without a licence and my Chinese sailor was able to convince us all he was not the one who perpetrated the dastardly deed. After all, don't all Chinamen look alike?

From this early experience of life I learnt a basic philosophy: unless I was extremely knowledgeable, I would not buy a secondhand Rolls Royce "wiv only twenny fousand miles on the clock, guv" from a back street car trader or at auction. I would prefer to go to an expert who has a reputation for fair trading that he wishes to uphold. So I would perhaps have to pay a little more, but the peace of mind obtained would be worth it.

So, we arrive back at our art fakes — no reputable dealer is going to handle one, his reputation and livelihood are too valuable to lose for a quick buck.

So where does this put the auctioneers? It is an unfortunate fact that the small firm of auctioneers — often an off-shoot of a much larger real estate firm — cannot be an expert in all aspects of "art". The large, specialist auctioneers suffer from being vast, metamorphic masses who, by sheer volume of turnover, weight of advertising, free, glittering press coverage of this and that world record price, can succeed in spreading the gospel of Utopia where the seller gets the best possible price and the purchaser gets the best possible bargain.

Remember also that a few odd mistakes made by a junior cataloguer for a large firm of auctioneers, whose blunder is missed by his superior due to a surfeit of after-dinner port, will not cause the Chairman any sleepless nights.

As President Truman said: "The buck stops here" and any reputable dealer is aware of this and will not play Russian roulette with his reputation.

Figure 10.

Figure 1. A ''five-position'' ship portrait in oils by H. Vale, the earliest recorded native English marine painter, dated 1714. From her construction the ship is probably a French prize taken in the War of the Spanish Succession, and so this painting is likely to have been commissioned by the captain who captured her.

Figure 2. A good example of the ''three-position'' ship portrait; in this case the East Indiaman ''Star of India'' off Tynemouth. Painted in oils by John Askew, c.1790.

SHIP PORTRAITS

by
Simon Carter

Figure 3. A most interesting water-colour portrait of the brigantine ''Grazia Dio'' by the Trieste artist Ferdinando Luppis, dated 1816. She flies the Austrian flag, and is shown on ten different tacks in the background and a scale of her measurements is provided. A huge Teutonic eagle hovers overhead bearing an inscription to her owners, the Minervi family. Three dimensional realism is provided by the cannon being made of intricately rolled paper.

The thought of ships makes people feel traditional: they personify them, and significantly call them ''she'', probably because it is known they can be fickle. The accomplishment of a voyage, especially in the sailing era, was always an event, since usually one's life and livelihood depended on it. On some occasions it was also a matter to be recorded for posterity, and from this feeling, similar to that which in Middle European countries impelled people to commission a naive picture from the local painter to commemorate their deliverance from some dramatic adversity, arose the art of ship portraiture. And art it is, however repetitive and primitive these rather simple yet laboriously detailed records may seem of sailing vessels, steam assisted sailing ships, paddle-steamers, screw-driven steamers, and even submarines, in the same way that the conventions of icon painting, which were laid down in Byzantine times, are still rigorously observed by artists today. This is not to say that there were schools of ship portrait painting — one cannot talk of the Liverpool or Bristol schools for example; however, over the years certain conventions in the portrayal of ships grew up, to which almost every painter in every port independently but slavishly adhered over a long period of time, and it is the consideration of these conventions that enables one to differentiate between a specific ship's portrait and a marine painting of a general kind.

The origin of ship portrait painting begins with the Dutch, the first nation to treat the sea seriously in their art, because, apart from other more aesthetic reasons outside the scope of this article, their economic life depended on their dominance of the maritime ''carrying trade''. It was quite usual for the burghers' syndicate who financed a ship to commission a painting of it, meticulously executed of course, to enhance their sober boardroom. Particularly popular were pairs showing the same ship in different situations: basking in calm blue sea at its exotic destination point, contrasted with a second showing her battling home through tempestuous grey seas to deliver the goods. In the 18th century and in Britain especially, which became the dominant naval nation during this period, the ship portrait became almost standardised into a long oblong format in which the ship, usually with all sails set, was viewed broadside on in detail in the centre of

the canvas, with small representations of the same ship tacking towards and away from the viewer on each side. Sometimes one of these small views would be dispensed with in order to include a piece of identifiable coastline, that would set the scene for the informed observer. These pictures were quite sophisticated affairs, undertaken regularly by all the leading marine painters of the day, such as Serres, Holman, Paton, Dodd, Luny, Huggins, Whitcombe, etc. and the majority of the vessels would be those of the Royal Navy or the East India Company. Paintings of smaller private trading vessels are fairly rare. Because of the precariousness of communication and the high incidence of wars and piracy, it was not general practice to have the name or style of one's ship visible from a distance, in case of the need for disguise; thus many of these early works appear to be of anonymous ships.

However, the long period of peace which followed the end of the Napoleonic Wars in 1815 and the abolition of the East India Company monopoly in 1833 brought a vast increase in mercantile shipping and shipyards of the humbler kind all over the European seaboard. With the suppression of piracy, ships could proudly fly their identification flags — from 1854 they had to anyway, under the terms of the Merchant Shipping Act which insisted that each ship fly its allotted official number: a series of four flags flown vertically from the mizzen mast, each of which represented a numeral. Private enterprise prospered, and a new class of owner/builder/captain came into being in most seaports from Aberdeen to Ancona — similar to the Onedins of T.V. fame. These people, who had unsophisticated but tradi-

Figure 4. A comparative example of the best English work of the same period as figure 3, a brig by Henry Collins of Whitehaven, dated 1814.

Figure 5. The sail-assisted steamship ''Beta'' shown off Dover by R.B. Spencer, c.1870. She flies the Red Ensign at the stern, the statutory flag of the British Merchant Navy from 1864, but in common use by the merchant service since at least 1800. The owner's house flag is at the aftermast, and the Mercantile Marine Jack on the foremast. This was the Union Jack enclosed by a white border, introduced in 1817 to denote that a pilot was required.

Figure 6. A standard prototype ship portrait: the barque ''Vikingen'' off Sandefjord, 1883. Painted by the Norwegian artist Anders Lind, it shows the coastline to the left and the same ship going away to the right. She flies her official number four-flag sequence, and the combined merchant flag of Norway and Sweden, in use between 1844 and 1898.

Figure 7. The Yarmouth drifter ''Viking'', painted in oils on board in 1911 by Moule & Luck, the local pierhead firm. Although very primitive and mass-produced for sale to the trawlermen at about 2s. each, this kind is a pleasingly direct statement.

Figure 8. The "Barque 'Berwickshire' In a Cyclone Latitude 27°-45' South Longitude 62°-39' East" reads the inscription on this oil by the Chinese artist Kwong Sang of Calcutta, painted in 1896. Clearly a commemorative work for the captain, grateful to have escaped a watery grave.

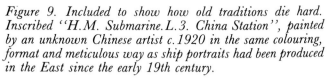

Figure 9. Included to show how old traditions die hard. Inscribed "H.M. Submarine.L.3. China Station", painted by an unknown Chinese artist c.1920 in the same colouring, format and meticulous way as ship portraits had been produced in the East since the early 19th century.

tional and exacting tastes, were particularly desirous that their ships should be commemorated; they had after all in many cases personally both built them and sailed them at considerable hazard over long distances, and in all kinds of conditions. But this new-fangled photography would not do: it had to be a proper hand-done painting, preferably by one of these "pier-head artists", who sat on the quay of every port painting a likeness of every ship that docked, if they felt she had had a good run and the skipper had a little money to spare.

These artists were quick — they had to be, otherwise the ship might leave before they finished; they were cheap — they had to be, because it was a buyer's market, and anyway sailors never have much money, or at any rate not for very long; they were accurate about what they painted — they had to be, because every detail of the vessel must be impeccably correct, but that was usually no problem since most of the artists had been sailors in their time themselves. In Germany their pictures are known as "Kapitänsbilder" — captain's paintings, and in Denmark as "Kadrejerbilleder" — literally bumboat pictures, because when the shipchandlers rowed out in their kadrejer to any newly-arrived ship to solicit custom, they would take with them examples of the local ships' portrait painter's skill.

Their pictures followed a time honoured formula which evolved little over almost three hundred years: a large broadside-on view of the ship with all sails in place and flags flying, a small stern-on view of the same ship to one side and a horizon view of the port of origin or destination on the other. By the early 19th century the "three-view look" seems to have passed out of vogue, and the "two-view look" becomes rare after about 1850. Possibly because of the influx of smaller merchant vessels commanded by less literate masters, from about 1825 the fashion began to have a strip beneath the water on which would be inscribed, frequently and charmingly misspelt, the name of the ship and the master, together with the date.

Presumably with mechanical innovations, principally steam power, shipping did not stay so long in harbour. To meet departure date the painters had to speed up their methods, and from about the 1870s, with a few exceptions, one has the impression that mass-production began to creep into ship portrait painting. Going or gone is the meticulous but quite individual representation of each vessel produced by the early 19th century artist, typified by Giuseppe Fedi of Leghorn who, as well as being a sailor-painter, must have had training as an heraldic artist, because of his highly-mannered flags which lovingly fly in baroque curlicues and his immaculate lettering. In comes a much larger volume of work, any examination of which leads one to suppose that the stereotyped sea, background and sky were all pre-painted long before the ship was even viewed, and that the ship was dashed in at the last moment, and often not very well at that.

This impression is particularly true of what are known as China Trade ship portraits, i.e. ships painted in the Far East by Chinese artists, either in Calcutta, Canton or, after its annexation in 1842, Hong Kong in particular. Chinese ship portraits are especially inscrutable; though finer and more meticulous in their ship detail than even their best European counterparts, they are completely lacking in individuality, serving only to indicate their Chinese authorship by their anonymity as far as painter goes — unquestionably the majority of them were produced by teams of hacks at piecework rates — and by their invariable use of the same cool blue-green palette, ranging from black in the foreground of the sea to a duck-egg turquoise in the sky. An overall wide craquelure of the paint surface is also usually visible, since they were obviously painted in great haste, varnished too quickly and then subjected to violent extremes of temperature on their voyage home.

The end for ship portrait painting came inevitably with the supremacy of photography. For years all over the world painters had done ship portraits from photographs, from the Chinese, to Gregory & Boistel who worked for the Adelaide Photo Co. of Sydney, Australia, or Moule & Luck, Military & Civil Photographers of Lowestoft, Suffolk, but finally in the 1920s, with the end of the sailing era, the camera proved if not stronger, at least irresistibly cheaper than the brush.

A COLLECTOR LOOKS AT DELFTWARE

by Norman Stretton
F.R.S.A.

Figure 1. Lambeth bleu Persan *plate.*

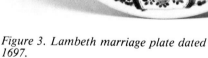

Figure 3. Lambeth marriage plate dated 1697.

Figure 4. Lambeth ointment pot and cover.

Early in March I received a catalogue of an important sale of delftware to be held at Sotheby's in London on the 25th of that month. The sale included a large number of choice pieces from the well-known collection of Mrs. Marion Morgan and Mr. Brian Morgan, from which ninety pieces were shown at a number of museums in the United States under the auspices of The International Exhibitions Foundation, an illustrated catalogue being published with the title "Fair as China Dishes". The volume is splendidly illustrated and each item has detailed and scholarly entries by Brian Morgan.

I thought it might be fun to assume I was a delft collector of reasonable means and after careful perusal of the well illustrated catalogue I decided that there

were a dozen lots which particularly appealed to me. So I made a trip to London, viewed my selection and made a note of the bid I would put forward.

Working systematically through the catalogue the first lot to study with a purchase in mind was a *bleu Persan* plate. Comparatively few examples of this type of decoration have passed through the salerooms in recent years and so it was exciting to see the octagonal shaped plate with its rich blue ground decorated in white with a China-man seated in a landscape, the same design being adapted for the rim (figure 1). It is likely that the English potters took the idea from French pottery made at Nevers in the middle of the 17th century. Persian potters as early as the 14th century used a dark blue ground with designs in white, which led the French potters to name this style of decoration *bleu Persan*. The octagonal plate

illustrated was made in Lambeth towards the end of the 17th century. A similar shaped *bleu Persan* plate but with a rather sketchy painting of a symmetrical spray of stylised flowers and leaves passed through Sotheby's rooms in May 1978 and fetched £800. I thought the Chinoiserie decoration of the plate in this sale was more attractive and, in view of the increase in values over the past two years, considered a bid of about £1,000 would be appropriate, taking into account some slight wear on the rim.

Blue dash tulip chargers are very colourful and I have often thought a good example would show up handsomely on my oak dresser. The catalogue contained four such chargers which I examined carefully. One was a

Figure 5. Bristol double-handled cup.

Figure 6. Lambeth jar.

Figure 7. Liverpool vase.

particularly fine specimen with lively and vigorous painting of tulips and carnations issuing from a tiny spherical vase, but the estimated price of £3,000 to £5,000 made me realise that I must try for a less expensive piece and I finally settled on a tulip charger probably made in London in the third quarter of the 17th century (figure 2). 16ins. in diameter, it was a good large size with a wide border of leaves, fruits and diaper which seemed to concentrate my vision on the central theme of three carnations and a tulip painted in bold tones of ochre, yellow, copper-green and blue. I found the whole conception aesthetically satisfying so thought it right to value this handsome charger at £1,800.

I am not alone in my liking for dated pieces and so when I saw a "marriage plate" with the initials and date IBM 1697 (figure 3) I felt this was something I should consider carefully, particularly as the attractive decoration in bright blue included a pair of storks standing near flowering plants. The plate had a small hair crack but one can hardly expect a piece of delft over 280 years old to be absolutely perfect. I liked the plate very much and the fine painting of the subject together with the early date influenced me to mark my catalogue with a bid of £650.

Many medical accessories were made in delftware in the 17th and 18th centuries, the most common being drug jars of various shapes and differing types of decoration. Seven examples were in the sale, together with a pill slab and cylindrical ointment pots, but one unusual shape caught my fancy. This was a late 17th century ointment pot with its cover (figure 4). Small in size, just over 3ins. high, the depressed globular body with a lug type handle was painted with trailing flower sprays in blue, the decorative design probably originating from K'ang-hsi porcelain. Such an unusual ointment pot would be a handsome addition to any collection but when deciding its value I had to take into account the fact that there was a little chipping around the rim of the pot and some restoration to the flange of the cover. But how marvellous that the cover had survived nearly three hundred years. I felt I had to make a handsome bid and so decided that if I could secure it for £600 or a little over the expenditure would be well worth while.

A double-handled cup just over 5ins. high caught my eye as being somewhat unusual (figure 5). Based on a silver shape, the deep bowl was supported on a short spreading foot, the decoration of scattered flowers with elaborate floral borders to the rim and foot being intricately painted in blue. This well potted piece made at Bristol in the early part of the 18th century had unfortunately some cracks in the bowl which, although not disfiguring the piece, made me value it rather conservatively at not more than £300.

The rather naive decoration on the Lambeth jar illustrated in figure 6 is uncommon, being an early example of European figures painted in polychrome, the colours used being blue, red and green. One side depicts a man walking in a wood, his body outlined in blue and his garments picked out in red, while the reverse shows a lady with a small child ahead of her being held by leading-strings. The combination of these homely subjects on a piece of unusual shape made quite early in the 18th century resulted in a very desirable lot and I wondered what I should bid. Obviously the jar lacked its cover, and there was some slight restoration round the rim, so I decided not to overdo things and thought an appropriate valuation would be £600.

To my mind one of the most handsome pieces in the sale was a tall vase of inverted baluster shape (figure 7), a little over 12ins. high. Painted in soft tones of blue of varying shades, a continuous estuary scene is depicted with Orientals in conversation amid trees and rocks and others plying sampans on the wave rippled estuary. The vase had to be seen for the full merit of the painting to be appreciated. Made about the middle of the 18th century, it was attributed to Liverpool, although a possibility of a Dublin origin was also mentioned. An exact pair to this vase in the Victoria and Albert Museum is almost certainly decorated by the same hand, and the same design is known on a large vase and cover of Liverpool porcelain. The graceful shape of this vase with its fascinating

Figure 2. Lambeth blue dash tulip charger.

Figure 8. Dublin basket.

Figure 9. Dublin serving dish.

Figure 10.
Liverpool plate.

Figure 11.
Lambeth plate:
Nancy Dawson
dancing.

well painted design running round the surface was most attractive, but should it have a cover? If so, the lack of it would detract from its value and even though a vase of similar shape and comparable but slightly less pleasing decoration, also without a cover, was sold in the same rooms in November last for £190, I thought this lot warranted my bidding up to £300.

There were a few pieces of Irish delftware in the Morgan Collection and I hoped this might be an opportunity to acquire an example for my collection. Delftware was made in Ireland by a number of potters from the end of the 17th century and through the 18th century, the greatest activity being about fifteen years on either side of 1750. When I viewed the sale the Irish piece which appealed to me most was a fine circular basket with its sides formed by interlaced circles beneath a scalloped rim. The interior was painted in blue with radiating panels, each of which contained a flower: the attractive design of the basket is illustrated in figure 8.

Sotheby's catalogue suggests that the dish was probably from the factory of John Chambers who was working in Dublin c.1735 to c.1739. There is, however, a jug in America at Colonial Williamsburg with the same pattern inscribed "Mr. White 1750" and this date fits the Dublin factory of Davis & Co. at Worlds End who were in production until approximately 1752. It is interesting to note that in 1750 Mrs. Delaney wrote to her friend Mrs. Dewes: "Tuesday went to Dublin on business; first to a place called the Worlds End, where I spent an hour and a half in choosing out a set of earthenware for the Duchess of Portland such as yours, and a dozen baskets for Mrs. Montagu, as she desired…" The basket was in excellent condition and although not the easiest of things to display I felt it must merit a valuation of £600 or perhaps one more bid if "I was on the wrong foot".

My second choice of a piece of Irish delftware was the well painted attractive large 19ins. dish illustrated in figure 9. The decoration in blue showed a land-

scape with two figures standing on an outcrop of rock beside a tall column, with a group of buildings featured in the background. Several pieces from this service are known, all with a border of swags of drapery arranged over leafy scrolls. A large dish painted by the same hand is in the National Museum, Dublin. The service can be ascribed to Henry Delamain's factory in Dublin and was made about 1755. I noted a bid of £300 against this lot which I thought might be on the low side, but I made a mental reservation that as I particularly wanted a good piece of Dublin delftware I would increase this by £100 if I did not secure the basket previously mentioned, which was due to come up two lots earlier.

The plate illustrated in figure 10 was decorated in a style not normally found on delftware; in fact it gave me the impression that it might have been enamelled by a painter who was accustomed to working on salt-glazed wares. The amusing subject in the well of the plate was a Chinese mother and child

Figure 12. Bristol shell-shaped dish.

seated on a rather sad looking horse with a body nearly twice as long as it should have been. The group was depicted among flowering shrubs growing from rockwork, the whole painted in "jewelled" famille-rose enamels of the type found on some salt-glazed wares. The plate had an elaborate border with trailing sprays and scrolling "fish-roe" panels. The Glaisher Collection in the Fitzwilliam Museum, Cambridge, has a Liverpool delftware bottle painted with a Chinoiserie subject in similar enamel colours with leafy sprays and a rim border somewhat akin to that on the plate illustrated, and it may be that these and one or two other pieces of delftware with comparable enamelling were decorated in Staffordshire. I felt bound to try for this unusual plate, the peculiarly proportioned horse carrying the mother and child was quite hilarious; but how could

I value such an uncommon piece? Well, if it appealed to me it would obviously be desired by others and I could envisage considerable competition, so I marked my catalogue £750 to £800.

Pottery and porcelain with decoration which can be traced back to an original print or painting has always interested me, so when I saw the sale included a delftware plate painted with an adaptation of "Nancy Dawson Dancing the Hornpipe" (figure 11) my mind went immediately to *The Ladies Amusement* of 1762 which has a print of this subject which may have been the inspiration of the painter. Sadler & Green of Liverpool made use of this design which is to be found on transfer-printed delft tiles sometimes with the signature "J. Sadler Liverpool". The subject also appears on early creamware and I have a bowl of about 1765 which has this print. The

delft plate in the sale was ascribed to London, about 1760, though I thought a Liverpool attribution should not be ruled out. This attractive piece was painted in pale shades of blue, green, yellow and manganese with rather stylised sprays of prunus tied with ribbons round the rim: Nancy Dawson was wearing a yellow dress while her companion had a yellow waistcoat. Obviously I should like this plate to tie up with my creamware bowl and the print in my copy of *The Ladies Amusement* and I hoped it might come my way if I thought in terms of £300.

One of the smallest pieces in the sale was a rare Bristol shell-shaped dish painted in shades of blue with two figures crossing a steeply hump-backed bridge on the far side of which was a leafless tree (figure 12). The delicacy of the painting was charming, the design well conceived to fit the shape of the shell, and I really coveted this particular lot, although it was fairly late for delftware, having been made about 1760. The exterior of the shell was fluted and it stood on three short feet. Measuring 3¾ins. its great charm meant that it must surely be worth at least £100 an inch, so it had to be a bid of £450, despite a very small chip. Shell shapes are fairly common in 18th century porcelain, but when should I next see one in delftware?

It now remains to be seen how successful my bids will be: some of my friends call me a "mean buyer", but perhaps when I feel the excitement of the saleroom I may be led to exceed the prices marked in my catalogue. I hope not.

WHAT ACTUALLY HAPPENED AT THE AUCTION

On the morning of the sale it soon became obvious from conversations with a number of dealers and private collectors that the fine examples of delftware on offer had aroused a great deal of interest and consequently prices were likely to be high. This is often the way when an important collection comes on the market accompanied by a well illustrated and informative catalogue.

Once the sale was in progress and the first few lots had been sold, it was apparent that competition was extremely keen and a new level of prices for fine and important delftware was being set. This was confirmed when the fourth item from the Morgan Collection, a rare London "pomegranate" charger, was bought by a leading dealer for £2,400 as compared with Sotheby's pre-sale estimate of £800-£1,200. So I knew immediately that my pre-sale values as a collector were likely to be much below the standard now emerging. This was confirmed when, four lots later on, my first selected piece, the *bleu Persan* plate illustrated in figure 1, was bought by the same dealer for £2,400 as compared with an estimated value of £1,000 made by me when viewing the sale.

A list of "hammer prices" and "actual prices" realised by the twelve items illustrated in this article is given below and I can claim that only three of my suggested prices were fairly near the figures achieved in the saleroom, while in the other cases my values were well below the final bids. Without doubt, there has been a substantial rise in the price of fine English delftware during the past twelve months.

Figure	Description	Auctioneer's Estimate	Author's Estimate	Hammer Price	What items cost the Buyer
1.	Lambeth *bleu Persan* plate	£800-£1,200	£1,000	£2,400	£2,676.00
2.	Lambeth blue dash tulip charger	£1,200-£1,800	£1,800	£2,900	£3,233.50
3.	Lambeth marriage plate dated 1697	£500- £700	£650	£2,100	£2,341.50
4.	Lambeth ointment pot and cover	£400- £600	£600 +	£680	£758.20
5.	Bristol double-handed cup	£400- £600	£300	£280	£312.20
6.	Lambeth jar	£600- £800	£600	£1,600	£1,784.00
7.	Liverpool vase	£300- £500	£300	£580	£646.70
8.	Dublin basket	£400- £600	£600 +	£750	£836.25
9.	Dublin serving dish	£300- £400	£300-£400	£720	£802.80
10.	Liverpool plate	£500- £700	£750 +	£2,100	£2,341.50
11.	Lambeth plate: Nancy Dawson dancing	£300- £400	£300	£500	£557.50
12.	Bristol shell-shaped dish	£300- £400	£450	£340	£379.10

Tunbridgeware
by
Derek Roberts

A fine Tunbridgeware table by Barton, c.1870. The base is made of solid ebony and coromandel is employed on the top. Note the wide variety of techniques and woods used, including the green in the centre.

Figure 1. Some idea of the variety of Tunbridgeware available can be gained from this picture showing tea-caddies; work, handkerchief and pin boxes; a brush, ruler, cribbage board, watch stand, pin wheel, taper and counter holders and a book rest. The cube design seen on the box at the top left predates the end grain mosaic but continued to be made throughout the 19th century.

It was in 1606 that Dudley Lord North, a young nobleman in the court of James I, visited Eridge House, the seat of Lord Abergavenny. The purpose of his visit was to try to recover his health after having led a somewhat dissipated life. It was whilst out walking that he noticed the peculiar appearance of a stream which had a shiny mineral scum upon its surface. It occurred to him that this water might possess similar medicinal virtues to that of some of the spa towns which already existed at that time, both in England and on the Continent, and thus he sought medical advice on the matter. It was as a result of this that the spa town of Tunbridge Wells, as it subsequently became known, was born.

As the number of visitors to the Wells increased, so did the local production of gift ware to sell to them. Indeed by 1650

it had grown to such proportions that one manufacturer alone was employing no less than twenty-two people.

Tunbridgeware, as it came to be known, was, in its early days, very similar to the gift ware produced in other spa towns throughout the country, consisting mainly of trinkets, boxes and toys. Thus, unless an early piece of Tunbridgeware is marked with the manufacturer's label, it is virtually impossible to prove that it was indeed made in or around Tunbridge Wells. These remarks would hold true until well into the 18th century.

One of the earliest manufacturers was Boyce, Brown and Kemp who were working from 1623 until 1927 when they closed their factory. The oldest known piece of Tunbridgeware is a back-gammon board, now in the Victoria and Albert Museum, which can be dated to 1624.

One of the main characteristics of Tunbridgeware throughout the 18th and 19th centuries is the large number of different woods which were often highly figured, had a great variety of colour and were always carefully polished. In the early days these were all of local origin but by the 19th century large numbers of imported woods were also being used. Indeed it has been estimated that the leading makers employed as many as 160 different types.

By around 1800 transfer and painted ware was starting to be produced in quite large quantities and this continued until the advent of the "new mosaic", as it came to be known, which William Burrows is believed to have invented in 1827. It is thought that the idea arose from his seeing an Italian producing mosaic wood work in a hut near Tunbridge Wells. However, it probably

Figure 2. Eridge Castle depicted on the lid of a glove box.

Figure 3. A Tunbridgeware block together with a veneer cut off it.

goes back a lot further than this as a similar ware was being produced either before or at this time in Damascus and it is thought the original concept goes back as far as the Phoenicians.

Sorrento Ware

Sorrento ware, which is still being made today in southern Italy, was first produced at about the same time as Tunbridgeware. Whether it pre- or antedates it has always been a matter of some controversy. The main differences are that Sorrento ware employs dyed woods — red, for instance, which is never seen on Tunbridgeware, being frequently employed — and that the designs depicted, except occasionally on the border, also differ markedly.

Prior to the introduction of the new mosaic, manufacturers had been producing marquetry and parquetry boxes such as that shown at the top left of figure 1, but with the advent of the new ware they were able to create far more intricate designs and could now

depict, for instance, insects, animals, flowers and buildings (figure 2).

Method of Manufacture

The exact way in which Tunbridgeware was manufactured has long been a matter of debate and it seems likely that the methods used varied considerably from one craftsman to another. Certainly all the different designs seen cannot be accounted for by any one technique. However, the basic method of construction for the majority of Tunbridgeware is almost certainly as follows:

1. A design is created on a piece of graph paper and the wood to be used is indicated on each of the squares.

2. This pattern is now copied line by line. Veneers approximately 1/16in. thick and 6ins. long are glued together in exactly the same order as on the graph paper, one block being made for every line of the design. This may well involve making thirty to forty blocks.

3. These blocks are now sliced into

veneers 1/16in. thick, each one thus consisting of a row of square wood sticks. One slice is now taken from each block and these are laid down and glued together on top of each other, thus creating the whole of the original design. It can now be seen that this technique is only applicable to relatively large scale reproduction as the minimum number of final blocks produced is probably thirty to forty which, with an average of sixty slices from each of these, means that the final number of veneers produced, all of the same design, will be around 2,000.

4. Slices are now cut from the block (figures 3 and 4) with a circular saw and glued to the box or other object that is being decorated. When the block is relatively large, brown paper is sometimes stuck to the end face before the veneer is separated so as to protect and strengthen it and stop it disintegrating when it is being transferred to the box or other object. Although the term "end grain" is commonly used to describe the

Figure 4. Sample veneers which were on display in Burrows' workshop.

Figure 5. Many small pieces were produced in Tunbridgeware. Examples of stickware are the counter box, thread waxer and pin poppet, pin stand and pin wheel. In "The New Mosaic" may be seen stamp, pin and puzzle boxes and a needle case.

Figure 6. A tea caddy decorated with the coarse mosaic which is generally only seen on Tunbridgeware produced between 1830-50.

Figure 8. A fine floral design by Barton set on a white ground and contrasted by coromandel.

mosaic, this is really a misnomer as careful examination of the tesserae will show that they are usually long grain.

Stickware

Another type of Tunbridgeware produced at the same time is known as stickware. In this blocks are built up as for the mosaic, but the size of the sticks incorporated is normally much larger. Instead of cutting slices off these blocks they are then turned to produce small decorative items such as the counter box, pin poppet and thread waxer, pin stand and pin wheel seen in figure 5. At the same time veneers may also be cut off these relatively coarse blocks to produce decorative designs similar to those on the tea caddy in figure 6. These are normally seen on the earlier items produced about 1830 and 1850.

Items Produced

The range of items produced in Tunbridgeware is almost limitless, but they are nearly always of a functional nature and generally for use around the home (figure 1). Three of the biggest groups comprise those connected with needlework, writing and toys and games. Some idea of the range will be gained by listing just a few of the items produced.

For needlework, needle boxes, pin boxes, button boxes, needle books, glove menders, knitting pin sheaths, pin trays, tape measures, weighted blocks for holding down material, table clamping candle arms to see by and boxes, trays and work tables for carrying the work around in were all manufactured.

To assist in letter writing beautifully fitted cabinets and writing slopes (figure 7) were produced, stamp boxes were made, stationery boxes, paper knives, paper cutters and book markers, inkstands and desk sets and even beautifully made sealing wax outfits with which to close your letter when it was written.

Various toys were produced such as yo-yos and tops, and boards were made for draughts, chess, cribbage and bezique.

Boxes and cabinets were produced in an almost bewildering variety for such purposes as keeping jewellery and trinkets, hair pins, buttons, gloves, handkerchieves and cigarettes. Tea at that time was a very valuable commodity and thus a wide variety of caddies were produced, often of superb quality, to keep it in (figures 1, 6, 7). Sometimes these had just one compartment and on other occasions two or, very rarely, four. When they had more than one compartment a glass jar was often provided to enable the owner to blend her various choice flavours of tea.

Probably the first designs depicted in the new mosaic, as it was then termed, were very simple ones, but more elaborate designs rapidly evolved. Initially these were probably based on flowers (figure 8) and leaves, but were quickly extended to insects, birds and animals, the moth in particular being seen quite frequently on early boxes.

As their skills developed still further, so the complexity of the subjects being shown increased and thus in a relatively short space of time buildings were being incorporated in the designs (figures 2 and 7). Initially these tended to be of local interest, for example Eridge Castle (figure 2), Tonbridge Castle, Penshurst, Hurstmonceux (figure 7), the ruins at Bayham, Battle Abbey, The Pantiles in Tunbridge Wells (figure 7), Knole,

Figure 7. Some idea of the range of subjects depicted on Tunbridgeware may be gained from this picture. Top, left to right: Hurstmonceux; Battle Abbey Cloisters (by Barton); Muckross Abbey. Bottom, left to right: a bold floral design surrounded by oak leaves; The Pantiles, Tunbridge Wells; a stag.

Figure 9. St. Helena's Cottage, Tunbridge Wells. Note the realistic effect achieved by using individual tesserae for each tile, stone, block, etc., of the building.

Hever and St. Helena's Cottage (figure 9). However, in time more distant buildings such as Windsor Castle, Malvern, Eton College, Muckross Abbey (figure 7) and Shakespeare's birthplace were also used.

In the vast majority of cases the buildings were all built up with tesserae of equal size but in a few instances (such as Fenner and Nye's masterpiece of Battle Abbey) every single stone, window, archway and even the fencing was represented by an individual piece of wood. The overall effect is superb but must have been extremely time consuming and costly to produce. Figure 9 shows a view of St. Helena's Cottage produced in this way and one can see how lifelike it really is.

Only the natural colour of the wood is normally used in Tunbridgeware, no dyes ever being employed. However, there is one particular colour which is always highly prized by collectors, and this is green. This was achieved by finding oak, birch or beech trees which had fallen into the surrounding bogs and been attacked by a fungus which turned it this colour. Unfortunately only a very limited amount of this material was available and in the latter half of the 19th century the waters in the Chalybeate springs were used to dye such woods as satinwood a similar colour. Holly, satinwood and maple were often used as backgrounds to make the picture depicted show to the best advantage (figure 8), but the timber most commonly employed for making or veneering the boxes was probably rosewood. Coromandel and ebony, because of their hardness and also the dark background they provided, were also used quite frequently.

Tunbridgeware Manufacturers

The manufacture of Tunbridgeware was very much a family business and certain families produced it over an extremely long period of time. The most famous of the makers producing Tunbridgeware in Tonbridge itself was **Wise**; George started the business in

1685 and it continued until the death of John Wise in 1899. Unfortunately relatively few of the Wise family's signed pieces still exist. Whether this was because their output was relatively small or because they signed very few it is difficult to assess, but the quality of some of their pieces is quite exceptional. When they employed the Van Dyke design on their boxes they also incor-

porated a thin dotted line around its border and this is a characteristic feature of their work.

Both **Fenner and Nye** were well-known manufacturers in Tunbridge Wells who worked both separately and also in partnership. A considerable number of signed pieces by Nye still exist and they are almost invariably of very fine quality. His designs were frequently of great delicacy and he was very fond of using satinwood as a background.

Thomas Barton, who was probably the most famous of all Tunbridgeware manufacturers, joined Edward Nye in 1836 and continued with him until Nye died in 1863. After this he took over the business, initially signing his pieces Barton late Nye and subsequently solely with his own name. He made extensive use of ebony, and coromandel (figure 7), and this contrasted strongly with the white background of satinwood, box-wood or holly on which he placed his mosaic (figure 8). He made extensive use of the green wood and thus achieved by far the most spectacular colour effects of any Tunbridgeware manufacturer. Some of the flowers he produced such as roses and peonies (figure 8) are beauti-

Figure 10. Cribbage boards and boxes, tea caddies, glove, pin, string and trinket boxes; watch and ink bottle stands and a paper knife. In the centre may be seen a glove box decorated with Russell's individual form of marquetry.

fully executed. It is interesting to note that nearly all the Tunbridgeware furniture one sees such as games, work or occasional tables are by Barton (figure 11, left).

The **Burrows family** commenced manufacture in 1685 and continued right through into the 20th century. They manufactured both in Tonbridge and Tunbridge Wells, **William Burrows** being almost certainly the first to start producing the "new mosaic". Sample veneers from their factory may be seen in figure 4.

One other manufacturer worth mentioning here is **Russell** as his work is often extremely individual. Besides the standard form of mosaic he also decorated his boxes with a form of marquetry and scroll work peculiar to him (figure 10, centre).

Forming a Collection

There are many different ways in which Tunbridgeware may be collected. Thus some people may acquire items in what appears to be a relatively haphazard fashion so as to try to illustrate all the different types of mosaic and the ways in which it is used while others concentrate on one group of items, needlework, for instance, being particularly popular. An interesting collection may be built up of all the different animals, birds and insects depicted and an even wider field is the collection of all the buildings including the numerous ways in which each has been illustrated. This task is almost insurmountable when one realises that one building such as Eridge alone has been shown in more than twenty different ways.

Another aspect is to collect only signed pieces and try to find examples of all the known Tunbridgeware manufacturers' work. Examples by Barton and Nye are reasonably plentiful, but one has to search much harder to find pieces by Burrows, Russell, Wise and Medhurst, to name but a few.

What to Buy

Probably the best advice that can be given to any collector is never to buy any Tunbridgeware that is damaged. This is to overstate the case somewhat, but it must be a very fine piece before one can justify the time and expense involved in restoring it. Very few people are available who can carry out the delicate restoration required once the tesserae are damaged or missing and this is inevitably both time consuming and costly. The loss of even a relatively small piece of the ware will probably cost £20-£30 to replace and extensive damage can easily extend to £100-£150. Obviously if one has the skill and the patience to restore it oneself then this argument does not apply nearly so forcefully. Where the veneers other than the ware itself are damaged then this is obviously not nearly so critical and they can normally be restored with relatively

Figure 11. Left: a fine cigar table by Barton. Right: a rosewood games table.

little effort.

A common defect with Tunbridgeware, particularly with later examples, is that the varnish or lacquer with which they have been finished has become relatively opaque so that the colour and beauty of the veneers beneath it cannot be seen clearly. In these instances it can be very rewarding to remove the dead lacquer gradually with very fine wire wool and a little turps and then restore the piece to its former glory by waxing and polishing it.

A point to guard against is poor repair of Tunbridgeware. It is relatively common to see examples, a part of the mosaic of which has been lost and then filled in with wood filler and the design painted on this. In these instances the piece either has to be accepted for what it is, which may possibly be indicated if, for instance, it depicts a rare view and the price is favourable; or the cost of what may be a very expensive restoration has to be carefully assessed.

The Price of Tunbridgeware

It is impossible to give an accurate guide to the price one might have to pay for any particular item of Tunbridgeware as the quality of each individual piece can well vary the value by 100%-150%. A maker's label will always command an appreciable premium, as also will a rare view or a

particularly fine picture of an animal. Certain items such as toys, pens and pencils which are easily damaged and thus in very short supply also command quite a heavy premium. Examples of the very fine mosaic such as that used to depict the Queen's head on the top of a stamp box (figure 5) are also much sought after. The smaller items of Tunbridgeware such as patch and pin boxes, needlecases, thread waxers and other small items may usually be purchased for between £15 and £40. The medium sized pieces such as handkerchief, glove and jewellery boxes and single caddies will normally fall into the price range £40-£120. However, a particularly fine signed item may well go for appreciably more than this.

To buy a good writing slope or needlework box with fitted interior or large caddy would cost around £300 and if one wants a piece of furniture (figure 11), which will usually be either an occasional, games or work table, then one is likely to have to pay something in the region of £500-£700.

In conclusion, it cannot be stressed too strongly that the pieces which will give you most pleasure and inevitably in the long run prove the best investment are those which are in the most perfect condition. The purchase of a badly damaged piece is almost inevitably sooner or later regretted.

Meerschaum pipe, amber mouthpiece with yellow metal band, 11ins. long overall, fitted case. £950.

Toned Meerschaum pipe, amber mouthpiece with metal band, 5½ins. long overall, fitted case. £500.

Meerschaum pipe, vulcanite mouthpiece, well toned bowl carved with head of, probably, a Napoleonic soldier, 7½ins. long overall, fitted case. £400.

Meerschaum pipe, cylindrical bowl carved in high relief with the royal arms of the Netherlands above inscription "Je Maintiendrai", hinged and pierced Austrian white metal mounts and back plate, 5½ins. wide. £300.

Rare Meerschaum double pipe, the heads and shoulders forming the covers, 5ins. wide, brass stand. £700.

Partly toned Meerschaum pipe, amber mouthpiece with metal band, 6½ins. long. £260.

Meerschaum pipe, amber mouthpiece, bowl carved with the head of Dante in cloth cap set with oak leaves, 7½ins. long overall, fitted case. £220.

Meerschaum pipe, amber mouthpiece, 6½ins. long overall. £260.

Meerschaum cheroot holder, carved with man in 19th century German costume, amber mouthpiece, 7½ins. long overall. £85.

Meerschaum pipe, amber mouthpiece, bowl carved with man in 16th century dress, 6ins. long overall, fitted case. £850.

Meerschaum pipe, partly toned bowl, amber mouthpiece, 7ins. long overall, fitted case, £800.

Meerschaum pipe, amber mouthpiece, 7ins. long overall. £950.

Above: Briar pipe shaped as train engine with four metal wheels, vulcanite mouthpiece, 4¾ins. long. £75.

Right: Large Meerschaum pipe, well carved bowl, square tapering amber stem with darker amber beading, 16½ins. long overall, bowl 8ins. high, fitted case. £3,300.

Rare briar pipe, bowl carved with head of a knight wearing hinged visor with separate cheroot holder and feathered metal cap, bearded face, carved in Meerschaum, cedar stem in two sections and with separate amber mouthpiece, fitted case with dark blue silk tobacco pouch, 21ins. long overall. £950.

CONVERSATIONS OF A VETTING COMMITTEE — 11

by Peter Philp

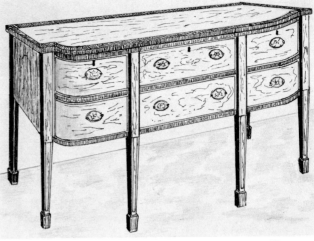

One of the more mysterious cults practised by the Anteeksandart people was known as Investment — a word which, in the 16th century, meant what it said: "the act of putting clothes or vestments on" (especially by the priesthood, as represented in the sagas by the High Priest, the Second Priest and the Priestess). Indeed, in our own culture, Shakespeare refers to the Lord Archbishop "whose white Investments figure Innocence". For us, of course, an investment is still something that is white and innocent — only that and nothing more — but it would appear that, early in the 17th century, the Anteeksandart tribe invested Investment with a new and very different significance bound up with a magical, protective barrier called A Hedge Against Inflation, probably derived from yet another early use of Investment to mean "the surrounding or hemming in of a town or fort by a hostile force".

What was really under attack was not a town or fort but the value of money. The Anteeksandart unit of currency (the Kwid) was being "invested" in the military sense, i.e. beleaguered. To counteract this, the people turned the word inside out, to mean its opposite, so that when they spoke of "investing two thousand kwid" in a fetish, as a Hedge Against Inflation, they firmly believed that, far from laying siege to their own money, they were protecting it, on the principle that, as the kwid fell in value, the fetish would increase. Eventually this led to the fetish becoming not so much a Hedge Against Inflation as a symbol of inflation, and Investment became a dirty word.

In spite of all this, the fact remained that those who chose wisely and bought the right kind of fetishes at the right sort of price succeeded in maintaining and even improving their financial standing. The danger lay in the temptations thus put in the way of artisans who created their own Hedges Against Inflation by faking fetishes, or embellishing genuine but unfashionable ones, and selling them at high prices as Investments. The Saga of the Sideboard is one of the moral tales told to illustrate this theme.

The fair — one of hundreds in the packed Anteeksandart calendar — was due to open to the Pun Terz (the public) on the following day. The vetting committee, comprising the High Priest, the Second Priest and the Priestess, were met to perform the sacred rite of the

casting out of devils. They stood in solemn silence before an object which, according to the ticket, was a Sheraton mahogany sideboard c.1790.

"The owner," said the Priestess, who disliked these wordless reveries in which the High Priest was wont to indulge, " — he hasn't been in the trade very long — is very proud of this. He told me that, at two thousand *kwid*, it would be a very good investment for someone."

"Do you agree?" asked the High Priest.

"I haven't really looked at it properly," replied the Priestess, evasively.

"That crossbanding on the top," ventured the Second Priest, "doesn't look original to me. It doesn't quite match the banding on the edges, and I'm never quite happy when sideboards have that wide crossbanding across the back of the top."

"It *can* be perfectly genuine," said the High Priest. "I have seen very fine sideboards — especially satinwood ones — with their tops crossbanded in rosewood or kingwood all the way round. But I do like to see some traces of the flange plates which held the supports for the brass rail that was usual on sideboards of this kind in the late 18th and early 19th centuries. And there's no sign of them here."

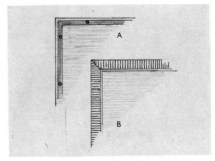

Figure 2 (detail). A. Rear left-hand corner of the top, seen from above, showing the kind of mark that would have been left on a plain mahogany top, without crossbanding, after removal of a wood splash-back. B. The same corner with the tell-tale marks concealed by wide crossbanding.

Figure 1. The sideboard on offer, purporting to date from about 1790. It has the square-tapered legs and oval brass handles consistent with the style of that time. The surface of the top, as well as its edges, is crossbanded; but the crossbanding does not, on close examination, match up too well with that on the edges of the top and on the front of the carcase. The lack of interest at the centre of the front, where there is often an arched "kneehole", is something of a disappointment. Otherwise, if entirely genuine, this would be a very saleable commodity.

"Perhaps," suggested the Priestess, "it was in order to hide marks of that kind that the crossbanding was either replaced, or possibly added."

"Not quite of that kind, I think," said the High Priest, "but marks, certainly, of one kind or another. I can't prove it, but I suspect this sideboard originally had a wooden splash-back which ran right along the back of the top and was continued at the ends. It would have had a rather ornate scrolled profile."

"But that's a much later feature," cried the Second Priest in alarm.

"It was in by about 1825," warned the High Priest, "so even if it were still on the sideboard, we wouldn't reject the piece on those grounds alone — although I agree that it usually indicates a date of about 1840 to 1850."

"But we'd chuck it out if we could prove the splash-back had been removed to enhance the appearance and make it seem forty years older than it really is," insisted the Second Priest.

"How old is it, anyway?" demanded the Priestess, examining a drawer-lining. "This looks pretty good to me, but some of those late Victorian and Edwardian copies of Hepplewhite and Sheraton sideboards can look very convincing indeed. Shall we take a peep at the back?"

The sideboard was lifted out from the wall, and the triumvirate knelt, as in prayer, to peer at the outside back.

"Not Edwardian, anyway", pronounced the High Priest. "You can see clearly the ends of the through-tenons — the rear ends of the two

boards which are in line with the inner front legs, and which divide the interior of the carcase into three sections. It's a useful, if not infallible, rule of thumb. I've never seen it on a reproduction — not even on a late 19th century copy. Equally, I have never seen a period sideboard without it — except for one or two where the back was replaced at some time, probably to get rid of worm-eaten pine, which was the usual timber for the purpose, originally.''

"How long did they go on making sideboards with through-tenons in the backs, do you think?'' asked the Second Priest.

"In my experience, until about 1850. So, if my theory about a feature such as a splash-back on the top is correct, the construction of the carcase, on the evidence of the through-tenons, is still consistent with it, and with a probable date of manufacture of about 1840.''

"But surely'', objected the Priestess, "at that date the legs would have been heavily turned — not square-tapered, like these?''

The High Priest paused to light his pipe. It was well known that it was a pipe, not of peace, but of war — and the lighting of it at such a moment was a danger signal portentous in its implications.

"I want you,'' he said sweetly, "to examine those legs rather carefully. Each one should, of course, be a single piece of mahogany running down through the carcase to the floor, with no joins anywhere along its length.''

The Priestess and the Second Priest went down on their knees once more. The Priestess peered at the legs through her lorgnettes, while the Second Priest

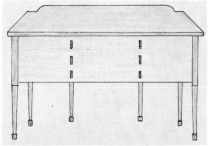

Figure 3. The sideboard viewed from behind, showing the ends of the through-tenons which are in line with the inner front legs — a constructional feature normally present in sideboards made c.1780-c.1850, but seldom after that. The number of tenons varies.

made great play with a pocket torch, casting its beam first on the upper end of the legs, then on the lower. (He was very fond of flashing his torch around like this, not always for very clear reasons, but it gave him something to fiddle with when he wasn't too sure what he was looking for, or even at. On this occasion, however, he was in no doubt, and for once the torch was serving a genuinely useful purpose.)

"These legs *have* been joined!'' he exclaimed. "The upper ends, jointed to the carcase, have a different, more clearly defined grain than the legs proper — or should I say 'improper'?''

"You certainly should,'' said the Priestess. "They've even tried to simulate a continuation of the grain with a brush, carrying it over the join, which must be just below the bottom edge of the carcase, where the turning of the original legs would have started.''

"You're right'', said the Second

Priest, his voice — not to mention his torch — quivering with excitement. "There's a definite line, not very obvious because it coincides with the upper edge of that horizontal bit of satinwood stringing.''

"Coincides?'' echoed the High Priest. "That, my boy, is no coincidence. The stringing has been set at that point quite deliberately to make the join seem natural — but you can see where it extends each side of the stringing, and goes around the corner. Incidentally, the stringing on these legs was the first feature to rouse my suspicions. Usually, when it occurred — as so often it did — on the genuine article, it was repeated elsewhere on the piece — and almost invariably on the upper part of the leg. Here it is on the lower part only.''

"So,'' the Priestess summed up, "this was originally an early Victorian sideboard in the late Georgian tradition, with a mahogany splash-back, heavy turned legs and wooden knobs. You can see from the inside surfaces of the drawer-fronts where the dowel-holes have been plugged; but of course wooden knobs, and turned legs of a lighter kind, occurred in the late Georgian period. If it had looked attractive, they would no doubt have left it alone, but it didn't. It was the type that is extremely difficult to sell, so they put a wide cross-banding on the top to hide the marks of the splash-back, sawed off the turned legs and replaced them with square-tapered ones, inlaid with satinwood stringing at the critical point. Is that about right?''

"Very well put,'' purred the High Priest. "I'm afraid we shall have to ask the owner to remove his prize exhibit. If he's a newcomer to the trade he's probably the innocent victim of someone else's deception. I'm sorry for him, but he has to learn the hard way. I don't think it would have been a good investment at two thousand *kwid*, do you?''

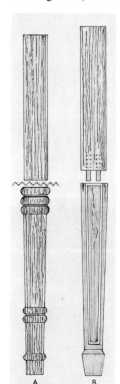

Figure 4 (detail). A. A turned leg c.1840. The jagged line between the upper and lower section denotes, in Anteeksandart symbolism, a saw-cut. B. The lower section — the heavily turned part — having been removed, is replaced with a square-taper. The join is effected with dowels glued into holes drilled for the purpose. The replacement leg is decorated with an inlay of satinwood, or boxwood, stringing — the top edge of the horizontal set exactly against the upper edge, so that it goes some way towards camouflaging the join. More camouflage is added by simulating the grain of the original.

Figure 5. The sideboard as envisaged before being "improved". It has the original splash-back, turned legs and wooden knobs to the drawers. An honest article of good quality, it would be preferred by the true collector to the botched attempt at greater elegance into which it has been converted, and might well prove to have greater "investment potential". A rather similar sideboard with turned legs and splash-back, but with a more interesting centre, is illustrated in The Price Guide to Antique Furniture by John Andrews (Antique Collectors' Club), where reference is made to the practice of changing the legs.

Pot-lids

by
A. Ball

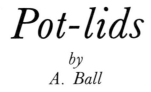

Author of The Price Guide to Pot-lids and Other Underglaze Multicolour Prints on Ware, 2nd Edition

Bear's Grease Manufacturer, Price Guide No. 3. The world record price of £3,000 was paid for this lid.

Queen Victoria and the Prince Consort, Price Guide No. 152. A commemorative lid much in demand. £150-£200.

Over the last year pot-lids have maintained their steady rise. The salerooms have continued to attract much attention and it is noticeable that collectors are becoming more discriminating in their purchases. Even if the item being sold is of the common variety, one can be reasonably certain that the price realised will be correspondingly higher if the lid is in particularly good condition. Prices in general seem to have increased by at least 20%, with rather more emphasis on the rare and scarcer items, where condition does not seem to play such an important part in governing the price. It is still possible to make good buys, particularly in the field of wares, although they also have seen an increase in demand and price.

Now, to mention certain lids. The very high prices realised in the latter half of 1980 for a number of scarce and rare lids were due entirely to several collections appearing in the London sale-rooms over a correspondingly short period of time, which meant that all the collectors were competing for items which rarely appear in sales and have not been on offer for many years. This situation, coupled with the inflationary spiral, gave us prices which would not have been dreamt of only three or four years ago. For instance, we are now seeing many lids reaching the almost unbelievable price of £1,000 or more, and 1980 saw the world record price being paid for "Bear's Grease Manufacturer". After allowing for the buyer's premium and the V.A.T. payment, the staggering price of over £3,000 was reached. This was not just an isolated instance as quite a number of other equally scarce lids also reached hitherto unknown heights, for instance (1976 prices shown in brackets):

Jenny Lind £1,300 (£500-£800)
The Truant (large lid with base) £2,000
(price by negotiation)
Felix Edwards Pratt (small plaque)
£1,900 (£150-£250)

Arctic Expedition £700 (£100-£150)
Our Pets £500 (£80-£120)
The Boar Hunt £800 (£150-£250)
Belle Vue Tavern (with cart)
£700 (£200-£300)
The Closing Ceremony £1,000 (£100-£150)
Bears Reading Newspapers £2,200
(£250-£350)
with many others in the region of £250-£750.

Of course, it must be realised that these prices are the exception rather than the rule. The majority of lids are sold for £30-£60, but only a few years ago they could have been bought for £10-£30.

Another point which should be mentioned is that a rather larger increase was noticeable in commemorative lids, particularly those with royal subjects. This is not in any way related to the news of Prince Charles's engagement, as the prices referred to relate to 1980.

To sum up, it appears that prices for lids or items of ware in good condition are likely to continue to rise in 1981, as they have in past years.

The Village Wedding, Price Guide No. 240. A common but very popular lid. £30-£40.

Interior View of Crystal Palace, Price Guide No. 138. A lid which shows extraordinary detail. £100-£150.

Cabbages to Kings
The
Book Market
in
1980-81

by

Simon Houfe

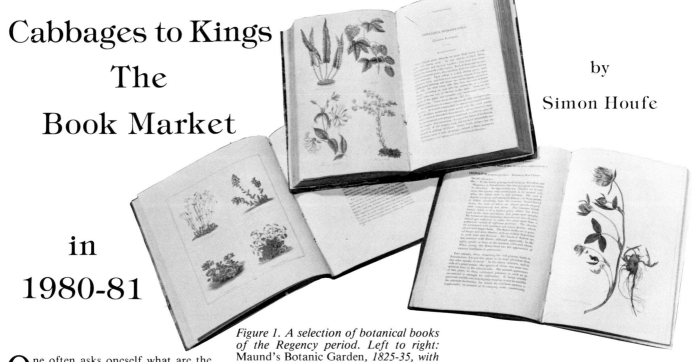

Figure 1. A selection of botanical books of the Regency period. Left to right: Maund's Botanic Garden, 1825-35, with hand-coloured plates by E.D. Smith; The New British Domestic Herbal by Waller, 1822, with 132 plates; Hortus Gramineus Woburnensis by Sinclair, 1824, a treatise on grasses.

One often asks oneself what are the permanent seams that run through book collecting today, where are those areas of rich bedrock which never seem to shift and remain a stable ground to quarry in even the most difficult times? It is certainly a question that needs an answer at the start of the 'eighties with the book market quiet and many collectors having to be more ruthlessly discriminating than ever before.

Perhaps the Provincial Booksellers Association have the answer in the thirty or so provincial fairs they hold up and down the country during the course of the year. Among them I visited Oxford, Cambridge and Solihull, all of which showed a trend towards well-tried areas of collecting. There was a strong concentration of interest in natural history books, books with botanical illustrations and books with colour plates, and at the same time a marked increase in special subjects such as gardening, sports and collecting. Open volumes showing plates of great cabbagey hand-coloured roses vied with the handsome monographs on royal collections of the past, the odour of fine paper mixing with the bouquet of old morocco, literally everything from cabbages to kings.

The tradition of collecting botanical books in this country is certainly a long one; the fashion for rare plants in the Georgian and Regency periods created a spate of volumes, collected first for their scientific accuracy, then for their beauty and finally for their rarity as individual prints. Fortunately that last phase that involved the book breaker has been stemmed in recent years with the price of complete volumes outstripping their breaking value.

Certainly in the 19th century there are two distinct types of botanical book: the specialist publication, the discourse on a certain species with its hand-coloured plates and calf binding, and the table-book, a happy little compendium where flowers are arranged rather than shown, portrayed rather than analysed. Both sorts turn up with agreeable regularity in the shops, both are highly collectable.

Typical of the first category is Maund's Botanist in four volumes and the part volumes of Maund's Botanic Garden, 1825-35 (figure 1), the former now fetching as much as £750 for a complete set. Maund, bookseller, botanist and enthusiast, brought a clarity to his publications, fine type, wide margins as well as the exquisite hand-coloured engravings by E.D. Smith, milestones in depicting English flora. A more general book that I have seen for about £75 is The Florist and Garden Miscellany of 1830. Packed with colour plates, it leads the way to the garden magazines and supplements of the 1840s, 1850s and 1860s, hand-colouring slowly changing to colour printing and chromo-lithography.

The Floricultural Cabinet and Florists Magazine, 1856, is in many ways a purely Victorian book, with twelve hand-coloured plates and magnificent spreads of begonia and anemone. It is none the less earthy and practical in its designing of shrubberies and borders, and is about £50.

With a peculiar attraction of their own are the herbals, more popular today I think with the revival of herb cooking. Among the most delightful is Culpeper's Complete Herbal, 1828, with numerous hand-coloured illustrations, which I saw in Oxford for £60. A few years earlier is The New British Domestic Herbal or A Correct Description of British Medicinal Plants by John Augustine Waller, 1822 (figure 1), with 132 plates from adder's tongue to corn poppies in brilliant colours, making around the same price. Slightly less dramatic flora may be less expensive to acquire. One might mention Hortus Gramineus Woburnensis by George Sinclair, 1824 (figure 1), a study of grasses; the various books on ferns are also a rich area to collect.

The empress among Victorian lady gardeners was surely the redoubtable Mrs. Jane Loudon, who produced a score of books between 1840 and 1860 together with her architect husband, J.C. Loudon. Her books are recognisable in trim green publisher's cloth with blind stamping and a little gilding with titles like The Lady's Country Companion, 1845, The Villa Gardener, 1850, and many others. Mrs. Loudon's works have remained at a reasonable price because none of them was coloured, and yet they are packed with period detail, the heating of conservatories, garden statuary and seating, the pond, the terrace and the summer house with delightful wood engraved plates of fountains and arbours. Her Botany for Ladies, 1845, at £25 would be a useful departure for any collection and The Ladies Companion to the Flower Garden, 1853, is yet another Victorian gem which I recently found for £17.50.

Mrs. Loudon would certainly have approved of more slender books with a practical bias. Particularly attractive are Indoor Plants and How to Grow Them by Maling, 1861, and Song Birds and How to Keep Them, 1862, uniform

volumes with coloured frontispieces and for sale at £5.50 and £7 respectively. Rather more superficial but very pretty is *The Sentiment of Flowers or Language of Flora*, 1839, a small square book with decorative hand-coloured bouquets on each page, intended for the table rather than the library. This is about £22.50 and a similar book, but at only £7, was glimpsed at Oxford — *Flowers and Their Poetry*, 1851, an example of early colour printing by Orr.

There has been quite a shift of emphasis towards Edwardian gardening books and they are to be seen everywhere. A few years ago many booksellers would scarcely have given them house-room; now they are sought after as the trend setters of the small picturesque garden!

High on the list I would place all and every work of Gertrude Jekyll, that talented accomplice of Sir Edwin Lutyens in so many country houses. Full of photographs of Edwardian planned irregularity of border and clump, I would recommend *Lilies For English Gardens*, 1903, at about £25, and *Wood and Garden*, of a year earlier, for around £20. One of her most celebrated studies, *Home & Garden* of 1900, can be

found for a little less, say £18 for a reasonable reading copy, and she also roamed with her pen through such subjects as *Old West Surrey*, 1904, and *Old English Household Life*, 1925, dealing with antiques.

Some very nice things are still on the shelves for £5 or under. I think in particular of *Our Garden*, 1899, by S. Reynolds Hole, doyen of the Rose Society, and H.H. Thomas' *The Book of Hardy Flowers, Trees and Shrubs*, 1925.

If Edwardian gardening has come into its own, so has Edwardian collecting. There is definitely a resurgence of interest in books of the 1900s about antiques, carried forward I think not by pure nostalgia but by the excellent background they contain. Their photographs are often execrable but where in modern books could you find so much of the romance of collecting and the sort of catalogue appendices that modern printing prices often preclude?

First on my list would be *Chats*, those dumpy volumes that tell us so much of our grandparents' taste. They began to appear in 1905. The best are probably *Chats On Old Prints* by Arthur Hayden, 1906, *Chats On Old Pewter* by Massé,

1911, *Chats On Old Copper and Brass* by Fred W. Burgess, 1914, *Chats On Household Curios* by Fred W. Burgess, 1914, *By-Paths in Curio Collecting* by Arthur Hayden, 1919, and *Chats On English China* by Arthur Hayden, 1922. They are usually about £10 each in early editions; reprints up to 1925 should be no more than £5. I do stress that these books, like the ones I am mentioning below, are lovely to own and enjoy for the history of collecting; they are not the prime textbooks on the subject today.

Low printing costs and high standards enabled the Edwardians to publish books on almost every major collection, often in limited editions, usually sumptuously illustrated. These were considered useless by antiquarian booksellers a few years back. Referring to them as "plugs", one bookseller told me that of the limited edition of 350 copies of a Royal Collection, he was sure that he had 349 in his basement! One immediately thinks of W.H. St John Hope's monumental *Windsor Castle*, 1913, in two volumes with some excellent colour plates, the *John W. Wilson Collection*, Paris 1873, and William Younger Fletcher's *English Bookbindings in the British Museum*,

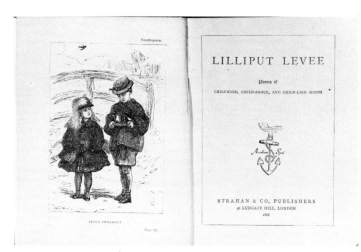

Figure 2. Title page and frontispiece of Lilliput Levée, *1868, a selection of poems illustrated by Millais and others.*

Figure 3. "Ride a Cock Horse", an illustration by Paul Woodroffe to his Booke of Nursery Rhymes, *1897. Items of this sort can still be found for around £20.*

Figure 4. Title page and frontispiece by H.K. Browne for Dickens' Dombey & Son, *first edition, 1848. The price of such classics has risen steeply in the last five years.*

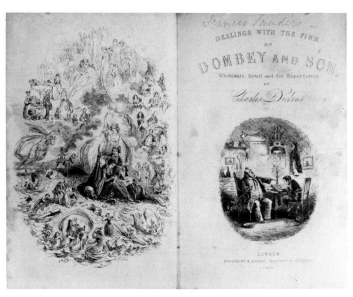

Figure 5. Cover of The Butterfly, *an illustrated art magazine of 1899-1900. The little magazines of the 'nineties now fetch £20 or over depending on condition and quality of illustration.*

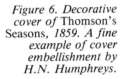

Figure 6. Decorative cover of Thomson's Seasons, *1859. A fine example of cover embellishment by H.N. Humphreys.*

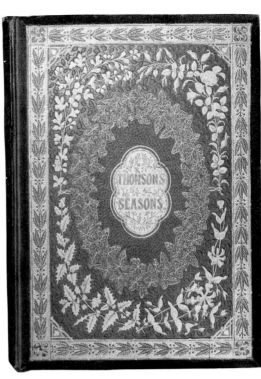

1895, with sixty-six magnificent plates chromo-lithographed. The Burlington Fine Arts Club was responsible for some masterpieces in the 1890s such as their *Catalogue of European Enamels*, 1897, in a very grand format. Such work will not be done again and, as this is recognised, the value of such items creeps up; many of these titles can still be found for under £100. One collector was recently amazed to see copies of *Sèvres Porcelain in the Royal Collection* on sale at the Queen's Gallery bookstall, eighty years after it was published! He was told that they were selling off surplus stocks!

Sporting books continue to have a wide popularity and the early publications on classic games are very much in demand. I have seen *The Cricket Field* by the Rev. James Pycraft, 1862, an attractive volume with two plates, selling for £38, golf and football being equally popular in print or covers.

The perennial favourites of the sporting bookshelf seem to be the Badminton Library series, not very glamorous volumes in their brown cloth covers but somehow catching the romance of Edwardian leisure and relaxation. The one on *Motors*, 1902, is usually the most expensive at £20 to £30. *Football*, 1908, is around £12 and then there are the more recondite numbers such as *Archery* by Longman and Walrond, 1895, which can be £25, and *Coursing and Falconry* by Cox and Lascelles, 1892, which could be £30 and over. Humorous sporting books also join this league so that light-hearted glances at hunting like *The Sporting Adventures of Mr. Popple* with illustrations by G.H. Jalland would be £15 to £20 and Cecil Aldin's incomparable two

volumes of *Handley Cross* of 1911 is priced at £25.

Children's books are such a convenient market that some dealers can specialise in them alone. The attraction is above all the recognition that there is a Peter Pan in most of us and that the infant library of a hundred, seventy-five or even fifty years ago is both colourful and plenteous. Kate Greenaway rules the roost in the years before 1900; her books are still reprinted but the originals are eagerly hunted. Her *Almanack* for 1883 was £30 at the Solihull Fair with a less good *Almanack* for 1886 at £25; a repaired *Baby's Opera* was £15. Incidentally, a charming period guide to older infants' books is *Forgotten Children's Books* by Andrew Tuer, 1898-99, in two volumes, elegant and spacious, now selling for about £45.

Although Greenaway, Caldecott and Potter are so celebrated, minor figures in illustration deserve recognition. For my money I would look out for the work of Paul Woodroffe, a superbly imaginative book artist who was designing nursery rhymes in the 1890s. I illustrate in figure 3 a fine piece of black and white work from his *Booke of Nursery Rhymes*, 1897, which fetches from £25 to £35. This is not to forget that great rarities emerge from attics still in the 1980s — Beatrix Potter's *A Happy Pair*, 1890, a totally unknown title, was sold at Sotheby's last November for £1,850.

Although fine bindings have always been desirable to the specialist collector, I think there is a more general appreciation of them now, particularly the examples of the 19th century. From the 1820s to the 1860s, commercial bindings had as much richness and variety as

those ordered for private libraries. Characteristic of the late Regency were the embossed "cathedral" bindings on keepsakes and prayer-books, Gothic tracery or arabesques. The craze for showy cloth bindings in the 1850s gave rise to some remarkable books. One thinks especially of the designs of H.N. Humphreys (figure 6) such as his *Psalms of David*, 1862, with maroon cover and floral sprays in gilt, now in booksellers' lists for £80. Humphreys also designed bindings to imitate carved wood, such as his *Miracles of Our Lord*, 1848, a very attractive book. The labels of these binders, Leighton, Edmonds and Remnant and others, are often found on the back end-papers; they are worth while looking out for.

Topography remains a very stable area for collecting, the views of English landscape prior to 1800 commanding a fairly high price. The picturesque scenes published as *Jones Views* and including both countryside and mansions, 1829, make at least £145 for a full set; one hundred only were on sale bound for £116. Aquatints are particularly prized, accounting for the high price of £225 asked for P. Holland's superb *Select Views of the Lakes*, 1792. Ireland's aquatints of the *Avon*, 1795, were £120. Bartlett's Middle Eastern series are seldom seen under £50 and Joseph Nash's *Architecture of the Middle Ages*, 1838, is well over £200.

At the present time collectors are choosing carefully and deliberately. Dealers seem to be offering water-tight selections, but for the specialist there is always a surprise.

Sale Review: *Sotheby's Oak Sale, 29th May 1981*

by Victor Chinnery

Figure 1 (lot 108). A single-leaf withdrawing table, late 16th century.

Figure 2 (lot 110). A six-legged dining table, late 16th century.

On 29th May last Sotheby Parke Bernet held a sale of "good English oak furniture" at their Bond Street premises. While there were some good pieces, the sale contained a wide selection of quality and condition and prices underlined the state of the market. Up until the end of July good and unusual pieces were fetching consistently high prices while poor and restored pieces found little or no demand. Since the start of August the strong dollar has resulted in improved demand at the utilitarian end of the market.

My favourite piece was a rare and very attractive single-leaf withdrawing table shown here in figure 1 (lot 108). The design of this table is a beautifully restrained example of Elizabethan classicism, which suffers from none of the excesses often associated with other aristocratic oak furniture of that period. The supports take the form of simple columns surmounted by Roman composite capitals, and the frieze is composed of a band of double-S scrolled strapwork, punctuated with bold applied oval bosses and diamonds.

The patination is a lovely thin and dry grey-brown, which will by now have responded very well to a coat of wax and a vigorous polish with a dry cloth. The whole piece is in a good and original state, very grey and dry underneath, with all four stretchers intact (though lacking the full height of the feet and some of the applied bosses). Single-leaf withdrawing tables are very rare (but with no practical advantage over the double-leaf type) and it was no surprise that this one cost £8,800.

Figure 3 (lot 116). A panelled and inlaid chest, early 17th century.

Figure 4 (lot 183). Unusually elaborate chest for the period, dated in marquetry over the arches A.D. 1653.

Figure 5 (lot 153). An unusual wall cupboard, c.1700. Courtesy Louis Stanton.

Figure 6 (lot 158). A low dresser, 1690-1730.

A companion piece to the draw-leaf table was the less impressive six-legged table in figure 2 (lot 110). Both tables were apparently by the same hand, sharing certain peculiarities of construction and decoration. They both came from Bridwell House in Dorset, where they were reputed to have been rescued when the original Elizabethan house burned down, the present house being a rebuilding of 1762. Unfortunately, the six-legged table appears to have spent a considerable number of years in the kitchen at Bridwell. The result is that the top is heavily scrubbed, and over a long period of time the entire table has been bleached of any colour by the action of water repeatedly soaking into the surface[1]. This would not seem a failing with a Georgian or Victorian kitchen table, but it detracts seriously from an otherwise fine Elizabethan dining table. The lack of patination and one or two small patches kept the price down to £5,610. No doubt some colour will return after a liberal waxing, but too much damage has already been done.

In between these two tables (not illustrated, as lot 109) was one of those marvellous Victorian confections which had been 'judiciously compiled' from a few early fragments of carving. This was known as the Altar of Bulfestra, and had a provenance from Buckfast Abbey, where it was recorded as already 'ancient' in a catalogue reference of 1914. A few years ago such pieces were readily available in provincial salerooms, and discriminating buyers would acquire them and break them up to retrieve the early panels and figures which they contained. Then, in the wake of an influx of competition from an *avant-garde* of French interior decorators, the prices bid for these wondrous pieces began to equal and surpass those for genuine and intact period furniture. It was no longer possible then to buy such things *and* still see a profit in

the sale of the component parts. Yet it seems that even those inflated days may have passed, for the Altar of Bulfestra failed to sell and was bought in for £1,900.

Nevertheless, it contained some very interesting late gothic fragments, including linenfold and tracery panels, a succession of small saintly figures and a fine pair of aumbry doors carved with an Annunciation scene. On one side was the angel, and on the other the Virgin Mary, both seated in high-backed box-base armchairs surmounted by canopies. These date from around 1500.

From a number of chests and coffers in the sale, only one seemed to me to have any real merit, and I have illustrated it here in figure 3 (lot 116). At £1,210 it was not the most expensive chest in the sale, but it was relatively clean and attractive, with a good rich colour. The marquetry stars had been rather over-cleaned, making them

appear excessively bright and sharp, and the lock-plate was an 18th century replacement; but the applied decoration was intact and boldly carved, and the whole piece of good early 17th century date. A much higher price was reached by another chest at £2,860 (figure 4, lot 183). This was a flamboyant piece with a great deal of marquetry and deeply carved terminal figures or caryatids. It came with a fine provenance (Crofts Collection; illustrated by Percy Macquoid in his *Age of Oak*, plate 202), but somehow for me it lacked the appeal of the simpler chest, being of inferior colour and not in the best of conditions.

Another very satisfying piece is the small wall cupboard in figure 5 (lot 153). This is one of a small regional group of similar cupboards which seem to derive from the Southern Welsh Border area[2].

Figure 7 (lot 160). A boarded stool, 16th century.

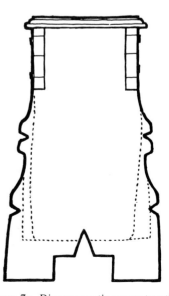

Figure 7a. Diagrammatic reconstruction of the original appearance of the plank supports of the stool in figure 7. The dotted line indicates the remaining portions of the two boards.

The construction, and the resultant silhouette, are most unusual, since the top and sides are formed from a single length of riven oak which is curved over into an arch and secured with nails. I know of at least five other specimens, and would like to hear of more; but this one is unique so far in having a square panelled door. The whole thing is of good colour and, apart from a split in the door panel, is in good original condition. It must seem a little cheap at £1,210.

An excellent colour, combined with a very simple and practical format, was no doubt the reason for the bid of £1,760 which secured the rather plain low dresser in figure 6 (lot 158). Despite a deceptively clean appearance, this three-drawer dresser had in fact been cut down from its original length of four drawers (and probably for very good and practical reasons). In order to retain a balanced appearance, the centre leg had been sawn off; and the inquisitive viewer would find the stump hidden under the lower moulding between the second and third drawers.

Also included in the sale was a boarded stool of the 16th century, which might be expected to reach a good price, since items like this are rare and seldom appear on the market. The stool was rather low at £1,375, and for good reason. This particular stool (figure 7, lot 160) had lost most of the shaping to the buttressed edges of the plank supports which are such a distinctive feature of more complete specimens. In figure 7a I have attempted to reconstruct the

Figure 8 (lot 163). A turned armchair in yewtree, 17th century.

original height and profile of the boards, to give some idea of the missing decoration. In a complete state, such a stool might well fetch twice the price reached here. The damage was apparently due to a poor choice of timber by the carpenter who made the stool, for the plank had contained some sapwood down the outer edges, which succumbed to the effects of woodworm and had been trimmed to make them tidier.

Such is the nature of things that a good fake can occasionally slip past the discerning eye of even the most experienced cataloguer; and just such a piece appeared in this sale as a 16th century trestle table (not illustrated, lot 162). This remission was fortunately spotted by Sotheby's own experts before the sale, and the auctioneer was able to announce before bidding started that the item was of later date; thus the lot was bought in at £1,000.

The large and heavily built yewtree armchair in figure 8 (lot 163) brought a respectable price of £2,640; rather high in view of the battered and repaired condition of the main structure. Turned armchairs of this sort have never been a popular commodity with collectors, but this high price may be a sign that they are at last being understood and viewed with real interest. The history and development of turned chairs is a matter of some fascination to specialist furniture historians, and involves a long tradition stretching from pre-medieval times down to the 19th century and even later. Once their story is more accurately revealed, they may find a more respected niche in the scheme of things.

Most of the early bedsteads which reach the salerooms are in a highly restored or fragmentary condition. They are often made up from remnants of panelling and posts, and the various bits often do not belong to each other. It was therefore something of a pleasure to see the relatively complete bed shown here

Figure 9 (lot 165). A tester bedstead, early 17th century.

Figure 10 (lot 175). A child's high chair, late 17th century.

Above Figure 11 (lot 208). A small side table, c.1700.

Right. Figure 12 (lot 216). A large curved settle, mid-18th century.

in figure 9 (lot 165). Lacking only the foot and side-rails of the bedstock, which originally stood free of the posts which hold up the tester, this is a good quality bed from the early years of the 17th century. The headboard has a pair of large marquetry panels of vases filled with sprays of leafy flowers, flanked by formal caryatids.

Had the bedstock not been so badly missed from this bed, it would have contributed towards a much higher price than the eventual £4,730. The purchaser in this case was the Bradford Metropolitan Council, so we may eventually see the bed put in an appearance on public display at one of their early houses such as Bolling Hall or Ilkley Manor.

Three child's high chairs of 17th century date put in an appearance at this sale, but the most interesting was the one shown here as figure 10 (lot 175). This seemed a little later than as described in the catalogue, but was certainly of the earlier panel-back form. Nail-holes in the cresting-rail showed that it had once sported a crest of some form, and the seat-board in birch was almost certainly an old replacement; yet the colour was good and such chairs continue to be harder to find. The final bid of £1,815 might seem a little high for such an article so less than pure, but children's furniture of any period is always a delight for the collector.

Another small piece was the X-stretcher side table with a drawer, illustrated here as figure 11 (lot 208). The attractive size was further enhanced by a number of decorative features such as the pretty shaped frieze and the unusual square knops to the turned legs. The table was in good original state, except for a replaced handle to the drawer and a small finial missing from the crossing of the stretchers. This condition, and the good, if rather dry, colour contributed to a final price of £814.

At the opposite end of the scale was a very large but elegant country-made settle of semi-elliptical shape. This probably started life in a large inn or farmhouse in the middle of the 18th century, and was equipped with three cupboards in the space under the seat. The colour and condition were good, so the hammer price of £580 must seem rather low. However, it is well to bear in mind that this piece was subject to an addition of V.A.T., as well as the buyer's premium of 10% (which for the previously quoted examples has been added on), giving a final cost to the purchaser of £734. The settle is shown here as figure 12 (lot 216).

1. See my comments in *Antique Collecting*, July 1981, page 23.
2. For three further examples, see Victor Chinnery, *Oak Furniture — The British Tradition*, page 330.

Marine Painting ~ A British Success Story

by Denys Brook-Hart

Author of *20th Century British Marine Painting*

Colin Verity, R.I.B.A., R.S.M.A. (born 1924). "Picking up the pilot", oils, 10½ins. × 14ins. Exhibited at the R.S.M.A., Guildhall, in 1977.
This painting shows a tramp steamer in the early 1900s picking up a pilot offshore from a pilot cutter prior to entering estuary waters. It is an incident invented by the artist with no particular location in mind, but typical of hundreds of places around the British Isles and in European waters.
Colin Verity believes that marine painting should not be undertaken without careful thought and analysis. He feels that it is essential to have the ability to observe and draw, because ships are particularly unforgiving to the indifferent draughts-man and no amount of "arty verbosity" can disguise this fact.

Rowland Hilder, P.R.I., R.S.M.A., (born 1905). "Iron grain ship", 8ins. × 10½ins.
This drawing was sketched from the embankment in front of the Royal Naval College, Greenwich, in the summer of 1926. It is indicative of Rowland Hilder's very fine draughtsmanship, one of the qualities for which he is notable.

The interest in and demand for marine painting has reached such large proportions and is shared by so many people that it may be useful to outline the history of this peculiarly British success story.

It is possible to date quite accurately the beginning of the great movement of marine painting for which British artists are deservedly world renowned. The year was 1674, when the Van de Veldes, father and son, came to Britain from Holland. They were appointed official marine painters to King Charles II and for some thirty years they produced a wealth of marvellous sea pictures, both drawings and oils.

From these beginnings there emerged many illustrious artists such as Peter Monamy (1670-1749) and Charles Brooking (1723-1759) who were influenced by the Dutch tradition. These 18th century artists created a form of sea painting that is now regarded as a classical style. Their methods were carried well into the 19th century and continued until an entirely new concept was displayed in the work of J.M.W. Turner (1775-1851) and John Constable (1776-1837). There are few good marine artists who have not fallen under the magic spell of Turner and the effects of his genius are still strongly felt today.

From about 1820 the Dutch style of marine painting gradually became superseded by a wholly British concept which treated the sea, ships, harbour, and coast scenes in a realistic and sometimes romantic manner. This can be exemplified by pictures painted by artists such as Clarkson Stanfield (1793-1867),

Victor (Vic) Ellis, D.S.M., R.S.M.A. (born 1921). "Trading days: in the Jenkin Swatch", oil on canvas, 20ins. × 30ins. Exhibited at the R.S.M.A., Guildhall, in 1978.
This painting tells of trading days in the earlier part of the 20th century, as the buoyage indicates. The "Jenkin Swatch" (now known as the "Nore Swatch") is the channel between the Nore Sand and the Kent shore. The barge "Hawk" in the fore-ground, was one of five of that name all operating at the same time. She was owned by the Bowman family of Southend-on-Sea and is shown here in a stiff northerly blow together with other barges bound from London to the river Medway.

Frank Joseph Henry Gardiner (born 1942). "Reflections — Maldon", watercolour, 16ins. × 21ins. Exhibited at the R.S.M.A., Guildhall, in 1979.
Painted on a late summer afternoon, this peaceful scene gives the interesting feeling that the viewer might well be sitting at water level in a small boat looking towards the shore.
Frank Gardiner is a professional illustrator and has exhibited at the R.S.M.A. since 1971.

Charles Murray Padday, R.I., R.O.I. (fl.1890-1940). "The yacht race", oils, 18¼ins. × 26ins.
This very fine painting shows the elegance of yacht racing in Edwardian days. The composition is beautifully balanced between the two calm figures in the foreground and the other yachts ploughing through the water behind them. It was probably painted about 1908, as the artist was then living at Hayling Island and this address is inscribed on the reverse of the canvas. The scene is obviously in that area of the south coast. The picture is in the collection of Roger Hadlee, Esq.
By courtesy of the Royal Exchange Art Gallery, London

Peter Leath (born 1935). "J-class yachts, Velsheda, Endeavour and Britannia", oils, 20ins. × 30ins.
This painting shows J-class yachts racing off the Isle of Wight during the summer of 1935. The yachts are heading for the Nab Tower off the eastern extremity of the island; they "round" this mark and return westwards up the Solent to Cowes.

The vessels shown are the famous yachts Endeavour, Velsheda and Britannia. The picture gives an excellent impression of the huge size of the J-class mainsails and their enormous booms which, even with their very large crews, must have been extremely difficult to handle in anything more than a gentle breeze.

Peter Leath is a self-taught artist who has had a lifetime of experience in small boats, including designing and building his own fishing trawler. He lives in the Isle of Wight and paints mainly in oils and acrylics.

Derek George Montague Gardner, V.R.D., R.S.M.A. (born 1914). "Winter North Atlantic", oil on canvas, 32ins. × 48ins.
This painting shows the Loch Tay running before an Atlantic gale, outward bound for Adelaide, Australia. The Loch Tay was an iron-hulled vessel built in 1869, and she carried main skysail yard and stunsails. In this picture, the skysail yard at the main has been struck down to reduce top hamper. In later years she was converted to barque rig. On one voyage, this ship averaged 285 miles a day for nine consecutive days in the roaring forties. Derek Gardner aims for complete accuracy in his paintings, and always carries out considerable research.

Terrick John Williams, R.A., R.I., R.O.I. (1860-1936). "Brixham harbour", oils, 20ins. × 30ins.
The work of Terrick Williams has become more widely acclaimed in recent years. Whilst his painting shows the influence of the Impressionists, his style is original and distinctive. His exhibition record in the early part of the 20th century is impressive (including 142 pictures at the Royal Academy and 111 at the R.O.I.) and his work is now sought after by discerning collectors. He painted both marine and landscape pictures, many of them being harbour scenes. He studied in Antwerp and Paris and was at one time President of the R.I. and Vice-President of the R.O.I.
By courtesy of the Louise Whitford Gallery, London

Peter MacDonagh Wood, R.S.M.A. (born 1914). "The West Indiaman Thetis off Bolt Head", oil on canvas, 27½ins. × 40ins. Exhibited at the R.S.M.A., Guildhall, in 1977.
The artist has had practical seafaring experience from an early age and is a specialist in square-riggers — facts which show clearly in this painting. Of this picture, he says:
"This shows an early 19th century merchant vessel, of a type which I find very attractive, reaching up Channel with just about as much wind as she wants for full sail. I have hoped to convey in the action of the Indiaman and foreground lugger some of the pleasurable excitement of sailing on a fresh, lively day.
"The West Indiamen were, of course, much smaller than the warshiplike big East Indiamen, but were impressively lofty and heavily sparred and canvassed."

E.W. Cooke (1811-1880), Henry Redmore (1820-1887) and Henry Moore (1831-1895) — to mention a few names from a galaxy of talent. By the end of the century, some thousands of sea pieces had been exhibited in London art centres such as the Royal Academy, the British Institution, and the Royal Society of British Artists.

Towards the end of the 19th century, the French Impressionist movement rose to its height. Although it made little immediate impact in Britain, a handful of artists including Walter Richard Sickert (1860-1942) and Philip Wilson Steer (also 1860-1942) introduced similar ideas to the U.K. The so-called traditional style of marine painting then marched side by side with the new impressionist methods into the 20th century and this co-existence has continued up to the 1980s.

At the beginning of the 20th century, although sailing vessels were yielding to steam-propelled ships, there was still plenty of picturesque material for artists and during the first fifty years a multitude of fine painters was at work: men like Thomas Somerscales

(1842-1927), Julius Olsson (1864-1942), Frank Brangwyn (1867-1956), Stanhope Forbes (1857-1947) and W.L. Wyllie (1851-1931) — the full list would seem almost endless. Then, the Second World War abruptly interrupted the careers of most men, including painters, but fortunately there was an enlightened policy which resulted in the appointment of official War Artists. There is therefore a magnificent fund of marine art from this period, much of it housed at the Imperial War Museum in London.

Since the war, the guiding body of British marine painting has been the Royal Society of Marine Artists, formed in 1939. Membership is fairly exclusive — there are just under fifty elected artist members — but non-members are able to submit pictures to the annual exhibitions which maintain a very high standard.

It is during the last ten years that the popularity of marine painting has risen to such extraordinary proportions, chiefly based on the international demand for 19th century British sea pictures. As a specialist dealing in marine art, my own work has been com-

pletely bound up in this field for well over a decade. I have therefore had the opportunity to observe the magnitude of the subject and the enormous mine of artistic talent which has been a feature of the past 150 years in this country. As a result of my studies, in 1974 I completed the book *British 19th Century Marine Painting* which to my great pleasure has become the standard reference work on this subject and continues to bring me many new friends.

However, three or four years ago, I saw the first signs that the supply of good quality 19th century marine pictures would not be inexhaustible. Prices rose steeply and have continued upwards. High prices for the good quality pictures have inevitably resulted in a flow of poor and mediocre paintings into the salerooms from both private and trade sources, and these have been fetching prices which in many cases are far above their real worth. Therefore I began to turn my attention more and more towards the work of 20th century painters, and I was surprised to find a large number of excellent artists, some of them outstanding, whose work is

Trevor Chamberlain, R.O.I., R.S.M.A., N.S. (born 1933). "Martello tower and boat", oils, 9½ × 13½ins. Exhibited at R.S.M.A., Guildhall, in 1977.
A nicely balanced composition. The artist set out to portray a bright morning with a slight breeze, and with the subject matter bathed in an almost silvery light. The nearly unique features of the Kent coastline coupled with the characteristics of the local craft make a most interesting combination.
In the collection of M.K. Collins, Esq.

Terence Lionel Storey, R.S.M.A. (born 1923). "Old Gaffers", oils, 24ins. × 36ins. Exhibited at the R.S.M.A., Guildhall, in 1979.
The artist made sketches of a number of boats and composed this imaginary scene from them. The figures on these vessels give life and credibility to the subject; in some marine pictures the lack of figures on ships makes them appear to have been abandoned.

Hugh Boycott-Brown, R.S.M.A. (born 1909). "Before the start", oil on canvas, 23½ins. × 29½ins. Exhibited at the R.S.M.A., Guildhall, in 1977.
A view of the "cut" from the end of the quay at Blakeney in Norfolk, showing the yachts ready to go to the start of the handicap race in the harbour. For many years after the war, the artist had a cottage at Blakeney where he used to both paint and sail. He says that "in pre-war years I had great help from Sir Arnesby Brown, R.A., and in addition there was my admiration for Boudin and the Impressionists — therefore Blakeney was a wonderful and ideal place to begin to study the sky, the clouds, and the magic light of East Anglia. The lessons I learnt there have never been forgotton in my work — with the sky and the light always forming the dominant element in all my paintings".

Richard Eurich, R.A., Hon. R.S.M.A., Hon. N.E.A.C. (born 1903). "Survivors from a Torpedoed Ship", oil on canvas, 14ins. × 24ins.
Richard Eurich was an Official War Artist to the Admiralty from 1939 to 1945, with the rank of Hon. Captain Royal Marines. A number of his war paintings became famous including "Withdrawal from Dunkirk" (now in the National Maritime Museum) and "Air fight over Portland" (Imperial War Museum).
This picture is both striking and poignant. The half-frozen men are held together by a negro clinging to an upturned ship's boat, which they dare not try to right. When first shown in 1943 it caused such a shock that it was withdrawn. Richard Eurich asked the Merchant Navy whether they objected to it, but they said "far from it, we can't deal with the number of men who want to join, and this is just the sort of picture which is true and admirable".
After the war, when the picture was put into the permanent collection at The Tate Gallery, Sir Winston Churchill considered it to be one of the best paintings to come out of the war.
Courtesy The Tate Gallery, London

insufficiently recognised and clearly undervalued.

With the co-operation of the R.S.M.A., I undertook an in-depth study of 20th century British marine painting. As well as analysing hundreds of exhibition catalogue entries and other records, I had lengthy discussions with many distinguished artists whose views and comments proved invaluable in forming an overall picture of this vast field of activity. The result of these three years of work may be seen in my forthcoming book *20th Century British Marine Painting* which is intended as a logical continuation from the 19th century one.

There are some marine artists painting today whose pictures command quite high prices. But there are many others of considerable merit whose work deserves greater consideration. There is also a large store of rather neglected work by artists who painted in the first fifty or sixty years of this century. Since many thousands of people are still looking for high quality marine paintings, either to study or to buy, it is my hope that this new book will help to create a greater interest in our talented and in many cases underrated 20th century artists.

There have been significant technological developments in this century which have had subtle and sometimes powerful effects on art. Colour photography and television, for instance, have influenced people to require new levels of artistic competence and imagination. Photography and modern means of travel by ships and aircraft have given marine artists new tools and a new outlook on the sea. Although there are still artists painting very successfully in the idiom of the 19th century, most are using colours and styles to which 20th century man is more accustomed. Whilst I am a firm admirer and advocate of 19th century painting, I also believe that the time has come for a wider and greater appreciation of what is being created today. There is a large amount of modern marine art which is being quietly appreciated and purchased — but a good deal more light needs to be thrown on the whole subject so that more people can see what is available and who the talented artists are.

Cast brass soup tureen with turned foot and lid, engraved with contemporary arms of the Jopp family, Hampshire, c.1720. 9½ins. high, 12½ins. wide. About £800.

A CAST BRASS SOUP TUREEN

by Rachael Feild

Dear Aunt Augusta,

How sweet of you to ask me to choose something from the lumber room for my Christmas present. Of course, now that you are moving from The Dower House to Channel View you won't have so much room for your family treasures. All the same it is very generous of you. I don't think I really need the dressing-up trunk, and there isn't much wall space for the antlers, both of which you suggested. You're quite right though — I loved them when I was little. I used to imagine I was the Beauty and they were the Beast!

Actually I have a confession to make. When Greaves told me to go up and look round, I made a beeline for what you always called "the brass pot". Do you remember it was on Tibbles' grave in the Shrubbery for ages? Amazing he lived so long, with all the poison the farmer kept putting down. Fourteen, wasn't he? Anyway, I found the lid in the Flower Room just after you first took to your bed, and put them both up in the lumber room. I'd quite forgotten till the other day!

I'm sending you a photograph of it after spending hours with a tin of Brasso polishing away like mad. Don't you think it's come up beautifully? I know it belongs to your side of the family and not Nunc's because I asked the Royal College of Heralds and they said definitely Jopp of Hampshire, around 1720. Wonder what other hidden treasures there are in the attic!

Your loving niece Vinny

Dear Lavinia,

I cannot for the life of me think how a valuable piece of *silver* came to be up in the lumber room. However, I made my offer in good faith and would not dream of asking you to return it because of a silly mistake. I shall rely on your conscience to do what is right.

Yours ever,
Aunt Augusta

Oh dear Aunt Augusta,

Here is a *colour* photograph of the brass pot and as you can see it didn't come out of the silver cupboard. You know I would *never* do a sneaky thing like that. Actually, it's the most marvellous sort of silky gold — a lovely buttery colour. I showed it to Nigel who works for You-Know-Who and he says it's worth about £800! He always exaggerates, but all the same! He says you're spot on to mistake it for silver

from the photograph because silver-smiths sometimes worked in brass and of course they followed the lines of silver though in a different metal. They even put imitation hallmarks on their pieces (see the one on the brass pot?)

Nigel says he could have dated it before the 1780s from the colour alone, because brass-founding was a very hit-and-miss affair till then, and often the alloy had too much zinc in it — like the brass pot — or too much copper which made it almost pink. I must stop calling it "the brass pot". It's a tureen, and it holds about fifteen pints of soup! Strictly speaking it should be one of a pair, one for thick and one for clear which is the way soup was always served.

Nigel also said to tell you it is cast brass but I said you knew that — you took it down to Tibbles' grave so you know it's pretty heavy! But wasn't it lucky I found the lid? Without it some people might think it was a punch bowl but Nigel says that's ridiculous because (a) it's far too deep and (b) nobody ever used brass for punch or anything like that because acid has a ghastly reaction with metal and apart from ruining the shine it might actually kill a guest or two (I said he always exaggerated!). But the lid itself is pretty spectacular — it was turned on a lathe and engraved before the handle was put on. Can you see the sort of bulls-eye pattern in the middle?

Just one other thing, and Nigel had to clear it with his boss before he could be definite. The imitation hall mark *does not* necessarily mean it was originally silvered, though some pieces obviously were because you can still find bits of silvering in odd corners or on the base. It just means that the brass pot (sorry, tureen) was made by a silversmith and he was entitled to put a mark on it to show it was his work. So it wasn't ruined in the butler's pantry, or by me and my Brasso!

Your loving niece
Lavinia

My dear Vinny,

What a splendidly chatty letter! Your nice young friend Nigel seems very knowledgeable. Would you like to bring him to tea one day after Christmas? We are sure to have some of the Cake left, and he might be interested to see what other little "trouvailles" we have here. Greaves has already brought down several more things and is busy rubbing them up in the pantry. I cannot get used to the idea of *brass* being *valuable!*

With best wishes for Christmas,
Aunt Augusta

P.S. I hope the insurance premium on £800 won't be too much for you to bear. If it is, I will gladly take the brass pot back in exchange for something else. Greaves mentioned the existence of a similar pot in the old Gun Room but he thinks it was thrown out when they came to put in the boiler.

An English Oak Book Rest

by
Thomas Crispin

I am not a covetous man, especially at this season of goodwill, so that when the Editor approached me with the suggestion that I should write an article on "what I would like for Christmas", I thought at first that I would place him in an embarrassing position (which I would dearly love to do), and walk around his home and say "now that I would really like for Christmas" ... However, it is the season of goodwill, and I think that it would be much kinder to place myself in his position, and write about an article of mine, that a dear friend, whom I shall call Willy, always admires, and I know secretly desires... perhaps even for Christmas!

Now the article so desirous to my friend, is an oak book rest of folding form, the back supported by a strut, adjustable to two positions, to raise and lower the angle of the book placed upon the rest. It is a simple, small and beautiful article, intended to support a book or manuscript, although in all probability a Bible, in which case it could be used as a portable lectern. However, because of the lack of documentary evidence it could have been used for either religious or secular reading. The motifs, of lozenge, scroll and rose, carved upon the front of the rest, can also be found either adorning the panelwork of church pulpits, or upon various items of late Elizabethan furniture. The designs mentioned reached their zenith in the Jacobean period, declining as the Commonwealth approached. Thus the rest was probably made at the beginning of the 17th century. Although it is not possible to designate the area of manufacture, an interesting comparison may be drawn between the deeply carved scroll motif upon the top of the rest and the cresting rails of 17th century oak chairs ascribed to the North Midlands, and loosely referred to as "Derbyshire Chairs". (Factual evidence — as opposed to speculation — being exceedingly difficult to trace at this early period of domestic oak.)

That the rest when not in use was originally intended to be hung up folded is obvious, as all the decorated frontal surfaces would then be shown. However, this example shows no signs of holes for hanging when not in use, so it can be assumed that most of its early life

Figure 1. An oak book rest of folding form, the back supported by a strut, adjustable to two positions. The front is carved with lozenge, scroll and rose, combined with punchwork. English, early 17th century. Length 17½ins., width 9¾ins., folded depth 1¼ins.

Figure 2. Front view of oak book rest, folded for hanging, showing detailed carving.

was spent in use, although equally it could have been folded flat and stored away.

When I look at this book rest, as I do daily, I never fail to marvel at the basic skill of the craftsman who made it. That such rests were not widely in use is evidenced from the very few 17th century rests that survive today. What has to be understood is that the rest was constructed from a single plank of oak, the only addition being that of the back strut. A small plank of oak would be taken (approximate size 18ins. x 10ins. x 1in.), upon which the basic cut lines would be marked out, some of these lines still being visible. The board would then be cut from both ends into half depth, to a point where the central hinge was to be, the surplus wood being cut away from both sides. The central hinge would have to be chiselled away from back and front, so that, when finally cut through, the larger back board could separate from the smaller front board. When opened, the top of the back board forms the base of the book rest; the base of the front board forming the foot of the book rest.

After the basic construction the decoration would be laid out and carved. Finally, the back strut would be attached with wrought iron hinges and nails. These hinges are beautifully constructed, and time should be taken to study them, the attention to detail of the cut-out ends of the hinge bars, and the birdlike finish of the scroll hinges. Bearing in mind that these hinges were unseen, such details show the pride of a craftsman in his work.

Now that I have put upon paper so much about this small piece of domestic oak, I can really see why my dear friend so admires it. I now look at it in a different light, in fact "all I want for Christmas is my second book rest".

Figure 4. Back view of oak book rest, showing the strut in detail and the wrought iron hinges. Note cut lines of wooden hinge, visible below shaped foot of strut.

Figure 3. Side view of oak book rest, folded, showing hinged joint.

A KENMAC CRYSTAL SET

by
Anthony Constable

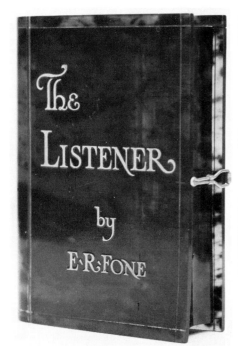

Three views of the Kenmac book crystal set made of imitation tortoiseshell. When connected to a pair of headphones and a good aerial and earth, a gentle tweaking of the "cat's whisker" brings about instant reception of the more powerful or the local radio stations. Tuning is effected by sliding the pointer along the scale. (This crystal set was kindly loaned by Jonathan Hill and photographed by David Baughan.)

Despite the celestial wanderings of Santa Claus and his reindeer, from quite an early age I recall seeing pictures of his sack full of very down to earth presents. Nothing has ever convinced me that there also exists a Santa Claus who hands out those rare and expensive gifts for "the collector who has everything".

My own collecting interests lean strongly towards those very rare and expensive relics of wireless history which I instinctively know I must not ask Santa to try to acquire for me. Even so, my modesty in asking for an inexpensive present, which I know will be handled through the agency of my wealthy Uncle Charles, will not induce me to select one which lies in the normal price range of the presents I shall receive from my immediate family. Thus, I conclude that this special present will lie outside the £10 range (the family limit) and yet will not come near to the maximum price (approximately £1,000) so far recorded for a rare specimen of radio history. A notional value of £100-£150 seems a reasonable target for me to aim at and I think that within this range it should be possible to find a small item of good quality in the "medium-rare" category which will comfortably fit into my moderately proportioned stocking.

Most readers will have seen and perhaps owned one of the multi-valve radio sets of the 1930s, '40s or '50s but fewer will recall those delightful sets of the 1920s which had brightly glowing valves on a control panel, numerous batteries and a curvaceous horn loudspeaker. It is this era of the 1920s from which I wish to select my Christmas present but my price restrictions forbid me to request one of these valuable multi-valve receivers. It was in this age, however, that the classical crystal sets were in widespread use by a hard working population unaccustomed to luxury.

Crystal sets came in all shapes and sizes and well preserved examples can be found in many of the collections which have been lovingly gathered together by enthusiasts all over the world. Among the few I have in my own collection is one made by Kenmac Radio Ltd., of Dalling Road, Hammersmith, London, W.6. It is in the shape of a book 4¾ins. x 3½ins. x nearly 1¼ins. thick and, in gold embossed lettering, the front cover bears the unforgiveable words, "The Listener by E.R. Fone". The binding is red leatherette and, when opened, the book reveals a well made crystal set just as capable of receiving radio transmissions as other considerably more elaborate versions. This rather "gimmicky" crystal set appeared in 1925 and at that time cost £1 1s. in red, blue or green colour.

The Kenmac company also made an imitation tortoiseshell version costing £2 2s. and this is what I would like for Christmas. It should still be possible to find one of these within my price range in mint condition though I am not at all sure where to suggest Santa should start looking. Perhaps he should keep his eye on the quality salerooms and be prepared for some very brisk bidding because I suspect there will be others wanting a similar present this year.

So, all in all, dear Santa, I should be very pleased with one of these small crystal sets (tortoiseshell, remember) in mint condition please, to keep my red leatherette version company. There is a possibility that one may turn up which does not bear the dreadful title previously referred to. The Kenmac Company did offer to supply these sets at no extra cost with any desired lettering, for example: Merry Christmas from Uncle Charles.

A CHRYSOLITE AND DIAMOND BROOCH

by
Anne Clifford

Left: Figure 1. 18th century chrysolite and diamond brooch from S.J. Phillips of Bond Street, £1,200.

Right: Figure 2. 18th century paste brooch with Saint Esprit pendant. (Private collection.)

I am very well accustomed to combing shops, markets and salerooms with a non-existent relative whom for years I have known as Money No Object. As nowadays I generally limit my explorations to what I suppose one can call the "upper reaches" of the trade, I usually come back with a shopping list as long as my arm but nothing else. Not that I am bemused by high prices and naturally gravitate to the limit for in practice I find I very rarely pick on the most expensive things — not for me a diamond as big as the Ritz, let such things be bought and worn by the sort of people who buy and wear them. In fact my Money No Object relative would have a comparatively easy time of it, although of course he would be asked to operate in financial realms which I rarely enter.

This generous person, despite his name, does like to get his money's worth and, if in his generosity to me he also has the satisfaction of feeling that he has made an investment which will appreciate in value, then his pleasure is not less. This Christmas he is giving me (would that he were!) the chrysolite and rose diamond brooch from S.J. Phillips of Bond Street shown in figure 1.

"Ah!" he will say, "but you already have brooches of that pattern, would you not prefer a change?"

"Excellence" I reply, "is excellence and there are subtle differences. It is true that I am lucky enough to own the paste brooch with the Saint Esprit (figure 2) and I also have a not dissimilar bow brooch with pendant drop in chrysolite and I love them both dearly, but I want this as well and I will tell you why.

Variations on the bow and pendant motive are common in 18th century brooches. The pattern was used throughout Europe so that it is rarely possible to say in which country any particular brooch was made, but the design always speaks to me of 18th century elegance and good manners.

"Although portraits show brooches of this style being worn at any time between 1740 and 1770 it is not easy to date any one brooch precisely because few people discard a precious jewel when it is a year or two out of date. The design certainly had its origin as early as the 17th century and copies are still being produced today.

"What is so special about this one? Firstly it is special because it is the only one I have seen which combines chrysolite *and* rose diamonds. Secondly, it is lighter and more elegant than my paste Saint Esprit. Thirdly, it is inexpensive for what it is. If you need a fourth reason then let it be that this brooch once graced the collection of Doctor Joan Evans, the great expert and collector of jewellery, many of whose finest pieces are now in the Victoria and Albert Museum. Its date? On the late side, I should judge; its lightness and the openness of the design suggest somewhere about 1755. Where was it made? Spain or Portugal, probably Portugal because the source of chrysolite in the 18th century was Brazil and Brazil was part of the great Portuguese Empire."

"But why choose chrysolite when I should be pleased to buy you diamonds? And this place is full of wonderful things besides — emeralds, rubies, pearls,

enamels, everything, a dragon's cave of jewels."

"Because everyone wears diamonds but only the discerning wear chrysolite. I prefer glow to flash. Besides, chrysolite brooches are more rare than diamond ones and a good deal cheaper."

"Will you wear it?" he asks.

"Not when cooking or doing a morning's shopping but at Glyndebourne and the Savoy...when you take me. Besides, what if I don't? I had a much loved and very generous aunt once (a real one, not like you) who used to say of her jewellery: 'There's such a thing as a joy in possession'. Jewellery is certainly to wear but it is also to be taken out of a case and looked at and admired. This piece is certainly wearable. I *have* seen a chrysolite bow brooch solidly pavé set that would have been a bit much even for a Royal occasion unless one had wanted to upstage the principal; nevertheless, I should have adored to have had that but you weren't with me at the time so someone else is gloating. This is definitely more wearable."

"But is it worth the money?"

"You will not find another like it. Antique jewellery of real quality is going up all the time. £1,200 is little enough for a beautiful piece of history. The Saint Esprit? Ah, yes, I believe it cost me £25 but that was some years ago and now it is worth perhaps twenty times as much, so you see how values are changing. Bearing in mind that this is chrysolite and rose diamonds and that the year is 1979, I think you will be well advised to get rid of those decaying pounds as quickly as you can. Chrysolite and diamonds are for ever."

Silver Napkin Rings *by Ole Lachmann*

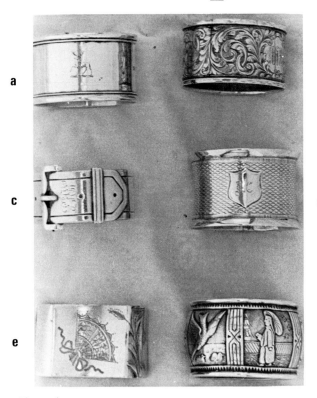

Figure 1

a. Plain ring with engraved crest (deer). Marked CR over WS, London 1852. Weight 20g, diameter 4.5cm.

b. Ring engraved with scrolling foliage. Marked A & S, Birmingham 1858. Weight 20g, diameter 4.4cm.

c. Napkin ring in the form of a belt. Marked William Summers, London 1866. Weight 30g, diameter 4.4cm.

d. Engine turned ring. Marked W.E., London 1879. Weight 25g, diameter 4.7cm.

e. Unusually shaped, almost square ring engraved in the Oriental style with fan, bird and rush. Marked London 1879, unclear maker's mark. Weight 30g, length of side 4.3cm.

f. Ring decorated in the Oriental style with chased motifs showing a swallow, a pelican, a mandarin and a Chinese woman. Marked London 1882, unclear maker's mark. Weight 30g, diameter 4.5cm.

Figure 2

a. Pierced and engraved napkin ring. Marked George Unite, Birmingham 1864. Weight 20g, diameter 4.5cm.

b. Pierced and engraved ring with a mistletoe and holly motif. Marked George Unite, Birmingham 1883. Weight 20g, diameter 4.5cm.

c. Silver-gilt ring with chased decoration showing signs of the zodiac (one of a pair showing all twelve signs of the zodiac). Marked W.E., London 1875. Weight 30g, diameter 4.5cm.

d. Ring chased with vineleaves and grapes, one of a pair. Marked E & J Barnard, London 1867. Weight 30g, diameter 4.3cm.

e. Silver-gilt ring engraved with flower basket motifs. One of a set of several from which I have two. Marked J, E, W & J Barnard, London 1875. Weight 40g, diameter 4.5cm.

f. Ring with elaborate bright-cut decoration. One of a pair. Marked London 1880, unclear maker's mark. Weight 40g, diameter 4.7cm.

Napkin rings, because they are inexpensive and fairly common pieces of small silver, are highly collectable and offer a fine opportunity for the study of European decorative silver styles and techniques from about 1830.

Literature on napkin rings, though, has been very scarce. *The Collectors' Dictionary of the Silver and Gold of Great Britain and North America* by Michael Clayton has a few lines on them, mentioning early English examples from 1821 and 1830, and in 1969 the magazine "Silver" ran a series of articles on figural napkin rings, an interesting but exclusively American speciality. Finally, a scientific study of Swedish silver from 1830 to 1915 has statistics showing how silver napkin rings first appeared in Sweden c.1840 and became very common at the turn of the century, outnumbered only by cutlery.

In the last two years, however, articles in English and Swedish antiques magazines have proved a growing interest in napkin rings, and Margaret Holland's *Phaidon Guide to Silver,* published in 1978, classifies them as small collectables and states that they date from as early as c.1760.

After three years of regular visits to silver shops, antique dealers and antique markets in Copenhagen and London, I have seen and handled several thousand silver napkin rings, and bought about 250 examples, of which sixty-one are illustrated in this article.

The oldest English and Scandinavian napkin rings I have seen are from 1844 (Danish), 1847 (Swedish) and 1852 (English), but a single day's visit to silver shops in Paris brought two older examples — one marked between 1835 and 1838, the other before 1835. The number of mass-produced German silver napkin rings from c.1850 found in Denmark suggests that silver napkin rings also started early in Germany.

The prices quoted in this article are October 1979 prices in shops in London (for English and Russian rings) and Copenhagen (for Scandinavian rings). Remarks on the price of silver metal are based on £9-£10 per ounce — and members will have to adjust for the continuous change in this price. Auction prices are relevant only to Russian enamelled rings, English Arts and Craft rings and a few cased sets of four to six Victorian rings. Other napkin rings are

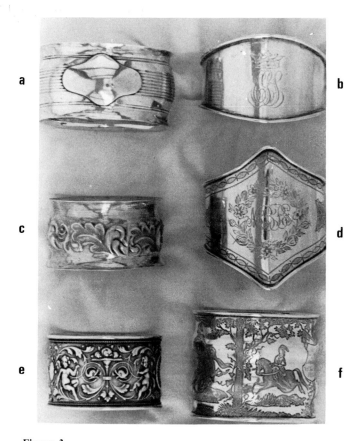

Figure 3
a. Oval Danish ring with "wavy" profile. Marked Anton Michelsen, Copenhagen 1844. Weight 25g, diameter 4.8cm-5.6cm.
b. Danish ring in special shape engraved with crowned initials. Marked Anton Michelsen, Copenhagen 1857. Weight 30g, diameter 5.4cm.
c. Primitive Swedish ring with "wavy" profile and band of chased flowers. Marked Gustaf Möllenborg, Stockholm 1847. Weight 14g, diameter 4.9cm.
d. Inside gilt Danish ring in a unique aesign, engraved with flowers on front and ornaments on side and back. Marked Peter Hertz, Copenhagen 1873. Weight 30g, diameter 5.2cm.
e. Inside gilt machine stamped ring in Swedish neo-renaissance style. Marked with a maker's symbol not known to me, the Swedish three crowns and 830 for silver quality. Weight 17g, diameter 4.9cm.
f. Danish ring with "wavy" profile. Machine stamped with hunting scene. Probably mass-produced German export. One of a pair, the other with a different motif. No marks but inscription with date 1854. Weight 22g, diameter 5.3cm.

Figure 4
a. Superb silver gilt ring engraved with scrolling foliage including two griffins. Initial under a royal crown. Marked M and 830 for Scandinavian silver quality. Weight 55g, diameter 5.1cm.
b. Superb silver gilt ring embossed with medieval inspired scrolls and leaves. Marked with full name TOLSTRUP (Norway) and 950 — a most unusual silver quality in Scandinavia. Weight 60g, diameter 5.3cm.
c. Danish silver gilt ring with engraved Viking motif. One of a pair. Marked A. Dragsted, Copenhagen 1902. Weight 40g, diameter 4.6cm.
d. Danish ring with stylised Viking motif. One of a pair. Marked Peter Hertz, Copenhagen 1903. Weight 35g, diameter 4.4cm.
e. Silver gilt ring engraved with Viking style motif. Marked IT for Tolstrup (Norway) and 830 for silver quality. (Motif used on coffee set in 1901.) Weight 30g, diameter 4.3cm.
f. Danish ring with very stylised Viking inspired motif. Machine stamped. Marked N.N. Hviid & Co., Copenhagen and 826 S for silver quality before 1914. Weight 15g, diameter 4.6cm.

still part of mixed lots at auction.

From 1976 to October 1979 almost all categories of silver napkin rings rose in price by 150%-200%. In the case of the average ring, which is valued only a little above the price of the silver metal it contains, the rise is entirely due to the steep rise in the price of silver. For collectable rings like the ones illustrated, the rise to a price of three to six times the price of the silver metal is a result of the growing interest in silver napkin rings as a collector's item.

Victorian silver napkin rings

Figures 1 and 2 show typical examples of Victorian silver napkin rings. The whole range of decorative styles and techniques known from other silver of the period was employed on napkin rings.

The oldest English ring I have seen is illustrated in figure 1a, hallmarked London 1852. The belt-form in figure 1c was used for several decades, but this early example is naturalistic whereas later rings in this design became more stylised.

The ring with the signs of the zodiac in figure 2c and the bright-cut ring in figure 2f are both unusually good work for napkin rings. The mark of the maker of the zodiac ring (W.E.) is found on several good Victorian rings. While the pierced ring in figure 2b is definitely Victorian, the waving lines of the holly and mistletoe are traits of the developing art nouveau style.

Though the value of the silver content in a Victorian napkin ring is now close to £10, it is still possible to find good rings for under £20, but in specialist shops in London the best examples will cost £50-£100.

Early Scandinavian silver napkin rings

Swedish statistics give the following numbers of silver napkin rings produced in selected years: none in 1830; six in 1840; 225 in 1850; 1,500 in 1905. The number of silver napkin rings imported by Sweden was 115 for the whole period 1840-49, but rose to 5,500 for 1905.

Figure 3 shows some early Scandinavian silver napkin rings and obviously, from the above statistics, the ring shown in figure 3c, marked 1847, is among the very first Swedish silver napkin rings. It is also very primitive, although made by the greatest Swedish producer of silver at that time, Gustaf Möllenborg.

The oval ring in figure 3a is made by Anton Michelsen, the best Danish silversmith in the second half of the 19th

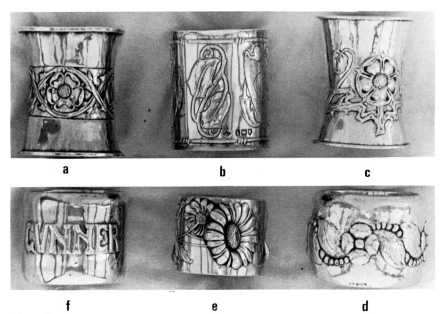

a   b   c

f   e   d

Figure 5

a. Unusually shaped, handmade arts and craft napkin ring with beaded surface and chased band of Tudor roses. Marked Omar Ramsden & Alwyn Carr, London 1901. Weight 45g, largest diameter 4.9cm.

b. Unusually shaped, handmade art nouveau ring chased with leaves and a large shield. One of a pair, the other ring with narrower leaves. Signed FR (THR ?) and marked THR in a lozenge (French manner), London 1905 + tiny French import mark.

c. Unusually shaped, handmade art nouveau napkin ring with beaded surface and chased Tudor rose with "floating lines". One of a pair, the other ring with a Scots thistle motif. Marked Omar Ramsden & Alwyn Carr, London 1909. Weight 32g, largest diameter 4.5cm.

d. Handmade ring with beaded surface and band of chased flowers. Marked Evald Nielsen (Denmark) and 830 S for silver quality after 1914. Weight 55g, largest diameter 5.5cm.

e. Machine stamped ring in very heavy silver with art nouveau flower motif used on several German made silver items. Marks: Horse in lozenge (maker's mark ?), Gratchev (Russian) and St. Petersburg mark c.1896 with large cyrillic letters PT (import mark ?). Weight 45g, diameter 4.2cm.

f. Handmade ring with beaded surface and name as decoration in large chased letters. Marked Georg Jensen with three different early marks and 826 S for silver quality before 1914 (probably made 1904-06). Weight 35g, largest diameter 4.7cm.

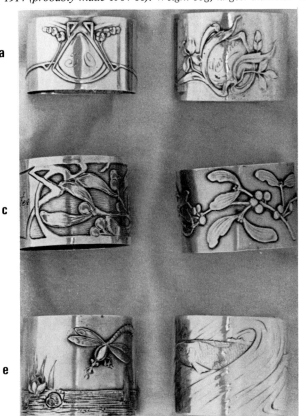

a

c

e

b

d

f

century. Michelsen was established in 1844 and made this ring only three years later. It is by far the earliest non-circular ring I have seen.

The ring in figure 3f is an example of the most common type of North European silver napkin ring from c.1850-65, with a characteristic "wavy" profile. These rings are normally unmarked and were probably mass-produced in Germany.

Prices for the rings in figure 3 are in the £20-£40 range.

Danish and Norwegian revival style

The napkin rings in figure 4 demonstrate the development of the Danish and Norwegian revival of Viking style (dragon style) and medieval style.

The very good ring in figure 4a with crowned initials has apparently belonged to a member of the royal family in one of the Scandinavian countries and the superb ring in figure 4b is decorated with medieval ornamentation. These two would be priced between £40 and £60 in Copenhagen and the others in this illustration would be in the £20-£30 range.

Arts and Crafts — art nouveau

This interesting period of experimentation produced many napkin rings in silver plate and a much smaller number in silver. Figures 5, 6 and 7b and 7c demonstrate the wide range in quality of art nouveau silver napkin rings, from primitive handmade "oddities" (figure 6e) and machine stamped rings with motifs "in the art nouveau taste" (figures 6a and 6b) to fully designed machine stamped examples (figures 6c and 5e) and handmade or hand decorated rings of top quality in workmanship and design. The best rings from this period are very collectable and include such English makers as Liberty & Co. (figures 7b and 7c), Haseler (figure 7d) and Omar Ramsden and Alwyn Carr (figures 5a and 5c). Prices for good Liberty, Haseler or Ramsden & Carr rings vary from about £20 to £200 in specialist shops. The other art nouveau rings cost from £20 to £60, depending on quality, country and type of shop.

Figure 6

a. Semi-circular ring with flat back. Machine stamped with art nouveau motif. Marked N.N. Hviid & Co. (Denmark) + (NHN) (in one symbol) and 826 S for silver quality before 1914. Weight 25g, "diameter" 4.8cm.

b. Machine stamped ring with French type art nouveau motif of flowers and fluid lines. Marked 800 for German silver quality. No maker's mark.

c. Inside gilt, machine stamped ring with mistletoe motif and shield. Marked Sweden and 830 S for silver quality. No maker's mark. Weight 33g, diameter 4.9cm.

d. Ring with soldered on mistletoe motif. Marked with French grade 1 silver, maker's mark unreadable. Weight 40g, diameter 5.0cm.

e. Inside gilt ring chased with a dragonfly over a lake with water lilies. Marked with French grade 1 silver. Maker's mark: ARO and a vertical bar with hooks on both ends, all in a lozenge. Weight 40g, diameter 4.9cm.

f. Inside gilt, handmade ring chased with two fish and waves in art nouveau style. Marked S.J. and 830 S for silver quality. Country of origin uncertain. Weight 50g, diameter 5.0cm.

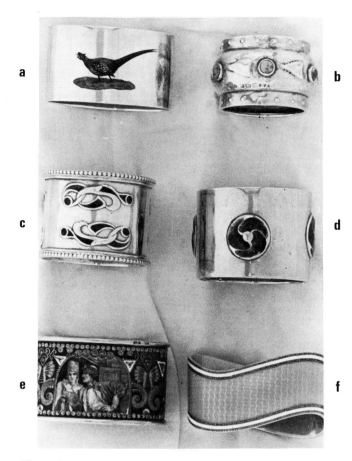

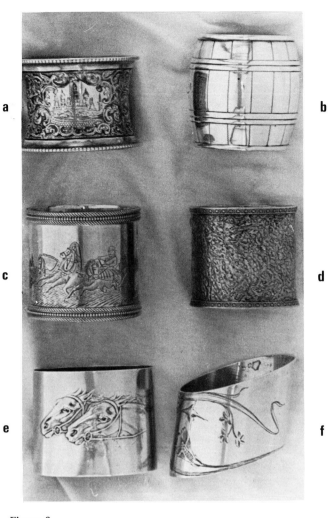

Figure 7

a. Oval English art deco ring with enamelled pheasant in natural colours. One of a pair — the other ring with a pheasant hen. Marked Collingwood and an O (for the enameller ?), Chester 1928. Weight 45g, diameter 3.5cm-5.7cm.

b. Unusually shaped — Indian inspired art nouveau ring set with six pieces of turquoise matrix in cabochon. Marked Liberty & Co and a design number 574, Birmingham 1916. Weight 20g, largest diameter 4.7cm.

c. Enamelled art nouveau ring with Edwardian border. Marked Liberty & Co, Cymric and design number 5144, Birmingham 1903. Weight 45g, diameter 5.1cm.

d. Enamelled art nouveau ring with Celtic inspired motif. Marked W.H. Haseler & Co, Birmingham 1904. Weight 40g, diameter 5.1cm.

e. Superb oval, Russian silver gilt napkin ring with cloisonné enamelling and painted figural scene in the "Old Russian Style". Marked Fedor Rückert, Moscow 1908-17 (inscription in cyrillic with year 1913) and 87 for the better than normally used grade silver. Weight 70g, diameter 4.8cm-6.3cm.

f. Superb unusually shaped, oval napkin ring with sky-blue translucent enamel over an engine turned pattern and "empire" border with white opaque enamel. Marked with full name Fabergé in cyrillic letters and A.N. for workmaster Anders Johan Nevalainen, St. Petersburg 1896-1907 and 87 for the better than normally used grade silver. Weight 70g, diameter 3.9cm-6.0cm.

Figure 8

a. Early Russian napkin ring with niello work on Kremlin motif and flowers. Marked ee (listed as not identified master), Moscow 1862 and 84 for silver quality. Weight 50g, largest diameter 5.2cm.

b. Napkin ring made like a barrel. Marked JAL (listed as unidentified master) and a poor mark — probably St. Petersburg last quarter of 19th century. Weight 35g, smallest diameter 4.1cm.

c. Ring engraved with troika ride on one side and revival style ornaments on the other side. Marked Alexander Alexejew Muchin, Moscow, c.1880. Weight 65g, diameter 4.9cm.

d. Silver gilt ring with "Samodorok" surface. Marked E.K. in cyrillic letters and St. Petersburg, last quarter of 19th century. Inscription with year 1890. Weight 50g, diameter 4.1cm.

e. Inside gilt ring with embossed horseheads. Extra material soldered on for the horseheads. Marked 2A for second "artel" (collective silver workshops established shortly before the revolution), Moscow 1908-17. Weight 40g, diameter 3.8cm-5.2cm.

f. Obliquely cut ring with art nouveau flower motif. Marked IP, St. Petersburg. Weight 45g, diameter 4.7cm-5.2cm.

Art deco

The only art deco napkin ring illustrated in this article is the superb ring with an enamelled pheasant in figure 7a. This would cost at least £80 in a specialist London dealer's shop.

Russian silver napkin rings

There are more Russian silver napkin rings on the market in London and Copenhagen than one would expect. Figures 7e and 7f and figure 8 show a range of high quality Russian rings which include special Russian techniques such as niello work, samodorok surface

and enamelling and special Russian motifs such as the Kremlin and a troika.

The ring with the horseheads is made by one of the thirty or so collective silver workshops (artels) set up in Moscow in 1908-17. The two enamelled rings by the Fabergé workmasters, Nevalainen and Rückert, are of absolute top quality in work and design. The design of the ring made by Nevalainen demonstrates Fabergé's inventiveness and is the only ring I know of with translucent enamelling and a full Fabergé mark. Fedor Rückert sold both through

Fabergé and through his own shop. The ring in figure 7e, having no Fabergé mark, was sold through his own shop. It was made in 1913, the year of the tercentenary jubilee of the Romanov empire when the "old Russian" style was at its peak.

Prices for "ordinary" Russian silver napkin rings range from £30 to £85. The enamelled rings are priced from £150 to about £300 for normal cloisonné enamelling and more for exceptional quality such as the two rings in figures 7e and 7f.

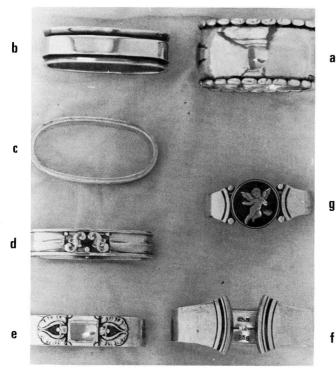

Figure 9
a. Oval ring with beaded edge and pearl border. Marked G.I.
830 S — an "impossible" combination since G.I. should only
appear with 826 S. The ring must have been made in 1914 or
1915. Also design no. 7. Weight 25g, diameter 3.9cm-5.2cm.
b. Narrow oval ring in typical design from Georg Jensen. Black
oxydised edges. Marked Georg Jensen, design Harald Nielsen,
design no 22 A (the A means a slight change of original design).
Also 925 S for sterling silver quality. Weight 40g, diameter
2.8cm-5.5cm.
c. Side view of ring in b. (same shape and thickness as rings in d
and e).
d. Narrow oval ring with pierced decoration. Marked Georg
Jensen, design no. 110 A (design by Johan Rohde but not
marked with his name). 925 S for sterling silver and London
import mark 19). Weight 30g, diameter 2.8cm-5.6cm.
e. Narrow oval ring with pierced flower motif. Marked Georg
Jensen, design no. 238 A, designer Gundorf Albertus. 925 S.
Weight 30g, diameter 2.8cm-5.5cm.
f. Large narrow oval ring with opening. Marked Georg Jensen,
design no. 258. No designer's mark but typical Harald Nielsen
style (see also the similarity with g). Also 925 S. Weight 45g,
diameter 2.8cm-6.5cm.
g. Small narrow ring with circular plate with putto on
background of blue enamel. Marked Georg Jensen, design
Harald Nielsen, no design number (probably unique). Also 925
S. Weight 25g, diameter 2.3cm-4.7cm.

Figure 10
a. Ring with beaded surface and pearl border. Marked Gran &
Lakly, Copenhagen 1916. Weight 30g, diameter 4.2cm.
b. Ring with beaded surface in very "clean" design. Marked
Frantz Hingelberg (Århus), and STERLING. Weight 30g,
diameter 4.2cm.
c. Inside gilt ring with moulded on decoration. Part of a
popular art nouveau pattern called seaweed. Marked Gran &
Lakly, Copenhagen 1920. Weight 25g, diameter 4.2cm.
d. Inside gilt ring with moulded on decoration. Marked Cohr,
Copenhagen 1911. Weight 35g, diameter 4.7cm.
e. Ring with beaded surface in very elaborate design and work.
Marked JVM (not in the official Danish register — probably
made as a test piece), Copenhagen 1934. Weight 35g, diameter
4.2cm.
f. Unusual design for a napkin ring, carried over from popular
design for bowls and tea and coffee sets from 1920s, used by
several Danish silversmiths. Marked Copenhagen 1926, no
maker's mark. Weight 25g, diameter 4.7cm.

Danish silver napkin rings 1910-39

The name in Danish silver of this period is Georg Jensen. After his first exhibition in the Copenhagen Museum of Industrial Art (Kunstindustrimuseum) in 1904, the director of the museum wrote "The rightly earned reputation of this young artist's exhibition was primarily based on the fact that one could buy even cheap items in full artistic form. Here were nice items: a tea set... hat pins, napkin rings...etc.

Even the smallest button was given all the abundance in form obtainable from the material".

One of Georg Jensen's very early rings is shown in figure 5d and some of the company's later and more lasting designs are shown in figure 9. Figure 9a is Georg Jensen's own and very popular design, later produced circular in several sizes.

Figure 9b (and 9c) is designed by Harald Nielsen in a shape later used by other designers from the company like

Johan Rodhe (figure 9d) and Gundorf Albertus (figure 9e) and widely copied by other Danish makers. The ring in figure 9g has no production number and is probably a unique piece.

Figure 10 shows the good design and workmanship of a number of Danish silversmiths from this period, including the mass-producing manufacturers, Cohr and Gran & Lakly.

Prices for the Georg Jensen rings are £30-£40 and for the rings in figure 10 £12-£20.

IS IT IVORY?

by Denis Szeszler

Reproduced by courtesy of
The Antiques Dealer

Celluloid   *Ivory*

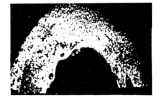

Above: A cross-section of a piece of bone showing characteristic holes.

Right: Magnified piece of bone cut lengthwise to display channels (dark lines).

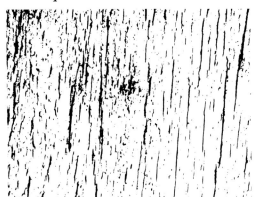

Cross-section and lengthwise view of ivory. In this high-contrast illustration, the characteristic "engine-turned" grain of the ivory is easily visible. This same effect can be seen on smooth surfaces of carved pieces with an ordinary magnifying glass.

Several people have written to me asking for help with the identification of ivory. The problem breaks down to two separate questions: distinguishing man-made materials from natural ones, and distinguishing ivory (the tusk of either the African or the Asian elephant) from bone, antler, and the teeth of other animals.

Man-made Materials

Man-made imitations of ivory include celluloid, "ivorene" (ivory dust mixed with an epoxy resin), and just plain white plastic. Objects made from these materials are moulded, and quite often the mould-marks are carefully eliminated by hand before the pieces are sold. We cannot, therefore, depend on finding tell-tale seams on the sides of objects made from these materials. We should, instead, look for the grain of the material.

Examination of any smooth area of the object in question with an ordinary magnifying glass will reveal the presence or absence of grain. Each of the natural materials (ivory, bone, antler and the teeth of various animals) will show its own distinctive grain. All of the mad-made materials, with the exception of celluloid, will show no grain at all.

Celluloid, a substance made from chemically treated plant-fibre derivatives, was widely used as an ivory substitute in the early part of this century. Since it is possible to cast it in thin layers of alternating lighter and darker yellowish colour, it appears to have a grain. This "grain", however, is unlike that of any natural substance, since it remains the same, whether cut with, or across, the "grain".

Since ivory, bone and the teeth of all animals are formed by tubular cells running lengthwise in the material, they will look different when cut *across* the grain than when cut *with* the grain. As our simplified drawing shows, since celluloid was cast in *layers,* the lines continue across the transverse section of a piece.

The piece of ivory, on the other hand, shows its characteristic "machine-turned" effect when cut across the grain, and all of the natural ivory-like substances will show their own characteristic patterns when cut across the grain — patterns that are different from those that appear when the material is cut with the grain.

If, after careful examination of the piece in question, you are still in doubt as to whether it is made of man-made materials, a simple test will provide the conclusive answer. The tip of a pin or pocket-knife, heated to a red glow, will melt any and all of the made-made materials, and none of the natural ones. This test should, of course, be done on a non-prominent feature of the piece,

and extreme care should be taken if you suspect that the material might be celluloid. (Although the hot tip of your pin or pocket-knife should only melt a very small dent in the material, the use of celluloid was discontinued years ago because of its highly flammable nature.)

Distinguishing Ivory from other Animal Teeth, Bone and Antler

There are, of course, various scientific tests, such as examination by spectroscope, ultraviolet, and polarised light, that will make clear distinctions between the materials under discussion. I have, however, restricted myself in this article to those differences in these substances that can be seen with a simple magnifying glass, so that the reader may with reasonable certainty identify the materials of objects that he is interested in.

While just about all cultures produced carvings in ivory as well as bone, animal teeth and the antlers of native deer and related animals, the identification of the particular material used is perhaps the most important for those who deal in netsuke and other Japanese art objects.

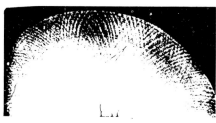

Two views of the grain of mammoth tusks, quite similar to that of modern ivory. The major differences are a markedly brownish colour, and a network of fine crackling that tends to appear on the surface of carvings of mammoth tusk.

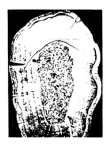

Walrus tusk is easily identified by core. What appears in our illustration as white centre mixed with darker dots is actually almost translucent material with irregular opaque spots.

Especially in netsuke, the Japanese tended to use every material known to them, and the small size of the pieces makes identification often quite difficult — while the collector to whom we offer the pieces often wants to know the material as specifically as possible.

Ivory
By the term "ivory" in this article I mean the material of the tusks of elephants. The tusks are the incisors (*not* canines) that have grown to great lengths in the upper jaws of elephants. When cut across, this material shows lines of alternating colours in arcs of a circle, producing a sort of "engine-turned" effect. This effect is due to the enormous number of minute tubes of which the ivory is composed, radiating outwards from the pulp cavity in the centre (this pulp cavity is reduced to a thin nerve passage in the outer halves of mature tusks).

When fresh, the pores of the ivory are filled with an oily substance, which accounts for the polish that ivory is able to take, as well as for the rejuvenating effect that oiling has on antique pieces.

The grain, looked at lengthwise, consists of long, parallel lines of alternating lighter and darker materials, sometimes relatively straight, and sometimes quite wavy.

The natural colour varies between a very pale yellow and light brown and, since ivory is rather porous, it is easily stained either intentionally, or through unintentional contact with coloured materials. Exposure to sunlight will bleach it to a nearly opaque white, and we often see old carvings that are dark brown in the back and quite light in the front where they have been exposed to the light.

Mammoth Ivory
Carvings from the tusks of the mammoth, a close ancestor of the modern elephant, display very similar patterns of graining. The material tends to be much darker, probably due to colour absorption from the earth.

The surface of carvings from mammoth tusks also tends to show a fine overall network of dark crackling, undoubtedly due to the loss of most of the natural moisture of the material through the millennia.

Walrus Tusks
The walrus has two large tusks (elongated canine teeth) projecting downward from the upper jaw. These tusks, often reaching 2ft. in length, have been extensively carved as ivory for centuries in Scandinavia, Persia, China and especially in Japan. Most Eskimo carving was also done in this medium.

Walrus tusk carvings are usually easy to identify, because much of the interior of the tooth is filled with a mottled, almost translucent substance that is harder and more resistant to carving than the rest of the tooth. Netsuke and other figural carvings of this material almost invariably show this translucent core at the top and bottom.

Teeth of the Sperm Whale
The sperm whale, an inhabitant of tropical and sub-tropical seas, has teeth running the whole length of its enormous lower jaw. Those in the middle tend to be the largest, often attaining a length of more than 6ins. to 8ins. Approximately one third of each tooth is hollow at the base.

When cut across, the teeth display a pattern of concentric circles and, lengthwise, the outside shows parallel lines while the inside grain follows the shape of the hollow pulp cavity.

We are most familiar with sperm whale teeth as the medium for the scrimshaw work of seamen, but they were also used extensively as ornaments by various inhabitants of Pacific islands. The Japanese often used the material for carving netsuke and other small figures.

Bone
All bones are hollow, the cavity being filled with a spongy material. Since the bone itself is relatively thin, carvings of any size will show some of this spongy material.

Cut across, bone shows a pattern of minute holes looking like dark dots. Lengthwise, bone displays many narrow channels which appear to be dark lines of varying lengths. Polished, bone is more opaque and less shiny than ivory.

Saleroom Report

Left: Crested hat pin set of two long-shafted pins, four buttons, and a brooch, floral design in pink and ivory enamel with gilt highlights and silver mounted, velvet and satin-lined case with simulated leather exterior. £80. Phillips.

Large Wedgwood Fairyland lustre bowl. £690. Henry Spencer & Sons.

Rare Battersea bottle ticket designed by James Gwin and engraved by Simon-François Ravenet, inscribed "Canarie" and transfer-printed in red and softly coloured, c.1755, 7cm wide, slight chip (apparently unrecorded, not listed by Penzer, Cook or Watney). £1,250. Sotheby's.

Part of a collection of seventeen items of headgear, including peaked caps c.1910-1960, a boy Scout's hat, military berets, a glengarry, forage caps, a Balmoral and two top hats, most in very good condition. Sold for £30. Sotheby, King & Chasemore.

Two Liberty & Co. "Cymric" silver and enamel vases, Birmingham 1904. Left, design attributed to Archibald Knox, £3,800. Right, design attributed to Harry Silver, £2,800. Sotheby's Belgravia.

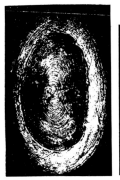

The tooth of the sperm whale. Concentric-circle pattern with band of contrasting colour outside. Lengthwise grain runs in parallel lines outside, one following conical shape of pulp cavity on inside.

The spongy centre of antler is harder than that of bone and less likely to disintegrate with time. Most antler carvings show some evidence of this core. Viewed from the side, the grain looks more like irregular dots than dark lines.

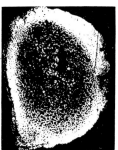

Antler

Antler

In areas where deer and related animals are found, the inhabitants have, since prehistoric times, made use of the antlers of these animals. In most cases, the material was used practically intact, and is easily recognisable.

Many cultures used antlers as knife and dagger handles, for example, changing the natural appearance of the material hardly at all. The Japanese, however, carved netsuke and other small objects from antler (commonly but incorrectly called "staghorn" in books on Japanese art), completely removing the characteristic outer "bark" of the material. The appearance of these objects, therefore, somewhat resembles that of bone and ivory.

The centre of antler consists of a spongy mate_ial, resembling the centre of bone, and the two materials can be confused if only their cross-sections are compared. Looked at lengthwise, however, the graining is quite different. Instead of the narrow, regular channels (seen as dark lines) which are characteristic of bone, antlers show a profusion of irregular holes under a magnifying glass.

The reasons for going into such detail about the various materials discussed above are twofold. First, I am sure that you have all found, and will find, that the more you know about the objects that you want to sell, the easier your job becomes. Second, the recently enacted pieces of legislation prohibiting the importation of objects made from ivory makes it necessary for all of us to become expert in the identification of materials that we want to bring in from abroad. The agent at Customs is much more likely than not to assume that anything that looks like ivory is indeed ivory, and therefore prohibited. If you can explain that, as a matter of fact, the carving in your possession was made from bone or antler, for example — and if you can point out the differences between these materials — your problems at Customs will most likely be greatly reduced.

As Mr. Szeszler mentions in his article, which was written for the American antiques trade and first published in *The Antiques Dealer,* there has recently been considerable legislation prohibiting the import and export of endangered wildlife and their derivatives, and the Department of the Environment has supplied the following guidelines on the importation of ivory into the United Kingdom.

1. The import and export of all ivory, whether or not worked and including antique ivory, is subject to licensing under the Endangered Species (Import and Export) Act 1976, which implements the controls specified under the Convention on International Trade in Endangered Species of Wild Flora and Fauna (CITES).

2. Export documentation must be provided with imports of any CITES listed species and a valid export permit or acceptable documentation must be obtained from the exporting country and presented to Customs upon the consignment entering the United Kingdom.

3. Controls on ivory are applied according to the status of the species as listed under CITES. The Asian elephant (*Elephas Maximus*) is listed as an Appendix I species (i.e. endangered) and as such trade in its parts and products is prohibited. Exceptions have been made, however, where the article is known to have been in trade prior to either 1st January 1976, the date licensing commenced for unworked ivory, or prior to 19th January 1979 when worked ivory became licensable.

4. The same dates as above apply for African ivory (*Loxodonta Africana*) but as the species is listed only on Appendix II (vulnerable) licences are generally freely given.

5. Narwhal (*Monodon Monoceros*) are now listed as Appendix II and their tusks are subject to the same controls as African elephant ivory. Walrus tusk (*Odobenus Rosmarus*), although not listed under CITES, requires licensing, but export documentation does not need to be provided unless it comes from Canada.

6. Persons wishing to import or export ivory should apply in advance to the Department of the Environment, Room 310, Tollgate House, Houlton Street, Bristol BS2 9DJ. Application forms are sent upon request.

7. All applications for the import of any specimen in Appendix I will be considered by one of the scientific authorities appointed by the Secretary of State, and a separate application will be required for each species involved. Each licence will be valid for one consignment only and will normally be valid for nine months. In considering each application the factors the scientific authority will take into account will include the status of the species in the wild and the origins of the specimen.

8. Over fifty countries now operate CITES controls including Australia, Botswana, Brazil, Canada, Chile, Costa Rica, Cyprus, Denmark, Egypt, Equador, Finland, France, The Gambia, Federal Republic of Germany, the German Democratic Republic, Ghana, Guyana, India, Iran, Madagascar, Malaysia, Mauritius, Monaco, Morocco, Nepal, Nicaragua, Niger, Nigeria, Norway, Pakistan, Panama, Papua and New Guinea, Paraguay, Peru, Senegal, The Seychelles, South Africa, The Soviet Union, Sweden, Switzerland, Toto, Tunisia, The United Arab Emirates, The United Kingdom (and Ascension Islands, Belize, Bermuda, Channel Islands, Falkland Islands, Gibraltar, Gilbert Islands, Hong Kong, Montserrat, St. Helena, Tortola, Tristan da Cunha), The U.S.A., Uruguay, Venezuela and Zaire and many others (including Bolivia, Holland, Indonesia, Ireland, Israel, Thailand, Yugoslavia and Zambia) issue comparable export documentation.

Triptych by Toyokuni III, climactic scene from Kabuki play. The price for such sets (three prints meant to be looked at as one) is slightly less than three single prints in comparable condition by the same artist. In this case: about $250 each, $600 for triptych. In London the triptych would probably fetch between £150 and £200 at auction, but these three prints, if sold separately, would realise about £40-£50 each, if in good condition.

An Introduction to UKIYO-E:

JAPANESE WOODBLOCK PRINTS

by Denis Szeszler

Reproduced by courtesy of *The Antique Dealer*

I hesitated for quite some time before deciding to write about Japanese woodblock prints, since the complexity of the subject is so great that I was afraid that I might not be able to impart enough information in a brief article to help our readers much in dealing wisely with the examples that they encounter. However, the popularity of Japanese woodblock prints has increased so rapidly in recent years, and so many antiques shops across the country *(This is equally true of the U.K. Ed.)* have started carrying them, that I decided that as much information as possible, including a fairly comprehensive list of signatures of major artists, should be provided.

Background

The word *ukiyo-e* means "pictures of the present, temporary world", in contrast to the eternal paradise of the afterlife promised by religion. Originally, *ukiyo* (e means picture) denoted that this life, filled with toil and trouble, is a kind of hell that one would long to leave. The meaning of the word changed at the end of the 16th century, however, when Hideyoshi, the son of a peasant, managed to become the supreme ruler of Japan. This event convinced many people that a world where a man can rise to the top through talent and ambition alone cannot be so bad after all, and *ukiyo* gained a positive meaning. Artists became more interested in illustrating the lives of the common people — their occupations, pleasures and interests.

During the 17th century the Kabuki theatre evolved, providing a need for posters and programmes. The wood-block print proved to be ideal for producing these, and the popularity of the medium increased together with that of the theatre. The early black and white prints were soon enhanced by hand colouring, then printed in two colours, and ultimately in full colour — a development introduced in 1764. Such multicolour prints required the carving of a series of blocks: a design block that printed all of the black lines on the paper, and a separate block for each colour which, after careful matching of the areas, was printed on the same piece of paper.

Although this was a painstaking process, the results allowed the artists a much greater degree of personal expression than the earlier prints. It goes without saying that the immediate commercial success of the full-colour prints did a great deal to encourage artists to produce them, and the majority of prints made after 1764 were in full colour.

The variety of subjects depicted in woodblock prints was almost endless. It included actors (all roles in the Kabuki were by then, and are today, performed by men); beautiful women; famous places and scenes; suma wrestlers; birds and flowers (as well as other flora and fauna); historical and legendary events, etc. In many cases woodblock prints served as fashion plates, allowing people to emulate the costumes and styles worn by the most popular actors, heroes and courtesans of the time.

As the popularity of woodblock prints increased through the late 18th and early 19th centuries, more and more artists began to work in the medium. They generally studied the styles of several masters, becoming pupils of one of the living greats, forming "schools" of artists working in individual but related styles. It was customary for the pupils of a master to take an art name that incorporated one of the syllables from the master's name, which accounts for the repetition of so many sounds in the list of signatures.

Some of the schools were quite large: for example, in 1828 the pupils and second generation pupils of Toyokuni I gathered at his grave site for a memorial service, and signed their names on the back of his gravestone. The ninety-seven signatures found there include such famous names as Kuniyoshi, Kuninaga, Kunitora, Kunimasa and Kuniyasu.

Towards the end of the Tokugawa era (1603-1868), Japan was torn by both internal strife and external pressures. There were several uprisings against the Shogunate (the succession of military rulers who had been in power since 1603), and the United States joined the efforts of several European powers to force Japan to abandon its longstanding policy of total isolation.

As usually happens during periods of great political turmoil, the arts suffered. Even the most famous woodblock print artists were unable to get more than the equivalent of a few dollars for their designs, and necessity forced most artists to begin having more concern for quantity than quality. The printers started using the newly imported chemical inks to make woodblock prints, which resulted in colours of an unprece-

Signatures of the Most Prominent Japanese Woodblock Artists of the 18th and 19th Centuries

(A number of the signatures reproduced below were used by a succession of artists who were followers of the innovator of a style. While they are generally known as "so-and-so II or III", the characters used in the signature tended to be the same, so that other considerations, such as the paper and colour used, must be weighed to determine which of a group of artists who used the same name made a particular print.)

Ashihiro c. 1820
Ashikuni fl. 1775-1818
Ashimaro 1803-40?
Ashiyuki early 19th C.
Banri early 19th C.
Buncho fl. 1762-92
Bunro c. 1800-10
Choki late 18th/early 19 C.
Eiju c. 1790
Eiri early 19th C.
Eiri (aka Rekisentei) c. 1790
Eisen 1790-1848
Eishi 1756-1829
Eisho c. 1780-1800
Eisui c. 1790-1823
Eizan 1787-1867
Enkyo 1749-1803
Enshi c. 1785-95
Fusatane fl. 1849-70
Gakutei 1786?-1868
Goshichi late 18th/early 19th C.
Hanzan fl. 1850-82
Haruji c. 1760-70
Harunobu 1724-70

Harushige 1747-1818
Hidemaro early 19th C.
Hirokage fl. 1855-65
Hiroshige 1797-1858
Hisanobu fl. 1801-15
Hokkei 1780-1850
Hokuba 1771-1844
Hokui early 19th C.
Hokuga early 19th C.
Hokui c. 1830
Hokuju late 18th/early 19th C.
Hokusai 1760-1849
Hokushu early 19th C.
Hokutsui mid-19th C.
Keisei (aka Eisen) 1764-1824
Kikumaro ?-1830
Kiyohiro c. 1737-76
Kiyomasa c. 1800
Kiyomasu c. 1700
Kiyomine (aka Kiyomitsu II) 1787-1868
Kiyomitsu 1735-85
Kiyonaga 1752-1815
Kiyonobu 1664-1729
Kiyoshige c. 1720-60

Kiyotada fl. 1720-50
Kiyotsune c. 1757-79
Koryusai fl. 1764-88
Kuniaki fl. 1850-60
Kunichika 1835-1900
Kuniharu 1830-84
Kunihiko
Kunihisa 1832-91
Kunikazu fl. 1848-68
Kunimaru 1794-1820
Kunimasa fl. 1773-1810
Kaigetsu (aka Kaigetsudo) 18th C.
Kunimitsu fl. 1801-18
Kunimori fl. 1818-43
Kuninaga ?-1829
Kuninao 1793-1854
Kunisada 1786-1864
Kuniteru mid-19th C.
Kunitomi fl. 1804-44
Kunitsuna 1805-68
Kuniyasu 1794-1832
Kuniyoshi 1797-1861

Kyosai 1831-89
Mangetsudo c. 1760
Okumura Masanobu 1686-1764
Kitao Masanobu 1761-1816
Masayoshi 1764-1824
Masunobu 18th C.
Morofusa 17th C.
Moronobu 17th C.
Ryukoku early 19th C
Ryu-unsai late-18th C.
Sadafusa fl. 1825-50
Sadahide 1807-73
Sadahiro fl. 1825-75
Sadakage fl. 1818-44
Sadanobu 1809-79
Sekiho early 19th C.
Sekijo fl. 1800-1807
Sencho fl. 1830-50
Sharaku c. 1794-95
Shigeharu 1803-53
Shigemasa 1739-1820
Shigenaga 1697?-1756

Shigenobu 1787-1832
Shigenobu (aka Yanagawa) c. 1820
Shigenobu (aka Hiroshige II) 1826-69
Shikimaro c. 1810
Shiko late 18th/early 19th C.
Shinsai 1764?-1820
Shucho fl. 1790-1803
Shuncho fl. 1780-95
Shundo fl. 1780-92
Shunei 1762-1819
Shunjo ?-1787
Shunko 1743-1812
Shunkyo early 19th C.
Shunman 1757-1820
Shunro (aka Hokusai) 1760-1849
Shunsen (aka Katsukawa) c. 1790
Shunsen (aka Kashosai) 1762-1830?
Shunsho 1726-92
Shuntei 1770-1820
Shunzan fl. 1782-98
Sori (aka Hokusai) 1760-1849
Sugakudo fl. 1850-60
Sukenobu 1671-1751
Taito (aka Hokusai) 1760-1849

Terushige fl. 1715-25
Tominobu mid-18th C.
Toshinobu fl. 1717-50
Toyoharu 1735-1814
Toyohide 19th C.
Toyohiro 1773-1828
Toyohisa fl. 1801-18
Toyokuni I 1769-1825
Toyokuni II 1777-1835
Toyokuni III (aka Kunisada) 1786-1864
Toyomaru fl. 1785-97
Toyomasa fl. 1770-80
Toyonobu 1711-85
Toyoshige (aka Toyokuni II) 1777-1835
Tsukimaro ?-1830
Utamaro 1754-1806
Yoshiiku mid-19th C.
Yoshiharu 1828-88
Yoshikazu fl. 1850-70
Yoshikuni 1803-40?
Yoshimaru
Yoshinobu 18th C.
Yoshitora fl. 1850-80
Yoshitoshi 1839-92

aka - also known as; fl. - flourished

Left: An exceptionally powerful actor print by Toyokuni III (also known as Kunisada). It is enhanced in value by the mica particles that were applied to the print. (These are barely visible in our photograph as light-grey squares in the background.)

Right: Rare print by Yoshiiku (Kuniyoshi's pupil, mid-19th century); fine condition. The macabre subject, one of "28 Scenes of Glory", ensures a value near the top of the $50-500 range customary for most 19th century prints. London auction price about £15 in good condition.

Below: Typical actor print by Kunichika. The style is reminiscent of Toyokuni III, but the intense reds/purples indicate the second half of the 19th century. London auction price about £20, in good condition.

dented harshness and vibrancy. The reds and purples of this period stand out particularly, being much more intense than those used previously.

Although several artists continued to produce woodblock prints during the Meiji period (1868-1912), the public's interest and support was rapidly declining. The people's imagination had been captured by the West; they wanted imported goods, and raced towards westernisation. Around 1890, modern printing presses were imported — for all practical purposes closing the era of the Japanese woodblock print.

Judging Prints

Unlike other forms of Japanese art, woodblock prints can be produced again and again. A print pulled from a particular block fifty or a hundred years after it was carved would match an original print line for line. While it's true that — if we had the opportunity to examine two such prints side by side — we could see a thickening and cracking of some of the lines on the later print due to wear on the block, such opportunities seldom present themselves. Therefore, the factors that must be examined to determine when a print was pulled from the block are the paper, colours and printing method.

Paper. In order to examine the paper properly, the print must be removed from the frame, mat-board and backing. The paper used until the middle of the 19th century was thin and fibrous, so that when one looks at the *back* of a print from that period, the design and most of the colours can be made out with surprising clarity. Improvements in the paper after the middle of the 19th century made it much more opaque, allowing less of the design to show through to the back. Prints made at the beginning of the 20th century were done on such thick paper that practically nothing of the design can be seen from the back.

Colours. As I mentioned earlier, Japan's opening to the West brought with it the importation of chemical inks and dyes whose colours were much more intense than those of the Japanese. Coming across a print signed by an artist who died in, let's say, 1840, which contains some areas of particularly vibrant or brilliant colours, would indicate the possibility that the print might have been made considerably after the artist's lifetime. In such a case, all of the other factors that might prove this should be examined particularly carefully.

Printing Methods. The traditional method of pulling prints from woodblocks consisted of inking the carved block, placing the paper on it, and rubbing the back in overlapping circles with a spoon-like tool to make the impression. There are two tell-tale signs which indicate that this was indeed the method used: the back of the paper will reveal spiral or circular rubbing marks,

and the unprinted areas on the front of the print will bulge slightly outwards, since the pressure of the "spoon" met no resistance and stretched the paper.

Looked at from the *front,* the lines on these prints seem to be *impressed* into the paper. On the other hand, prints made on modern printing presses show no rubbing marks on the back and tend to be flat, or the accumulation of ink needed to make the design actually makes the lines, rather than the spaces, bulge slightly toward the front of the print.

Pricing

Japanese woodblock prints range tremendously in value, from a few pounds for a minor print in poor condition to up to £50,000 for some rare masterpieces, such as a pristine print from the first run of Hokusai's "Great Wave", or a fine Sharaku (a great artist who worked only for a total of ten months in 1794-95). Such valuable prints are quite rare, of course, and I would strongly urge the "general practitioner" in antiques to consult a specialist if he thinks that he might have run across one of these.

The type of genuine woodblock print that we encounter most often is the work of prolific 19th century artists such as Kunisada (also known as Toyokuni III), Kunichika, etc. These prints generally retail today somewhere between $50 and $500 (with some exceptions), depending on factors such as condition, aesthetic appeal, subject and rarity.

Condition. The value of a print will be substantially reduced if it is very faded, due to either over-exposure to light or washing; if the print is completely pasted down to its backing; if it has sharp creases from having been folded; if it has had more than very minor trimming of its sides; and, of course, if it has obvious damage, such as large tears and holes.

Foxing (the appearance of some reddish-brown dots on the paper) and worm holes on the less important parts

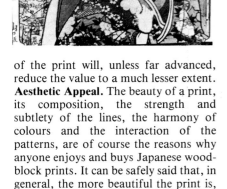

Left: Typical actor print by Toyokuni III (a/k/a Kunisada). If a good impression and in good condition — around $250. London auction price about £20 in good condition.

Right: Hiroshige II print from "36 Views of Tokyo" series. The style is practically indistinguishable from Hiroshige I, the signature the same, but brilliant red (imported from the West) indicates Hiroshige II (who survived his adoptive father by eleven years). About £30 at London auction, if in good condition.

Below: Unusual print by Yoshiiku; several worm holes. Some feel the aesthetic appeal (portrait-like face, look of curiosity/humour) compensates for the condition (see text). London auction price about £15 if in good condition.

of the print will, unless far advanced, reduce the value to a much lesser extent.

Aesthetic Appeal. The beauty of a print, its composition, the strength and subtlety of the lines, the harmony of colours and the interaction of the patterns, are of course the reasons why anyone enjoys and buys Japanese wood-block prints. It can be safely said that, in general, the more beautiful the print is, the greater its value.

Subject. Some prints demand higher prices because of the subject they depict. Any print whose subject is highly unusual, erotic, or grotesque, would fall into this category.

Rarity. Everything else being equal, prints that tend to be more valuable because of their rarity include: good prints by seldom-seen artists; rare subjects by more prolific artists; and unusual printing techniques used in the making of an otherwise not too unusual print. The term "unusual printing techniques" includes *gauffrage* (lines impressed into the paper without colour); the application of mica particles to the print; and hand-painted or lacquered details.

It is my hope that this brief guide and list of signatures will prove to be of help in the understanding and handling of *ukiyo-e* prints, which were the primary means of illustrating Japanese life and legend until they were superseded by the printing and photography of the New Age.

Recognising the Signature

Most *ukiyo-e* prints have an abundance of characters and marks on them, which might make it difficult for those unfamiliar with the language to recognise the signature. These include: the censor's mark(s), usually round, about the size of a dime; the printer's mark, which is often four characters in a vertical rectangle; the title of the print or of the series that it is part of, which usually appears near the upper-right corner of the print; explanations, clarifications,

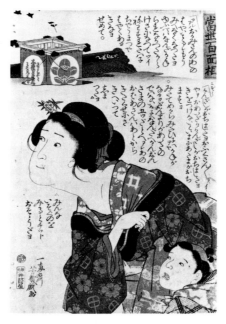

stories and poems, which run across the top of the print; the names of the characters depicted which are usually in vertical rectangles near each figure; and of course the signature, which is usually found in either the lower right or lower left part of the print. The characters of the name by which the artist is known are almost invariably directly *above* one of the three characters illustrated here:

Ga   *Fude*   *Dzu*

(The meaning of all three is "painted, drew or designed".)

Editor's Note on Prices

The apparent discrepancy between the American $ prices given by Mr. Szeszler and the £ sterling prices kindly provided by Kimi Mitani of Christie's is due to the comparison of retail prices and auction prices. Most of the buyers at Christie's sales of Japanese prints are dealers and, since the unit prices of Japanese prints in general are fairly small, the dealer has to double or sometimes triple the price to take account of travel expenses, the cost of framing (which is not cheap), cleaning, etc. Mr. Mitani feels that in general there is not much difference between New York and London prices for Japanese prints, except for a certain type of modern print.

Wistful print from Kuniyoshi's "Famous Poets" series; notable for strong feeling, Western perspective. In good condition this would fetch between £80-£120 at London auction.

A very finely made Meissen porcelain and ebony veneered cabinet made purely as a decorative item and with little practical use. The very fine quality solid porcelain panels on the four doors are painted on both sides with portrait panels after the painter N. Largillierre and harbour scenes after J.B. Weenix. The drawers are painted with numerous tavern scenes after David Teniers the Younger. In this instance the carcass is well finished with an ebony veneer but only veneered on to a pine carcass, which is hardly substantial enough for such a magnificent amount of porcelain. The metalwork is poor and, like the carcass, is only there for necessity and care has been taken not to draw the eye away away from the panels. The panels have the familiar Meissen crossed sword marks in under-glazed blue. The back of the cabinet bears a red wax seal stamped 'st. Dresden'. A similar cabinet was exhibited at the Paris International Exhibition in 1878 by Mr. William Oppenheim, an agent for the royal factory at Dresden. Late 1870s. £20,000/£30,000.

A fine 19th century marquetry writing table in Louis XVI style. The 18th century masters were very fond of pieces with these complicated writing drawers. This one has two hinged side pieces and an adjustable reading or writing flap. The quality of this piece is superb. The top is inlaid with muses representing astronomy and mathematics seated at either side of an armillary sphere. The colours are still very fresh, giving some indication of the brightness that the 18th century cabinet makers obtained in the colours of their period examples, colours which by now have faded dramatically and only the occasional opening of a hidden, long forgotten drawer will reveal the freshness of the king-wood and tulipwood veneers. It is not recorded who made this desk but the firm of Alfred Beurdeley is known to have made several examples with and without the fitted writing drawer. 1870s. £8,000-£12,000 but probably 20% to 30% more with Beurdeley's stamp.

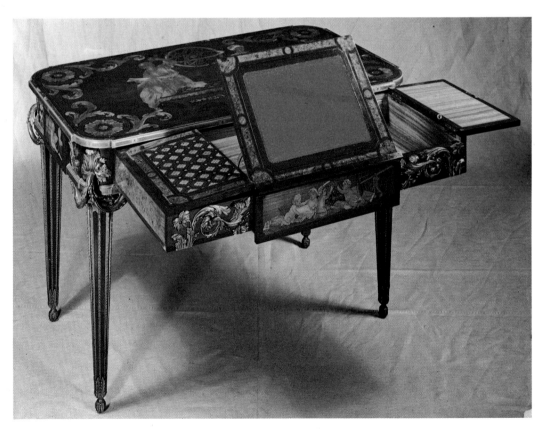

Continental Furniture and Napoléon III
by Christopher Payne

Author of The Price Guide to 19th Century European Furniture
to be published shortly by the Antique Collectors' Club

Figure 1. A lacquer and thuyawood cabinet, 1860-80. Sold at Sotheby's Belgravia on 11th March 1981 for £920.

The heyday for 19th century Continental furniture was a heady period from 1974 to 1976 when there was a great influx of buyers from a beleaguered Lebanon in fierce competition with Persian and Middle Eastern collectors. As the knowledge of any particular field of collectors grows, there is greater discernment, which creates a tendency to push the prices of the better quality items higher and higher, leaving a morass of lesser items that are difficult to sell both for the dealer and the auctioneer.

It is certainly wrong to say that prices have not caught up with those days five to seven years ago. A good piece new to the market will invariably realise a high price. The first major sale in the Sotheby's Belgravia equivalent in New York at York Avenue saw as its star lot an elaborate *bureau-de-dame* by the master of marquetry and ormolu, François Linke. Made in the first few years of this century — in the teeth of European art nouveau period — it realised £24,000. This and another magnificent 19th century copy of the Roi de Stanislas desk in the Wallace Collection, which realised £54,000 in Holland, set new trends and possibilities for the major items of European late 19th and early 20th century furniture. Unlike the British furniture of Mackintosh, Voysey or Burges, provenance, although always an advantage, is not absolutely necessary. Buyers are simply after fine quality impressive pieces in good condition. Contemporary furniture from France in a traditional style is just what the progressive architect designers in England rebelled against and abhorred, but the sophisticated architect designed pieces are generally only sought after by the *cognoscenti*, not the public at large.

It is not often that a piece bought in a major auction is reoffered within a three year period, so it was interesting to see a good quality *bureau-de-dame* made in the late 19th century bought in 1977 for £4,000 by a private Middle Eastern buyer against fierce trade bidding sell in the same saleroom in 1980 to a Continental dealer for £5,000 — not a huge profit for the collector, possibly, but a healthy trend in so short a time.

Certainly people collecting the better quality 19th century Continental furniture must consider their investment a long term one. Five years would be the minimum advisable turn around but ten years a more realistic period and sufficient length of time for the investor to reap some worthwhile benefit financially.

Suites of drawing room furniture have never been very easy items to sell. A settee, two armchairs and four side chairs in Louis XV or XVI style is not the type of furniture that is often bought for the modern, average sized home. It is amusing to note that auctioneers always describe these suites as "comprising a *Canapé*, two *Fauteuils* and four side chairs" — the French is either considered unnecessary or too involved to describe the side chairs. The ebullient Louis XV suites are rarer and more popular than the plainer rather refined Louis XVI suites. Seven pieces of the former can easily realise between £2,000 and £3,000, whilst the latter have to be very good quality to realise much more than £1,000. The price of Louis XV style furniture is steadily and slowly increasing, while the Louis XVI style suites are struggling to maintain the prices of previous years. To be fair, the Louis XV chairs were a revived fashion in the third quarter of the last century, whilst the Louis XVI revival for the larger commercial firms was the last quarter of the century and there was, in many cases, a distinct falling-off of quality during the transition of these styles. The Empress Eugenie may have thought she was Marie Antoinette c.1860 but the neo-classical revival for most was later than the height of royal Parisienne whim.

The small *tables de cheveret, tables ambulante* and *gueridon* tables have all increased in price recently, realising £300-£500, £500-£700 and £250-£450 respectively on average as against £250-£400, £300-£500 and £200-£400 during the preceding twelve months. These small, very useful items are highly conducive to modern city dwellings

Figure 2. A marquetry table de cheveret, c.1880. Sold at Sotheby's Belgravia on 12th November 1980 for £520.

which accounts for their increasing popularity.

A stamp or *marque au fer* is an enormous advantage nowadays in selling a piece and likely to become more and more so as the search for any type of provenance or "handle" filters through to the Continental field. It is difficult to give an overall figure for this advantage, as many of the named pieces are better quality than the unsigned items, thus showing the inherent good sense of the makers of *meubles de luxe* — no one wants to sign an indifferent piece! At a rough "guesstimate" the *meuble d'appui* in figure 1 might realise £1,200-£1,600 if it bore the stamp of, let us say, Henri Dasson. Dasson always signed his mounts and/or carcasses "Henry Dasson", with a "y" on Henry an indication, possibly, that he was manufacturing for the wealthy English and American markets. Without any stamp the cabinet realised £920.

Boulle is slowly and steadily increasing but not as fast as it had done in the previous year. The better made pieces from the remainder of Europe are increasing at a very healthy pace, although direct comparison of one piece with another in terms of price from one year to another is difficult as the furniture is usually highly individual and unlikely to be repeated — a definite "plus" as an investment factor.

Collecting Christmas Cards
by Maria Hubert

When I took my highly cultured mother-in-law into our library to show her my treasured collection of cards, her reaction was one of puzzlement, a sort of "Why are you wasting your time on bits of paper?" attitude. Likewise, an eminent local antique dealer friend refers to me as "an important collector of those expensive pieces of paper". Yet the greetings card, and perhaps now especially the Christmas card, is becoming a very popular collectors' item and has a very wide field of appeal.

There are essentially two types of Christmas card: the Christmas postcard, and the type designed to fit into an envelope.

The Postcard Type

These are usually the easiest to identify, having as a rule the artist's name on the front and the publisher or number of series on the back, with often the added bonus of a date if the card was postally used.

There are probably more postcard type Christmas cards around than any other type, and they can still be picked up for 15p-20p. If one is more expensive, take a hard look. Has it got a name to the picture? Does it do anything unusual, such as a flap opening to reveal

An attractive rosehip design attributed to Walter Crane and published by Marcus Ward.

another picture underneath? Or try holding it up to the light; it may prove to be a "transparency" which shows a completely different scene, or black and white which turns to colour. Or there may be "lighted" windows/stars/candles, etc. These "Hold-to-light" cards can fetch as much as £10, and the Santa Claus ones are highly prized. However, it is quite possible to pick these up for a few pence from an unobservant dealer with many thousands of cards to sell.

Still on the postcard, occasionally one can find an advertising card published by a large company to attract Christmas trade or to wish customers the compliments of the season. These are rare, much sought after and expensive. It is not impossible to find them priced at £30. I was lucky enough to come across a very tatty album recently for £9 which has one of these well preserved within its pages together with several other gems.

The most commonly found postcards date from around 1900-1920, but the Christmas postcard actually dates from 1870, one of the earliest publishers being John Day, London. These early cards were smaller than those we know today, being about 4ins. × 3ins. and were lithographed designs. America was quick to follow in 1872-73, soon after the American government issued their first ordinary postcards, and the rest of Europe started around the same time. The Germans, always artists in the field of printing, produced many excellent designs which were imported into Britain, and theirs were some of the first novelty cards.

Raphael Tuck are perhaps the best known and most prolific of the British publishers of Christmas postcards. They produced in series, and some collectors

Mr. Christmas, M.P., by Walter Crane, 1875, and four other cards of his from the same date.

A typically mid-Victorian design: "Evening Primrose" by Marcus Ward. Large cards with flower designs were particularly popular in the 1880s.

A page from a hand painted Victorian Christmas card scrap book. This one shows the still alive pre-Christian element of thinking of this season as a time to look forward to Spring and new life. The cards date from the 1870s.

A popular design in the late 1880s. This card is in willow pattern blue illuminated in gold.

Early shaped cards are difficult to find but well worth seeking. The design is continued on the reverse, and the card opens to reveal its accompanying verse. These two are in unusually good condition and their verses are as follows: "Put up with its shape for in hail or in damp/It will prove like my friendship a trustworthy gamp" And "If life is like a pudding, let others have the crumbs;/ But you my friend, to you I send, best wishes for the plums" by F.E. Weatherly, Raphael Tuck, late 1880s.

will seek only one specific series, or the cards of one publisher. Tuck's "Oilette" series was and is most popular, emulating, as the title suggests, an oil painting. These can be picked up for about 30p at most stalls. Wildt & Kray produced some fine cards including a very attractive bevelled gold edged card, which can usually be had for around 50p.

After 1900 the Christmas postcard became more and more elaborate, with designs in velvet, glass beads, seaweeds, glitter and sequins and a host of other materials. There were cards printed on cork and aluminium, and Ireland put out peat cards. These, though printed as postcards, were banned by the Post Office and had to be sent in envelopes. It is unlikely that these will go unnoticed by even the most harassed dealer, so expect to pay between £1-£5 plus, depending on condition, age etc.

There are, of course, catalogues which value cards (for example *The International Postcard Market Catalogue,* published annually from Kingscote Station, East Grinstead, Sussex), but it is really very much a case of demand. If you need a card badly to complete a collection, you may be prepared to pay over the odds rather than let it slip through your fingers. I once paid £12 for a card valued at only £7, but I needed it badly enough to bid high in order to persuade the reluctant owner to part with it.

Some of the fine illustrators at the turn of the century include Margaret Tarrant, whose work is executed in the most beautiful jewel colours and whose cards are getting quite difficult to find outside the specialist shop, perhaps especially her religious scenes. Louis Wain cards, especially cats, are now becoming quite expensive (I was offered one for £12 recently) and the pretty Regency children of Kate Greenaway are most popular. Mabel Lucy Atwell is rapidly becoming a much prized illustrator amongst card collectors; though her Christmas illustrations are not as prolific as one would have thought, her style lends itself so well. Earlier illustrators of note were Coleman, most famous for his scantily clad young girls posed as nymphs; Walter Crane, who did some early comic cards, then became better known for his attractive art nouveau designs and Horatio Coudrey whose puppy and kitten paintings must have brought many an "aah" in the '80s and '90s! The list goes on and on and includes many Royal Academicians.

The Christmas Card as we know it

This began life in 1843 when Sir Henry Cole commissioned a card designed by John Calcott Horsley, depicting a family at dinner toasting absent friends. It was hand coloured by Jobbins of Holborn and finally published in 1846 by Joseph Cundall. There were only 1,000 published and the idea did not catch on too

well. It was in 1862 that the firm of Goodall took the risk and published the first commercially produced card and the Christmas card industry was born. It blossomed and boomed throughout the '60s and '70s from the tiny "carte de visite" types — the earliest and almost impossible to find gems by C.H. Bennett between 1865-68 — to the elaborate concoctions of the 1890s — re-allocated Valentine card designs with a Christmas message added, fringes, padded satins and woven silks — to the mechanical, which were often more like toys than mere greetings cards. These latter covered everything from the immensely popular fan, which had many leaves stapled together to open out like a fan with a message on each leaf; the pull lever type, which moved part of the

design to show a verse or another picture underneath; the pop-up or three-dimensional pictures. There were doors which opened, concertina panoramas, etc., etc., etc.

The German school of oleographs were the next big thing on the market. They were highly coloured and often had a religious theme, not a strongly popular idea in England as a rule but, although it did not catch on with the British publishers, these cards were imported in their thousands, and there are many examples still around for a few pence.

Many of the early designs are very delicate and very beautiful with all their paper and silver lace, paper springs to make them three-dimensional. However, because of their delicacy, really fine specimens are hard to find. I made do with several damaged items before I came across a perfect one. Some had padded and perfumed centres, and most of these were produced by Eugene Rimmel in the 1870s-80s.

The carte de visite cards were designed to be left at an acquaintance's home by personal delivery. These tiny 3ins. × 2ins. cards make a delightful collection on their own. In the 1870s they became larger and verses began to appear,

A very rare Russian card showing a glitter spangled Santa Claus child's greeting from 1880.

usually on the backs, but the folded card did not arrive really until the 1890s. These single sided cards are most attractive. They can be round, triangular, diamond and square shaped, or even crescents, Chinese screens, barred gates, cut-outs of angels, birds, stars and

houses. Many are sprinkled with a very delicate glitter which was made from glass or even shell. All these cards I have found in quantity for as little as 50p, though you may have to pay £1.50 plus to a dealer in cards. They are still at the cheaper end of the market and make a good starting point. Early celluloid cards are still fairly easy to find at around the £1.50-£4 mark. These are very pretty, often hand-painted, embossed and glittered designs usually of a romantic nature. From around 1890-1925 there was a wealth of cut-away designs; small often foliated cut-out edges, some so intricate they are almost filigree. These are still to be had in their thousands for 50p-£1.

Raphael Tuck again was very high on the list of publishers as were the de la Rue Company, both starting in the early 1870s. The pioneer Goodall Company we have already mentioned; the pioneer of the American Christmas card was Louis Prang in 1874. Marcus Ward was another early publisher, starting in Belfast in 1866 but extending to London and later New York. Many of the companies, including Ward, Prang and Hildesheimer, held competitions for the best designs, and these cards can be quite an interesting find, often with the designer's name and the prize on the reverse.

Many fine early collections were wiped out in the Blitz of 1940-41, notably those of the de la Rue Company, which consisted of samples of all their published and unpublished work since they began, and the private collection of Jonathan King, who was undeniably the most knowledgeable on the history of Christmas cards and whose collection had some 163,000 types and was said to weigh over six tons! Consequently those cards left have become a precious part of our social history.

Preservation

Postcards are easy to store. An excellent filing system can be made from shoe boxes and the cards themselves can be stored in cellophane sleeves.

Two pretty art nouveau cards (the photograph does no justice to the butterflies which have pearly wings), c.1910/20.

Two "Hold-to-light" cards: a cottage in winter with snow on the branches and smoke from the chimney with the verse "Bathe this bleak spot in sunlight's glow, Summer will come to melt the snow!"; geese with the verse "You need but hold this card against the light, to see these geese all in a pretty plight!" The second illustration shows the hidden parts revealed by light: the winter scene changes to one with swallows flying, blossoms on the branches and leaves on the trees; the geese's plight is shown in the shape of a fox (top right) and their wings extend in flight.

The other type is not so easily dealt with. As they come in all sorts of odd shapes and sizes and are often not as strong as their postcard counterparts, they require careful storing. I evolved a series of albums made from polythene photograph sleeves which come in various sizes and can be bought from any good photographic supplier. By making punch holes at the edges and tying them together with picture cord, a most practical solution is to hand. For conventional cards with blank backs I use the albums called ''Magnetic'' with clear plastic leaves. These keep the cards clean and dry and do not spoil the backs.

When handling cards one's hands should be clean and dry and, if possible, lightly talced. Invisible moisture and acids from the hands cause serious deterioration. There are a number of archival preserving products available for the really serious collector.

The Future

I was asked recently what, in my opinion, would be the collectors' game of tomorrow. Personal opinions always bring criticism but I will stick my neck out and say almost certainly the World War II cards, the 1950 glittercards and pop-ups, and the Walt Disney cards, the modern Caldicott type humour of Thelwell, the fine verses of Patience Strong and, for publishers, I would say Gordon Frazer. He first began to publish cards in Cambridge just before the Second World War, and gradually introduced a totally new concept in Christmas cards based on modern design. His ideas were all simple, to the point, and bright, a concept which has brought him to the top of the tree. And Hallmark, the American company who with a modest beginning in the 1920s, rose in thirty years to be the very top publishers. Keep these thoughts in mind next Christmas — who knows, in fifty years' time someone may be very glad you did!

These three cards will help to solve the common problem of differentiating between Louis Wain cats and Helen Maguire cats. The two Wain cards on the left show fairly cartoony expressions, typical of the Wain hand. The Helen Maguire card on the right shows the softer prettier faces common to this artist.

Many cards had clever picture puzzle verses such as these three. The fourth card with a crown pin is unusual. The crown is made from gilt and plastic.

Left: A rare card produced for the golden jubilee of the penny post.

Just to prove that even the experts can be at a loss sometimes! Perhaps my favourite card. Artist initials T.L. and published by W.A.M&Co. Possibly 1880s. If anyone can identify this, I will be ever grateful!

An Onion Wine Bottle

by Roger Dumbrell

Figure 1. A good condition onion wine bottle c.1700 of classic shape and with almost full surface gloss. The bottle has everything going for it, the typical "squat" onion form, and in really dark lustrous glass. This present would cost you somewhere in the region of £80-£90.

Figure 2. So called "straight-sided" onion bottle, normally regarded as a somewhat later form, but dated examples testify that both forms were produced concurrently, so here it is a matter of choice. The bottle has not quite full surface gloss and is in much paler coloured metal. Say £60-£70 for this.

As a collector of wine bottles myself, it seemed very appropriate to consider their suitability as gifts at Christmas time, all the more so when one considers that in the past bottles must have figured very prominently at all social gatherings, feasts, festivities and celebrations.

For the gift seeker who would eschew the more "usual" antiques for his collector friends, the wine bottle must be high priority. Sealed examples, that is those marked on a circular pad of glass with the owner's name, date, locality, etc., are normally expensive and really only to be considered as gifts by the more prosperous amongst us. So, for the purposes of this short article I shall deal only with plain bottles, and furthermore with one in particular — the "onion" wine bottle.

The onion wine bottle has probably fired the imagination of more people than any other form. Suffice it to say here that bottles both before and after this were very different but, possibly because of the onion's distinctive shape, it has become more popular and widely known. In the form shown here, the bottles first appeared on the scene c.1700 and, appealing though they undoubtedly are today, such squat, stubby necked bottles must have proved far from easy to handle and pour from. However, the onion's greatest advantage was stability and, who knows, an attractive container was probably just as desirable then as now.

Study the photographs. To my mind the onion bottle conveys much more feeling of age than many antiques available today. I say available, as such considerations are of no mean importance. Most antiques of the 17th and 18th centuries are very scarce and prohibitive in cost, but not so the present article; at least not in comparison.

A totally free-blown and hand made piece of glass, nearly three centuries old, the onion bottle ranges in price from £45—£110, according to condition — and this is precisely what the buyer must define. A bottle dug out of the ground or recovered from a river bank, pond, etc., is rarely going to be worth as much as a cellar found example. Considerable pitting and degradation of the surface glass renders the bottle more of an artefact and less of an antique, if you see what I mean. Surprisingly enough, poor condition bottles from provenanced sites (wrecks, for example) often fetch alarmingly high prices, but that is a market all of its own. Generally speaking, bottles with what collectors call "full surface gloss" are the most desirable and obviously at the top end of the price range, but to my mind they are well worth the extra cost involved. One has to bear in mind that one is dealing with glass items and it is hard to appreciate the excellent reflective qualities of bottle glass, let alone the attractive colours involved, when the surface condition is not ideal.

Chipping is not as frowned upon in onion bottles as it is in the case of other glass items (e.g. wine glasses in particular), especially where the string rim only is affected, but none the less it is best avoided. The one major fault, and surprisingly one that is occasionally notoriously difficult to detect, is small star cracks and hair-lines in the body of the bottle. These render plain bottles of very little value indeed. Examine carefully from all angles, and in different light situations. Hold the bottle both against the light and away from it. Looking down and carefully revolving the bottle will often reveal the smallest of imperfections without the aid of artificial light. Indeed, to find a small "star" is often nigh impossible against the light. In any case, price should be commensurate with condition. Let's just say that a fair condition onion bottle with mostly full surface gloss and no chips or star cracks is presently worth somewhere in the region of £75, but that's not to say that you will not find one for less.

To my mind there is one condition that is perfectly acceptable and even desirable from a purchaser's point of view, but it is unfortunately not easy to define, especially on paper. Certain bottles, even when retrieved from the water, are found not to be pitted, but very lightly abraded, almost as if the very finest grades of wet and dry paper have been applied to their surface. Such bottles can often be bought relatively cheaply and, should the owner so wish, a good cleaning followed by very hard polishing with cerium oxide often restores a remarkable polish to the surface, albeit of a rather subdued nature but none the less attractive.

Having covered condition and price, if I have whetted your appetite for wine bottles, you will now wish to know where to find them. All the usual places are worth a try, especially the London markets, auction rooms and antique shops, but if you need to "score" in a limited amount of time you will need recourse to the main glass and specialist bottle dealers. If you are prepared to bid in the auction rooms you may well buy a little more beneficially. Plain onion bottles have quite recently sold in the larger London rooms for £30-£40. This is often the case when they are over-shadowed by much "rarer" bottles being present in the same sale. 17th century seals, for instance, at £1,000 plus, make the plain onion bottle seem a very humble antique indeed.

However, with prices rising virtually all the time, perhaps the day will come when we will all be giving Christmas presents in the four figure category!

Anyhow, until that evil day, I for one would be very happy to receive a nice glossy "black" onion wine bottle for Christmas. How about you?

Figure 1.

CAN ANYONE HELP?

*A*nthony D. Ealer's article in the January magazine (page 43) has brought forth some extremely interesting correspondence and, as the Editor remarks on page 1, an "Alice in Wonderlandish" tale. The story is not yet complete, and several people who are interested in different aspects and from different points of view are researching further. We shall of course publish all the information which may come to light but, in the meantime, here is the story so far.

It started with two letters from Club members.

Dear Sir,

I read Anthony D. Ealer's "Can Anyone Help" plea in this January's magazine. According to *A Hand-Book of Mottoes* by C.N. Elvin, published London 1860, the motto "Praise God for All" is listed as that belonging to the Bakers' Company of London and Exeter.

Hope this helps!

Yours faithfully,
M.M.A., Berks.

It certainly did help and had just been sent off, with a copy of the January magazine, to the Worshipful Company of Bakers at Bakers Hall, Harp Lane, London E.C.3, when the next letter arrived.

Dear Sir,

With reference to the article on page 43 of this month's *Antique Collecting,* I am of the opinion that figure 2 is the arms of the "White-Bakers Company", London, and figure 4 is the arms of the "Brown-Bakers Company", London. Certainly the charges are very similar (if not identical) to those of the "White-Bakers" and "Brown-Bakers" Companies c.1681.

Is it possible that both Companies, in the year 1722, combined to form one Company — at which time the panel illustrated in figure 1 and the panel illustrated in figure 2 were taken from different chests to form part of one chest? If such is the case, it may be that the centre panel, illustrated in figure 3, confirms the event.

With regard to the four names, it may also be that in the *early* part of 1722

Charles Jellec was Master of the "White-Bakers"
and William Briscoe was Master of the "Brown-Bakers"
whilst in the *latter* part of 1722 (i.e. the time of amalgamation?)

Robert Bower was Master of the "White-Bakers"
and William Ball was Master of the "Brown-Bakers".

I'm afraid I have no knowledge of the "Bakers" Company in the 18th century. However, I'm quite sure a perusal of the relevant records will prove or disprove my theory. If I am correct I would, if possible, like to be advised.

Yours faithfully,
T.W., Lincs.

This second letter really made us feel we were on to something and swiftly joined the first at Bakers Hall, where considerable interest was being aroused, resulting in this letter.

The Worshipful Company of Bakers

BAKERS HALL, HARP LANE, LOWER THAMES STREET, LONDON, EC3R 6DP

Dear Sir,

The fascinating photograph in your January journal leaves no doubt in my mind that this oak chest originally formed an item of the furnishings in the third Hall of the Worshipful Company of Bakers in Harp Lane in the City of London.

The intriguing question at the moment is how to prove it.

The first Hall on this site by the River Thames was an adapted manor bought by the Bakers' Company in 1506 and destroyed in the Great Fire of 1666. The Hall built in its place by 1675 was likewise burnt down in 1715 and the rebuilding of the third Hall was commenced in 1719 and completed in 1722 — the date on the chest.

The construction of this Hall was unusual in that the several trades engaged were personally supervised by the Master, Wardens and Members of the Company during that time. There must have been many joiners employed, for the Hall was heavily timbered and, although some pinewood was used, it was mainly in oak. Particular features were much oak panelling, a minstrel gallery and richly carved oak screen in the Dining Hall and then a broad and lofty staircase, the stairs of which comprised solid baulks of oak. All this seems to indicate the craftsmen were well experienced with oak and that most of the furniture would naturally have been in the same timber.

There are few of us now who can remember much detail about the pre-war Hall and, of course, an oak chest would have been a rather small item. Perusal of immediate records to hand throws no light on the names carved on the chest. They could be those of members of the Company who played a particular part in the rebuilding or possibly of the principal joiners. Further research will be made among the Company's old records.

At the outbreak of war in 1939, some of the more easily removable possessions in the Hall were taken to different safe retreats by members of the Company who lived out of London. Fortunately so, because the Hall was destroyed in the "Blitz" of December 1940 and when the present fourth Hall was completed in 1963, most of the Company's treasures were returned to it.

However, the most substantial clue to date is undoubtedly the two armorial bearings so well carved on the chest. These provide a positive identity with the Bakers of London rather than any other city, such as Exeter, where Guilds have flourished through the centuries but had no connection whatsoever with those peculiar to London — the "Livery Companies".

The arms on the left in the photograph are those of the "White-Bakers Company" and on the right are those of the "Brown-Bakers Company". The fact that both of these are on the chest clearly indicates its origin in the City of London where the two Companies existed during the Middle Ages for perhaps three hundred years.

Although there was a Guild of Bakers in London in the 12th century, no baker was allowed to make both white and brown bread. The bakers of brown bread, who were in the majority until the 14th century, had eternal disputes with those of white and, probably in 1312 and definitely by 1440, broke away and formed their own Guild. But, due to pressure by the City Fathers, the two Guilds were again amalgamated in 1486 for the control of the whole trade in London. It received a Charter of Incorporation at this time and in 1536 the Company obtained an official Grant of Arms from the College of Arms and, later, the motto "Praise God for All" was added. These armorial bearings were therefore for the combined Bakers' Guilds in London but became loosely identified more with the "White-Bakers" for the following reason.

In 1544, after further continual disagreement, the Brown-Bakers separated once more, purchased their own Hall and in 1572 their own coat of arms. Nevertheless, their numbers were steadily diminishing and despite having received their own Charter of Incorporation in 1621, they were finally forced to reunite with the White-Bakers into one Company in 1645.

There has been ever since, until recently, a tendency for the two armorial bearings to be used indiscriminately, and undoubtedly this confusion was much stronger in the earlier years following the reunion, so it is quite natural that both coats of arms were carved on this oak chest — the one of 1536 on the left being those of the Worshipful Company today.

I will let you know in due course the result of my further researches but in the meantime it would be most valuable if previous owners of the chest could be traced.

Yours faithfully,
Kenneth Mostyn
(Past-Master of the Company)

We have been quite fascinated by this chest and, on discovering that most of the Company's records had been donated to the Guildhall, one of our staff visited the Manuscript Department at the Guildhall Library. We hoped we might be able to identify the four names carved on the chest, and even find some reference to the chest itself — who ordered it and when, and possibly even the name of the joiner. Unfortunately, however, so far we have not been able to unearth any mention of any of the names, or of the chest itself, but both we and Mr. Mostyn plan to persevere.

As far as the chest's recent history is concerned, it was bought at a London auction in October last year, and we are hoping that the vendor will give the auctioneer permission to put us in touch with him or her, and that we may be able to trace it back to Bakers Hall at the outbreak of the Second World War.

* * * * *

In the meantime, Victor Chinnery, author of Oak Furniture — The British Tradition, *and contributor of many articles on oak to this magazine, had joined in the hunt, independently.*
Dear Sir,

I was most intrigued to see the photographs of the carved oak chest in your article by A.D. Ealer in your issue of January 1981 (page 43). Perhaps my observations will be of interest:

Without being able to see the chest itself for a close physical examination, I would certainly like to say that it looks perfectly genuine on the evidence of the very large photographs which you sent me, and in addition it would seem to have a very interesting provenance hidden somewhere.

Figure 2.

Figure 3.

Figure 4.

The texture and condition of the polished surfaces are very convincing, and a careful study of the patination and the inner surfaces would quickly confirm or deny its authenticity. The construction and structural decoration are perfectly compatible for a piece of this date (except that the lid *should* have a moulded edge, and may therefore be a replacement). The deeply-fielded panels with thumb-moulded edges to the framing-members are entirely typical of the period, and may be compared with several illustrations on pages 517-29 of my book, notably a press cupboard of the same date in figure 4:272. The fashion for fielded panels of this type ran through the second half of the 17th century and the whole of the 18th. The brass keyplate is identical to my drawing on page 147 (bottom row, no. 3).

The handling of the carving is likewise very typical, and should be compared with the decorative carving on cane chairs of this date and a little earlier. This is especially true of the nice curly scroll-work in the mantling of the armorials, and in the treatment of the flowers in the oval wreath. The floral wreath is squashed rather uncomfortably into the central panel, but this should be seen as an unsuccessful attempt to fit the design into an unsuitable space, rather than casting doubt on the authenticity of the carving. This deficiency would rather support a suggestion that the chest was made as a standard product a little *before* 1722, and that the carving was added as a special commission at that date.

Figure 2 is the coat of arms of the Worshipful Company of Bakers of London, though without the tinctures. A small mistake seems to have crept in with the omission of a pair of anchors from the upper register of the shield. The helm, crest, mantling, supporters and motto are all correct. Bakers' Hall in Harp Lane, near the Tower of London, was burnt down in 1715; to be rebuilt and re-opened (guess when!) in 1722.

Figure 4 is evidently a very closely related coat, with only slight changes and omissions. It may be nothing more than a casual variation of the legitimate version, or the two coats may represent the traditional division between the White and the Brown Bakers. Provincial companies sometimes adopted or adapted the arms borne by the London companies, but I doubt if this is the case here.

It seems a fair assumption that the chest was presented to the London Bakers' Company by Messrs. Jellek, Briscock, Bowyer and Ball to mark the opening of the new hall in 1722. They should be identifiable as freemen of the company, and probably as holders of some office such as warden or bailiff. Unlike Mr. Ealer, the significance of the letters A and S escapes me. They surely cannot belong with the date. Could they be the initials of the Latin terms for white and brown respectively, *albus* and *spadix*?

We should wonder how the Bakers' Company came to lose possession of the chest, for it to turn up anonymously in some saleroom. Such things were often taken as perquisites by retiring officials in the past, or it may have been removed to some place of safety on the outbreak of war in 1939. If the chest *was* in their possession until 1939, then it may appear in the photographic files of the Royal Commission for Historical Monuments at the National Monuments Record.

Altogether, this is a fascinating piece of furniture. It is very rarely that a new piece emerges with some clear provenance from this date, and further research may identify the donors (if such they be), and hopefully the joiner who made it.

Yours faithfully,
Victor Chinnery

So, Mr. Chinnery is as fascinated as the bakers and we are about this chest, and we are all hoping that our further researches will reveal the whole story. In the meantime, if anyone has any ideas or suggestions about the significance of the mysterious letters A and S — and it will be interesting to have Mr. Mostyn's reaction to Mr. Chinnery's suggestion — or any other information, we should be delighted to hear.

AUCTION FEATURE
Sotheby Beresford Adams, Chester
12th and 27th March

Pair of Royal Worcester vases painted and signed by H. Stinton, purple printed mark including date code for 1931, 5¾ins. £720. Royal Worcester pot-pourri vase and cover, painted and signed by K. Blake, pierced gilt cover, purple printed mark including date code for 1925, 6½ins. £120.

Left: George III mahogany stick barometer, silvered register with vernier scale and subsidiary thermometer inscribed Crichton, 112 Leaden Hall St, London, late 18th/early 19th century, 39ins. £320.

Unusual marble and gilt-bronze mantel clock, lever platform escapement, striking on a bell, revolving white marble sculpture of a pair of cupids, signed A. Moreau, rouge marble and gilt-bronze base, mid-19th century, 31ins. £1,300.

Chinese Chippendale giltwood wall mirror, later rectangular bevelled plate, third quarter 18th century, 53ins. × 26ins. £780.

CONVERSATIONS OF A VETTING COMMITTEE — 10
by Peter Philp

The annals of the Anteeksandart people are rich in anecdotes concerning a strange practice which translates as "the later carving of chests". At one time this was interpreted as meaning the slicing of meat from the chest of an animal, e.g. breast of lamb, but recent research has shown that the reference is to the decoration of wooden chests by chipping them with a chisel. In mitigation of the error, it should be noted in passing that confusion was worse confounded by the unfortunate translation of a popular synonym for chest as "cougher", whereas it should have been "coffer". This led the earlier interpreters of the text to assume that the animal (or even, according to one sinister deduction, human) chest in question was bronchial and subject to coughing fits. The rest is history . . .

"**O**ak," said the Priestess, "is really not my scene. I only know that, about a hundred years ago, the Victorians liked to furnish their tiled halls with heavily carved pieces, and that the dealers of the day were happy to oblige in one way and another. I hope that what we see before us never suffered such attentions."

The vetting committee had assembled on a low dais enclosed by walls on three sides — one of the many such constructions, known in the Anteeksandart tongue as *stands* (because the chairs were for selling, not for sitting on) that occupied most of the floor space in the temple. This particular stand was dedicated to the kind of artifact that used once to be described as "curiously wrought". At this moment, however, the most curiously wrought — indeed overwrought — thing in sight was the standholder, who was promptly dismissed from the scene by an awesome glance from the High Priest.

"At first sight," said the Second Priest, "all these things appear to be basically 17th century. Nothing looks as though it were assembled from various bits and pieces in 1880. But what I find difficult to judge, very often, is whether the carving was done originally, or added much later. Now take, for example, this coffer — sorry, chest —"

"No need to apologise," the High Priest assured him. "It's true that the coffer was first made by the cofferer, or coverer, who covered it with leather, and pedants try to insist that the term should be confined to travelling trunks and boxes of that kind. But wooden chests with no leather on them have been described as coffers since the 15th century. The proof of that is to be found in a petition addressed by the guild of coffer makers to Richard III in 1483, when they were having a recession and wanted to stop the importing of Flemish furniture. They succeeded, too."

"Does BL know about this?" asked

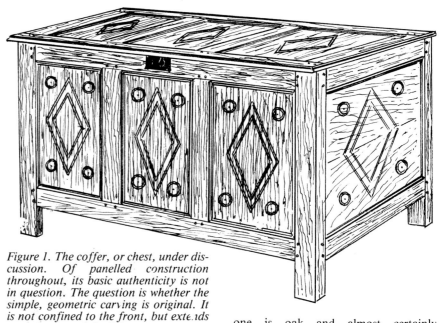

Figure 1. The coffer, or chest, under discussion. Of panelled construction throughout, its basic authenticity is not in question. The question is whether the simple, geometric carving is original. It is not confined to the front, but extends to the ends and the lid.

the Priestess, thoughtfully. The High Priest, intent on his theme, chose to ignore her.

"Then again," he continued, "direct equivalents of the word 'coffer' are found in the French *coffre* and the German *Koffer,* both of which are used to describe wooden chests of various kinds. So if you want to call this chest a coffer, I don't see why you shouldn't."

"Most instructive," said the Second Priest, "but you will forgive me if I say that it's not a lot of help in deciding whether the carving is original."

"I was coming to that, sonny," said the High Priest. "For a start, the panels of the lid are carved. In the 17th century, it was usual for them to be plain, so that things could be stood on them, or for people to sit on them. But there are always the exceptions that prove the rule, and I have seen one or two examples with carving on the lids which appeared to be, if not strictly original, at least to have been executed, perhaps by an amateur enthusiast, very shortly after manufacture."

"Weren't some of the early Continental chests carved on the lids as a matter of course?" asked the Priestess.

"Small ones, yes. They were known as 'Cyprus' boxes, but the name is misleading. It is really a mis-spelling for cypress, most of them being made of that wood, or of cedar. The larger ones, most of which came from Italy or Bermuda, have plain, boarded lids. This

one is oak and almost certainly English."

"Then what is wrong with the carving itself? If the lid were plain, would you still be suspicious?" persisted the Second Priest.

"More than suspicious," said the High Priest. "These conventional motifs are quite correct for the period, but rather poor examples of the simple technique known as 'scratch' carving, executed with a narrow, V-shaped gouge. On a chest of this fairly high quality, with panelled construction throughout, I would expect the carving to be rather better — joiner's work, perhaps, nothing very fancy, but done with an assured hand using a U-shaped edge for at least part of the pattern. These lines are narrow, mean and shaky — the work of someone who was certainly not a skilled carver, and was struggling with the additional difficulty of carving the panels after they had been built into the chest. It is too often forgotten that as much of the carving as possible on any piece of furniture was executed before the piece was assembled, and only the finishing, if any, was done afterwards. And there is one more very significant detail. See if you can spot it."

The Priestess and the Second Priest peered at the carving. "Too clean", declared the Priestess promptly. "Surely old carving should have a greater accumulation of old wax and dirt — unless the whole thing has been cleaned off, which this obviously has not. A good patina elsewhere with plenty of build-up of wax in the crevices."

Figure 2. Detail: a panel of the chest. Note the lack of precision in the "scratch" carving.

Figure 3. Detail: a panel of a chest carved simply but with assurance, using a fairly wide, slightly curved gouge. The lightly incised construction lines, made with a marking knife, are still faintly visible — a characteristic often seen in early decoration employing a geometric pattern.

"This carving has been coloured down with stain and acquired only a little patina," agreed the Second Priest. "When do you think it was done?"

"It's pure guesswork," said the High Priest, "but I would estimate about 1900, when there was a great fashion for woodcarving as a polite accomplishment among ladies and gentlemen. If you know your H.G. Wells, you will recall that young Kipps is introduced to a woodcarving class by the aristocratic young woman he is in love with. Well, that's that. I'm afraid the coffer will have to be rejected."

"Before we press on," said the Priestess, "is it true, do you think, that English chests were never carved at the ends, even when they were carved on the fronts? I've seen several where the ends looked as though they had been worked on by other and less skilful hands. And yet the carving looked old."

"And so it probably was," the High Priest assured her. "In some areas, where money was a little more plentiful than in others, it was quite customary, in the 17th century, for the ends to be carved. It is said — although the evidence doesn't entirely convince me — that Gloucestershire chests often had carved ends, but those over the border in Somerset usually had not. As to the difference in quality, it is only too well established that economies were effected by giving the decoration of end panels and other inconspicuous areas to the apprentice."

The High Priest paused to light a reflective pipe. "To jump a century or so, even Thomas Chippendale himself was not above using second-grade ormolu mounts on the rear corners of his highly expensive commodes, while dressing the window with top quality ones at the front. Anyone got a match?"

"Do you want to set fire to this lot, then?" asked the Priestess.

"Not a bad idea, at that," said the High Priest.

Saleroom Report

Victorian electro-plated ear trumpet, engraved, F.L. Prinz and Son, 6¼ins. £170. Christie's South Kensington.

Right: Edwardian satinwood and mahogany oval two tier etagère in the Sheraton style. £500. Phillips of Leeds.

.22 L.R. Parkerifled conversion of a rare Frank Wesson bicycle or buggy rifle, serial nos. 190 and A367, complete with detachable walnut shoulder stock, octagonal blued barrel rotates to right for loading, hooded bead foresight, screw elevating notch, peephole rearsight, Wesson address and patent date, nickel plated frame, rosewood grips, crisp and Grade 1 plus with most original finish, barrel 18ins. £210. Weller & Dufty.

Left: One of an unusual pair of Doulton stoneware bottle vases by Arthur Barlow, 11¾ins. £520. Christie's South Kensington.

Right: George III mahogany longcase musical clock by Edward Shepley, Manchester, 106ins. £4,800. Christie's South Kensington.

GOLFING ANTIQUES

by Ian T. Henderson and David I. Stirk

Figure 1. Long-nosed shallow-faced driver by Hugh Philp (1782-1856).

Figure 2. Wooden putter by Willie Park, Sen. (1834-1903).

Authors and publishers of *Golf in the Making*

Just as cricket has caught the imagination of collectors and regular auction sales are held of "cricketana", so golf and "golfiana" is now rapidly joining the collector's field.

Ten years ago the Golf Collectors' Society was formed in the U.S.A. It now has members all over the world — some forty in Britain — and a membership of over seven hundred. They are interested in every form of golfing antiquity. Sotheby's, Christie's and Phillips have now all had sporting sales where golfing items have appeared and dealers may find golfing antiquities appearing as people realise their potential values. Hickory-shafted golf clubs ceased to be made fifty years ago, being replaced by steel-shafted clubs.

GOLF CLUBS
Wooden Clubs — Long-headed

Until the late 1880s all wooden clubs were long-headed, the heads measuring 5ins.-5½ins. The shafts were hickory, fastened to the head by what is known as a scared-joint, and the leather grips of these scared-head clubs were much thicker than those of the modern club. Most of these clubs bear the name of the maker incised on their head, the best known names being McEwan, Philp (figure 1), Forgan, Dunn, Park (figure 2) and Morris. Of these Hugh Philp, who really founded the Forgan business, is the name to conjure with, followed by the McEwans who started making clubs in 1770. Philp clubs (particularly putters) have always commanded a

premium and a genuine Philp in good condition will change hands at around the £600 mark or more. Here are prices that have been realised in a recent auction:

Long-headed driver by William Park £400
Long-headed spoon by William Dunn £400
Long-headed driver by McEwan . . £320
Long-headed driver by Forgan £300

It is impossible to date these clubs with any accuracy simply from the maker's name stamp on them, and therefore a premium is paid for any documentary evidence of ownership and date of use.

Wooden Clubs — Short-headed

In about 1888 the shape of clubheads underwent a dramatic change. With the exception of wooden putters (which were being replaced by the iron putter), the heads became shorter and the faces were deeper and convex instead of concave. Drivers of this type came to be known as "bulger drivers" (figure 3) and short-headed brassies, spoons and wooden niblicks appeared, still with scared-head joints and hickory shafts. These were produced only for a period of just over ten years as the present-day socket-joint appeared at the turn of the century, and so are a class of club which is likely to be in limited supply. Depending on condition, clubs will fetch anything between £45 to £100 (for a well-known maker).

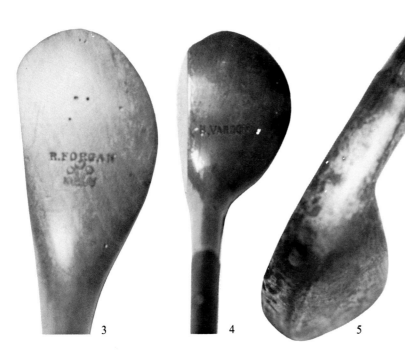

Figure 3. Bulger driver by Forgan.

Figure 4. Brassie by Harry Vardon (1870-1937).

Figure 5. Rut-iron — with face only 2ins. long.

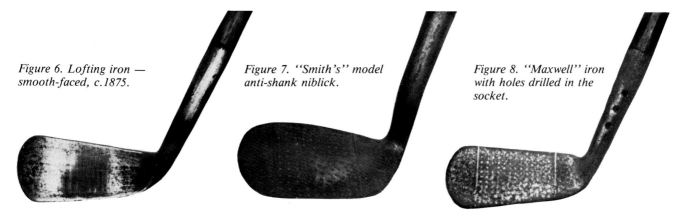

Figure 6. Lofting iron — smooth-faced, c.1875.

Figure 7. "Smith's" model anti-shank niblick.

Figure 8. "Maxwell" iron with holes drilled in the socket.

Wooden Clubs — Socket-headed

Socket-headed, hickory-shafted wooden clubs continued to be made up to around 1930 when the first steel-shafted clubs appeared. The small heads of the early part of the century gave way to clubs with larger heads. These are difficult to price, although the well-known names such as Vardon (figure 4), Braid, etc. will always attract buyers. The first steel shafts in clubs with their wooden imitation colour may well become collectors' pieces in due course.

Iron Clubs

Until the 1840s "sets" of golf clubs were mostly wood. The irons were the track irons, sand iron, rut iron (figure 5) and later niblick and one of these would be included in each set of clubs. There then appeared the cleek and the lofting iron (figure 6). These clubs were made by local blacksmiths, shafted by the clubmaker, and carried no name or mark of origin. Now and then some very old clubs indeed appear — going back to the turn of the 19th century. Two such clubs recently fetched over £1,500 each. Other smooth-faced clubs are in growing demand and are capable of fetching anything up to £150. They are likely to remain in limited supply.

At the end of the 19th century the manufacturers appeared (figures 7 and 8). The club faces were marked and on the back were stamped the names of the professionals for whom the clubheads were made, but the manufacturers used their own form of identification mark to indicate that the clubhead was made by them: for instance Stewart of St. Andrews had a pipe (figure 9) and Gibson of Kinghorn a star (figure 10), and there were over twenty-five such makers' marks. The first matched sets of clubs began to appear and a host of different designs and patterns representing a most interesting field for the collector. Prices for this type of club can still be modest at £10 to £15 a club. Later mass-produced irons, although hickory-shafted, have little value.

THE GOLF BALL

The ball in use until the middle of the 19th century was what was known as a feathery (figure 11, above). This was a leather ball, not unlike a fives ball to look at, stuffed with wet feathers which, when dried out, became very hard. They disappeared from use soon after the gutta percha rubber ball (figure 11, below) appeared in 1848. They are now collectors' pieces and have changed hands at auction for up to £850, and will probably continue to rise in price. Examples of pure gutta percha balls with random markings are rare and are likely to fetch well in excess of £100 each. The gutta was followed by the "gutty", a composite ball, and the manufacturers appeared, each producing their different design-markings and qualities. These gutties in good condition are relatively scarce and can fetch £20-£30 each.

The arrival of the U.S.A. Haskell core-wound ball in 1902 (figure 12) was to produce a host of different manufacturers, markings and claims of excellence. The First World War, however, reduced the number of manufacturers substantially, and this early field is eminently collectable apart from the fact that examples seem scarce. Given good condition, prices appear to be around the £10 to £20 mark and a case of ten Silvertown golf balls in a presentation box, entitled "The Cavalcade of Golf", c.1935, recently fetched £300.

Figure 9. Cleekmark — a pipe for Stewart of St. Andrews.

Figure 10. Cleekmark — a star for Gibson of Kinghorn.

Figure 11. Examples of feathery and gutta balls.

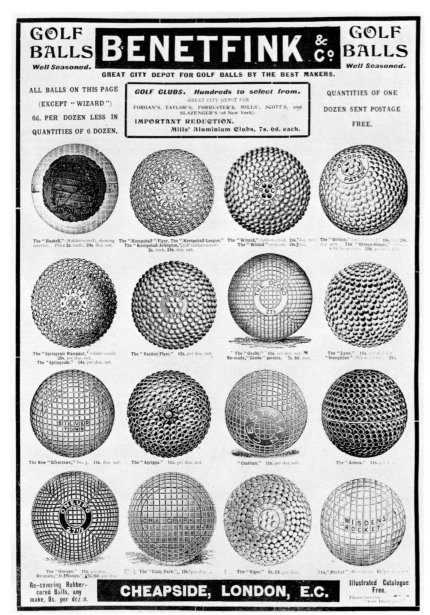

Figure 12. Benetfink advertisement for Haskell rubber-cored balls and guttas.

Patents, etc.

The great golf craze started in the 1880s. Between then and 1914 some seven hundred British and two hundred American patents relating to golf were taken out, covering every subject related to golf from golf bags to tee moulds, every form of aid for learning golf and any number of golf parlour games. Anything in this line will have undoubted interest and value.

Books

Within the last few years interest in golf book collecting has developed enormously and it is increasingly difficult to obtain golf books which appeared before 1900. For anybody collecting or intending to start, it is essential to be armed with *A Library of Golf 1743-1966* (with the current supplement) by J.S.F. Murdoch. One of the most significant is the *Badminton Library-Golf* edited by H.G. Hutchinson, first published in 1890 with subsequent editions, now costing up to

Figure 14. Doulton tankard c.1900.

Figure 13. Selection of golf buttons.

Figure 15. Mid-19th century "daisy plate".

Figure 16. Cartoon from "Rules of Golf" by Charles Crombie for a Perrier table water advertisement.

Figure 17. Cartoon by John Hassell.

£10 to £15. Rare books such as *The Golf Book of East Lothian* by Rev. John Kerr last changed hands at over £300, as did a copy of *Chronicles of Blackheath Golfers*. Copies of all early golf magazines and golf annuals are keenly sought after.

Silver

Golf prizes often took the form of silver cups, replicas, spoons and medals (some gold) and are probably one of the most likely items to come within the antique dealer's scope. There are also such items as tiepins, brooches, statuettes and buttons (figure 13) for golf jackets.

Ceramics

Golfing subjects on ceramics appeared at the turn of the century and were used as decoration for such items as mugs, bowls, tankards and tea-sets. Some were offered as golf club prizes and Doulton, Copeland, Spode, Grimwade and Minton all produced such wares which are keenly sought after (figures 14 and 15). These were followed by souvenir items by W.H. Goss, marked with the Goss falcon mark, and by his imitators, marked Arcadian and Carlton. The German souvenir manufacturers also imported items like illustrated ribbon plates and tobacco jars prior to the First World War.

Golfing Prints and Pictures

There is a considerable demand for these and there are a host of modern reproductions, but old prints, paintings and drawings are becoming difficult to find. At a recent sale a print of Henry Callender of Blackheath fetched £140, four pen and wash drawings by Charles Crombie (figure 16) £150 and a cartoon by John Hassell (figure 17) £120, while a set of four Louis Wain cat cartoons (figure 18) fetched £600.

A word of warning about fakes of old clubs and even balls. Clubs by Hugh Philp were faked, almost in his lifetime, and many reproduction copies of old clubs are now appearing which will deceive anyone who has not some knowledge of what old clubs really look like and who has not handled the genuine article. A feathery ball looks just like a fives ball and one has been known to be sold as a feathery. If you are offered golf antiques, it really is important to know where they come from. If from an attic of an old house, you can be pretty sure that they are genuine.

There are a number of golf museums in North America; the Japanese Golf Association has just opened its museum in Tokyo; and Scotland has its first private museum, "The Heritage of Golf" at Gullane, East Lothian. Finally there is an exhibition at the Russell-Cotes Museum, Bournemouth, called "Golf in the Making" which covers the development of the game. This is open until September.

It is clear that the market is international and will remain so, because this country remains the only source of supply and demand will exceed supply for anything one hundred years old or over.

Figure 18. "Holed Out". Cartoon by Louis Wain.

SOME FACETS OF FAN COLLECTING
Part I — The Finer Examples

by
Hélène Alexander

Figure 1. Queen Elizabeth I by Gheerardt. Hever Castle, Edenbridge. The Queen is holding a rigid gem-studded feather fan.

Fans, as objects for cooling the air, have existed in one form or another, in hot climates, from time immemorial.

There is evidence of fans being collected for their beauty and the delight of their owners in 15th century China, when the rigid screen fan was regarded as a work of art, either as a painting, or a poem, which might be signed by some of the greatest artists of their day.[1]

In England it could be said that Queen Elizabeth I was the first collector of fans[2, 3]. Most of hers were of the rigid type, made from feathers and having gem studded handles, which appear in many portraits of the Queen (figure 1). She did also possess folding fans, but few of either type have survived to the present day.

It is of interest to note that James I, on his accession to the English throne,

sent many items from the old Queen's wardrobe to his wife, Anne of Denmark, who was still in Scotland at the time. A close comparative study of the portraits of Anne of Denmark in which she carries a fan, and those of her predecessor similarly equipped, reveals the re-use, by the later Queen, of some of the gems and even handles with feathers of varying size, shape and colour.

It is possible that this procedure was adopted by most of the nobility who owned jewelled fans, and that it would partly account for the rarity of such objects. There is one fan of this type in a famous private collection[4], and another, somewhat later, in the Costume Collection at Bath.

Of the early European *folding* fans, such as may be seen in Elizabethan portraits, a delightful embroidered example, in unusually good condition, was acquired by a private collector at an auction sale at Phillips, about two years ago.

Recent research has shown that many brisé fans of the late 17th century were made in the East[5] not, as was hitherto supposed, in Holland, and these fans were exported to the West, via Holland and the other trading nations.

These brisé fans form a fascinating set, or "family". To anyone familiar with the history of dress, they are fairly easy to distinguish; they are often painted as showing a "genre" scene in which the rather clumsy figures appear almost like caricatures; of greater relevance is the fact that their clothes, and the way they "sit" upon the wearer, are totally misunderstood, thus proving that they were painted by someone unaccustomed to Western dress (figure 2).

It takes some courage to remove the ribbon from one of these fans, but in most cases the ribbons are a later

addition to the fan. More often, the removal of the ribbon reveals a set of two small holes at either side of the blades (figure 2), which would originally have been threaded through with a silken thread (figure 3), fairly slack at the top, so that, when the fan is closed, a tiny delicate ruffle appears along the edge.

Within this category one can also place a number of other brisé, ivory fans; in one particular "set" the blades are pierced and painted, usually with a larger motif at the top and smaller designs on the gorge (often birds and fish) in colours that emulate the very popular lacquers, golds, rich orangy-reds, sepias and black. Often these fans are reinforced around the pivot with tortoiseshell, and they are small, measuring about 18cm in length.

Following on from these fans, and no doubt "descended" from their popularity, is the much sought after so-called Vernis Martin type (figure 4). Equally small, measuring approximately 15cm, they are also brisé ivory fans, and they too can be grouped into quite closely defined categories. It is usually agreed to date them within the first half of the 18th century.

The finest of these fans are exquisitely precise. Classical subjects decorate the span of the open blades, executed in the very highest order of miniature painting, with clear eggshell finish, while the additional motifs of decoration, either in the "Persian" or "chinoiserie" manner, are frequently repeated on the ribbon which unites the blades. It seems fairly certain that a group of these fans

Captions to colour plates:

Figure 5. *Early 18th century brisé fan showing a theatrical scene (possibly Racine's "Andromaque").*

Figure 6. *Another so-called Vernis Martin fan. This fan has sadly received a coat of Victorian yellow varnish.*

Figure 8. *French fan c.1765. The leaf is painted with a vivid scene showing Bacchus and Ariadne; the mother-of-pearl sticks and guards are delicately pierced, silvered and gilded.*

Figure 9. *French fan c.1760. The quality of the painting is complemented by the richness of the mother-of-pearl sticks enhanced with gold leaf.*

Figure 9A. *Detail of the sticks.*

Figure 9B. *Detail of the leaf.*

Figure 12. *Lace and blond tortoiseshell, and diamond initials. This lovely marriage fan is dated 1894.*

Figure 12A. *Detail showing the initials JM.*

Figure 13. *A painted fan, the mother-of-pearl guards applied with pierced gold panels enamelled in subtle pinks, yellow and green, with lilies, daisies and carnations in the art nouveau style. Made in Berlin by the Roumanian Court Goldsmith Paul Telge in 1899 for Princess Elizabeth of Wied, Queen of Roumania, who wrote romantic poetry under the pseudonym of "Carmen Sylva".*

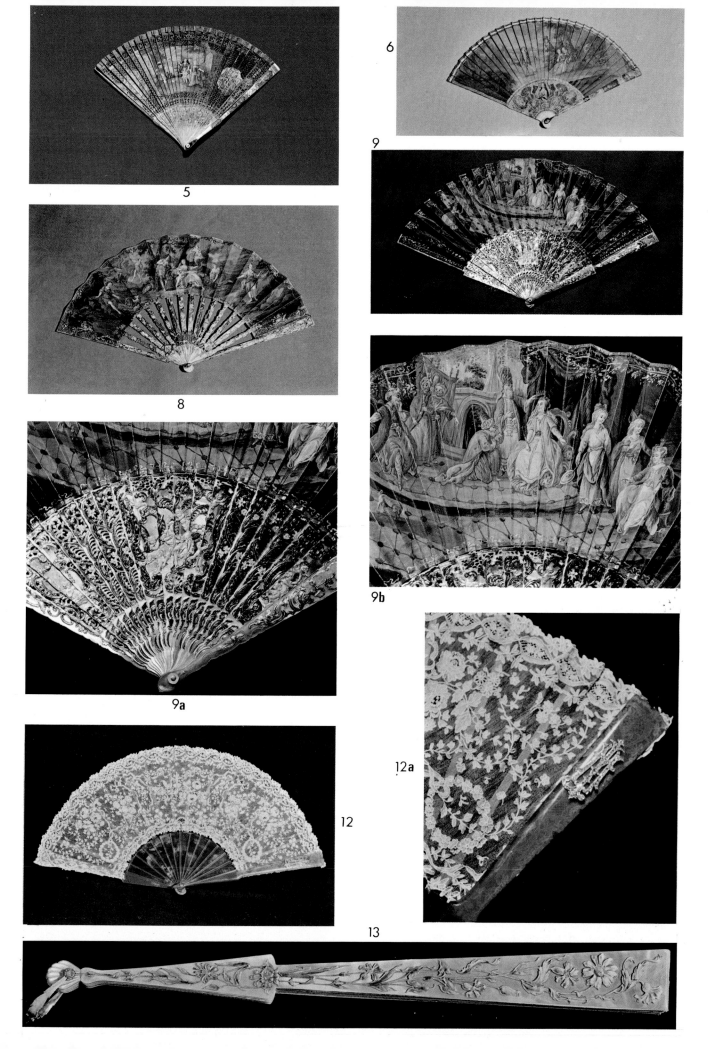

5

6

9

8

9a

9b

12a

12

13

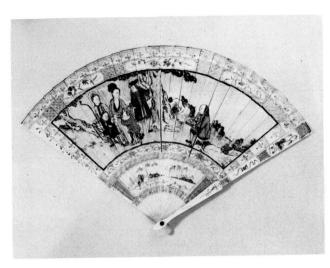

Figure 2. Early 18th century "export" fan. The painted figures show a curious mixture of styles and clothing. Here the ribbon has been removed leaving a double set of holes.

Figure 2A. A "famille rose" bowl of the same period showing the same type figures.

centuries, only a very few come on to the open market; this is hardly surprising, as they are the kind of object likely to be handed down in a family, from generation to generation.

Fine paintings have always been appreciated by the connoisseur, and fan leaves of quality will be collected by the amateur collector of pictures and the fan collector alike. It seems that, when they are mounted, these paintings of merit are always accompanied by equally well worked sticks and guards (figure 10).

Thanks to the encouragement of the Finance Ministers at the Court of Louis XIV, the Sun King, luxury goods became synonymous with "made in France", and fans are certainly no exception. The late 17th and 18th centuries in France were indeed to produce the very finest, richest and most elaborate fans. Although sticks and fan leaves often came from different workshops, with top quality fans the utmost care was given to the matching of sticks to leaf.

Figure 3. Early 18th century "export" fan showing the looped silk thread which unites the blades.

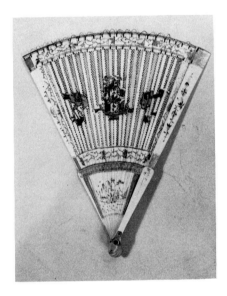

was manufactured in Spa in Belgium[6]. They all bear a family resemblance, however remote. Those more closely affiliated to the earlier Eastern ones form a set in which the outer blades are pierced and painted. A cartouche depicting some theatrical performance (figure 5) — a great favourite was the sacrifice of Iphigenia immortalised by Racine's verses — occupies the central part of the span, while the gorge is decorated with chinoiserie motifs. In almost every one of these fans the guard sticks bear a quite distinctive male or female figure (figure 7) on a roughed background (usually blue).

In the 19th century, with the renewal of interest in fans old and new, many of these so-called Vernis Martin fans were copies and found their way into the markets of Europe, while some of the original ones were also "touched up", re-varnished (figure 6), painted in, "restored", "re-ribboned". They can still be purchased, and undiscriminating buyers have been known to pay relatively high prices for them.

The market for early fans is somewhat capricious because of the lack of knowledge and clear understanding of these objects. Furthermore, many of them are offered for sale in glazed fan cases which are sealed down so that only one side of the fan is visible, and proper examination thus precluded.

Mica fans are another of the prized

rarities for any collector. Since the formation of the Fan Circle[7] some four years ago, and because of the exchange of ideas which such a society engenders, quite a few more of these fans are now known to be in private collections than was at first supposed. Broadly speaking, there is one particular group, c.1690-1700, which presents similarities so striking as to suggest they might emanate from the same workshop. Mica fans, and fans with mica insets are still rare, and prices increasingly high.

Of the precious jewelled fans, the gem studded Court fans of the 18th and 19th

Figure 3A. The same fan fully opened. Note too the angle of the fully expanded fan, and the imitation of the "Chinese Imari" style porcelain.

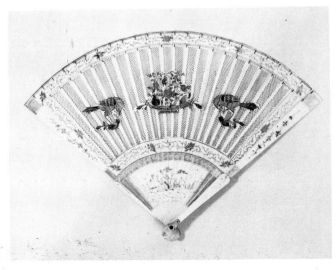

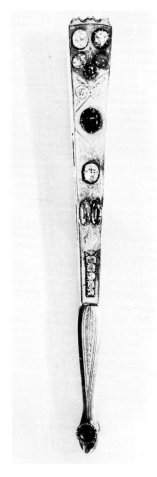

Figure 4. So-called Vernis Martin brisé ivory fan, first half of the 18th century, probably Dutch. The subject is the sacrifice of Iphigenia. Note the "Chinoiserie" subject on the gorge, and the scolloped edging round the central scene.

The political upheavals suscitated by the French Revolution did not stop the round of social activities in which beautiful women with their fans had a place; but it was a new social order with a different moneyed class, and from the beginning of the 19th century fans no longer "say the same thing". This is not to say that they are, in their own way, any less fine. Indeed, Directoire fans (notwithstanding the "austerity" of that difficult period), and then Empire fans, can be most richly decorated (figure 11). In Victorian times, from the 1840s, though the quality of the painting is, on the whole, rather mediocre, the materials used in the making of fans were of the most lavish, and certainly much more varied than ever before. Gorgeous lace and diamond studded blond tortoiseshell fans became the order of the day for wealthy brides from the 1870s onwards (figure 12). Gadgetry too was favoured, discreet, but with less of the naïvety of the previous century, and of special interest to collectors.

Fans and fan leaves reflect the quality of life of their time and so they remain, to instruct and delight.

Figure 7. Three early 18th century fans showing the dancing figure on the guard, the tortoiseshell reinforced pivots and similarities of style.

Figure 10. The exquisitely painted leaf of this English fan, c.1765, is perfectly complemented by the finely carved and painted ivory sticks and guards.

Figure 11. Directoire ivory fan. The guards are chased gold studded with gem stones. The pivot is malachite.

Foundation for British Art. 1969. Frontispiece and plates 108, 135, 140 and 143.

4. *A Collector's History of Fans*. Nancy Armstrong. Studio Vista. 1974. Plate 104.

5. *Fans from the East*. Debrett's Peerage and the Victoria and Albert Museum (in association with the Fan Circle). 1979. Page 30.

6. *The Book of Fans*. Nancy Armstrong. Colour Library International. 1978. Page 67.

7. *The Fan Circle* — a society for *anyone* interested in fans. Hon. Sec. Mrs. Morris, 24 Asmuns Hill, London NW116ET.

Acknowledgement

All the colour illustrations in this article are reproduced by courtesy of Colour Library International. The black and white photographs are by K.B. Cameras Ltd.

1. *Fans from the East*. Debrett's Peerage and the Victoria & Albert Museum 1979 (in association with the Fan Circle). Page 27.

2. *Elizabeth R*. Roy Strong and Julia Trevelyan Oman. Book Club Associates 1971. Pages 30 and 31.

3. *The English Icon*. Roy Strong. The Paul Mellon

Figure 10A. Note the fine reverse.

1

2

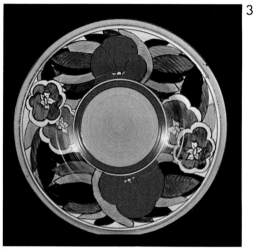

3

4

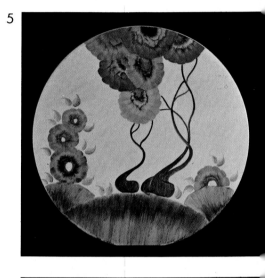

5

6

7

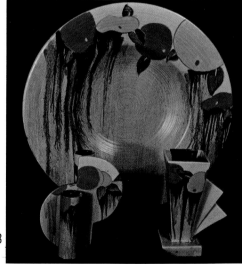

8

9

10

Ten years ago pieces like this vividly enamelled blue and yellow breakfast set (figure 1) designed by Clarice Cliff in the 1930s were never seen in the international salerooms; this July, an eight piece two person set was auctioned at Sotheby's for £190. Whatever has happened? Why have collectors all over the world gone crazy about Clarice Cliff?

Like all designers of the 1920s and '30s she has swept in on the recent wave of deco discovery. Her work is also easy to identify, almost every piece bears some form of her unmistakable signature (figure 1A). But it is the vitality and irresistible gaiety of her style which really counts — the dazzling daubs of blue, yellow, orange, green, crimson, scarlet and purple with the sharp black and brown accents which she lavished on every type of table ware and novelty (figure 11).

For inspiration, she seems to have absorbed every contemporary movement in European art and design from the flamboyant Ballets Russes — for colour — and the stark modernism of the Bauhaus (figure 3) to the cosy cottage of the garden suburb (figure 8): there are traces of Matisse (figures 2, 6 and 9), Cubism (figures 5 and 6), the blue and yellow tea set is pure Sonia Delaunay (figure 1) and withal she managed to mix it in a truly English fashion with her passion for flowers and gardening: "Crocus" (figure 4) was best seller for years — and is still the most popular — and "My Garden" (figure 7) appeared on a vast range of novelties. Most of her pre-war output was hand-painted earthenware with the odd experiment with printed patterns (figure 5) and a few richly glazed stonewares.

Clarice Cliff was born in 1899 at Tunstall, one of the six Staffordshire pottery towns. Her talent was encouraged at school and at thirteen she was apprenticed enameller at a local pottery where she learned the art of free hand painting. Meanwhile she studied fine art at evening classes, studies which she completed much later, in 1927, with a brief visit to London's Royal College of Art to do sculpture.

Figure 1. Classic geometric two person breakfast set decorated with vivid blue and yellow circles on a cream ground. "Bon Jour" shape. 1930s. £190 Sotheby's July 1979.

CLARICE CLIFF ~ DECO DESIGNER

Figure 1a.

by Caroline MacDonald-Haig

Figure 2. Left to right: Stylised fruit and flowers in purple, pink, yellow, green. "Latona" pattern. 21cm. Early '30s. £70 Sotheby's December 1978. Geometric design in orange, green, brown and blue. 20.5cm. Early '30s. £45 Sotheby's December 1978. Traditionally shaped vase with red and blue zig zag band on yellow ground, blue above red below. 18.75cm. Late '20s. £30 Sotheby's December 1978. Geometric design in shades of blue, orange, green, aubergine and yellow. 20.5cm. Early '30s. £55 Sotheby's December 1978.

Captions to colour plates:

Plate 1. "My Garden" jugs and vases. Mid-'30s. £10-£30 a piece.

Plate 2. "Inspiration", one of the few stonewares — the green colour is derived from a copper oxide. Mid-'30s. Bowl £35-£50. Dish £65-£80.

Plate 3. "Bizarre" wall plaque, 45cm diameter, "Fantasque" pattern. Early '30s. £280.

Plate 4. Harvest jug with embossed modelling. 1936/37. £30.

Plate 5. "Rhodanthe" wall plaque, 45cm diameter. Early '30s. £125. (The same pattern in pink/blue is called "Viscaria".)

Plate 6. A collection of early geometrics on both traditional shapes (the tapered-sided vase, plate and large bowl, all c.1929) and on the new modernistic shapes patented in 1931 (teapot, milk jug and sugar bowl). Vase £10. Teaplate £15-£20. Bowl £15-£20. The teaset, as a group, £65.

Plate 7. "Lotus" shape vase with "Crocus" decoration. '30s. £65. (This was Queen Mary's favourite pattern but only on traditional shapes.)

Plate 8. "Delicia", a style developed by running one colour into another. Early '30s. 45cm plaque £250. The vases are an extreme and quite rare example of Clarice's geometric style, £60 each.

Plate 9. "Delicia" breakfast set, Stamford shape, from the same range as plate 8 but this time in a poppy pattern. Early '30s. £250.

Plate 10. Novelty wall mask. Mid-'30s. £50-£70.

All these colour illustrations were taken during the Brighton Exhibition in 1972 and are reproduced by courtesy of Brighton Museum.

Figure 3. Part of a dinner service with black and orange line decoration on a honey ground. "Biarritz" shape. 1930s. Complete six person set. £220 Sotheby's April 1979.

Figure 4. Orange, blue, purple and green "Crocus" pattern plates. Six side plates and one serving plate. £25 Sotheby's April 1979.

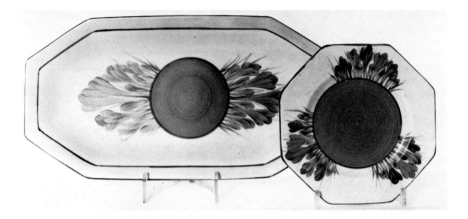

Figure 5. Orange, yellow and green banding and flowers on pale cream: the litho printed outline was a short lived experiment, it was too expensive and too regular for Clarice's style. "Conical" shape. Date marked 1931. £140-£200.

In 1918 she joined the firm of A.J. Wilkinson Limited, Royal Staffordshire Pottery, Burslem where she worked through all the decorating departments mastering lithography, modelling, gilding and firing. Round about 1925 her flair caught the attention of Wilkinson's managing director Colley Shorter (she married him, as his second wife, in 1941). Recalling this period, the mid-1920s, her younger sister Ethel, with whom Clarice then shared her bedroom, said "...The walls and woodwork were orange and yellow, the ceiling metallic gold, the wardrobe and chest of drawers orange with black relief and the iron bedsteads were encased in orange coloured leatherette. A nightmare to most people, but described by Clarice as bizarre''. How prophetic!

The next stage in Clarice's career is best told in her own words, written a few months before she died, in 1972, for the first retrospective exhibition of her work which opened at Brighton Museum in January that year.

"In 1920 the firm of A.J. Wilkinson acquired the adjoining factory, the Newport Pottery Co. Ltd. which (later) provided me with a studio cum workshop. The warehouses were stacked with (blank) bowls, vases, jugs and candlesticks etc., mostly of the art nouveau period. This huge stock had always interested me and presented a challenge. Eventually about 1925/26 I was allowed to experiment. First with one or two girls who had learned how to use the decorators' wheel round shapes were covered from top to bottom with coloured bands. Between guide lines they drew simple diamonds which in turn were filled in with bright colours by other girls. Then the articles were passed on to be banded at the top and bottom by others. Meanwhile a sizeable amount of goods was accumulating. These were a source of much merriment and derision to travellers to whom the idea of having to offer for sale so much crude colour, after selling only traditional prints and enamels and lithos, was a shock. However, after much persuasion the largest car on the factory was filled

with an assortment and to their amazement it was quickly sold and within two days they were back for more!''

This first collection was called Bizarre by Clarice, but it was Colley Shorter's brainwave that they should apply the name to the whole range and "Hand Painted Bizarre'' by Clarice Cliff was launched. The vase (figure 2, centre right) is almost certainly from this first period; it not only fits Clarice's description (left) but the shape and decoration also tally with illustrations from one of the first Bizarre sales brochures. The first sixty dozen pieces were sold in October 1928 and by the end of 1929 the entire production of the

Newport factory was given to her designs. Bizarre was a sell-out. The more high minded critics raised in the relative sobriety of the arts and crafts tradition never took to her — "A triumph of ugliness'' railed the *New Statesman and Nation* in 1935, a typical remark — but the china buying public in the smarter shops like Harrods, Selfridges and Lawleys had no doubts and back at the potteries Clarice could hardly keep pace.

In her heyday years 1929-35, up to twenty-seven new designs a week poured from her studio attached to the decorating shop where she retired to work on new ideas, getting inspiration from her growing collection of art and

Figure 6. Scarlet and orange poppies with red, blue, turquoise and purple streaked glaze on a honey coloured ground. "Delicia" pattern, "Stamford" shape. Early '30s. Two person breakfast set. £250.

Figure 8. Stylised landscapes with cottage. The plate, jug and teacup are orange, yellow and black and the teapot and toast rack in a traditional shape are orange, green and black. The mixed six person tea set £340 Sotheby's December 1978.

Figure 7. Large cream coloured vase with blue and pink sweet pea forms modelled on the handle plus a painted butterfly. "My Garden" from a very large range of bowls, jugs, cornucopias, trays, vases, candlesticks etc. Mid '30s. £15-£25.

garden books. At this time the work force totalled over 1,000 with over one hundred and fifty decorators alone. *Pottery Gazette* gives us the flavour of these times perfectly; in 1931 "...this is a courageous personal effort to attract business during a difficult period and richly deserves success ...(Clarice Cliff is)... a pioneer of advanced thought, blazing a trail of shapes with decidedly original decorations."

From the start Clarice felt the bold geometrics and simple landscapes cried out for shapes other than the traditional (figures 2, centre right, and figure 8 the teapot). New shapes based on cones, squares, circles and triangles were evolved: "Conical" patented in 1931 was the first (figure 5) and once the flat triangular handles were modified — they were hot and slippery to hold — it sold exceptionally well. In addition there was "Biarritz" with rectangular plates (figure 3) and semi-circular veg dishes; circular "Bon Jour" (figure 1) and the abrupt, Cubist "Stamford" (figure 6).

Just to give some idea of the extent of her range, and there is still much research to be done in this field, in table wares alone there were eleven different shapes to which any number of patterns could be applied: for example, the land-scape (figure 8) is a mix of traditional and modern shapes with a marked

change in pattern from one to the other. Nearly seventy patterns, as distinct from the shapes, have so far been tracked down and this does not include ranges like "My Garden" (figure 7) where shape and pattern were integrated. The flexibility of the Newport set up meant that customers could order their own patterns to be worked out from a picture of a house or garden: it was a marvellous free for all.

Quite apart from the day to day table wares which poured out of the factory in great quantities, Clarice also had a passion for novelties, flying swans, wall masks; there is "Subway Sadie", a cheeky face hollowed out into a fruit bowl... the sort of thing which even her devoted admirers find hard to take. But then Clarice is like that, you either like her but concede that she could lapse into dreadful vulgarities, or you loathe her! Take what you like and leave the rest, that's part of her charm.

For the precise identity of shapes, pattern, date etc., backstamps don't always help and are inconsistent. Any one, two or three of the available trade marks — A.J. Wilkinson, Newport Pottery or Royal Staffordshire Pottery — might be used; and then there are the marks of the trimmer (Clarice was very insistent on good trimming and liked to be able to trace back any poor pieces);

the initials of the decorator; occasional date marks and names of suppliers. Handwritten marks indicate the first pieces of a new range, established patterns had printed marks, and towards the end of the '30s the inevitable signature sometimes appeared in relief.

For serious collecting it is important to distinguish between the run of the mill table wares produced in such quantities and the really striking designs like this tea set (figure 1) or the magnificent 45cm wall plaques (see colour). Noel Tovey, a leading deco dealer at L'Odeon, 56 Fulham High Street, London S.W.6., who has supplied several museums with splendid Clarice pieces, warns that non-specialist dealers tend to over price the bread and butter wares and underprice the top quality stuff; they just see the name and slap on anything over £20 which comes to mind which may be far too much, particularly for smaller individual pieces. Prices for this first category went mad three years ago and are beginning to stabilise, even drop a little, whilst the best pieces have steadily appreciated. To give an example, in a recent Sotheby's sale the estimate for these "Crocus" plates (figure 4) was £20-£40, they fetched £25, while the estimate for the complete "Biarritz" dinner set (figure 3) was £175 and it fetched £220; compare too the out-standing tree decorated water jug (figure 9) estimated at £30-£40 which fetched £140 and its pleasant but comparatively wishy washy neighbour, estimated at £30-£40 which fetched £30. At the most recent sale, this July, quite a few pieces were unsold and a group of small "My

Figure 9. Left to right: Large water jug, the ribbed body decorated with stylised flowers and trees in yellow, orange, blue and green. 30cm. 1930s. £140 Sotheby's December 1978. Large pitcher, the ribbed body decorated with stylised shrubs in pastel pinks, blues and greens. 30cm. 1930s. £30. Sotheby's December 1978. Angular vase decorated with stylised landscapes in orange, green, blue and brown. 25cm. Early '30s. £95 Sotheby's December 1978.

Figure 10. Dinner plate with a rim of gazing pink faces banded in yellow and green. Designed by Dame Laura Knight. Brighton Museum.

Figure 11. Popular novelties. Left to right: Rimmed green ashtray with girl in orange spotted beach pyjamas, £40-£80. A landscape decorated powder bowl in turquoise, lilac, blue, green and orange with a kneeling figure on top, £60-£100.

Garden'' vases (figure 7) fetched just £18. So be careful and make sure the enamel is in good condition. Into the de luxe category come two of the stonewares (see colour), well worth looking out for, ''Inspiration'' and ''Persian'' with their deep rich blue and green matt glazes which even *Pottery Gazette* in 1933 reckoned to be ''...heirlooms of the future''; certainly it was the first time such glazes were widely available at a reasonable price. Some of the most highly prized and highly priced pieces at the moment, though not always aesthetically the most successful, are those decorated in collaboration with distinguished contemporary artists like Duncan Grant, Vanessa Bell, Paul Nash, Graham Sutherland and many more. The idea sprang from a chance meeting on a train by Clarice with Dame Laura Knight who contributed some cheerful circus patterns (figure 10). The designs were produced in bone china by Foley Pottery and earthenware by A.J. Wilkinson. The pieces were marked with a facsimile of the artist's signature plus ''Bizarre by Clarice Cliff''. The venture started in 1932 but was never really a commercial success; however today's prices make up for it and earlier this year

four big meat platters from the Dame Laura Knight dinner service (figure 10) were sold for £1,600.

Towards the second half of the 1930s, demand for the vividly coloured wares began to tail off. Softer more restrained patterns were wanted, although the modernistic shapes still sold well, and Clarice, sensitive to the slightest change in taste, toned down the decoration and turned towards softer celadon type glazes and Oriental novelties. When the war came the army claimed all the workers and the factory was turned over to making white hotel wares. Post war Britain was mono-chrome and cautious, and only the most popular patterns like ''Crocus'' (figure 4) lingered on into the mid '50s. The market had changed completely; also skilled workers were hard to find. Printed transfer and litho decoration was rapidly replacing free hand painting in the potteries. The company moved over almost entirely to traditionally styled underglaze transfer decorations but the pieces still bore Clarice's signature: there was no call for pottery with all the hectic gaiety of the pre-war years. Clarice stayed on as art director till 1963 when she nursed her beloved husband through his final ill-

ness. Running the factory became too much for her and in 1964 it was sold to Midwinters, now part of the Wedgwood Group. Clarice retired to the home she and her husband had built up together with its lovely garden and collection of Oriental ceramics, some of which she presented to Newcastle-under-Lyme Museum in his memory. When she heard Bizarre was beginning to be collected in the late 1960s it is said that she expressed amazement that anyone should want to collect pottery with ''great globs of colour'' on it. To the end she was shy and retiring about herself although always remarkably energetic and extrovert when it came to Newport Pottery and publicity for its products; who else could have dreamed up a teepee teapot for the Canadian market and sold it too?

It is too soon to assess her place in the history of English pottery but she had an enormous influence on her generation of designers throughout the potteries and helped to keep the industry alive and flourishing during a world wide recession. People loved her cheerful patterns (no wonder; they were pretty grim days) and now her designs are collected precisely because they are the very brightest examples of the factory produced pottery of their time.

The author wishes to thank Sotheby's Belgravia for photographs 1, 2, 3, 4, 6, 8 and 9, and the Brighton Museum for photographs 5, 7, 10 and 11 taken during the retrospective exhibition in 1972. She is indebted to Noel Tovey at L'Odeon, 56 Fulham High Street, London S.W.6 for information and the loan of the book on Clarice Cliff by Peter Wentworth-Shields and Kay Johnson published by him in 1976. It is the only book on her to date and there are a few copies left (of a limited edition of 1,500), price £12.50 including post and packing.

Figure 1. Oak hutch dated c.1600-1650 and measuring 82.5cm (33ins.) long, 65.6cm (26¼ins.) high and 30cm (12ins.) deep.

A Closer Look at an Early Oak Hutch

by Michael Nellist

Figure 2. A back view of the hutch showing a centrally placed pair of holes on the top board. These holes were probably made by iron lugs used to support the food-cupboard on a wall.

Family inheritance can sometimes bring to light old furniture which had been regarded as attractive or utilitarian rather than unusual (or even rare) but which, when passed on to a new generation, may evoke instant curiosity. Such an item of furniture is illustrated in figure 1 and was eventually identified as being a "hutch" or food-cupboard, dated c.1600-1650.

A hutch, derived from the French word *huche,* meaning a chest or other receptacle with one or more doors in front, had an interesting evolution.[1] During medieval times (c.395-1500) the hall became the principal living room where the whole household assembled for meals. As security and prosperity returned towards the end of the period, it became common practice for families to place and display their cups and plates on a "cupboard" within the hall. This was not the modern-day enclosed structure with a door, but was literally a board on which to place the items, although it might be fitted with a super-structure of shelves or "desks" as described by a George Harrison in 1562:

> "a cup board, being as long as the chamber was in breath, with six desks of height, garnyshed with guilt plate."[2]

Unfortunately there appear to be no examples of this type surviving.

Inventories of the 15th century indicate that the cupboard was sometimes provided with an enclosed space and door(s) beneath the shelf and was then described as a cupboard with an ambry or almery. Contemporary descriptions of the words "hutch" and "ambry" were:

"Hutch — Vide Ambrie."[3] and "An AMBRY or like place where any thing is kept. It seemeth to be deriued of this Frenche worde *Aumosniere,* which is a little purse, wherein was put single money for the poore, and at length was used for any hutch or close place to keepe meate left after meales, which at the beginning of Christianitie, was euer distributed amõg the poore people, and we for shortnesse of speache doe call it an Ambry."[3] These definitions indicate that when such an enclosed item of furniture contained any food, the term "hutch" was used. The word "almery" is thought to be derived from the fact that the contained left-overs were distributed to the poor in lieu of alms. An important feature in an ambry's design, due to its use as a food store, was that its front and sides were pierced for ventilation, either with small holes or often in the form of carved openwork tracery with "haire cloth" stretched behind to prevent flies, etc. from entering. (This could well have been the prototype of

the modern perforated zinc or metal gauzed larder cupboard.[4]) Further support that the ambry was used principally for the storage of food is that it was often listed in the pantry, buttery or kitchen; it could also contain "drinke", "mylke" or was even used "pro candelis". When used for drink, it had by necessity to be of table height and stood in the middle of the hall or by a window, so that it could be approached from all four sides. It usually contained a pot-board below.

However, in the 16th century the rich started eating in smaller, private parlours, away from the servants, and this change in domestic life affected the design of furniture, for space now became important. Thus the drink cupboard tended to disappear, whilst wall-hung furniture, although not novel, was an obvious way of utilising available

Figure 4. The basic design of the strapwork, about 23.7cm (9½ins.) in length, present along the upper borders of the hutch.

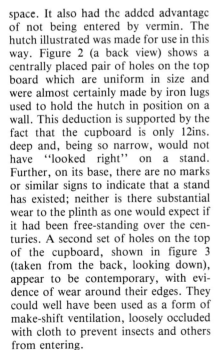

Figure 3. Detail of the top and back of the hutch showing the two pairs of holes discussed in the text.

Figure 5. Arcaded inlay on the door of the hutch in the form of a bowl of flowers resting on a crossbanded plinth. The escutcheon and key are not original.

space. It also had the added advantage of not being entered by vermin. The hutch illustrated was made for use in this way. Figure 2 (a back view) shows a centrally placed pair of holes on the top board which are uniform in size and were almost certainly made by iron lugs used to hold the hutch in position on a wall. This deduction is supported by the fact that the cupboard is only 12ins. deep and, being so narrow, would not have "looked right" on a stand. Further, on its base, there are no marks or similar signs to indicate that a stand has existed; neither is there substantial wear to the plinth as one would expect if it had been free-standing over the centuries. A second set of holes on the top of the cupboard, shown in figure 3 (taken from the back, looking down), appear to be contemporary, with evidence of wear around their edges. They could well have been used as a form of make-shift ventilation, loosely occluded with cloth to prevent insects and others from entering.

The dating of the piece comes from its style and construction. Rectangular panels below (inlaid with a hollowed diamond shape in bog oak) and arcaded panels above are characteristic of the Elizabethan period. Such an arrangement also exists on the sides of the hutch, whilst an intricate design of strapwork (figure 4) is present along its

upper borders. However, craftsmen were conservative people and new ideas and designs travelled slowly to the provinces; consequently much of Elizabethan designed furniture was produced in the Jacobean (1603-1625) and Carolean (1625-1649) periods. The inlay on the door of the cupboard (figure 5) is also indicative of the late Elizabethan period when it became common as a method of decoration (particularly plant forms), being introduced through Germany and Flanders from Renaissance Italy. It consisted in laying small carved pieces of different kinds of woods (holly and bog oak in this case) into shaped recesses in the solid wood (see *English Furniture Styles, 1500-1830* by Ralph Fastnedge, plate 6, page 54, for a similar inlay design dated c.1595). Only at a later date was inlay or marquetry laid on top of the wood. Other dating features are the small wedge hinges on the cupboard's door, typical of late 16th and early 17th century work, whilst oak was still the principal wood in

the first half of the 17th century, as it was only after this period that the walnut planted in Elizabeth's reign (1558-1603) began to supersede oak.

Thus, this is an example of an unusual and attractive piece of early English oak furniture.

1. R.W. Symonds: *The Evolution of the Cupboard. The Connoisseur,* December, 1943.
2. Victoria and Albert Museum: *A Short History of English Furniture.* H.M.S.O., 1966.
3. John Baret: *Bareti Dictionarium. An Alvearie or Quadruple Dictionarie, containing foure fundrie tongues: namelie, English, Latine, Greeke, and French,* 1580.
4. John Gloag: *Short Dictionary of Furniture.* Allen and Unwin, 1969.

Figure 1. The case. Gold outer (diameter 64mm) with owner's monogram. Hall-marked 1779, casemaker I.M. Silver gilt inner case with gold pendant and bow hall-marked 1779, casemaker. . .B.

A SEAMAN'S WATCH

by Terence Camerer Cuss

One of the benefits of being a dealer is the opportunity of seeing and sometimes owning just about every type, period and style one's subject has to offer. Consequently, one almost inevitably acquires a very broad taste and to choose just one watch for Christmas is especially hard!

Captain John Inglefield was the first owner of my choice in 1779. His remarkable voyage in 1782, a distance of nine hundred land miles from Newfoundland to the Azores in a ship's boat after the sinking of the seventy-four gun "Centaur", is well documented. The "Centaur" had been caught in a hurricane and the single boat that got away when she finally sank contained twelve men, eleven of whom survived the sixteen day journey. They had only a blanket for a sail and their provisions consisted of a small ham, a bag of bread, a piece of pork and two quart bottles of water. They had no compass or quadrant, so how did they manage to make good over fifty miles a day?

Fortunately, Inglefield had his watch — my Christmas present — which, as it kept very good time, not only allowed him to estimate the longitude but also enabled him to use it as a compass. One points the hour hand at the sun and divides the angle between this and twelve o'clock to find south. No wonder he had the watch inscribed "My watch and compass in the Centaur's boat 24th of Sept. 1782 J.N. Inglefield".

One of the rules of dealing (one is often told) is that one should not let one's view of a piece be unduly influenced by its history or background, but in this case I find it hard to resist.

Horologists will know that the escapement has much to do with the accuracy of a watch and also that an accurate timekeeper was required if longitude was to be successfully determined at sea. Apart from the robust but inaccurate verge, the cylinder was effectively the only one available when the watch was made. The virgule was unproven and anyway unsuitable and John Arnold had produced no spring detent chronometer and only a few pivoted detents. Part of the watch's attraction must be that the cylinder escapement, even when exceedingly well made, is generally considered as too inaccurate for a marine timekeeper. Ya-boo to established theory!

The watch has many late 18th century characteristics and exhibits the charming piercing and engraving that was soon lost with the onset of the 19th century when, with the exception of signatures, any engraving to a watch movement is very much a hangover. But the watch also combines a utilitarian feel (and don't waste gold on the inner case) and taste for precision that the 19th century mastered. A compromise, maybe, but to my mind a very satisfying one.

Of course the watch is unusual (there are so many unusual watches — can they all be rare?), but, if one excludes the historical connection, not particularly valuable — in the region, say, of about £1,500. But for me it is something out of the ordinary. The Inglefields too must have shared this view for their family motto is "the sun is my compass".

Figure 2. The dial. Black numerals on white enamel. Layout very reminiscent of those used on early levers produced a few years later. Gold hands.

Figure 3. The movement. Signed Jno. Brockbank London No.1211. Dust cap also signed and numbered. Pierced cock table with large diamond endstone, engraved with military emblems and a bust with DOMI AUG XII either side of neck. Keywind fusee and chain, start/stop lever acting on plain steel balance. Early example of watch main-taining power. The escapement is cylinder with a gold escape wheel and steel shell. Almost certainly a ruby shell was originally fitted although there are no signs of this. It is just possible a steel one was used as it could have been considered more robust. Compensation — curb pins set in free end of brass ring at some 345° circumference, the fixed end fitted to the regulator rack. Flat steel spring and light plain steel balance.

CRANBERRY

by Jack Ellson

"Cranberry" glass is a name that developed in the United States, and refers to the glass that we in Great Britain call "ruby".

It is mostly not expensive. Little Victorian pieces can still be found for a couple of pounds or so, and the price range for run of the mill items such as bowls and jugs of smallish to medium size is from around £8 to £18.

In my view the attractiveness of the transparent pinky-red of Victorian ruby glass is enhanced when it is combined with clear glass and this is shown in several of the illustrations.

Because of the appeal of ruby glass to American collectors, great quantities have been shipped over to the United States. It has also been very collectable in this country, with a special appeal for women collectors. Until recently, the supply has seemed inexhaustible. As fast as it has left the antique shops so it has been replaced by more "bits and pieces" from millions of homes up and down the country.

However, there is little doubt that genuine Victorian ruby is now becoming scarce. It is still about, and still relatively cheap, but this will not last much longer. Better than average pieces are already fetching higher prices — for example, a table centrepiece combining a silver-plated centre stand and ruby glass flowerholders, all in 1880s style, was recently bought for £100 from a Southport antique shop, and a miniature ruby tea-service, of seven pieces only, for substantially more.

How did ruby glass develop?

The Egyptians and Syrians made red glass before the birth of Christ, and a little of this was of a ruby shade, no doubt by chance. The Romans also made red glass by including copper in the "frit" (the mixture of sand and other items from which glass is made), a practice which continued in various parts of the world up to and through medieval times, when manganese was introduced to produce a paler shade of red.

In about 1680 Johann Kunckel, of Potsdam in Germany, started to make good consistent ruby coloured glass by the incorporation of gold chloride into the frit. This was not a brand new idea but Kunckel developed and perfected it, and it made ground in the glass producing areas of Germany and Bohemia. A number of jugs and teapots made by Kunckel in ruby glass with silver mounts and accessories have survived, and can be seen in a number of Continental museums.

The ruby glass bottle, 17.5cm high with gilt metal top and foot, shown in figure 1, was made in Germany in the mid-18th century. This type of item would fetch a high price on the open market, certainly into four figures.

Strangely, coloured glass articles were not particularly popular in England in the period of Kunckel's developments or, indeed, in the following century. The emphasis in this country was on clear "glass of lead", plain, cut or decorated, right up to the repeal of the glass excise tax in 1845.

This is not to say that there was no coloured glass made at all in England in this period; certainly from 1750 it was manufactured in various glasshouses in the Bristol and West Midlands areas, mainly in blue, yellow, green and purple. What shades of red there were involved the use of gold, iron or copper, or mixtures of these, as colouring agents, and there was no emphasis at all on ruby, although, almost willy-nilly, a little was produced.

The finest English coloured glass articles between 1815-45 were without doubt made by Richardson's of Stourbridge, who had some excellent pieces in the Manchester Exhibition of 1845-46.

An engraved ruby sherry glass c.1825 fetched £7.50 at auction not so long ago, an example of the undoubted bargains that, with knowledge, can still be found.

From 1845, many coloured glass vases and bowls were imported into the United Kingdom from Bohemia. These included cased, overlaid, flashed and iridescent glass incorporating various shades of ruby. Many of these articles were directed at the lower end of the market, but the top quality Bohemian coloured glass was on the whole more interesting and better made than that of the English glassmakers, who at this time included Rice Harris and Son of Birmingham, George Bacchus and Sons, Davis Greathead and Green, and Lloyd and Summerfield.

However, the English manufacturers were quick learners and, starting at the Birmingham Exhibition of 1849, but mainly at the Great Exhibition of 1851 at the Crystal Palace, they exhibited much coloured glass up to the best Bohemian standards, plain, cased and decorated. Most importantly, from the point of view of present day cranberry collectors, this included much ruby, and for example, Rice Harris's colour-list specified both light and dark shades.

Figure 2 shows a custard cup, a simple little piece with ruby bowl and clear glass elsewhere. It is English, 9cm high, made about 1880, and would now sell at about £6-£8, although it cost me less than half that three or four years ago. These attractive little glasses are becoming more and more difficult to find because not only have collectors of cranberry and custard cups been hoarding them for the past few years, but they also make up into very nice punch sets.

In the '60s, '70s and '80s, cheap ruby ornaments for mantelpieces and trinket tables were churned out in the Birmingham and Stourbridge areas. They were free-blown, mould-blown, or possibly lightly blown into a mould to give an outline surface pattern and then taken out and completed by free-blowing. They were often decorated with clear glass frilling and wavy edges or with pincered trailings of clear glass in a sort of 17th century style. These cheap mantel ornaments could be bought in seaside bric-a-brac shops or won at the fair at hoop-la or skittles. Also for sale at this period were vast numbers of ruby articles for use on Victorian teatables and in Victorian sitting rooms and parlours including sugar basins, milk and cream jugs, wine glasses and beakers. These were normally better made and more substantial than the ornaments, with glass containing less blemish, and decoration more carefully applied.

The decorated basket shown in figure 3 is 20.5cm high. The ruby bowl is applied with fruits and leaves, possibly plums, in clear glass, and the handle, in the form of a branch, and the four feet, are also in clear glass. This very desirable piece was probably made in Stourbridge in the last quarter of the 19th century, and illustrates the 17th century style referred to earlier. However, it is much better made and considerably larger than the great majority of such ornaments and was almost certainly the product of one of the better firms of the area such as Stevens and Williams or Thomas Webb. I would estimate that if this basket appeared in auction it would command a price of around £100, whereas a more typical ornament, perhaps a third the size and with clear glass feet as the only decoration, would fetch only about £12-£15.

Towards the end of the century, and into the 1900s, decorative items of fine quality of, or incorporating, ruby glass, made their appearance in the dining and drawing rooms of the professional classes. These included epergnes and flower-stands made by such prominent firms as Dobson and Pearce, Boulton and Mills, and Richardsons. Such pieces, highly ornate, large and excellently finished, rarely come on the market. If they did, they would surely make many hundreds of pounds.

The late Victorian years also saw the production of hundreds of thousands of press-moulded articles in all types of glass, but, remarkably including little or

*A selection of 19th century ruby glass from the
Brierley Hill and Stourbridge Glass Collections*
(Dudley Art Gallery).

Figure 1

Figure 2

Figure 3

Figure 4

Figure 5

Four pieces of moulded applied glass frilling provide a stand for the beaker, which is 18cm high. It cost £12 last year, a rather good buy.

No one is really very clear how this particular type of glass got its name. Was a lady called Mary Gregory associated with an American glassworks, as has been claimed? Certainly some of this distinctively decorated glassware was made in the United States in the last century and Americans dearly love to collect it.

However, the great majority came from Bohemia, as in the case of the item in figure 5, particularly from the Hohn glassworks at Jablonec. By the way, sometimes the enamelled decoration involved with ruby Mary Gregory is of a pink shade, and other colours include green, yellow and clear with either white or tinged enamelling. Prices are very variable depending upon scarcity. A small ruby bowl or tumbler could probably be picked up at auction for about £8 even today, but a more unusual item, such as a ruby pintray of the same sort of size, would bring considerably more, perhaps around £50-£60.

There is a great deal of modern ruby glass about, which is easily distinguishable from its Victorian equivalent because of design. It is made in modern style by modern methods and can be bought in glassware shops and department stores. It also abounds in bric-a-brac shops and on some stalls at some collectors' fairs. This concerns and confuses some people. I do not see why. This glass is new, or thereabouts, looks new and is even collected by some people, and why not? A modern piece can be artistic, desirable and collectable in its own right.

Firms which made Victorian ruby have continued to make it and are still doing so, and there is no reason why they should not. In some instances, firms have resumed the manufacture of

certain glassware long since discontinued, such as Mary Gregory, and again, why not? It fills a gap at presumably (although not always) a cheaper price, and at the same time confirms that the earlier specimens are becoming, or have become scarce. This can bring comfort to the owners of earlier pieces!

It is what happens to recently made items after manufacture that might cause problems; but it should always be remembered that items that have been tampered with can usually be detected, provided the would-be purchaser does not rush to buy, or get carried away at an auction, as so often happens. The sensible approach is to look at the object long and hard, handle it, carefully consider the price or estimate (not just whether it's too much; is it too little?!) and come to a logical decision whether to buy. And stick to that decision once made.

Acknowledgements
Figure 1 is published by kind permission of the British Museum and the Pilkington Glass Museum, St. Helens. Figure 3 is published by kind permission of Dudley Art Gallery, Brierley Hill Glass Collection, as is the full colour illustration.

no ruby, at least in this country. However, some ruby pressed items were made in the major American glassworks, are now very rare and do not normally come on the market.

The small late Victorian bowl, 7cm high, shown in figure 4, is of a light ruby shade with clear glass "veins" providing an unusual decoration. It is not strictly ruby from a collecting standpoint, being "flashed" on clear glass. Its interest is that it was almost certainly initially blown into a mould and then given a free-blown finish. It has a well-ground pontil mark and very recently cost me £3 in a North West antique shop.

People appear either to love or hate Mary Gregory glass, the subject of figure 5. This particular beaker is in ruby decorated with a typical white enamelled little Victorian boy blowing bubbles.

Brunel seated before the launching chains, the official portrait.

Isambard Kingdom Brunel standing before the launching chains of the Great Eastern.

A PHOTOGRAPHIC PORTRAIT

by David Allison

My choice of an ideal Christmas present is somewhat predictable, yet I feel it demonstrates the ultimate in photographic portraiture. It is the much sought after photograph of Isambard Kingdom Brunel, standing before the launching chains of the Great Eastern, by Robert Howlett, taken in late 1857. Robert Howlett and Joseph Cundall were commissioned by *The Illustrated Times,* a popular rival to *The Illustrated London News,* to record the construction and launch of the largest steamship of the century. Engravings from the series of photographs appeared in a special "Leviathan (Great Eastern) Number", scheduled to coincide with the second launch attempt, on 16th January, 1858. This is one of the earliest examples of photographs being used for reportage purposes, a fact we all too readily take for granted in today's newspapers and magazines.

The revolutionary broadside launch had attracted much interest and some scepticism, the first attempt failing in November 1857. Howlett, "one of the most skilful photographers of the day..." the article accurately states, used a device commonly employed by many modern photographers: instead of focussing on the ship he caught the tense expression of those responsible for her, the engineers — Solomon Tredwell, John Scott Russell, Henry Wakefield and mentor Isambard Kingdom Brunel. Paradoxically, Brunel standing before the chains was in fact taken after what was supposed to be the official study — a rather formal studio-like portrait of him seated before the chains. However it is the uncontrived version that was instantly applauded, Howlett cleverly representing a highly respected figure in such a human and identifiable manner. In his choice of location, the photographer displays a strong empathy for his surroundings, selecting a backcloth of immediate visual magnetism symbolising the magnitude of the undertaking. Howlett was no stranger to this type of work, having the previous year taken some studies at the Derby to serve as studies for William Powell Frith's painting "Derby Day". Brunel fully complements this feeling for com-

position; with characteristic cigar, stove pipe hat, muddied boots and trousers, he surveys the site displaying his total involvement in the project. The study is simple in construction yet succinct — the ingredients for a successful picture in any media. It is fitting, however, that a man of such great achievement and innovation should be immortalised by the comparatively new art.

From my point of view I am afraid the photograph's obvious merits have not escaped the notice of a great number of collectors. I would have to forgo a large number of Christmas presents to meet the payment of an original. A photograph from Howlett's own hand sold at Christie's South Kensington in a sale of 19th and 20th century photographs in March of this year for £7,500, a record auction price for a British paper photograph. I would therefore be pleased to accept one of the small carte-de-visite versions produced by the London Stereoscopic Company after they acquired the negative in the early 1860s, now selling at auction for a less prohibitive price of around £40 or £50.

THE ENGLISH "REGULATOR"
by
Derek Roberts

A good mid-19th century mahogany longcase regulator with a mercury compensated pendulum, glazed sides and a bombé base; a feature which is sometimes used to provide the extra stability which is essential for accurate timekeeping.

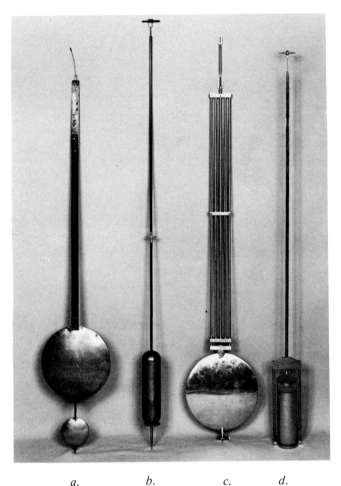

a.   b.   c.   d.

Figure 1. Regulator pendulums.
a. Wood rod with small auxiliary bob for fine regulation.
b. Invar pendulum with tray on rod for addition of small weights for fine regulation.
c. Five rod gridiron pendulum.
d. Mercury compensated pendulum.

The term regulator implies a precision pendulum clock which was designed for such purposes as astronomy and regulating other clocks and watches. Their origin probably began with the need of astronomers to measure the passage of various stars relative to one another and indeed some of the earliest regulators were those commissioned by Sir James Moore from Tompion for use by Flamstead in the New Observatory. The prime task of these clocks was to ascertain whether the earth rotated at a constant speed.

ACCURACY

The accuracy regulators achieve will vary both with their quality and the date of manufacture; thus it is unlikely that any regulator made prior to 1700 will keep time to within less than two to three seconds a day. However, during the first half of the 18th century compensated pendulums were developed by, amongst others, Graham, Harrison and Ellicott (figure 1) and this improved their accuracy to possibly one to two seconds a week. Indeed Harrison's regulator was recorded as consistently keeping time to within something less than one second a month.

It is doubtful if this performance was improved upon during the following hundred years and it is only when such problems as detaching the movement from the influence of the pendulum, allowing for changes in barometric pressure, and keeping the pendulum at a constant arc of swing were overcome that their performance improved much further. Thus it is interesting to note that the Royal Observatory in Edinburgh in 1864 specified an accuracy of plus or minus 0.1 of a second per day for their regulator.

By 1900 by, amongst other developments, controlling barometric pressure and detaching the escapement, astronomical regulators by Le Roy and Reiffler were keeping time to within 0.01 of a second per day and by 1920 Short had achieved a daily rate of 0.005 of a

A fine astronomical regulator by Parkinson and Frodsham c.1830. Note the fine wheel-work, even the maintaining disc being spoked out; the beat regulation; end "stops" or plates and substantial brackets holding down the heavy and beautifully finished movement. The maintaining power, including the spring, can be seen quite clearly.

Figure 2b.

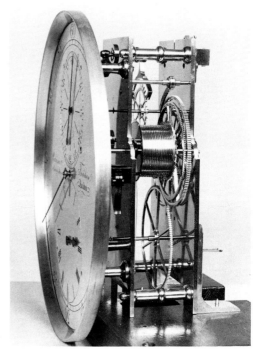

second and continued to improve on this until by 1940 the rate was down to 0.001 of a second. This marked the zenith of the mechanical, or possibly one should say the electro-mechanical, clock and thereafter the atomic clock and its derivatives took over.

MECHANICAL FEATURES

The main properties sought in an English regulator produced from around 1720 to 1920 are:

1. **Maintaining power** so as to keep it going whilst it is being wound, otherwise it might well lose ten to fifteen seconds every time this is carried out.

2. **A compensated pendulum** so that its effective length will not change with variations in temperature and thus affect the timekeeping.

3. **Some form of dead beat escapement** so as to prevent train reversal which occurs when escapements such as the anchor or recoil, as it is sometimes termed, are used.

Other desirable features which may or may not be present depending on the quality of the clock and the date of its manufacture are:

a. **Jewelled pallets.** These not only reduce friction but also minimise wear of the escapement and thus any variation in depthing of the pallets, which would result in the arc of swing of the pendulum varying and thus the timekeeping of the clock. It is interesting to note that the loss of time involved per day in an arc of one degree is 1.55 seconds whereas, if this is increased to three degrees, it is 14.8 seconds and six degrees over one minute.

b. **Fine pivots.** These are desirable to reduce friction to a minimum and can often be directly related to the weight required to drive the clock.

c. **Jewelled pivot holes.** Jewelling of the pivot holes assists in two ways: a. by

reducing friction; b. by minimising wear and thus any variation in depthing of the wheels and pinions throughout the train which could increase friction.

d. **End plates** (figure 2). These are used to limit the play of the arbors and prevent the shoulders butting on the plates and thus causing undue friction.

e. **A high count train.** The higher the count of the train the less power which will be absorbed by it; however, there is probably a point at which the gain is so small as to be not worth considering.

f. **Fine wheelwork** (figure 2b). Wheelwork should be both as light and as rigid as possible which implies that wheels should be delicately crossed out and usually of five, six or even sometimes of seven spokes in place of the usual four employed on longcase and bracket clocks.

g. **Plates and pillars** (figure 3). These should be as rigid as possible and firmly fixed to the case; similarly the case itself should be firmly anchored to the wall so as to prevent any movement whatsoever.

MAINTAINING POWER

As the precision of clocks improved during the 17th century, so the time lost during winding when the power was removed from the train became increasingly significant and thus quite early on a form of maintaining power known as bolt and shutter was developed.

Bolt and shutter (figure 4). With this a cord or lever is depressed which actuates a spring loaded bolt which engages on a wheel in the train and continues to supply power when the force of the driving weight is removed during winding. To make certain that it is employed, shutters are positioned over the winding holes which are only removed when the maintaining power is actuated.

This particular form of maintaining

power was used extensively on longcase clocks until around 1690 to 1700 and is occasionally seen on regulators even as late as 1800 to 1850. However, its popularity rapidly decreased with the advent of Harrison's going ratchet.

Harrison's going ratchet (figure 2b)

The disadvantage of bolt and shutter was the inconvenience of having to actuate it by a cord prior to winding. Harrison overcame this by employing an additional wheel which is normally cut with fine teeth and employs its own ratchet. This is positioned next to the great wheel and is linked to it by a spring which, when the power is removed from the train during winding, still applies pressure to it and keeps it going.

COMPENSATED PENDULUMS

The simplest form of compensated pendulum is that employing a wood rod with a heavy brass cased lead bob (figure 1a). Wood expands comparatively little in long grain when compared with iron and steel and this small amount is compensated for by the upwards expansion of the bob away from the regulating nut which supports it.

Mercurial pendulums

Nearly all the forms of compensated pendulum other than the wood rod are based on the differential expansion of various metals. George Graham commenced experiments in 1715 to try to measure these variations. His aim was to find two metals which, when used in opposition to each other in the construction of a pendulum, would have rates of expansion which would compensate or cancel each other out. However, he found that the difference between the expansions of brass and iron, the metals most easily available, was so small that he could see no way of utilising them and so gave up this particular line of investigation.

Figure 3. A typical fine quality Victorian regulator movement. Points to note are the screwed plates and dial feet; pulley offset; beat regulation and massive holding down bolts.

He subsequently turned his attention to the much greater expansion of mercury relative to iron and in 1722 produced a pendulum making use of this principle (figure 1d). Mercury contained in a jar is employed as the bob and will thus automatically expand upwards with any increase in temperature to compensate for any increase in the length of the pendulum rod. As mercury has a thermal co-efficient roughly six times as great as iron, if a column of mercury 6ins. long is employed in conjunction with a 36ins. long steel rod, i.e. a ratio of one to six, then the thermal co-efficients should exactly cancel each other out.

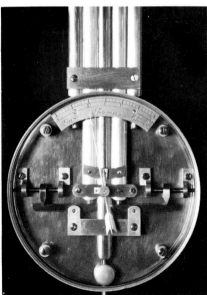

Figure 5. Ellicott's form of gridiron pendulum. This bob is from a French regulator but illustrates the principles of Ellicott's pendulum. Rods press on the pivoted levers and thus raise the bob.

In practice it has been found, because of certain additional factors which have to be considered, that the length of the column of mercury usually required is around 6.8ins. An advantage of this form of thermal compensation is that it can be finely regulated by the addition or removal of small quantities of mercury from the jar.

Gridiron pendulums

The relative expansions of steel and brass are approximately three to five; thus, if a 5ft. steel rod in a pendulum expanding down could be opposed by a 3ft. brass rod expanding up, then theoretically the length of the pendulum would remain unchanged. In practice the simplest way that this can be achieved and, indeed, the way described by Harrison is by employing several shorter sections of rod but still keeping the ratio of steel to brass the same. Thus the five (figure 1c) or nine rod gridiron pendulum was evolved. Variations of the gridiron pendulum were produced by several well-known clockmakers during the 18th and 19th centuries but, whether they performed any better than Harrison's original design, is open to doubt.

Ellicott's compensated pendulum

Ellicott devoted a lot of his time to the design of compensated pendulums developing more than one different type to try to overcome the errors he felt were inherent in some of the other designs. The main objection to Harrison's gridiron was that it was difficult to adjust to correct for any inaccuracies in the degree of compensation being achieved. Although Ellicott and others produced tables to show the relative expansion of metals, these figures varied considerably depending on such factors as the exact composition of the metal used and the way in which it had been prepared by tempering, hammering, polishing, etc. To overcome this problem, it was necessary to measure the exact co-efficients of expansion of the metals being used in the pendulum after they had been prepared. Alternatively some method of adjusting the degree of compensation achieved had to be provided and this is what Ellicott achieved (figure 5).

Basically, a flat bar of brass is fixed to the iron pendulum rod by screws passing through slots in the brass and allowing a sliding movement of the two relative to each other. The pendulum rod is extended beyond the brass and widened. To this is fitted two pivoting levers, on the outer ends of which rest two screws which support the pendulum bob; the brass rod presses on the inner ends of the lever and thus on expansion depresses them and raises the bob. The relative lengths required of the two ends of the lever will depend on the difference in co-efficients of the two metals. However, corrections can be made by moving the screws of the pendulum bob in or out

Figure 4. A relatively simple regulator movement with bolt and shutter maintaining power.

and thus varying the point at which they act on the lever.

Zinc/steel compensated pendulums

A combination of zinc and steel was occasionally made use of during the 19th century. These were of several different forms, the commonest probably consisting of a central steel rod expanding downwards and supporting a skeletonised zinc tube expanding upwards which in turn supported an outer steel tube which carried the pendulum bob.

Invar

Many more forms of compensated pendulum were invented during the 18th and 19th century and some of these are described in Rees's *Clocks, Watches and*

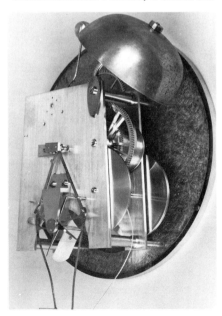

Figure 6. A gravity escapement, in this case four legged, as devised by Lord Grimthorpe for Big Ben and produced by Dent.

Chronometers. However, the problem was finally simplified and virtually laid to rest by the invention at the end of the 19th century of invar (short for invariable) by Dr. Guillaume. This is a nickel/iron alloy with small quantities of carbon and manganese. Its extremely low co-efficient of expansion, 0.0000013 per degree centigrade, or even less depending on its exact composition, meant that the changes in the length of a rod made of this material could almost be discounted (figure 1b).

ESCAPEMENT

The form of dead beat escapement seen on the vast majority of English longcase regulators was that perfected by Graham in the first part of the 18th century (figures 2b and 4). However, two other types were sometimes employed: a. the pin-wheel which was used much more on the Continent than in England; b. the gravity escapement.

Figure 7. The classic English regulator dial with concentric minute hand and subsidiary seconds and hours. Note that they are of identical maximum size which demands careful train layout. The numerals are clear but not unduly heavy.

Several forms of this were devised but that most frequently found was either the double three legged or the four legged (figure 6) which was developed by Lord Grimthorpe for use on Big Ben which Dents constructed. It is thus scarcely surprising that the majority of regulators, particularly the early ones using this form of escapement, were made by this firm.

Many more complex forms of escapement were devised for astronomical regulators but these were only ever produced in very small numbers.

DIALS

Dial layout on regulators is of particular importance, as their sole function is to be able to display the time clearly and accurately. Obviously with a regulator keeping time to within a few seconds a week the seconds hand is most significant and thus this is usually placed in the top half of the dial. Below and balancing this is the hour hand or occasionally an aperture showing the hours. The minute hand is concentric.

The layout shown in figure 7 is considered to be the classic English regulator layout and was used almost exclusively for a large part of the 18th and 19th centuries. It is only on the very early regulators and again increasingly on those made towards the end of the 19th century that a conventional longcase dial layout is used.

REGULATOR TYPES AND CASE STYLES

Regulators may be roughly divided into two groups: those of astronomical quality which were rarely employed for other than observatory purposes, and the domestic variety which were used primarily to regulate other clocks and watches. These were to be found in many of the finest houses and also came to be used increasingly in clockmakers' workshops and jewellers. Indeed, by the end of the 19th century one was to be seen in nearly every jewellers throughout the land.

Case styles varied considerably during the 18th and 19th centuries. The domestic variety roughly corresponded with the longcase clocks being produced but was generally somewhat smaller and simpler in form (figure 8). The astronomical regulators were of two types: those which remained in the observatory and were rigidly fixed in position, often even standing on a brick pier and being

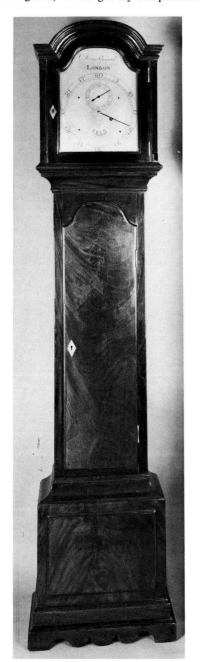

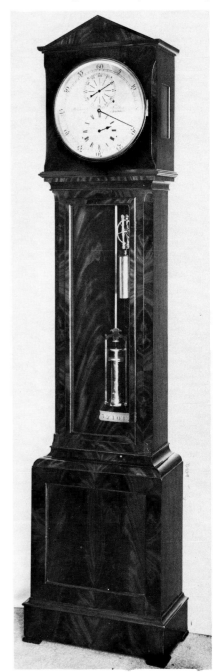

Figure 8. A typical George III mahogany longcase regulator with solid door and shallow breakarch, one of the styles favoured at this time. Height 6ft.6ins.

Figure 9. A classic regulator case of a type used by many fine makers such as Molyneux, and Parkinson and Frodsham during the first half of the 19th century. The architectural top was often omitted. Height 6ft.6ins.

Figure 10. Left: A fine quality dome topped regulator with mercurial pendulum and decorative pulley. This style was to dominate the second half of the 19th century. Height 6ft.1in. Right: A typical Regency domestic longcase regulator. Height 6ft.4ins.

bolted to the wall, and those designed to be portable. These latter were used, for instance, to record the transit of Venus in Tahiti in 1769.

Whereas during the 18th century the majority of regulators had solid trunk doors, by the early 19th century the glazed door became increasingly popular (figure 9), largely to show off the compensated pendulum and the brass cased weight. Regulators similar to the Regency longcase clock were also being produced (figure 10, right). The cases, particularly of observatory regulators, are extremely rigid and well made, the backboard and seatboard, for instance, often being up to 1in. thick. The seatboards are rigidly fixed to the case and the movement itself is bolted to the seatboard. Beautifully turned and knurled nuts (figure 3) or brackets (figure 2a) were often employed for this purpose, particularly on the later regulators.

As the industrial revolution progressed during the 19th century both the wealth and population of the country increased dramatically and so did the number of jewellers' shops throughout the land. This gave rise to a dramatic in-

crease in the number of regulators being manufactured, the majority being supplied by a few specialised firms. At the same time they became more standardised until by around 1860 the vast majority were of the style now known as the Victorian dome topped regulator (figure 10, left). The quality of these cases is nearly always excellent and they must have been made as fine show pieces in the jewellers, displaying as they did the impressive pendulum swinging backwards and forwards.

Whereas in the 18th and the first part of the 19th century the wood rod pendulum was most commonly used on domestic regulators, by 1850 the mercury compensated pendulum had largely taken over, although regulators were still sometimes made with a wood rod pendulum with a heavy lenticular bob or later still a cylindrical brass bob. Gridiron pendulums were also occasionally employed but not nearly so frequently as on the Continent.

SUMMARY

In a brief article such as this many factors, particularly of a technical nature, have had to be omitted, but in

conclusion it was felt that it might be of help to give the collector interested in this field of horology some guidance as to the possibilities.

The first thing to bear in mind is that regulators are only available in very limited numbers when compared with longcase clocks which means that not only is the choice far more restricted but also that they are rising in value far more rapidly — particularly now that so many people are appreciating the fine craftsmanship involved.

The next factor to consider is whether you are seeking an astronomical regulator by one of the famous makers such as Ellicott, Shelton, Hardy or Dent, which would probably cost upwards of £8,000, or whether a domestic regulator is acceptable, which would be anything from £1,000 for a very simple country made clock to £4,000-£5,000 for a good example in a fine mahogany case.

You then have to decide which period of regulator you require. The domestic variety made in the 18th and early 19th centuries (figures 8 and 10, right) usually had solid doors, wood rod pendulums and fairly simple movements, whereas the dome topped regulators made in the second half of the 19th century (figure 10, left) often have massive and superb quality movements (figure 3) and generally employ a mercurial pendulum (figure 10, left).

Factors which affect the price of a Victorian regulator are usually related to its quality and thus its cost in the first instance. These are:

1. The quality, proportions and size of the case, and the wood it is made of.
2. The type of pendulum — mercurial and gridiron pendulums are generally preferred to a simple wood rod.
3. The movement may to some extent be assessed by
   a. the size and finish of the plates and pillars
   b. the count of the train, the higher the better
   c. whether the pallets are jewelled
   d. whether there is any jewelling to the pivot holes
   e. whether end plates or jewels are provided.
4. The dial should be clearly laid out with seconds and hour rings of maximum size and exactly balancing each other (figure 7); the numerals should be easily read but not unduly heavy. Engraved brass dials are to be preferred to painted ones.
5. The weights should be brass cased and the pulley should be of fine quality. It is normal for this to be spoked out in a similar manner to the wheels in the train.

With Georgian domestic regulators the price is generally determined far more by the size, proportions and quality of the case than by the movement. It is usually only the astronomical regulators produced during this period which had very fine movements.

IN SEARCH OF CATS
Part II *by M.I.N. Evans*

Figure 11. Rockingham cats. Left. 3rd size, 1¾ins. Right. 1st size, 2⅜ins., incised No. 77. Courtesy Miss J.L. Hopkins.

Figure 12. Rockingham cat on rococo base, incised No. 77 and Cl 2 in red. Courtesy Clifton Park Museum, Rotherham.

The search for cats has, so far, been for older and more rare varieties — not that Rockingham cats (figures 11, 12 and 13) are particularly plentiful but they do come into the more modern group, and they are eagerly sought after, both by collectors of cats as well as Rockingham enthusiasts. This was the only porcelain producing factory in Yorkshire and operated for the short space of sixteen years, from 1826 to 1842, at Swinton near Rotherham — though pottery was produced by the Bramelds at Swinton for many years prior to 1826 and indeed up to the time of the factory's closure.

Rockingham cats are quite small and often the same cat is produced in three sizes. Figure 11 shows two of the three sizes with clear indications of their origin on the base. The cat on the right is incised with No. 77; it also has Cl 2 in red (a mark peculiar to the Rockingham factory, which sometimes appears in place of, as well as, the griffin mark) and 1st size (actually 2⅜ins.), whereas the cat on the left also has Cl 2 in red and 3rd size (actually 1¾ins.); the 2nd size would be 2⅛ins.

These cats, c.1826-1830, are black with gilt collars and are seated on tasselled cushions. The three sizes are

also known in white and gilt (see D.G. Rice's book *Rockingham Ornamental Porcelain,* page 143) and others are decorated in marmalade colours and seated on a green cushion. Figure 12 shows the same model but in this case seated on an oval green and white rococo base; it still bears the incised No. 77 and Cl 2 in red.

The delightful group of cat with kittens (figure 13) is white with gilt decoration on a base 3¾ins. long and is incised No. 107 with Cl 1 in red. The animals in the group would appear to be moulded separately and then placed on the plinth. This is a very comprehensive group compared with others which have, in one case, only the three kittens and, in another instance, the cat and kittens but without a saucer for milk.

This group is also known with marmalade and black animals, and can be seen in the Langton collection at the Castle Museum, Norwich. The other cats described can be seen in the Clifton Park Museum, Rotherham, where there is an exquisite collection of Rockingham ornamental items.

In auction, Rockingham cats fetch between £200 and £350, depending on type and condition.

Also in Rice's book, Plate 112, is a re-

cumbent cat from the Derby factory. This animal, c.1820, has the round Bloor Derby mark in red and is illustrated with an identical Rockingham cat, No. 104, showing, as Rice says, "the remarkable similarity of modelling practised at the two factories" — figure 14 shows this Derby cat. Early models are not usually marked whereas later ones generally have an incised number on the base. Two cats from this factory are in the above mentioned collection ... one c.1810-20 is a porcelain figure of a seated man with a cat on his right side (height 5½ins.). The base is marked with the incised No. 71, and crown, crossed batons and D34 in red enamel — the other is a mid-19th century undecorated porcelain group of three kittens playing on a rectangular base.

Other cats from this factory include large and small ones on cushions, modelled by Edward Keys who worked at the factory until 1826.

The last in this survey of the early 19th century cats with a good factory pedigree is a Chamberlain's Worcester model. The original Worcester Porcelain Company was founded in 1751 by Dr. Wall and five other men. Dr. Wall died in 1776, after which time the company changed hands several times until 1840 when they amalgamated with Chamberlain.

Thomas Chamberlain was one of the decorators at Worcester, who with his brother set up a decorating establishment, but soon turned to producing their own porcelain. Although most of Chamberlain's pieces were marked, sometimes small items such as cats and dogs were not, as in the case of the cat in

Left: Figure 13. Rockingham group of cat and kittens, incised No. 107 and Cl 1, 3¾ins. long. Courtesy Miss J.L. Hopkins.

Right: Figure 14. Derby cat, c.1820, black and white, 2¼ins. long. Courtesy Mrs. D.G. Rice.

Figure 15. Chamberlain's Worcester cat, c.1840, 2¼ins. long, 1¾ins. high. Courtesy Miss J.L. Hopkins.

Figure 16. Group of typical Staffordshire cats.

figure 15, which has dark grey tabby markings on a pale grey body, a white front, yellow eyes and orange collar. A similar cat is in the Langton Collection and is marked inside in red enamel "Chamberlains Worcester", whereas a kitten in the same collection has only "Chamberlains" on the base.

Over the next forty years, Staffordshire cats came into prominence but they cannot be attributed to any particular factory. In a group of typical Staffordshire cats (figure 16), the pair seated on cushions are probably the most common and are to be found in sizes ranging from a few inches to 8ins. or 10ins. and in colours of yellow, black, white with black spots or lustre spots of pink, and shown in colour on the cover of this magazine.

In many cases, this same type of cat is to be found reclining on a cushion. Good Staffordshire cats cost from £15-£30 but many of these cats are being reproduced and can be bought for as little as £5.

The wide range of cats seated on cushions tends to be monotonous but the Staffordshire factories produced various alternatives. One such variant is a pottery cat bank — costing only a few pence to produce, it was presumably to encourage children to save their pennies. These are not very plentiful since the only way to get at the savings was to break the ornament. A cream one with

Figure 17. Staffordshire pottery cat bank, c.1850, 5ins.

marmalade markings (figure 17) fortunately has survived.

Figure 18 is a pincushion of a white porcelain cat holding a ball of green wool. The cushion is of mauve velvet edged with brown cord and has the original, rather coarse pins, whilst another cream coloured ornament (figure 19) is of a pottery cat with green eyes and a black nose, crouching on a wall.

Utility wares include a biscuit coloured unglazed porcelain jam pot (figure 20a) with a black and white striped cat creeping up to two blue birds

which form the finial to the lid, while (figure 20b) is a green glazed pottery milk jug with a cat forming the handle.

Another more important jug is pictured in Godden's *Illustrated Encyclopaedia of British Pottery and Porcelain,* plate 389, which is a dressed cat representing a schoolmaster, c.1860, 10½ins. high.

No doubt, many such figures were produced but not many seem to have survived the hazards of the nursery and the kitchen.

Also known to exist is a salt drier in the form of a cat — almost life-size, it would sit in the hearth serving a useful as well as ornamental purpose.

Unusual Staffordshire cats in the Langton Collection include a colourful group of a cat and kitten seated in a basket — as well as a cat dressed as a woman pushing a barrow containing kittens similarly clothed, and a companion group of a cat dressed as a man pushing a barrow containing flowers and fruit. An attractive and useful item, only 2½ins. in height, is an inkpot. This is a cat and kitten seated, the latter looking at a mouse — all are on a moulded dome forming the inkpot. These are just a few of the enormous range of cats produced in Staffordshire — a great many of which still exist.

Moving toward the end of the 19th century brings us to fairings. Although the intention was to search for cats of

Left: Figure 18. Victorian porcelain pincushion, 3¼ins. × 2¾ins.

Right: Figure 19. Staffordshire pottery cat crouching on a wall, 5ins.

a   b

Figure 23. Goss cat, arms of Wolverhampton, c.1890, 3½ins. Courtesy Miss J.L. Hopkins.

a   b   c

Figure 21. Fairings. a. "Five o'clock Tea" (Elbogen). b. "A Triple Alliance" (possibly French). c. "Good Templars" (Elbogen).

Left: Figure 20. a. Unglazed porcelain jam pot, 4ins. b. Green glazed pottery jug, 3½ins.

Figure 22. Fairings. Match strikers and pin box from various factories.

British manufacture, the well modelled groups from the German factory known as Elbogen should be included, both here and in a collection. Made by the firm of Springer and Oppenheimer of Elbogen, as Elbogen is German for elbow they used as their trade-mark a bent arm or elbow within a waisted shield, and were made largely for the English market. Usually about 3ins. high, these ornaments were produced following careful instructions from England, and the captions were in English. At the outset, the maker probably received only one penny per ornament — whereas today the cat groups fetch about £45.

Early groups (1860-65) do not have a number on their base whereas later a number was incised and, after 1880, the number was impressed. Two of the later fairings are shown in figure 21.

Some fairings can be dated from their subject content and in his book

Victorian China Fairings W.S. Bristowe records that it is possible that "The Good Templars" (figure 21c) was issued after the American Society of Abstainers, bearing that name, had launched their campaign in England in 1868. After the success of the German fairings, there were imitators. A Triple Alliance (figure 21b) is from one of these

factories — probably French — as also are the two match strikers and the Manx cat in figure 22. This type of fairing in good condition would cost today between £15-£30.

This article concludes with an example from the well-known Goss factory which produced fine quality little ornaments in an ivory tinted porcelain, each bearing a brilliant coloured coat of arms of a town or city.

Figure 23 is of a Cheshire cat c.1890. It is 3½ins. high and bears the arms of Wolverhampton. Probably selling at that time for about one shilling (5p), today it would cost about £50. On its base is a printed falcon under which is W.H. Goss. The factory opened in 1858 at the Falcon Works, Stoke on Trent, and was taken over by the Cauldon Potteries in 1934.

Other factories produced similar wares, notably Arcadian, Carltonware and Willow Art China. A Willow Art China ornament of the head of a cat bearing the arms of Merthyr Tydfil and a Carltonware seated cat with the crest of Worthing are representatives from two of the last named factories (figure 24). These are relatively cheap and can be found for between £1 and £5.

Figure 24. a. Carltonware seated cat (crest of Worthing), 2ins. b. Willow Art China cat's head (Merthyr Tydfil). c. A present from Southend-on-Sea (foreign), 1½ins.

a   b   c

A MARINE DISASTER

Johannes Christiaan Schotel (1787-1838): Dutch Fishermen and Vessel off-shore in heavy seas.

Dear Charlie,

As usual I've started my Christmas shopping early. The Overseas League is so convenient for Christie's that I hobbled round there and had a look. I must say I rather like this picture. Don't you? Remember that big old yacht your Uncle Dick used to enjoy so much? He often said it needed half a gale to really get going properly. The picture's a bit expensive but rather jolly don't you think. Shall I go along on Friday and see if I can get it for your Christmas box?

Your loving Aunt Gemmy

My Dear Aunt Jemima,

I'm afraid this is an awfully difficult letter to write and I do hope that you are not going to be offended — you really are terribly kind.

The problem is that like Uncle Richard I *do* sail and to be honest I'm sure he would be no keener on it than I am. Do you remember that frightful row when Aunt Winifred fell out with you all and left Uncle Albert's art collection (all the money there was on that side of the family) to charity? If I remember correctly Uncle Richard was executor and was so furious he sent Alcoholics Anonymous the Italian "Bacchanalian Romp" and the Vegetarians got that early Dutch butcher's shop — incidentally did the Society for Purity and Light *really* refuse that rather curious painting that Oscar Wilde paid so much for?

Anyway this marine falls very much into that category. You see, Aunt, the whole thing is quite literally a marine disaster. The wind is howling in from the right of the picture and the boat in the foreground, because it has a great flat bottom and so no grip on the sea, is having a terrible job from being blown on to that sunlit shore on the left. What has just happened is that the rope holding up the sail (technically the main halliard which raises the gaff) has just broken so that long bit of wood half way up the mast and the sail will come tumbling down on deck. That in itself should kill somebody! Uncle Dick's ketch had a big diesel engine which got him out of this sort of scrape, but this boat will be out of control in a second and will be blown sideways at the mercy of the sea and wind. In these seas (about gale force nine, I would judge) it will either capsize or be wrecked on the shore. Anyway, I'd hate to be on board.

The big boat on the left has an anchor down but the two foremost sails (the ones set square) have been caught "flat aback" so they will be increasing the strain on the anchor rope which in this sort of weather will drag anyway. The boat in the distance is beating into the wind as best she can but can carry hardly any sail so won't be able to get away from that lee shore which looms up so horribly.

Surely nobody who sails would *choose* to live with this picture. Even with every modern refinement the sea is in command in these situations and gear can fail, as we all know. It's a "there but for the grace of God go I" picture made more menacing by the super way the artist (Schotel isn't it?) has

depicted that frightening sea. Frankly giving this to a sailing man is like giving a picture of Captain Oates, staggering off to his death in an arctic blizzard, to an Eskimo.

Look, Aunt, why don't we have a nice lunch at Overton's on Thursday and then go round and see what else Christie's have in that sale? They get some super things there. Let's leave that picture to the desk and jet-bound executive who dreams of getting away from it all to the clean fresh air and the sea, and who never will.

Your loving nephew, Charles

I think Charles is a little hard on this superb action picture. In fact it was sold for £6,000. Ed.

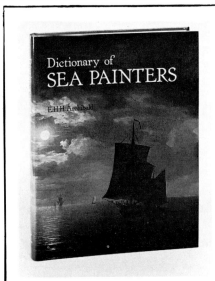

Dictionary of Sea Painters
by E.H.H. Archibald
11ins. x 8½ins. 453 pages, 700 black and white and 32 colour pages, together with 169 line drawings. ISBN 0 902028 84 7. Written by the Curator of Oil Paintings at the National Maritime Museum, this is an important addition to our art reference series and we expect that it will quickly be accepted as the standard work on the subject.

£29.50

NEWS AND VIEWS ON CATS
Members' Letters
and Reproductions

Figure 1. Foreign porcelain cat, c.1960. Grey with black stripes. 3½ins. long. Its head is detachable and can be moved round to any position. Courtesy Miss P.J. Evans.

Several people have written with queries about their cat models, but, without seeing either the animal or a photograph, it is impossible to give an accurate answer — but in reply to one member who has a green glaze pottery cat whose head is suspended on brass pins, allowing its head to nod, this is quite likely to be of German origin, late 19th century and known as a "nodder". This type was also made in Japan in 1920.

The only other one of this nodding or movable head type that I know of is of foreign origin. It is 3½ins. long and has an elongated neck on to which the detachable head can be placed at any angle (figure 1).

A cat which is reproduced in great numbers is a Staffordshire model (similar to the one illustrated on the cover of the February journal), but whereas those produced c.1850 appear to have been decorated with dark blue, black or lustre spots, and, more unusual, a mottled brown and underglaze blue cat on a yellow cushion which sold at Sotheby's in 1974 for £150 (figure 2), a member has written in to say that she has a pair of 7ins. cats "prettily decorated with flowers, consisting of a trailing flower not unlike a clematis with forget-me-nots at the edge which is also adorning the front facing leg — rather similar to the motif found on the Elbogen skirts and trousers". This is a type of decoration which I had not seen until visiting the Antique Cat Shop at

Gray's Antique Market in London recently. A cat of similar size and decoration had been in an exhibition, where it was catalogued as French early 19th century pottery and priced at £110.

Another reader tells me that he has in his bathroom some tiles designed by Nicholas Vergette for a friend who was the previous owner of the house. These tiles are in the form of two friezes, each of seven tiles across and three tiles down. On them are three tiger-like cats, one sitting, one stalking and one standing. They are in the same style as the cat by Nicholas Vergette shown in "In Search of Cats" Part 3, figure 33, being grey with black stripes on a pink and grey background. Unfortunately, they are not signed but have been authenticated by a neighbour of the same name who is a relation of Vergette.

I have recently seen a reproduction of "The Good Templars" cat fairing (figure 3) which was originally made at Elbogen. The reproduction is not as well modelled as the original, it is very shiny and the gilding crude; the price was £12.

Yet another reproduction which I purchased only three weeks ago is not only of great interest, but extremely well made. It is a black basalt cat, has pinky orange glass eyes and is an exact replica of the Wedgwood impressed model (figure 4) illustrated in "In Search of Cats" Part 3, figure 30. The measurements of my recent acquisition are 4½ins. tall and 3½ins. wide. The price paid was £2.75. The dealer who sold the cat said they were produced about twenty years ago by a firm which no longer exists, from a mould which escaped from the Wedgwood Pottery, but as the reproduced model is, I am told, one twelfth smaller than the original, it is more likely that a mould has been taken from an existing cat.

This could very easily pass as truly Wedgwood, it is so well produced, and the advice to anyone being able to purchase a cat labelled Wedgwood is — see that its measurements are larger than as stated above and that it has green eyes and not pinky orange.

I wonder how many collectors visited the Chelsea Fair (10th to 21st March) where there was a loan collection of cats? I don't know how many animals

Figure 2. Staffordshire cat mottled in tones of brown and under-glaze blue, seated on a yellow cushion. 7ins. Courtesy Sotheby's.

were exhibited, but I was dismayed to see illustrated in the catalogue part of the collection which included seven "Early Rockingham Cats 18th century", none of which was in fact from that factory. There is no record of earthenware cats being made at the Rockingham factory and the porcelain models (as illustrated in "In Search of Cats" Part 2, figures 11, 12 and 13) were not made until between 1826 and the closing of the pottery in 1842.

Acknowledgements

I would like to thank all those readers who have written to me about their cats, also all those people who have helped in providing information and photographs and not least, my husband Gwynant, who has so patiently photographed the cats from my own collection.

Mary I.N. Evans

Figure 3. Elbogen fairing "The Good Templars". A crudely made reproduction of this is selling at £12.

Figure 4. Reproduction black basalt cat of the type made by Wedgwood. 4½ins. high, 3½ins. wide.

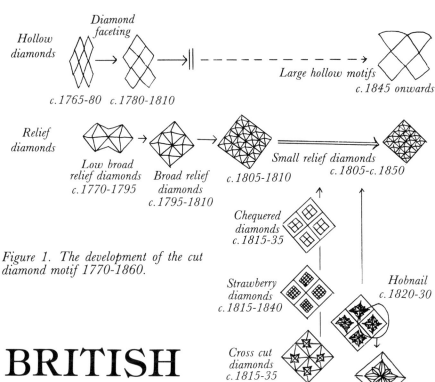

Figure 1. The development of the cut diamond motif 1770-1860.

BRITISH CUT GLASS
An Appraisal for Glass Collectors

by Jeremy T. Stedman

Figure 2. A wine glass with an ogee bowl; the stem cut with tall diamond facets. c.1775.

Figure 3. A late 18th century cruet bottle with Sheffield plate neck and lip; the glass cut in the broad shallow style. c.1785.

"For all manner of Cut-Glass. This is to inform the Nobility, Gentry, Merchants, Captains and Others, that Jerom Johnson is removed opposite the New Exchange in the Strand; where he continues to sell the finest Cut Lustres, Candlesticks, Salts, Desarts, all brilliant pollish'd, better and cheaper than has hitherto been done."
(London Evening Post 18th February 1749)

Lurking in kitchen cupboards with no longer a use on the modern dining table must be a fair number of small pieces of 18th and early 19th century cut glass. Items such as stands, small dishes, jars, cruet bottles and salts occasionally find their way into antique shops where they may remain unloved because of their chips and scratches until some knowledgeable collector snaps them up. These items were not the prestige products of the glass industry; nevertheless they were luxury goods which reflect the cutting skills and styles of their period. While the larger and more prestigious pieces of antique cut glass have become prohibitively expensive, these small items can often still be bought for a few pounds. They make a pleasing and representative collection which takes up relatively little space.

The history of glass cutting in England possibly begins in the late 17th century as there is a reference to "diamonding" in a patent taken out by John Roberts in May 1678 for cutting glass "by the motion of water and wheels". A group of simply cut scent bottles of the period c.1690-1720, identified by Edmund Launert in his book *Scent and Scent Bottles*, may be the earliest example of English cutting of glasswares other than plates of glass for mirrors.

Cut glass became popular after a sale of "very fine German Cut and Carved Glasses" held in London in 1709, which was disrupted by members of the Glass Sellers' Company. By the 1720s, helped perhaps by immigrant German craftsmen, the art of glass cutting was well established in England, being based in the capital. It is one of the mysteries of glass collecting that so little cut glass made in the first half of the 18th century survives today. No doubt its heaviness, combined with the flourishing market for cullet (the broken remains of glassware), encouraged 18th century households to part with their chipped or old fashioned pieces of cut glass. There are hardly any pieces of cut glass that can safely be dated earlier than about 1750, a fact which has hindered a

Left: Figure 4. A heavy glass caster or pepper pot cut with relief diamonds and prismatic steps. Star cut under the base. c.1810-1820.

Right: Figure 5. A fine water jug with prismatic grooves above panels of relief diamonds and strawberry diamonds. c.1825-1830.

Below: Figure 6. A straight sided decanter cut in typically horizontal arrangement with flat flutes above strawberry diamonds above printies above comb flutes. c.1825.

proper understanding of the early development of English cutting.

The cutting on the very early wares was probably restricted to shallow step cutting or fluting, shallow diamonds and rim scalloping. Certainly in 1722 Lady Grisell Baillie noticed among other things a "high scaloped glass" in the middle of the table laid for dessert at the dinner party of "Lord Carlile".

By the 1750s considerable progress had been made with various broad motifs being employed such as flutes, hollow diamonds and then hexagons, shallow sliced motifs such as lunar slices and also various rim cuts. Some broad relief motifs such as relief diamonds and relief triangles were also used.

A few salient features of 18th century cut glass and much glass cut in the first decade of the 19th century are useful if the collector is readily to identify a piece. It is of course always difficult to generalise but these features are as follows:

1. The metal of 18th century cut glass is dense and relatively heavy in the hand. It is almost always tinged with grey to a greater or lesser extent and it is never pure and "white" as is more modern metal. The heavy greyish metal persisted well into the early 19th century. Pictures and descriptions are inadequate and the collector must handle authentic specimens in order to get the feel of old glass.

2. The rule of thumb pertaining to the presence or absence of a pontil scar does not apply to 18th and 19th century cut glass. Except on drinking glasses the pontil scar was usually polished out, frequently as part of the

pattern. Not until about 1810 was the pontil scar under cut drinking glasses regularly ground away.

3. Motifs on 18th century cut glass are generally broad and shallow. Relief diamonds tend to be broad and low unlike later small sharp diamonds used in bands or fields. Central stars are broad and shallow with six or twelve rays unlike 19th century stars which are deeper and more complex. When small motifs were used they were often part of a larger overall design. 18th century cutting is never fussy as is some of the 19th century.

4. The scalloping of rims is a common feature of 18th century cut glass. Regular lobes and broad zig-zags were used and more elaborate edges resembling the moulded rims of contemporary porcelain and creamware appeared after 1750. Fan cutting came in towards the end of the century as a development of the trefoil

edge. Notched and scalloped rims continued into the early 19th century.

5. 18th and early 19th century cut glass should show signs of wear. This feature is most important and is all too often ignored by collectors in the quest for a perfect piece. Minor chips which would be unacceptable on a drinking glass are accepted on a piece of cut glass and cut rims which show no signs of wear should be regarded with suspicion as they may have been trimmed later. Scuffing often appears on the edges of relief motifs as well as on the rim, the sharp diamond motifs on cut glass after about 1810 being particularly prone to bruising. The most important wear to look for is at the point of contact with the table. This should take the form of numbers of minute *irregular* scratches, giving a matt slightly rough appearance on heavily worn areas. Scratches and scuffs may also appear on the upper surfaces of dishes which have been stacked or used as stands.

The exact dating of much 18th century cut glass is extremely difficult. Diamond faceting on glasses and broad cutting on glasswares continued until about 1810 having changed little since the middle decades of the 18th century. The reasons for the persistence of rather shallow cutting were technological rather than financial. The glass excise tax, imposed in 1746 and doubled in 1777, has been blamed for the stagnation in the development of cutting but this can be disputed. The scarcity of cut glass made before the excise and the fact that so little cut glass can be firmly attributed to Ireland where the excise did not apply (until 1825) means that evidence for theories is rather slim. In the late 18th century there was probably little to choose from between English and Irish cut glass despite competition from the growing Irish glass industry which

Left: Figure 7. An Anglo/Irish footed bowl c.1800-1805. Note the retained use of shallow cutting combined with a band of relief diamonds. Courtesy Sotheby's.

Right: Figure 8. A mid-19th century cut glass chandelier. The chandelier was the most fabulous product of the late 18th and early 19th century glass cutter. Courtesy Christie's South Kensington.

Below: Figure 9. A pair of covered sugars and stands, heavily cut with relief diamonds and flutes. c.1810-1820. Courtesy Delomosne and Son Ltd.

benefited from freedom from the excise and also from freedom of trade, granted in an act of 1780. The effects of the excise were probably less than have been supposed: it certainly did not hinder the development of deep cutting in the early 19th century. The real restraints on 18th century glass cutters were the slowness of the hand or water powered wheels and to some extent the dictates of the neo-classical style which called for restrained shallow cutting.

The broad, rather shallow style of cutting persisted until after 1800 by which time the graceful neo-classical style was giving way to the Regency style of glass with its formal shapes and heavier forms. The real impetus for a change in cutting came with the advent of steam powered cutting wheels which, according to G. Bernard Hughes, were introduced shortly before 1810. Fast smooth running steam powered wheels made possible the cutting of deep, sharp V shaped grooves which were the basis of the most popular motifs used from about 1810 such as relief diamonds, blazes and prismatic lines. This type of deep mitre-cutting was frequently combined with flat flutes which continued to be popular after 1810. Powered wheels also enabled cutters to execute some very extravagant patterns such as convex pillar fluting or reeding which was used on some luxury wares from about 1815-1835.

The small sharp relief diamond used in wide bands or in fields had developed from the earlier broad diamond and it was the key motif in the early 19th century. Variations on the relief diamond such as hobnail and strawberry diamonds appeared from about 1815 and these are shown in figure 1. On the best wares these variations were carefully executed but soon glass cutters tended to turn to simple cross hatching to achieve a

similar but less effective result. The small relief diamond was popular until the early 1850s by which time cutters were returning to shallow faceting and other broad shallow designs.

Collectors are helped by the existence of several sets of patterns from the 19th century, the most accessible of which are those kept by Samuel Miller, the foreman cutter at the famous Waterford glasshouse. These are reproduced in *Irish Glass* by Phelps Warren and are of the 1820-1830 period.

From patterns and surviving examples it is evident that most cutting between about 1810 and 1830 utilised bands of small motifs divided by horizontal grooves or prismatic lines. Motifs such as diamonds were used in bands or sometimes in fields covering

the entire surface of the vessel. Even prismatic lines were occasionally used to decorate the whole of an article. Scalloping continued after 1810 though the serrated or saw tooth edge was becoming popular. Stars appeared more frequently under decanters and quality tablewares after about 1810 and these were deeper and more complex than earlier stars. By the early 1840s stars with thirty-two points were in use.

Shortly before 1830 vertically arranged patterns began to appear and some attempt was made in the later 1830s and 1840s to follow the plainer, more formal cutting exemplified by the Biedermeier style. Plain fluting extending down the length of the article was the principal feature of this "broad flute" style of cutting. In addition to flutes, large shallow ovals

Figure 10. Six cut finger bowls and wine glass coolers, the earliest being the bottom left-hand example which may be very late 18th century. The others are variously c.1810-1840. Courtesy Delomosne and Son Ltd.

also became popular from the 1840s. Elaborate cutting of glass died hard in England but by 1851 it was obsolete; a truth brought sharply home by the bankruptcy of George Gatchell at the time of the Great Exhibition at which his Waterford glasshouse was exhibiting clear cut flint glass. Osler's crystal fountain, the centrepiece of the Great Exhibition, was really an ambassador from the past representing a pinnacle of achievement for English cutting skills.

The demise of elaborately cut glass was ironically stimulated by the repeal of the glass excise tax in 1845 which freed glassmakers from supervision, enabling them to experiment with new types of glass, particularly coloured types which did not require elaborate cutting. The rise of pressed glass also adversely affected the market for quality cut glass since it "cheapened" cutting by imitating it at a fraction of the cost. In addition there was a revival of interest in Venetian glass in the 1840s and early 1850s which speeded up the decline from favour of formal cut glass. Apsley Pellatt's descriptions of Venetian methods in *Curiosities of Glassmaking*, published in 1849, were probably more influential in turning glassmakers away from traditional cutting than John Ruskin's condemnation of cutting in *The Stones of Venice* published in 1852/53. It was not until the end of the century that elaborate cutting was resurrected in the so-called "brilliant" style.

To return to the task of collecting cut glass, the collector should be aware of the fact that reproductions of early 19th century cut glass abound. Most of these were never intended to deceive but as prices rise more and more will be passed off as genuine. Most reproductions can be distinguished from genuine pieces by their poor shapes, lack of wear and modern looking metal. Handles are a particular giveaway as reproductions usually have handles attached from the bottom whereas on genuine examples the upper terminal is thicker than the lower terminal. The collector should handle as many genuine pieces as he can so that he will gain the knack of being able to reject spurious pieces within minutes if not seconds.

At the present time many small pieces of 18th and early 19th century cut glass are underpriced and should be bought now. Larger items such as jugs and decanters are already costly but are I believe cheap when related to the amount of workmanship that went into producing them.

With regard to actual prices it can be said that cruet bottles, salts and other small items are still available for under £15 while larger items such as decanters, jugs and dishes frequently leave little or no change out of £100, especially if they are in fine condition and pre-1830 in date. It must be said that prices vary widely from place to place and with such a diversity of objects it is impossible to give a generalised view. What can be said is that the price of pre-1850 cut glass will continue to rise though those wares that are already expensive will probably rise more slowly in price than the smaller, undervalued pieces.

Figure 11. A selection of cut glassware with prismatic stepping and serrated edges, c.1820-25. Note the use of flat flutes on the drinking glass and the star cutting underneath its foot which was until about 1840 used only on some top quality cut drinking glasses. Courtesy Delomosne and Son Ltd.

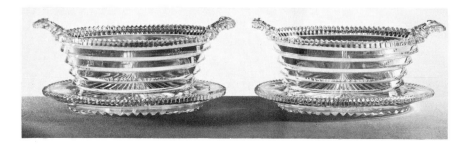

A set of sixteen Halifax bell-metal weights ranging from 56lb. to ½dr., inscribed Borough of Halifax, 1894, maker's mark De Grave & Co., London, the smaller weights in fitted mahogany case. £1,600.

Right: A Bradford brass standard yard measure, inscribed City of Bradford, with turned lignum vitae handles, maker's mark De Grave Short & Co. Ltd., London, in fitted mahogany case. £260.

Right: A Bradford bell-metal and brass 56lb. beam, inscribed City of Bradford, maker's mark W & T Avery Ltd., Birmingham, in glazed wooden case. £180.

Left: Another, similar, Morley. £140.

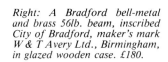

A set of sixteen Huddersfield bell-metal weights ranging from 56lb. to ½dr., inscribed Borough of Huddersfield, 1879, the smaller weights in fitted mahogany case. £1,000.

Left: One of a set of seven Leeds brass-bound copper conical measures ranging from three gallons to half-pint inscribed City of Leeds, maker's mark De Grave & Co., London, in fitted pine cane. £600.

A set of seven Halifax cylindrical bell-metal measures ranging from gallon to half-gill, inscribed Halifax, His Grace the Duke of Leeds, Lord of the Manor of Wakefield, 1824, maker's mark, Bate, London, Maker of the Exchequer Standards, in fitted pine case. £1,000.

Right: A set of thirty Halifax decimal bell-metal weights ranging from 30kg. to 1mg., inscribed County Borough of Halifax, in fitted mahogany case. £1,000.

Below: A set of three Dewsbury brass conical measures comprising four gallons, two gallons and one gallon, inscribed Borough of Dewsbury 1893, maker's name De Grave & Co., London. £650

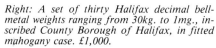

Right: A set of ten West Riding cylindrical bell-metal measures with turned wooden and ivory handles and inscribed West Riding of Yorkshire 1824, ranging from half-bushel to quarter-gill, quarter-gill dated 1879. £1,800.

A set of eight West Riding bell-metal cylindrical measures ranging from gallon to quarter-gill, inscribed West Riding of Yorkshire 1880 (sold with photostat copy of indenture dated 1880. £620.

Below right: One of a set of eleven Halifax brass conical measures ranging from five gallon to quarter-gill, inscribed Corpn. of Halifax 1893, maker's mark Doyle & Son, London. £1,350.

A set of four Halifax bell-metal weights ranging from 50lb. to 5lb., inscribed County Borough of Halifax, in fitted mahogany case with maker's mark De Grave & Co. £450.

One of a set of eight Huddersfield brass conical measures ranging from five gallons to one pint, inscribed Borough of Huddersfield, maker's mark De Grave & Co., London, in two fitted mahogany cases bearing inscribed plaques. £1,050.

Right: A set of eight West Riding bell-metal cylindrical measures ranging from 4fl.oz. to 1fl.dr., in mahogany case bearing brass plaque inscribed West Riding of Yorkshire Standard Apothecary's Measures, maker's mark De Grave Short & Co., London, dated 1879. £300.

A Wakefield 56lb. bell-metal beam scale measure inscribed City of Wakefield, in fitted mahogany case with brass inscription plaque. £250.

A set of sixteen West Riding bell-metal weights ranging from 56lb. to 1dr., inscribed West Riding County Council, Sowerby District, 1908, in fitted oak case. £1,000.

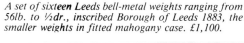

A set of sixteen Leeds bell-metal weights ranging from 56lb. to ½dr., inscribed Borough of Leeds 1883, the smaller weights in fitted mahogany case. £1,100.

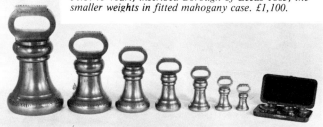

A set of fourteen Leeds cylindrical bell-metal measures ranging from bushel to one-sixth of a gill, inscribed City of Leeds 1906, and three later inscribed 1965, maker's mark W. & T. Avery Ltd., Birmingham. Unsold.

Figure 1. A selection of tiles, 1895-1925.

Pilkington's Tile and Pottery Co. Ltd.

by

A.J. Cross

Today, the firm of Pilkington's is known internationally as a manufacturer of high quality ceramic wall and floor tiles; what is not generally realised by the public at large is that for a little over thirty years the company also produced a decorative art pottery which won international acclaim and is now eagerly sought by discerning collectors.

Pilkington's Tile and Pottery Co. Ltd. was formed in 1891 at Clifton Junction, near Manchester, as a result of a chance discovery of a red marl suitable for tile making during the sinking of a new shaft by the Clifton and Kearsley Coal Company. The colliery was owned by four Pilkington brothers, related to the family making glass at St. Helens. To manage the new company, the Pilkingtons recruited the services of William Burton, then a chemist at Messrs. Josiah Wedgwood and Sons. Burton designed the plant and in 1893 production began.

Initially production was concentrated on tile making (figure 1), but as the company expanded potters were recruited and a small number of wares decorated with glaze effects only was made. From an early stage Burton sought the advice of and used the work of gifted artists, such as Lewis F. Day, Walter Crane and C.F.A. Voysey, who contributed greatly to the company's early successes.

In 1900 Burton took a small party of his artists to the Paris International Exhibition where Pilkingtons also exhibited floor and wall tiles, fireplaces and hearths. This visit enabled the artists to observe the then current trends in ceramics as developed by companies on the Continent. By now Burton was assisted by his brother, Joseph, who was responsible for the several thousands of

glaze trials, many of which were used to decorate vases and bowls which were shown at the first exhibition devoted solely to Pilkington's Lancastrian Pottery and held in 1904 at Graves Gallery, London. Glaze decorations were of four main types: crystalline, opalescent, textured and transmutation.

With crystalline glazes various effects were achieved. They could be filled with myriads of glittering crystals resembling the mineral sunstone; they could form radiating groups; or they could produce crystals, fine lines or patches, depending on the flow of the glaze on the pot. These glazes were known respectively as Sunstone, Starry Crystalline and Fiery Crystalline (figure 2).

Opalescent glazes were produced from leadless glazes fired at low temperatures. Transparent glazes were prone to develop opalescent patches, but careful research produced glazes in which the opalescence appeared as layers, streaks, curdled patches (figure 3), feathered or

Figure 3. Opalescent curdled glaze c.1905, 5ins. high.

Figure 2. Fiery crystalline glaze, 1908, 5ins. high.

Right: Figure 4. Vase in silver and copper lustre, with the legend "Ave Maria Gratia Plena", painted by Gordon M. Forsyth, 1908, 11½ins. high.

A lustre plaque painted by Richard Joyce
from a design by Walter Crane, 1918, 19ins. diameter.
Courtesy Richard Dennis.

Figure 5. Lustre vase by Richard Joyce, 1924, 11¼ins. high.

Figure 6. Silver lustre vase by William S. Mycock, 1913, 8ins. high.

Figure 7. Vase in copper lustre painted by Charles Cundall, 1907, 7ins. high.

clouded colour. These glazes are usually fired on terracotta which enhances the effect.

Of the textured glazes the most important is that known as eggshell. These were matt leadless glazes in which the active ingredient was lime, magnesia or zinc oxide. The usual colouring oxides were used, the final colour depending on the basic oxide used.

The term transmutation glaze was given to the effect produced when the actions of the fire gave two or more coloured glazes on the same piece, and usually gave a splashed or mottled effect.

Lancastrian pottery proved to be extremely successful and decorative glaze effects were soon followed in 1906 by the introduction of hand-painted lustreware. The lustre was produced by reduction firing, a technique first developed in the Middle East during the 10th century, and quite different from those used to make Staffordshire lustres and Wedgwood lustre ware. In the main, decoration was by silver lustre, although designs in copper lustre were also done. The artists decorating lustre ware were headed by Gordon M. Forsyth (figure 4), and included Richard Joyce (figure 5), William S. Mycock (figure 6) and Charles Cundall (figure 7), later to be elected to the Royal Academy. The firing process was very erratic; whole kilns would be lost and even successful firings produced different effects within the kiln. Thus, fine lustreware would have good iridescent lustre well developed over the whole of the piece. So successful was the pottery that, following a visit by King George V in 1913, the company was awarded a Royal Warrant and henceforth the pottery became known as Royal Lancastrian.

The period following World War 1 resulted in a decline in the demand for

Figure 8. Lapis jar designed and decorated by Gladys M. Rogers, 7¼ins. high.

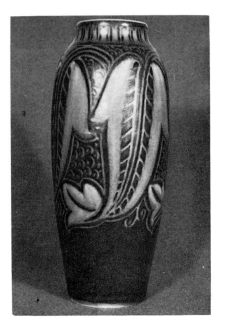

Figure 9. Sgraffito vase decorated by William S. Mycock, 1932, 7¾ins. high.

high quality decorative pottery and, as a result, sales of lustre pottery fell, apart from which several of the artists left. Those that remained carried on and new forms of decorative ware, less expensive to make, appeared.

An important innovation was the introduction of a new glaze effect known as Lapis, taking its name from the lapis lazuli stone. In this underglaze colours were used, covered with a lime based eggshell glaze. During the firing the two reacted, producing a diffused pattern on the surface of the glaze, the effect being partly determined by the flow of the glaze which itself was affected by the shape of the pots. Designs were drawn using simple broad brushwork, the main exponent being Gladys Rodgers (figure 8). In addition sgraffito, scratched and slip modelled designs were also used as decorative techniques. The sgraffito vase illustrated (figure 9) has the design carved through a blue glaze, the whole subsequently covered by a green glaze. With scratched designs, the pattern was scratched in outline on the glaze and the lines enhanced, usually with cobalt blue (figure 10). Other wares would have the design modelled in slip before being glazed (figure 11). Despite these innovations, the pottery department continued to lose money and subsequently closed, the last firing taking place in 1938.

From 1948 to 1957 Royal Lancastrian pottery was revived under the direction of William Barnes, an artist potter whose work was admired by Pilkington's directors. Barnes was assisted by Eric Bridges and John Brannan (figure 12) and the style of this new ware differed from that of the previous era mainly using the sgraffito technique. Again the economic problems of running a pottery department arose, Barnes left and once the outstanding orders were completed the department closed.

Left: Figure 10. Scratched decoration by William S. Mycock. The design is outlined in cobalt and coloured naturalistically. 1936. 8½ins. high.

Below: Figure 11. Slip modelled vase design and decorated by Richard Joyce c.1930. 7ins. high.

Right: Figure 12. Sgraffito vase decorated by John Brannan c.1950, 9½ins. high.

With Pilkington's the products are so varied as to suit the pocket of all collectors.

Tiles	£2- £10
Glaze effects	£10- £50
Lustreware	£50-£300
depending on size and condition	
Lapis ware	£10- £50
Sgraffito, scratched and	
slip moulded	£20-£100
Post-war	£10- £30

The prices quoted are for average sized pieces up to 8ins., rarities can cost much more.

The examples illustrated will be on view at an exhibition of Royal Lancastrian Pottery and Tiles to be held from 4th to 27th June at the Upper Chenil Gallery, 183 Kings Road, London. An authoritative book *Pilkington's Royal Lancastrian Pottery and Tiles* by A.J. Cross will be published by Richard Dennis to coincide with the exhibition.

SALEROOM REPORT

George III silver coffee pot, London 1804, maker Samuel & Robert Hennell, 30oz. £300. Capes Dunn & Co.

Lead characters from Charles Dickens (left), £22, and Lewis Carroll, £55, 86mm scale. Phillips.

Left. Regency mahogany sofa table, satinwood banding, brass inlaid frieze containing two drawers, brass inlaid legs, c.1820, 2ft.4½ins. high x 5ft.8½ins. wide. £1,150. Sotheby's.

Right. 19th century Irish folding top parquetry games table. £550. Phillips of Leeds.

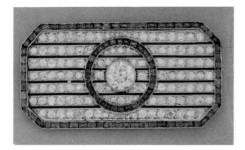

Figure 1. Edwardian diamond, sapphire and enamelled plaque brooch. £4,600 (28th April 1981). Another brooch of identical design with onyx, diamond and black enamel, probably by Lacloche, is expected to make £3,500-£4,000 on 30th June.

Figure 2. Ruby and diamond Edwardian earrings, sold on 28th April 1981 for £3,000.

Figure 3. Step-cut diamond ring weighing 3.11 carats flanked by baguettes. £6,500 (24th March 1981).

Right. Figure 4. Very small fine quality emerald diamond Georgian brooch. Sold on 24th March 1981 for £1,600.

Figure 5. Georgian diamond bracelet sold on 28th April 1981 for £10,000.

Figure 6. Fabergé small circular gold brooch set with a peridot bordered by rose diamonds with white enamel border and open-work decoration. Sold for £1,200 on 25th March 1980 (would have fetched £250 if by anyone else).

JEWELLERY
by Peter Beaumont
Phillips

Figure 7. Mid-19th century Holbeinesque pendant set with an oval garnet cabochon with pale green chrysolites and green enamelled decoration. £920.

It is interesting to note that with retail sales of new, good quality, jewellery at an all time low, demand for fine period items, whether antique or 20th century, continues to break all records. The accent at the moment is on pretty, well-designed, good condition pieces in all combinations of gemstones, but particularly sapphire or ruby and diamond (figures 1 and 2) from all periods right up to the Second World War. At present such names as Fabergé, Cartier, Boucheron, Lacloche etc. practically guarantee that any nice item, whether bracelet, earrings, ring, necklet or even brooch, will make a top price in the saleroom.

It seems likely that this situation is going to continue for some time. Inflation makes it necessary for one section of the community to be realising their portable assets, encouraged by the relatively high prices fetched at auction, and for another section to be hedging against further inflation, with gemstones and jewellery a particularly attractive proposition, thereby creating a very healthy market (but largely bypassing the conventional retailer with his very high costs and therefore large profit margins). In this country, where we pay a high rate of tax on earned income from a very low threshold, the capital gains tax concessions on "chattels" is an added assurance of stability.

In a short article it is difficult to do more than just sketch the outlines of the more favourable areas for the investor. Most people will have read of the chaotic state of the diamond market and it may be interesting to consider the best ways of taking advantage of the situation. While it is now possible to buy a reasonable quality brilliant cut diamond solitaire setting for a sensible price in the salerooms, the real weakness is in the fancy cut stones (emerald cuts, pendeloques, marquises, etc.). On 24th March Phillips sold a ring set with a good quality step-cut diamond weighing 3.11 carats (figure 3) for £6,500 which, after allowing for the cost of the mount, means a retail price of about £2,000 per carat!

In the same sale, a pair of certificated white brilliants of good clarity weighing 1.62 carats and 1.57 carats sold for £3,600 and £3,200 respectively, making fine investments for somebody as, with De Beer's substantial resources and marketing expertise, prices are bound to recover in the fairly near future.

In the field of coloured stones, good rubies and sapphires have held their prices well, due to scarcity, but, because of a big influx of poorer stones, the emerald market has dropped substantially for all except the best Columbian stones and it is possible to buy sizeable, pleasing emeralds at a few hundred pounds per carat usually mounted as rings, etc., with diamonds.

When it comes to buying jewellery for investment, from whatever period, the rules vary very little in principle. Always buy the best quality you can afford; go for tasteful design, good workmanship and quality stones. The professional buyer will examine stones for clarity with a 10x loupe but he will use a lower power, wider field instrument, usually of 6x magnification, to inspect any piece from several points of view. Firstly he will assure himself that the piece is "right", i.e. not reproduction. Then he will look at the condition of the item and carefully examine the reverse for signs of modification or repair, which will show as lines of solder of a different colour — all too often lead solder, like an electrician uses, which will have a marked effect on price, particularly when re-selling.

Sometimes pieces have been modified by adding complete clusters of stones or collets containing large coloured stones, often quite prettily, but long after manufacture and quite out of context.

Many Georgian and Victorian pieces come on the market which have been made up out of a series of clusters, perhaps from a tiara or other larger piece. If carried out properly and fairly contemporarily, this does not always have too bad an effect on value, but great care should be taken.

Perhaps I should stress that it is always possible to get qualified advice when viewing for auction. At Phillips there are always specialists available to help and auction house staff are relatively unbiased. With luck one may even be able to speak to the cataloguer of a particular piece if there is an important query.

When buying Victorian or Georgian jewellery, always look for the bi-metallic construction, silver front, gold back, as in figures 4 and 5. The actual demarcation will vary, but should always be clearly visible. Avoid pieces which have been replated all white or all yellow as this can conceal a multitude of evils.

With 20th century period jewellery prospective buyers should again beware of reproductions — there are some very clever ones about. Beware of any piece that has visibly been cast without adequate finishing (on the reverse). Catalogue descriptions such as "in the art deco style" or "thought to be by Cartier, Boucheron" etc., often indicate possible fakes. Look for the actual name and/or individual number engraved on the piece. Fabergé items (figure 6) are the major exception to this rule, many of the best fakes also having perfect workmasters' and other marks.

Having slandered fakes and imitations, perhaps I had better add that there are some very fine and valuable reproduction pieces on the market. Much of the work of Giuliano and Castellani were reproductions (of superb quality) of Renaissance, Etruscan and ancient styles and are works of art in themselves and command impressive prices. Phillips sold a mid-19th century Holbeinesque pendant set with a cabochon garnet and chrysolites (figure 7) recently for nearly £1,000 and there was a similar item in the recent Princely Magnificence Renaissance Jewellery Exhibition at the Victoria and Albert Museum.

And if none of these categories appeals there is the thought that all pearls and cultured pearls can be bought cheaply in the saleroom, as can be most modern brooches and clips which are often sold below "break".

A final word of caution. Beware of the (apparent) bargain!

AUCTION FEATURE
Burrows & Day
Ashford, Kent
3rd June

Left: Royal Doulton yellow glazed "Morrisian" pattern jug decorated with brown transfer of figures in medieval style dress on a terrace, 8½ins. high. £55. Right: Doulton Lambeth silver mounted brown glazed stoneware bulbous jug decorated in relief with portrait medallions and mottoes, London 1888 hallmark, 7½ins. £130.

"The Battle between Crib and Molineaux fought at Thissleton Gap Sept. 28th 1811", coloured etching published by Walker and Knight, 7 Cornhill, 9ins. × 13ins. £46.

Above: 18th century delft beer stein painted in green, blue, yellow and mauve with a woman in a landscape, domed pewter lid, inscribed "M.S.R.V. 1784", ball thumbpiece, 10ins. high (chipped). £460.

Left: wine cruet, supports with bead mounts and three shell and mask cartouches, 16½ins. high, and three slice and hobnail cut decanters, 9¾ins. high, and stoppers. £160.

Right: Dieppe wall mirror, oval bevelled plate 10ins. × 12ins., gilt slip, contained in ivory frame well carved with a ground of leaves, coat of arms with inscription "Montioye St. Denys", cupids, smaller coats of arms, bearded masks and cornucopiae of flowers, 34ins. × 22½ins. overall. £480.

Tom Cribb, coloured engraving by George Hunt after J. Jackson, published May 1842 by J. Moore, Upper St. Martins Lane, London, 15¼ins. × 11¾ins. £38.

Left: French miniature carriage timepiece, white enamel dial, eight day movement, brass case with moulded columns and bevelled glass panels, 3½ins. £115. Right: French carriage clock, white enamel dial, eight day half hour striking movement, brass and bevelled plate glass case, 4¾ins. high. £155.

Left: silver mounted glass claret jug, baluster body with heavy slice, hobnail and star cuttings, plain silver mounts, Birmingham 1902, 9ins. high. £240. Right: late Victorian silver mounted glass claret jug, waisted body with slice, diamond and fan cuttings, plain silver mounts, Birmingham 1899, 9¾ins. high. £125.

THE REVOLVING BOOKCASE MYSTERY — A TALE OF THE TABARD INN

by John Andrews
author of
The Price Guide to Antique Furniture

Right: Figure 2. "Queen Anne" cabriole-legged rush-seated corner chair from Willesley. Stained green and designed by Shaw, probably in the mid-1860s. Reproduced from Richard Norman Shaw *by Andrew Saint, published by Yale University Press, New Haven and London. These chairs are now at High Hall, Dorset.*

Richard Norman Shaw (1831-1912) was possibly the most celebrated of the Victorian domestic architects. Apart from his churches, the striped Scotland Yard on the Thames, chunks of Regent Street and a host of solid commercial buildings, he designed and "improved"

Figure 1. "Gothic" bookcase by Richard Norman Shaw, shown at the 1862 Exhibition. Now in the Victoria and Albert Museum after "discovery" in his daughter's convent in 1962.

many large houses and dominated domestic styling for a couple of decades. He was avidly copied and his protégés became the nucleus of the Arts and Crafts Movement. He was industrious, Scottish, family-minded (his brother founded the Shaw-Savill Line) but civilised and humorous. People liked him. Despite his single-minded purposefulness, he avoided the austerity of Voysey and the political involvement of Morris. The confidence of the balanced relationships with his clients that led to his success clearly came from inner strengths of character and humour. Is it possible that this busy and famous man could have designed bookcases for a lending library?

Shaw was as concerned with interior decoration and furnishing as he was with outer style. Yet little furniture directly attributable to him survives or can be identified. He started off designing in the Gothic manner, went over to "Old English" or Kent-Sussex Wealden style of tile-hanging and half-timbering, progressed — if that is the word — to "Queen Anne" and finished up with Edwardian Classical. So one would expect a great range of furniture in a variety of styles to be associated with him. It is not the case. His most famous piece — see figure 1 — is the grand Gothic bookcase in the Victoria and Albert Museum, illustrated with monotonous regularity in every book on the period and by everyone seeking to deal with the Reformed Gothic Movement.

But the fact is that Shaw rapidly tired of this piece, designed to accommodate his own papers and effects in his own office at a time when he was relatively impoverished. He gave it to

his daughter's convent where it turned up, forgotten, in the early 1960s. It is remarkable for its decoration, its Japanese motifs and the quality of workmanship — by his cabinet maker James Forsyth — compared with the other Gothic exhibits at the 1862 Exhibition which were not nearly of the same standard. And there it rests, a great isolated monument, not intended for domestic use.

Shaw never abandoned the Gothic style entirely for pieces like settles and sideboards but by 1870 the "Gothic" in his architecture became tempered by a "vernacular" or "Old English" style that he and his friend William Eden Nesfield (1835-1888) picked up travelling in Kent and Sussex. The artist J.C. Horsley commissioned Shaw to extend his country house, Willesley, at Cranbrook in Kent, now the Willesley Hotel on the Hawkhurst to Maidstone road. It is a staggering hotch-potch of an extension which no modern Planning Authority would allow. Shaw's timbered, tiled, Japanese-incised decoration bears no relation to the original Georgian house at all. Yet it is impressive in its way and many other commissions for Shaw followed its completion.

For Willesley we are told that Shaw designed some chairs — see figure 2 — and, here again, the jaw drops at the sight of them. They are corner chairs, stained green, with rush seats. Shaw liked the masculine corner chair and used it himself in his office. But it is the style which takes the viewer aback; it is "Queen Anne" with cabriole front leg, pierced splats and features of 1720-1740 in a much less robust form. The green stain and

rush seats may have been the influence of William Morris's "Sussex" chairs, but the style is unmistakably from the Queen Anne—George I and II period known under the generic title of "Queen Anne". And this was in the mid-1860s.

Shaw's taste was clearly quite eclectic, for from 1870 he also designed the great house, Cragside, near Newcastle on Tyne, for the armaments manufacturer, Sir William Armstrong. In the library at Cragside Shaw placed chairs in the Anglo-Japanese style, with ebonised turned galleries of spindles typical of the Aesthetic Movement. He patronised the famous dealer Duveen in his early days, obtaining antique pieces from him for his clients or having pieces made up or modified to suit the interiors he was providing. Duveen was already shipping "antiques" to America and was careful to separate the tasteful pieces for the discerning Shaw from those intended for his less knowledgeable American clients.

In 1877 the entrepreneur Jonathan Carr commissioned Shaw to work on the first Garden Suburb in Britain — Bedford Park, Chiswick. It was an ambitious scheme which eventually bankrupted Carr. He never fully paid Shaw his fee. Visitors to Bedford Park will now admire the pleasant leafy roads and calm "Queen Anne" red brick styling of the houses with their Dutch gables and brick or terra cotta mouldings. Carr had already involved the famous "Anglo-Japanese" architect and designer, E.W. Godwin, in his scheme but it was to Shaw that the main work fell, particularly the group of buildings adjacent to Turnham Green station — St. Michael's Church and the Tabard Inn.

The church, currently appealing for a £150,000 restoration fund, was completed by Maurice B. Adams (1849-1933) but was, for the major part, designed by Shaw. The Tabard Inn, its "rival in the field of spiritual refreshment" seems to have been entirely by Shaw, although Jonathan Carr's workmen executed it, with "limp brickwork and window detailing" in the objection of Shaw's recent biographer, Andrew Saint. (It is difficult for the layman to understand this comment, for the building is robust, with strong glazing bars.) The area became a focus for aesthetes and artists. Even today, the headquarters of the Victorian Society are to be found in Priory Gardens, hard by St. Michael's Vicarage.

The Tabard Inn was not just a pub, which it remains to this day (see figure 3). One end was a "stores" of the co-operative Civil Service type. There was a "coffee and commercial room" and a meeting room. And

Figure 3. The Tabard Inn, Bedford Park, as it is now. Note that the pub occupies the near right-hand end; the further part of the building contained the stores. The "meeting room" is on the first floor and is still used as such.

somewhere — it is something of a mystery where — within this building there must have been a lending library, perhaps within the meeting room.

The interior of the pub contained tiles by William de Morgan and by Walter Crane. These may still be seen by the visitor, but the other interior furnishings were changed by the brewers in the 1950s. Thus the original interior, where the aesthetes and adherents of the Arts and Crafts Movement met over a restorative pint, is not now visible. Shaw almost certainly had some hand in the interior decoration and his assistant, E.J. May (1853-1941) who lived in Bedford Park briefly and designed the vicarage, may well have had some part in it as well. In the Victoria and Albert Museum there is a rush-seated chair — see figure 4 — described rather cautiously as being designed "in the office of Richard Norman Shaw" for the Tabard Inn, Bedford Park. It provides a fascinating comparison with the green Willesley chair of figure 2. It is an Arts and Crafts Movement chair of distinct "Queen Anne" derivation, wholly suitable for the milieu for which it was designed. The back is very like the rather stiff Queen Anne chairs of c.1700 illustrated as item 122 in the *Price Guide to*

Figure 4. Oak chair from the Tabard Inn, designed "in the office of Richard Norman Shaw". There were also two-backed settees in the same style. The back is typically "Queen Anne" if a bit rigid; the lower half is typically Arts and Crafts Movement, particularly the rush seat and the incised ringing on the turned front legs. Said to be made by William Morris & Co.
Courtesy: Victoria and Albert Museum

Antique Furniture (see figure 5). The baluster-turned arm supports are similarly in period. But the Arts and Crafts version of the "pad" foot on the front legs is wholly late 19th century, as is the incised turned ringing on the legs and the flat stretchers between them.

This Tabard Inn chair was probably designed around 1879-80 and is therefore much later than the Willesley chair. Rush seating had become almost *de rigueur* for the Arts and Crafts designers, following William Morris's example, but the "Queen Anne" style, used by Shaw for the Willesley chair so much earlier on, had not so far been a feature of the Movement. Clearly, the Tabard Inn chair is more restrained and severe than the curvaceous Willesley piece, but it is not at all inconceivable that Shaw himself might have designed it as he did the green-painted pews in the church opposite. After all, his architectural designs had by this time become much more restrained and classical, particularly for town work. And he was clearly fond of the style, which was much more suitable for cities than the sprawling, vernacular "Old English" used for the country.

So what are we to make of the Tabard Inn bookcases, the subject of our mystery? The two examples illustrated here show distinct differences, much as the buildings designed by Shaw for Bedford Park show qualitative differences occasioned by cheaper execution of an originally more expensive and better design.

Carr's workmen cut corners with Shaw's house designs to reduce costs; did the same thing happen in the library?

The first example — see figure 6 — is made, as one would expect, in oak. It stands about 6ft.6ins. high and has a distinctive "Queen Anne" roof, tiled in the manner of a Burges piece, with a minor gable at the front. There is a small glazed cupboard and a deeper cupboard with a slot in it within the shelves. Around the architectural top, under the eaves, inscribed in Gothic lettering, runs the inscription "The True University of These Days is a Collection of Books — Carlyle". Down the sides of the

bookcase, which is mounted on a stand with central metal spigot to enable it to revolve, run the inscribed subjects "Biography", "Poetry", "Religion", etc. and armorial shields are also carved into the surfaces. The lower moulding, crisp in oak, is a Queen Anne profile. On the front door, with its brass slot, are incised the words "The Tabard Inn Library — Exchange Station". It was into this cupboard, via the slot, that requests for new titles were posted, written on cards taken from the glazed-door cupboard beside it.

One of the most confusing quotations, incised into a panel on the side of the bookcase, is the line "With all the Red Tape on the Box" in a rather shaky Arts and Crafts Movement lettering. Quite what this means is not clear. The reverse side — see figure 7 — is simply shelved with neat mouldings decorating the edge fronts.

Figures 8 and 9 show in close up the lettering and execution of the roof and door. Note the somewhat quirky design of hinge rather redolent of some of Shaw's Gothic work. Clearly, this is no half-thought-out bookcase, pushed into the lending library in order to serve an immediate function. The Tabard Inn's lending library was intended for People of Taste and the bookcases were to be original, properly styled for the building and suitably mottoed. The subscription library, headed by Boots and W.H. Smiths, was a prominent social feature of a period starting in the late 19th cen-

Above: *Figure 5. Genuine "Queen Anne" chair c.1700 with, originally, a rush seat, now covered over. Note the stiff, turned uprights and straight-sided centre splat, gently curved in this chair to give the comfort and support to the back which Shaw's chair forbids.*

Left: *Figure 6. Oak architectural bookcase from the Tabard Inn. Could Norman Shaw have designed it? Almost certainly, but so could one of his assistants. Note the brass slot in the solid door beside the glazed little cupboard and the incised Gothic lettering under the eaves of the gabled "Queen Anne" roof à la Bedford Park.*

Right: *Figure 7. Reverse side of the oak bookcase. The pivot is a large metal rod running up the inside centre. The small plaque on the side is incised with the motto "With all the Red Tape on the Box" in shaky Arts and Crafts lettering. Note the shields and subjects "Fiction", "Politics", "Mechanics" etc. incised in the sides.*

tury, reaching a peak in the 1930s and dying out in the 1960s. One feels that the Tabard Inn library would not somehow rely on the thrillers and westerns of popular taste; yet the shelves are not of a size to accommodate weighty volumes. Perhaps Aesthetic reading was lighter than we suppose. The Arts and Crafts Movement were avid campaigners for free lending libraries, however, and it seems more in keeping that a free exchange system might have been adopted for this communal bibliotheque.

What, then, of the second bookcase shown in figures 10 and 11? Outwardly it is made to the same design as the first example, but there are very important differences. It is not made of oak. It is a cheaper mahogany stained up to look a rich darker colour. This is entirely at variance with Reformed Gothic and the "honesty" of Arts and Crafts design. There is no inscription engraved under the eaves. The effect of the stain is to diminish the crispness of the mouldings, even though they are identical in profile with the first

example. The piece has the same subject titles and shields on it, "Poetry", "History", "Mechanics" and so on, and the same puzzling "With All the Red Tape on the Box". But the slotted door has no inscription at all and the glazed door is to be found, not next to it, but around the other side. Why? There is no mention of a library but, in the minor gables, the words "The Tabard Inn" are inscribed. The piece was obviously in the same library as the first one and is, in most other respects, the same. The lower hinge on the slotted door is

Right: Figure 9. Close-up of oak bookcase cupboards, with glazed door using "Queen Anne" glazing bars and solid door, inscribed "The Tabard Inn Library — Exchange Station" in various scripts. The hinges are a rather careful "Gothic" design. The inference is that cards with requests for titles and offering exchanges were posted into this cupboard.

Above: Figure 8. Close-up of the "tiled" roof showing the incised Gothic motto which runs under the dentilled "Queen Anne" eaves: "The true University of these Days is a Collection of Books — Carlyle". Very improving. The integrity of much Arts and Crafts design depended on the use of natural wood surfaces.

Left: Figure 10. Mahogany stained bookcase, identical in dimensions and profile to oak version, but with important differences. The glazed cupboard is on the reverse side; there is no "Gothic" inscription of motto by Carlyle; the words "The Tabard Inn" are inscribed in the minor front and back gables with similar inscribed "flowers" to those on the oak door. Note the long lower hinge on the solid door; the upper hinge is identical to the oak version. The plaque on the side is again inscribed "With all the Red Tape on the Box". What does it mean?

Right: Figure 11. Reverse side of mahogany stained bookcase. Note that the glazed cupboard is now on this side. Why? The plaque on the other inscribed side reads "All the good new books in the best bindings". Otherwise the subject inscriptions and armorial shields are identical to the oak version.

much longer than the upper hinge and a wooden knob replaces the inset lock of the oak version.

Could it be that this mahogany-stained piece, with no Gothic motto from Carlyle, was produced as a cheaper version at a slightly later date by Carr's craftsmen, just as they cut corners on some of the houses in Bedford Park? Could Carr's financial difficulties have induced him to have the extra bookcases necessary for the Tabard Inn library to be made at less cost, just as the woodwork and brick mouldings were skimped on some of the houses? Carr was, after all, committed by his own promotional publicity to providing the church, the club, the inn, the stores and tennis courts on the estate as part of the social structure of this new suburb. As time went on and it became clear that he had not the financial means to see the scheme through, many of the details which are so much more of the cost than originally imagined might have had to be passed over.

The more important question still remains, however: who designed the bookcases? It is tempting to ascribe them directly to Shaw and to draw the same parallel between Shaw's house designs, inadequately supervised in execution by Carr, and the second bookcase, inadequately finished when compared with the original oak version. Yet E.J. May, mentioned earlier, was Shaw's assistant in the scheme and designed much in Bedford Park. Could it be he?. Then there is the Tabard Inn chair, with the V. and A.'s cautious rider about its being designed "in the office of" Norman Shaw. It is, in many ways, a typical Arts and Crafts Movement chair. In Shaw's office around 1879 were the famous Ernest Newton (1856-1922), Shaw's chief assistant up to 1879; the even better-known William Richard Lethaby (1857-1931), chief assistant from 1879 and much associated with William Morris, whom he admired (indeed the Tabard Inn chairs were made by Morris & Co. to the "Shaw office" design); and Edward Schroder Prior (1852-1932) who was articled to Shaw in 1874 and assistant certainly up to 1880.

Newton, Lethaby and Prior are all "names" from the Arts and Crafts Movement. But, although, like Morris, the movement used traditional materials and designs as a basis for their work, the use of the "Queen Anne" style for town work is particularly associated with Philip Webb, Scott's pupils, Shaw and his friend Nesfield. One feels instinctively that the chair, like the Willesley chair, goes back to at least an idea from Shaw and the bookcases have the same ring. Perhaps May, dutifully interpreting Shaw's design ideas, actually put the design to paper. It is a fascinating speculation. About four of these bookcases are known to be still in existence; perhaps there are more. Like many pieces from this period there is much yet to be found out and identified. Any help from readers and members of the Club would, as always, be highly appreciated. Can you throw more light on the mystery of the revolving bookcases from the Tabard Inn?

The author is indebted to Mr. Tom Affleck Greeves, President of the Bedford Park Historical Society, for valuable comments and assistance, as well as for arranging a visit to the Tabard Inn Meeting Room. Also to Mr. Mike Jacks, architect and company designer for Ind Coope, Taylor Walker Ltd., who pointed out (over a pint of best bitter) the consistency of the incised lettering on the oak bookcase with the original Tabard Inn Sign lettering, hanging outside.

John Andrews' new book The Price Guide to Victorian and Edwardian Furniture 1860-1930 *is currently in production and will be published by the Club later this year.*

Prices of Marine Chronometers and Deck Watches

by Richard Garnier Christie's

MARINE CHRONOMETERS	Basic Value	Brassbound Box	Earlier Example e.g. convex glass	Plus Auxiliary Compensation	Gold hands	Damaged Detent	No Observation Lid	Basic Value No Box i.e. movement in bowl only
One day	£450	+£100	£100	+£75	+£50	−£150	−£80-£120	£300
Two day	£500/£600	+£125	£100	+£100	+£50	−£150	−£80-£120	£350
Eight day	£800/£900	+£150	£180	+£150	+£50	−£150	−£80-£120	£400
DECK WATCHES (LEVER ESCAPEMENT)				Free Sprung		Damaged Escapement		
One day	£300	+£50	—	+£150		−£150	—	£175 +
Eight day	£600	+£50	—	£150		−£150	—	£300

Prices for chronometers by early makers would be double or more.

N.B.   Note the difference between "early" and "earlier"
          "Early"   =   1780-1820
          "Earlier" =   1830-1870

These prices are for examples in good and presentable condition. Those in excellent condition would be 25% + or more.

Selection of post-war Dinky toy vehicles with advertising. Top row, left to right: £110, £30, £78. Second row, left to right: £62, £58. Third row and bottom centre sold together for £45. Sotheby, King & Chasemore, 15th May 1981. These prices represent an average increase of about 15% over the last year or two.

TOYS
by
Alistair Morris

Sotheby, King & Chasemore
Co-author of
The Price Guide to Metal Toys

"They're not toys any more", said the autojumble stallholder to a colleague as he pondered a selection of Dinky vehicles. Indeed they are not. Old toys, generally, have become a strong collectors' market and, strange though it may seem to collectors of "Fine Art", the prices now commanded for even the toys I enjoyed in the 'fifties allow consideration of market trends and investment theories.

At a glance, toys are toys, full stop, but to the enthusiast the permutations of collecting are numerous. The subject may be divided into half a dozen, or more, distinct categories, borders which some but not many will cross. I feel it is worth considering some of the differing forces at work within the sphere to appreciate the strengths and weaknesses of the market.

The collector of model trains will have his railwayana interest at heart, but even he must decide which gauge satisfies his eye, and which method of propulsion, steam, clockwork or electric, holds his interest. At present, there seems a definite trend for British made products in preference to German items, and pre-war Hornby "O" gauge, especially locomotives in fine condition, are on the up. Hornby's post-war product "Dublo" ("OO" gauge) has been tipped before now, and these items certainly appear to be getting scarce. As with some other categories, I cannot help but conclude that this interest, particularly with regard to post-war items, reflects nostalgia interest from new collectors, possibly now in their thirties and forties, endeavouring to recapture some childhood pleasures, even if this means acquiring a model longed for, but not to be had, years ago.

The collector of early tinplate novelty toys will feel his area encompasses one of great mechanical ingenuity and social interest. The spotlight has swung away from this field, along with some other

early tinplate items, and perhaps it is worth studying this group again in the near future, since prices generally do not appear too unreasonable.

In the case of tinplate transport, with its enormous range of developing styles and refinements, road vehicles appear to have superiority over nautical and aero toys. This is quite understandable in that collectors of automobilia (another vast collecting field) may also indulge their interest further by acquiring some or any realistic representations of a real life car. Whilst prices seem fairly steady, I like the potential of post-war Tri-ang Minics which are probably slightly cheaper than a year ago. Some of their post-war tinplate items in mint condition are still available at under £10.

Die-cast Dinky toys provide an interesting paradox. The prices generally for pre-war models appear to have fallen slightly. This may well be due to the high prices which scarce items command, or possibly to the fact that some (not all) pre-war Dinky toys suffer from a dreaded metal fatigue and can eventually crumble away. The post-war Dinky product is not normally prone to this fatigue and therefore represents a safer investment. Prices for post-war products are very healthy and show a marked increase particularly for mint boxed (factory fresh) examples. All post-war items bearing advertising remain popular. The keen interest from new collectors, as mentioned earlier, has no doubt strengthened this market.

I noted some months ago that Britain's model soldiers were tipped as a good investment, but I cannot say I have noted a great increase in price. It is, like the other categories, a vast field, with

much to offer, especially to the collector interested in military history, with numerous regiments long amalgamated, developments in uniform and equipment, casting varieties, etc. If you are tempted by this area try to buy sets in their original boxes. An average boxed set of infantry can still be had at about £30. Interest seems greater in Britain's civilian products, notably the "Miniature Garden" and "Home Farm" series. Mint items have in some cases doubled in price. Nearly all Britain's products are marked with their name — again seek out undamaged pieces.

There are some regions I have not covered — stationary steam engines which seem quiet, Mickey Mouse and other cartoon character novelty toys which will probably be ever popular, the list could go on. However, always remember the best advice to collectors — buy what pleases you and in the best condition you can afford, preferably mint and boxed if post-war. They will be the rarities that will accrue value far faster than items damaged or repaired. The market is obviously selective at present and discretion must be exercised.

As a postscript, one interesting investment tip appears to be for tractor toys, a demand from American farmer collectors who apparently are doing rather well at present and indulging a "home grown" interest in these items. For example, post-war Lesney Massey-Harris 745D tractors are items which are rising in price — even a damaged example can now be in the region of £80-£100. Certainly realistic tractor toys do seem to be selling quickly at present, and perhaps these collectors may extend their interest into other "agricultural" toys.

A Hornby "O" gauge 4-4-2 Flying Scotsman in attractive condition. Now about £225 (£125 a year or two ago).

"TRANSPORTS OF DELIGHT"
Part 2. Prints of the Canals and of the Air

by Elizabeth Harvey-Lee

Figure 14. F.J. Havell after Thomas Shepherd: "City Basin, Regent's Canal". Line engraving published in 1828 by Jones & Co. Current auction estimate £10-£15.

The days of canal construction like the days of coaching were, after 1835, to be numbered by the fast developing railway companies. In England the first modern canal was built by James Brindley for the Duke of Bridgwater and opened in 1761. Its most remarkable feature was the Barton aqueduct carrying it over the river Irwell and this is shown in several 18th century engravings with a sailing barge crossing above the river, sometimes with the Duke of Bridgwater standing in the foreground. There is a most attractive lithograph of the opening of the Glastonbury Canal, with many flags flying in and around the boats in the foreground on the new canal and a distant view of the town crowned by the Tor. To mark the opening of the Telford's Pontcysyllte

aqueduct on the Ellesmere Canal in 1805 an engraving of the aqueduct, which with spectacular grace carries the canal for three hundred yards 120ft. above the valley of the river Dee, was given to all shareholders. Engraved by Francis Eginton after George Yates of Oswestry, the print was published by Allen & Co. of Birmingham.

These prints have in common an ephemeral quality, being produced rather as newsworthy documents than pictorial decoration and in fact the majority of canal prints would seem to have been rather crude wood engravings which appeared in contemporary newspapers in lieu of today's photographs, for there was much to report. The Bridgwater Canal was the prelude to great activity in canal building and travel by

canal packet boat became quicker than by road until macadamising was introduced.

It is strange that few fine canal prints appear to have been made, although exceptions are to be found in John Hassell's book *A Tour of the Grand Junction Canal* which comprised aquatint views, and in the engravings published in 1828 by Jones & Co. after the series depicting the Regent's Canal by the London topographical watercolour artist Thomas Shepherd (figure 14). Both these sets of prints, however, are small in scale.

Larger prints were produced around 1831, but in the guise of railway prints. Although railways began when the waterways were at their peak of prosperity, the progress of the railway system alarmed many canal companies who sold out to the new railway companies. In T.T. Bury's series of "Six Coloured Views on the Manchester & Liverpool Railway" published in 1831 by Ackermann, a train is shown crossing the viaduct over the Sankey valley. Henry Pyall's serene aquatint shows sailing barges on the canal in the foreground (see colour plate). The same canal is seen in an original etching by Isaac Shaw (figure 15) from a set of four "Views of the Most Interesting Scenery on the Line of the Liverpool & Manchester Railway" published by Shaw in 1831. Alfred B. Clayton in a set of three lithographs of the railway included the "View of the Liverpool & Manchester Railroad at the point where it crosses the Duke of Bridgwater's Canal". In each

Figure 15. Isaac Shaw: "The Viaduct over the Sankey Canal". Etching, published by Shaw in 1831 as one of the set of four "Views of the Most Interesting Scenery on the Line of the Liverpool & Manchester Railway". Sold by Phillips in July 1979 for £40. The complete set of four, together with two other companions after Shaw, all hand-coloured, sold in Phillips' Fine Early Railway Prints sale in November 1977 for £1,500.

Figure 16. John Wallis (publisher): "General Alarm of the Inhabitants of Gonesse occasioned by the Fall of the Air Balloon of Mr. Montgolfier" (sic) (in fact showing Charles's balloon). Etching, published 1st December 1783. Current auction estimate £100-£200.

T.T.Bury. del.ᵗ   H. Pyall. sculp.ᵗ

Viaduct across the Sankey Valley.

London, Published Feb.ʳ 1831. by R.Ackermann, 96 Strand.

After Thomas Talbot Bury: "Viaduct across the Sankey Valley". Hand-coloured etching with aquatint printed in black, sepia and blue, engraved by Henry Pyall, from the album "Six Coloured Views on the Liverpool & Manchester Railway...", published in 1831 by Ackermann, which sold at Phillips in 1977 in the sale of "Fine Early Railway Prints" for £1,900; however, a single impression of this plate is likely to realise £100-£200 in a general auction today.

instance the canal is incidental to the representation of the railway and these examples mark the end of canal prints. Later in the 19th century photographers found sympathetic images in life on the canals and most of the later pictorial material available is photographic and beyond the scope of this article.

Aeronautical prints too were overtaken by the camera, but the early days of ballooning were long before the invention of photography and are well recorded in prints of many kinds.

Ballooning was a French invention. The Montgolfier brothers, papermakers, inspired by flakes of ash floating into the air from a fire, made experiments inflating paper bags with hot air which culminated in the creation of the first hot air balloon. After an unmanned demonstration in their native Lyons they were invited by the Académie des Sciences to Paris. There Etienne Montgolfier constructed a 74ft. high balloon which ascended successfully on 19th

September 1783 carrying a sheep, a cock and a duck in a suspended wicker cage. On 21st November the same year, in a larger balloon, Pilâtre de Rozier and the Marquis d'Alandes made the first manned flight. Hot air balloons were called "montgolfiers" after their inventor. Hydrogen balloons were invented almost simultaneously in Paris by Jacques Alexandre Cesar Charles and were named 'charlières' in his honour. The first unmanned ascent took place on 27th August 1783. The balloon landed outside Paris at Gonesse, to the consternation of the unprepared inhabitants. A manned flight followed on 1st December 1783. A spate of French engravings witnessed these momentous aeronautical inventions.

Although Englishmen themselves had not yet taken to ballooning, English prints appeared to record the French triumphs. Some were simply English versions of French prints such as that published by John Wallis on 26th

November 1783, "Representation of the Air Balloon of Mr. Montgolfier in the Field of Mars near Paris", which used a French plate by Blanchard but with an incorrect title in English added. The balloon portrayed is in fact a charlière. This mistake is repeated in Wallis's "General Alarm of the Inhabitants of Gonesse, occasioned by the Fall of the Air Balloon of Mr. Montgolfier", which shows Charles's fallen hydrogen balloon after its first unmanned flight being attacked with pitchforks and guns by the unwitting citizens who thought it a being from another world (figure 16). J. Lodge etched an original pair of prints, "The Ascent of the Aerial Balloon" and "The Descent of the Air Balloon", which really did show Montgolfier's balloon on its first Paris flight carrying its animal passengers.

It was an Italian who brought ballooning to England. He demonstrated an unmanned hot air balloon, which incident was recorded in an engraving

Right: Figure 18. Francesco Bartolozzi after H. Rigaud: "The Three Favourite Aerial Travellers". Line and stipple engraving, second state, published in 1785. A trimmed impression with repaired tear sold at Phillips in July 1979 for £60. An impression in good condition would realise in the region of £100-£120.

Figure 17. Francis Jukes after Brewer: "The First Balloon Ascent in England". The crowd gathered at the Artillery Ground, Moorfields to watch. Outline etching, proof before aquatint, with watercolour. Sold by Sotheby's in the sale of "Well Known Collection of Ballooning and Aeronautical Prints and Drawings" in March 1962 for £110. Current auction estimate £400-£600.

published on 1st December 1783 by I. Marshall & Co. of Aldermary Church Yard, Bow Lane, London, "The Air Balloon which was launched in the Artillery Ground Nov. 25 1783". Count Francesco Zambeccari did not experiment with his first manned flight until 23rd March 1785, by which time another Italian, Vincent Lunardi, had already made the first balloon ascent in England on 15th September 1784. This event is celebrated in an aquatint by Francis Jukes after Brewer (figure 17). Another print concerning Lunardi is the earliest example of a fine ballooning print by a leading engraver of the day. This is the stipple engraving by Francesco Bartolozzi (1728-1815), the only engraver thought worthy to be admitted to full membership of the Royal Academy for many years after its foundation. Lunardi is portrayed with Mrs. Sage and G. Biggin Esq. in the car of a balloon. First published on 13th May 1785 by Bori, a second state with the title "The Three Favourite Aerial Travellers" was issued on 25th June 1785 (figure 18). However, the weight of the three passengers was too great and the balloon failed to rise. The flight was actually made only by Mrs. Sage and Mr. Biggin, who landed safely at Harrow and were entertained by boys from Harrow School.

Thomas Rowlandson also put his hand to describing balloon ascents and in the hand-coloured etching "The First Crossing of the English Channel by Blanchard and Dr. Jeffries, January 1785, Dover" published by Fores 1794, showed the Frenchman's balloon over the sea near Dover castle with people waving on the cliffs.

Most ballooning prints were not by significant hands and though imbued with naïve charm are of historical rather than artistic interest, being produced to record the latest scientific exploits of aeronauts such as James Sadler, Richard Crosby, Sir Richard McGuire, James Decker, Major John Money, Charles Green, George and Margaret Graham. Exceptions are the aquatint by Havell, published in 1811, of "The Ascent of Mr. Sadler, the celebrated British Aeronaut, at Oxford at the Commemoration, July 7, 1810" (figure 19), where beneath the rather primitive drawing of the balloon itself lies a small gem of English topography, showing the towers of Oxford. Sadler was the first English born aeronaut. The ill-fated flight of Major Money from Norwich which ended in the sea off Yarmouth on 22nd July 1785, is portrayed by the noted engraver John Murphy in a mezzotint after Philip Reinagle, which shows him struggling with the balloon, while a boat is setting out from the sloop Argus to rescue him (figure 20). A mezzotint on this scale and of this quality is unusual among ballooning prints.

Figure 19. R. Havell after E.M. Jones: "The Ascent of Mr. Sadler at Oxford 1810". Hand-coloured aquatint, published by Jones in 1811. Current auction estimate £80-£120.

Figure 20. John Murphy after Philip Reinagle: "The Perilous Situation of Major Mony" (sic). Mezzotint published in 1789 by Murphy. Sold by Sotheby's, "Ballooning Sale", in March 1962 for £55. Current auction value £300-£500.

Figure 22. Geoffrey Watson: "Supermarine S 6". Drypoint. Sold by Phillips for £28 in July 1979.

Figure 21. W.L. Walton: "The First Carriage, the 'Ariel' ". Hand-coloured lithograph published in 1843 by Ackermann. This impression, trimmed, with a repaired tear, was sold by Phillips in July 1979 for £150. A print in good condition would currently realise £200-£300.

As early as 1835 a French colonel, Comte de Lennox, set up in England an Aeronautical Society to build an airship, "The Eagle", a scheme that collapsed that same year, but not before a lithograph had been produced. "An exact representation of the first Aerial Ship The Eagle, now exhibiting at the grounds of the Aeronautical Society Victoria Rd., facing Kensington Gardens" was published jointly by some of the leading print shops of the day, Ackermann, Reeves and McLean.

Equally anticipatory was the series of prints showing the "Ariel", a steam aeroplane designed by William Samuel Henson (1805-1888) in 1842. He and a Mr. Marriott formed the "Aerial Transit Company" to produce the plane, but his ambitious project for a steam-driven monoplane with a 150ft. wing span was never carried out due to lack of financial backing. The plane disappeared from history except for its appearance in numerous prints in which it is shown variously over London (figure 21), the Pyramids and, on handkerchiefs produced as advertisements, over China, with the title "The Flying Steam Company, to China in twenty-four hours certain".

It is sad that when the Wright brothers finally did get an aeroplane off the ground in 1902, it was not recorded by artists in print at all. Photography had taken over this function.

However, although generally modern print makers have not been inspired by aeroplanes, a fitting close to the genre of aeronautical prints is provided by the drypoint by Geoffrey Watson (figure 22) to celebrate the plane which won outright for Britain the Schneider Trophy. This famous international biennial air race, which started in 1913 to encourage seaworthiness in marine aircraft, developed into a race of absolute speed. The conditions laid down that any country which won three times consecutively held the trophy in perpetuity. Britain's "Supermarine S 6" achieved this in 1927, 1929 and 1931.

Reference books on transport prints are in general scant. However, coaching prints are well described in a section in F.L. Wilder's *English Sporting Prints,* 1974, and also in Ralph Neville's *Old Sporting Prints,* 1908. N.C. Selway has produced a three volume work on the paintings and prints of James Pollard. Nowhere have canal prints been collated and much remains to be discovered in this field. A very informative reference for aeronautical prints is supplied by the sale catalogue compiled by Sotheby's for the sale held in March 1962 of "The Well-known collection of Ballooning and Aeronautical Prints and Drawings, the Property of Col. R.L. Preston, C.B.E."

Fine early aeronautical engravings are in the region of £100-£500 and canal prints, though also rare, are still modestly priced in the range of £10-£100. Overall a small price to pay for such delightful didactic decoration.

Acknowledgements
Figures 14, 15, 18, 21, 22, courtesy Phillips. Figures 16, 17, 19, 20, reproduced from Sotheby's catalogue of "The Well-known collection of Ballooning and Aeronautical Prints and Drawings, the Property of Col. R.L. Preston, C.B.E."

What I've Decided To Keep For Christmas

by A.D. Ealer

There are occasions when one buys something cheaply, fails to appreciate its full worth and sells it, only to regret doing so later. It remains in the mind, which possibly over-exaggerates its good points, until it becomes an obsession. This very nearly happened with this picture.

I went into a furniture shop and looked round. There was very little, but as I had a van passing through the town I bought a couple of small pieces and, as a result, was taken round the premises. The picture was in a corner of the loft, dirty and with a few pieces flaked off.

I suppose because I like boats and sailing it put me off. The sea in the foreground is unrealistically rough, tiny waves with high crests, highly imaginative contrasts of colour in the middle distance and, unbelievably, a matronly woman in the foreground attempting to row an old tub of a boat into those impossible seas.

But then I looked at the signature — "A Vickers 1869" — and decided that for the modest price asked it must be worth the gamble. After all, even if messy and stylised it was a Victorian marine, and by a name that commands a good price.

It might have been restored and sold had not an odd incident occurred. Old friends had bought a boat and asked us down to the Solent for the weekend. Despite the large number of yachts out we had an enjoyable time round Cowes, Yarmouth and Beaulieu (indeed the Beautiful Place so christened by the Normans) and started back to Portsmouth at lunchtime on Sunday. The clouds scudded across the sky and the wind rose to a useful eighteen to twenty knots. The spring tide was ebbing hard as we approached Portsmouth harbour entrance and with wind against tide there was a fair tumble. The tide surged off the Hamilton Bank and, in company with the other boats, we clung close to the eastern shore to avoid being too knocked about. The wind increased and for a few moments it was quite exciting — the sea surged and foamed and spray covered the ten ton yacht as it crashed through the steep seas. The head of the boat was dragged back and forward and the helmsman had a busy ten minutes. For some reason I turned to look across to the Isle of Wight and felt an odd sensation, not the result of the sea but the strong feeling of having seen it all before, a genuine "déjà vu". For a nasty moment I couldn't understand why, and that made it worse. Then, with considerable relief, I realised that I was standing near to the shore where Vickers had painted that scene over a hundred years before.

On Monday morning I went round to the restorers and had a close look at the picture. It was all there — the gentle slope of the Isle of Wight tapering off to the left. H.M.S. Vernon now replaces the old fort but it is only a grander version. The dark cloud falls almost exactly on the Hamilton Bank. The square-rigger master must have local knowledge, for he has taken the shallow inshore route while the others in the distance are giving it a wide berth. The wind is obviously coming in hard and the tide going out fast which produces the dramatic effect which must have attracted Vickers, who indeed got the light on the green tinged water just right as was clear from the newly cleaned picture.

But what about the woman rowing in the foreground? The cleaning shows that the boat is firmly moored to the shore and in the relatively quiet edge of the tide all she is doing is keeping the boat's head out while the man amidships works his red fishing net in the water.

This picture is not going to be sold this Christmas. I'm taking it home as a happy reminder of an enjoyable little holiday. Besides, it's taught me a lesson about unknowledgeable prejudice, and that's something worth reminding myself about — at least that's my excuse for hanging on to it.

Figure 1. A pair of Georgian decanters of the so-called "classic" pattern, c.1815. £250-£300.

Movements in Values of English Glass
by Martin Mortimer *Delomosne and Son Ltd.*

Figure 2. A superb Irish boat-shaped fruit bowl on heavy moulded foot, c.1790. £350-£450.

During the past year recession has touched many aspects of collectors' glass. Only the rarest drinking glasses have continued to rise in value. Among these the neatest and best made (not necessarily the most unusual) baluster glasses have made exceptional prices. The inflated Beilbys too have held well but ordinary opaque twists have faltered and fallen back. Very simple glasses such as plain stems, short ales, jellies and so forth have increased somewhat under the influence of the high price levels now reached and mostly maintained by other more desirable glasses. Colour twists now seem to start at £500 if perfect, a general rise after a period of market indigestion.

But wineglasses are only a part of the picture. Good Georgian cut glass has continued to sell readily during the last year. This reflects its relative cheapness in relation to comparable products today: and certainly it is astonishing to be able to buy, for instance, a meticulously cut water jug which has been knocking around the cupboards for 170 years for the same or less than its machine finished equivalent. Investors should note the second-hand value of the latter is negligible!

Decanters, staple diet of donors of wedding presents, are the measure of the cut glass market. The commonest (and many think the nicest) pattern of Georgian decanter is the so-called "classic" (figure 1). It has a bulbous body, three rings at the neck, wide flutes above, fine or finger flutes below and either a mushroom or a bull's-eye stopper. Pairs of these in good condition have moved from about £8-£10 in 1960

to £30-£40 in 1970 and on to £250-£300 in 1980. Quite a change in the slope of the graph!

Well, it is easy enough to see what has happened in recent years but, as ever, impossible to predict what will. Since it is clear from the above that glass is capable of sustaining enormous rises in value it might be worth considering what category in the field has not risen to such a great degree in the last thirty or so years. Irish glass boat-shaped fruit bowls (figure 2) come to mind. £350-£450 (£80-£100 in 1960) will buy a nice one today and this does not seem excessive for what might be called the jewel in the crown of Irish glass. These bowls are large but elegant: they date from the early years of the emergence of Ireland as a major glass making area before the industry absorbed international styles, and so are strongly evocative of Irish taste. Each is a small miracle of survival combining as it does a thin and vulnerable upper part with a heavy integral stem and foot. They must be reasonable in price today standing as

they do at not much more than the price of a pair of relatively common Georgian decanters.

It is an odd thing about glass that quality is rarely linked to value. As technique advanced in the early 19th century, complicated patterns evolved such as pillar flutes or step (sometimes called prismatic) cutting. A really well finished piece of step cutting in good condition is a brilliant tour de force combining as it will a perfect glass recipe and technical mastery in cutting (figure 3). But though such a piece might command a reasonably high price, a poorly executed example will not be far behind. The same could be said about some wineglasses. The balustroids as a class contain some pretty dismal glasses, ill-formed, ill-proportioned and crooked. They have their devotees, however, and pull good prices.

It is clear there is room among glass collectors for more discernment. Poor pieces should be passed up in favour of refinement and prices will then take more account of quality.

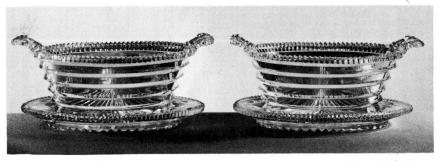

Figure 3. A brilliant pair of oval step-cut piggins and stands, c.1820. £350-£400.

Georgian Brown Furniture

by

Adrian Frazer

Christie's South Kensington

Two from a set of eight (six plus two) George III mahogany dining chairs of Sheraton design. £3,400 by Christie's South Kensington on 14th April 1981.

This article confines itself to Georgian mahogany pieces of the middle range, probably produced by the lesser makers in London or the better makers in the country; these comprise the well-made but unrefined and unadorned pieces that are still widely available in antique shops and auction rooms.

As far as investment is concerned, there are those who have invested and those who still intend to invest. The market has changed markedly over the last two years and this could affect both sides. Those who have invested in quality will probably find, when the time comes, that their returns will be handsome. Alternatively, there are many areas where the market has remained static or even dropped. This, of course, is to the benefit of the new buyer and in general terms furnishing a house now with good quality antiques of the lower end of the market has rarely been cheaper, bearing in mind inflation and the cost of newly manufactured items. In the difficult times of the last two years

A George III mahogany whatnot, 44ins. high. £920 by Christie's South Kensington on 14th April 1981.

the trade has become much more selective; the result is that better quality pieces in good condition realise more and more ordinary pieces make less. Foreign buyers' visits have become more erratic and this has noticeably affected certain areas.

In terms of prices the dining room still rules. Sets of chairs of four or more are still greatly in demand; any set of quality of eight or more is virtually impossible to price in advance. Wise buying in this area in the past would be greatly rewarded on re-sale. Alternatively, as long sets of chairs become scarcer the buying public widen their horizons and early to mid-Victorian sets of chairs, although already expensive, must still have investment potential. Everybody seems to want a circular table to go in their dining room so these are at a premium. Pillar dining tables are now at astronomic prices, around £2,000 to £3,000 a pillar, and that is not for the best. Tables with legs around the outside are still available at not too outrageous prices. Good sideboards of 5ft. wide or less now tend to cost over £1,000 but the late Georgian or early Victorian double pedestal sideboard can still be had for a few hundred pounds which must be reasonable.

Moving into the drawing room funny things have happened. Large bookcases are variable but are still about £1,000 to £2,000 for something very ordinary or altered, £2,500 plus for anything of quality. Small secretaire bookcases are very rare birds these days; larger, more boxy types can still cost over £1,500. Pembroke and sofa tables in the middle range have not really moved much in the last year. Middle range Georgian card tables are cheaper, on the whole, than a year ago and £200 to £250 could secure a perfectly nice, useful example. Ordinary tripod tables are about the same price, so in real terms are cheaper; with these in particular if you wish to be more ambitious and buy one over £500 go to the best dealer you can afford — it will pay dividends in the end. Bureaux, which five or six years ago were making

A George III mahogany bedside commode. 26ins. £700 by Christie's South Kensington on 14th April 1981.

£500 to £700 at auction, are now selling for £350 to £550 as a result of the lessening of foreign demand.

It is in the bedroom that the thump can loudly be heard this year. Late Georgian chests of drawers with straight fronts and over 36ins. wide are still available at £80 to £150 so have not noticeably moved in price. Bowfront examples are still £120 to £300. Clothes presses are very noticeably down; these were bought by Northern Europeans for their sitting rooms either with panel doors or converted to glass. A year or two ago even very ordinary ones were making £300 plus; these are now down to about half that. Tallboys also are noticeably affected. This, of course, does not apply to the top end of a market that appears to be starved of prime pieces; these still exceed even the wildest expectations when they appear but the magic difference is hard to define or describe to the untrained eye.

If I had £1,000 to invest in this field I would buy a good clothes press for about £200 to £250, a bowfront chest for £150 to £200, a respectable toilet mirror for £50 to £100 and with what was left the best bureau I could find.

The Cost of Lace
by Pat Earnshaw

Figure 1. Mrs. Winifred Millar, M.B.E., demonstrating the making of bobbin lace. The equipment includes a pillow, parchment pattern, bobbins, pins, a pincushion (here in the form of an elephant), and the maiden or stand on which the pillow rests.

Figure 2. A pricked parchment for use in bobbin lace making, a design known as "Lords and Ladies". Courtesy Mrs. W. Millar.

"We are all Adam's children but silk makes the difference" wrote Thomas Fuller in 1732. For "silk" substitute "lace" and we have an insight into the high value placed on lace as a discriminating agent. Those who wore lace were better than those who did not. "My dear! ten pounds would have purchased every stitch she had on — lace and all" was Miss Pole's scathing appraisal of Lady Glenmire in *Cranford*. The comment dates from the 1840s, but it has a timeless quality. Lace from the mid-16th to the early 20th century demarcated rich from poor, and the nobles from the plebs. Its value was as high as man's wish to be greater than his neighbour.

Much the same might be said of those days with regard to gold, jewels, and rich furs but, unlike the mineral status symbols, and the pelts which required no more than an animal's death and destruction, lace involved human skill, time, artistry and sometimes acute suffering. Its financial value was therefore a complex thing compounded of cost of materials, cost of labour, hours of labour and, inevitably, supply and demand.

From about 1540 to 1780 demand was high, and the costs of material and labour basically static. The hours of labour for equally skilled workers in fact never change except in relation to the fineness of the thread and the complexity of the work. Thus given the hours of labour for a precise piece of lace it should be possible to calculate its value at any period simply by multiplying number of hours by hourly rate of pay at that time. This would give a figure for what that lace *should* be worth, assuming of course that anyone wanted to buy it, and to this the cost of materials would have to be added.

Cost of materials

The materials, or equipment, required for lace making are, at the most: pillow, stand, patterns, pins, bobbins and thread (figures 1 and 2); or, for needlepoint or embroidered laces, pattern, needle and thread only. Of these, the most expensive items were in the past pins and thread. English brass pins were not manufactured until 1530, and only in 1543 was their price restricted to 6s. 8d. per 1,000. Fine flax thread was used, the preparation and hand spinning of which was both skilled and very laborious and, incidentally, unhealthy since it had to be done in cool humid conditions with no light except a single beam to illumine the thread which was too fine to be felt between the fingers. It was so expensive that it was weighed before and after spinning to make sure that none had been stolen.

The following figures are from various writers, and in no case is the actual "count" given. The count was calculated from the number of threads, each three hundred yards long, required to make up an English pound in weight and, obviously, the finer the thread the higher the count. The finest thread known — 17th and 18th centuries — had a count of 1,200; 19th century threads were no finer than 300-400; and today the finest machine thread is probably 170 and the finest that could be made by hand about 60.

1787. 1lb. Flanders thread £16 (one quarter the price of standard gold).

1790. Antwerp thread for droschel ground, £70 per lb.

Left: Figure 3. A Buckingham lace stole, 2ft. by 9ft., made in three strips, the joins visible only where the seam has slightly split apart.

Right: Figure 4. The lace border of a linen cloth 5ft. square, worked by Mrs. W. Millar. The charming design is a derivative of a Cluny technique.

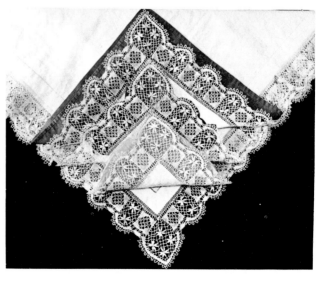

Figure 5. A handkerchief border of Bucks point ground lace, worked by Mrs. W. Millar. This shows the Wreath pattern and, in each corner, a girl holding a May Day garland.

18th century. Very fine flax thread £240 per lb.

1851. £100 to £120 per lb.

1868. Antwerp thread £95 per lb.

19th century flax thread exported from Northern Ireland to Valenciennes, 500 to 2,000 francs per lb.

1884. Thread fetching 3,000 francs per lb. had become a rarity, the finest flax available costing 2,400 francs.

1908. Machine spun Flanders thread at £70 per lb. was said to be nothing like so durable as the handspun.

The occurrence of antique foreign currencies in these figures is unfortunate, but there is as yet no simple way of converting them into accurate modern equivalents.

Cost of labour

Direct payments to lace workers in the 19th century varied, and there appear to be no statements of wages available for lace workers in earlier times.

1810. 9s. to 10s. a week (about 2s. more than an agricultural labourer would earn).

1850. South Devon — 5s. to 6s. a week.

1860. South Devon — "the payment", says a contemporary writer, "is now excellent — 7s. a week for a 10 hr. day." In the same year, however, as a result of competition from Malta, and from the machines, the Midlands lace industry was in decline, and wages were no more than 2s. 6d. to 3s. 6d. a week.

Children in France and England earned 6d. a day at the age of six or seven.

Two other systems of payment were practised by lace merchants: c.1870 a productivity deal in which the lace maker was paid as many shillings as it took to cover the piece she had made; and a barter system made use of, for example, by Thomas Tucker of Branscombe who employed as many as five hundred women in 1850. He gave groceries from his own shop in exchange for lace, at somewhat inflated prices, and since there was no one else to whom they could sell their lace, these rather harsh terms had to be accepted.

These figures had great significance when compared with the earnings of machine lace workers. In 1808 workers on the warp frame machines in Nottingham were paid £2.50 a week. Shortly afterwards, cotton was substituted for silk, and at the same time wages rose to £4 a week. The cotton cost only £15 a lb. — compare the figures quoted for flax thread. With the highly successful invention of machine blonde in 1820, skilled workers were paid the then astronomical sum of £10 a week.

Thus high cost of material and low cost of labour for hand lace battled with low cost of material and high cost of labour for machine made. As in time the machines became more efficient, the factories were able to produce lace much more cheaply. Heathcoat's bobbin net machine was at first very complex in its arrangements, one single hole requiring sixty motions, and one square yard of

Figure 6. A baby bonnet with mistletoe leaves and berries, designed and worked by Mrs. W. Millar. Some four hundred bobbins were used, and the work took a full six months of spare time to complete.

net in 1815 cost 30s. By 1860 the work had been simplified to six motions of the machine, and one square yard of similar net cost only 3d.

Hours of labour

The making of lace by hand is a very slow process, and nothing can be done to accelerate it except the use of thicker threads or simpler patterns. Thus figures for hours of work given below could be taken to apply to any century, except that when the thread used was very much finer, the time taken would be considerably increased. Though these figures are unsatisfactory in that they do not specify precise count of thread dimensions of lace, or intricacy of design, they do demonstrate quite clearly that results are not "instant".

1851. A flounce of Honiton guipure made for the Great Exhibition of 1851, five yards long, took forty women eight months to complete (or would have taken one person twenty-seven years).

1855. A dress of Alençon needlepoint made for the Empress Eugenie took thirty-six women eighteen months and cost £2,800.

A Buckingham stole presented to Queen Victoria in the late 19th century had been worked by three sisters in eighteen weeks, and each was paid 6s. a week, making a cost of approximately £16 for labour alone (figure 3).

1939. A cloth exhibited in Munich took sixteen women a total of 15,800 hours. To find a fair price multiply by the average contemporary cost of labour per hour.

1942. A triangular mantilla of black

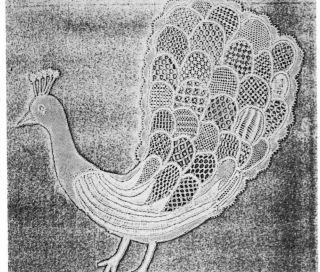

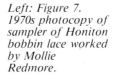

Left: Figure 7. 1970s photocopy of sampler of Honiton bobbin lace worked by Mollie Redmore.

Figure 8. Part of a needlepoint altar border worked by Lady Town. Photograph by Peter Hogben.

Figure 9. A Shetland shawl, 4ft. square.

silk made for the Milan Triennale took three women eighteen months to complete. It measured 1.2m by 2.6m and weighed 100g (just over 3oz.).

1970. A Bedfordshire border 5ins. deep for a large table cover took five hundred hours (figure 4); a handkerchief edging of Bucks lace, 3ins. deep, one year (figure 5); and a curved leaf approximately 1in. by ¼in., in a mistletoe design, an entire evening (figure 6).

1970s. A small rose and leaf Honiton motif eight to ten hours; and a sampler of Honiton lace stitches in the form of a peacock, 7½ins. long, over six weeks (figure 7).

1978. A needlepoint border for an altar cloth 5,500 hours (figure 8).

1979. A Shetland shawl hand knitted in 1-ply wool with size 18 needles, 52ins. square, took one hour for each row. Still uncompleted, but with approximately thirty rows to the inch, the total time required will be about 1,560 hours (figure 9).

Supply and demand: the retail price

A piece of lace at the time of its working would, in a straightforward calculation, be a product of the three sets of figures outlined above. However, lace designers and lace merchants also had to have their profit, often considerable; and, when demand exceeded supply, as for two hundred years it did, it was a seller's market.

During the 16th century lace was already expensive. We are told that luxury taxes were necessary to restrict imports into England of lace and other trimmings, which in 1569 amounted to £10,000. An inventory of Elizabeth I's apparel included "1 yd Italian cutworke, ¼ yd wide, 55s 4d; and 3 yd broad needlework lace of Italy, with purls, 50s yard."

In 1623 clergymen raved against the unbridled extravagance of the time when gentlemen were forced to sell their lands to deck their wives with lace. Pepys in 1662 was delighted with a lace collar which he bought for £3; but his wife was furious when he refused to buy her a flounce which she craved. Nell Gwynn trimmed her shoes with silver lace; and Charles II in 1684 spent £20 on a cravat

of Venetian lace for his brother James (figure 10).

In 1695 William III spent a total of £2,459 on lace. In 1710 Queen Anne paid £151 for twenty-one yards of Flemish edging; and in 1712 a total of £1,418 for Flemish laces, including Mechlin (figure 11)

In 1711 Roxana wore "a suit of lace worth £200" on her head. Defoe was obviously lace conscious for elsewhere he quotes Blandford (Dorset) lace at £30 a yard, in 1724. Certainly for the greater part of the 17th, 18th and 19th centuries lace was valuable enough to be smuggled when its importation was restricted, and to be stolen whenever opportunity arose. Moll Flanders c.1722 is recorded as having stolen £300 worth of Flemish lace; and Bishop Atterbury as, in 1732, he made his last journey from France to Westminster Abbey, had tucked away in his coffin lace worth £6,000.

In 1739 the trousseau of a French princess cost 625,000 francs. Madame la Marquise de Pompadour paid 60,000 marks for a lace dress, c.1750; and Madame du Barry in 1771, 2,400 livres for a headdress. A pair of ruffles for a gentleman's coat at that time cost 4,000 livres.

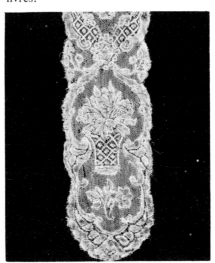

Figure 11. A lappet of Mechlin lace from the time of Queen Anne.

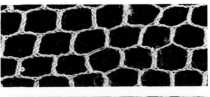
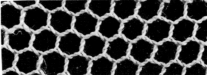

Figure 12. Droschel ground (above) and Heathcoat's 2-twist machine net (below). At this magnification, of × 6.6, the difference between them is obvious, but from even a short distance such as 3ft. each appears simply as a fine mesh.

Figure 10. Venetian gros point such as Charles II might have bought in 1684.

In 1787 we are told that an ounce of Flanders thread made into fine lace cost ten times the price of standard gold of equal weight. "Greek" said Dr. Johnson in 1780 "is like lace: every man gets as much of it as he can."

Alas, devastating changes were on the way. The Industrial Revolution had already begun. The French Revolution of 1789 guillotined the customers, and the market plummeted. There were other contributory factors to the sharp drop in the demand for lace, such as a change to extreme simplicity of fashion, and then the whole frenetic economic scene of wage spirals, inflation and taxation opening up in the 19th century, which made the excessively long hours and uncomfortable conditions of hand spinning and lace making quite ludicrously unrewarding. Lace, until the second half of the 19th century, when handwork revived as a craft, was primarily a commercial product, and its production ceased when it ceased to make a profit.

George III with his taboo on personal decoration played his part in making lace demodée, and in the time of George IV dresses were of shimmering silks and lawns, with trimmings of ribbons rather than lace. George IV himself was no boon as a patron of lace: there was in 1908 at Haywards of New Bond Street a fine piece of Brussels lace made for that monarch but never paid for. However, an era of royal, and noble, patronage was beginning: *they* paid a lot of money for individual pieces, specially commissioned. Queen Adelaide tried to order an application of sprigs of Honiton lace on a handmade ground, to support the workers, but no one could be found who remembered how to make it, so machine net had to be used instead. The handmade ground, known as droschel, had cost £15 in 1800 for an 18ins. square. Machine net of the same size about fifteen years later cost 15s., and by 1851 the cost had fallen to 15d. (figure 12). In fact, trying to support the flagging and completely uneconomic industry of handmade lace was a lost cause. Nevertheless the philanthropic attempts continued. Queen Victoria was a more efficient patron. The lace for her

Figure 13. Queen Victoria's wedding veil, Honiton appliqué on net, and her headdress. Reproduced by gracious permission of Her Majesty Queen Elizabeth II.

Figure 14. A photograph of Queen Victoria taken on the occasion of the wedding of Princess Mary of Teck and Prince George, Duke of York, on 6th July 1893. She wears her wedding flounce and veil over a dress of light black stuff. Reproduced by gracious permission of Her Majesty Queen Elizabeth II.

Figure 15. A baby bonnet worked entirely in Bucks point ground by Mrs. Winifred Millar, showing the type of bonnet back in vogue in the first half of the 19th century.

wedding dress in 1840 cost £1,000. It took two hundred women some eight months to complete, and comprised a flounce 4½yds. by 27ins., and a matching veil 1½yds. square. "A white satin gown, with a very deep flounce of Honiton lace, imitation of old" Queen Victoria says succinctly in her journal* (figures 13 and 14).

At the same time the rapid and inexpensive productions of machines were changing the whole attitude to life. In the 18th century the well-to-do bourgeoise would invest her savings in fine lace and wear it with pride all through her life. Even in the mid-19th century small specialised items such as the Bucks baby cap crowns invented by James Millward in 1820 were bought as expensive luxuries to be kept and treasured, and there was a flourishing export of them to America until the Civil War of 1861 (figure 15). But the machines and mass-production were progressively taking over. In 1837 the wife of the American Ambassador to Britain was given a Court dress of Nottingham machine lace, and was delighted to wear it; and Queen Victoria's daughters, at the christenings of successively younger siblings, wore dresses "trimmed with flounces of beautiful Nottingham lace"*. Lace was edging its way back into fashion. Whiteley's lace department in 1867 had a turnover of £3,500, the third largest of their seventeen departments; and in 1895 Peter Robinson's lace department sold £25,958. Much, perhaps the greater part, of this would have been machine made. Limerick tambour — hand worked chain stitch embroidery on net — began in 1829, and by the 1850s every woman had at least a collar or fichu of this lace (figure 16). The average price for a dress was 2gns. to 5gns., but the finest quality, especially that which by the use of two thicknesses of thread gave the effect of shading, could be worth 30gns. a flounce, still a bargain compared with

the special commissions of a decade earlier. This work held its price, and in late Edwardian times when the technique was copied in Ghent, a flounce of Ghent tambour, wrongly catalogued as "real old Limerick", sold at a London auction for £60.

Now a further aspect of cost arose: lace was becoming a collectors' item. At Queen Victoria's death in 1901 her wearable lace was valued at £76,000, and went to Queen Alexandra. It was in fact very rare for old lace to come on to the open market. However, in 1903 the christening garment of fine Brussels lace decorated with "N"'s, crowns and cherubs, which Napoleon had ordered at the birth of his son in 1811, was sold at Christie's for £120 — though one might assume it had cost a great deal more when it was made. A court train of lace sold for £140. In 1904 a 58ins. length of Point de Venise 24ins. deep sold for £600, and four yards of Point d'Argentan 25ins. deep for £460 (figure 17). In 1907 five yards of reticella 7½ins. deep sold for £33 (figure 18), and a Point Gaze parasol cover for £6 16s. (figure 19). Was this a lot to pay, or a little?

The old saying "A thing is worth what people will pay for it" is very relevant to any object of art, old or young, whether it is under consideration for investment, sale or purchase. The early investments in lace crashed with the First World War and the slump. In the ensuing bankruptcies, and the unsteadily increasing cost of labour, few had time for an esoteric conglomeration of threads which all too often defied identification. In the postwar world of the fast and

brittle 'twenties lace appeared again in an orgy of diaphanous garments as though it must be used and enjoyed to the full before it was snatched away in another cataclysm. There was a huge demand, both in Europe and America, for "corsets formed of priceless old rose point, chemises encrusted with the choicest laces of Buckinghamshire, or camisoles made entirely of the rarest Alençon". And then, suddenly, no one was interested at all: people moving house, or going abroad, could not even give away lace, because no one would take it.

These doldrums of apathy lasted for some forty years, and anyone who was perceptive enough to take an interest in antique lace during that time was on to a very good thing. Whether the revival of interest began as a fashion trend, or as a need to put money in solid objects at a time of high inflation, certainly since about 1968 interest in lace has grown with increasing rapidity. This interest has been reflected in the prices: in 1973 a Point de France flounce failed to reach its reserve of £100; in 1976 another shot up to £550; and in February 1980 yet another shook the lace world by reaching four figures, in fact nearly £2,000 (figure 20). Each was offered in a London auction house, each was of

Figure 16. Part of a long shawl collar of Limerick lace. This lace deteriorated after the early 1840s.

Figure 17. A fine panel of Argentan lace "Marquis et Marquise" made by nuns at the Abbaye Notre-Dame, Argentan. Such a piece, in terms of hours of work required, would cost in the region of £2,400 if made today. Reproduced by kind permission of the Abbess.

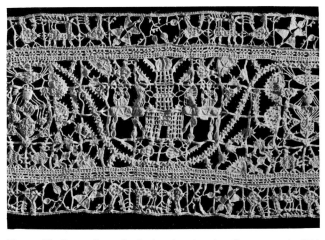

Figure 18. Part of a reticella border showing figures, early 17th century.

much the same size and quality, and about three times as deep as the modern needlepoint border for an altar cloth which took 5,500 hours to make. They were of considerably finer thread, and somewhat longer, and so probably represented a total of some 50,000 hours of work. Thus at the current secretarial wage of £2 upwards an hour, £100,000 might be regarded as a very favourable price.

It is relatively easy to say what the cost of antique lace *should* be, very hard indeed to advise what would be a fair price to ask, or to pay. The number of collectors is still so few that the absence of only one or two of them from a sale-room can make a vast difference to the prices reached. Bargains still slip through: inconspicuous lappets or crumpled droschel veils find their way into job lots of worthless oddments; really fine shawls of Chantilly or a point de gaze train can look so much too good

Figure 19. A 19th century parasol with a point de gaze cover. Ex Vivienne Pye collection. Courtesy of Harrods Auction Galleries, August 1980, £75.

to be true that they are mistaken for machine lace and sold as such; only two years ago several hollie point bonnets and baby shirts of the early 18th century were given away with a breadbin on a market stall for 25 pence. Fashion may favour bold chemical laces, or coarse Bruges, to such an extent that they are priced higher than the far more intricate and valuable laces of the 17th and 18th centuries. As far as these centuries-old laces are concerned, their value to a collector rests on age, scarcity, quality of thread and workmanship, and completeness. This latter point is extremely important. So extensive was the cannibalisation of Victorian times, and of the 1920s, that relatively little remains in its original form (figure 21). That even these few pieces should be damaged, now, seems little short of iniquitous. Yet in the last twelve months the following have been recorded: a square cut out of a small droschel veil to make a doll's party dress; a triangular panel cut from a lace parasol to make a jabot; a 17th century alb flounce complete at both ends and in perfect condition cut in half by a vicar's wife because she thought she would get more money for it as two pieces; and the value of a lappet decimated at one snip of the scissors when

the end was cut off to send as a sample to a potential purchaser.

In the next few years the value of lace will probably sky-rocket as richly-endowed museums turn their eyes towards antique textiles while they are still, relative to paintings, furniture and objects of vertu, greatly underpriced; and one can only hope that all the fine old pieces will be safely preserved for posterity before life again becomes so grim and so severe that nothing will be further from people's thoughts than the microscopic plant or animal fibres comprising those artistic fairylike gossamers which we call lace.

Acknowledgements

All illustrations are strictly copyright, and must not be reproduced. Photographs 1-6, 9-12, 15, 16, 18, 19 and 21 are by Ronald Brown.

* *These quotations, from Queen Victoria's Journal, are by gracious permission of Her Majesty The Queen.*

Figure 20. A long deep flounce of Point de France, almost certainly a Royal commission, late 17th century, which sold for £1,900 in February 1980. Courtesy Christie's South Kensington.

Figure 21. A bill dated 1906 from Haywards of Bond Street, listing laces refurbished for a customer.

BENTWOOD FURNITURE

By Gillian Walkling

Left: Figure 1. Thonet production no.4. The design of the back of this chair is similar to those supplied to the Café Daum in Vienna in 1849. The Café chairs were constructed of laminated veneers rather than solid pieces of wood as in this case. Courtesy the Victoria & Albert Museum.

Figure 2. Illustration from the Art Journal Illustrated Catalogue 1851 *showing a Thonet table shown in the "Luxury Furniture" range at the Great Exhibition at the Crystal Palace, London. It is described as "rosewood, so bent that the grain of the wood invariably follows the line of the curve and shape required, by which means lightness and elasticity is gained with the least possible material".*

Bentwood furniture, both antique and modern, is today a familiar sight in homes throughout the world. Examples of 19th century bentwood chairs can still be bought for as little as £3 to £4 while rarer examples of hall stands, tables and screens can now fetch as much as £1,500. Rocking chairs, for which the original maker, Michael Thonet, is probably best known, range in price from £30 upwards depending on

condition and complexity of design. The best selling chair, Thonet's production chair no. 14, is reputed to have sold over fifty million since its first appearance in 1859. During the 1870s the Thonet factories are recorded as producing over 1,200 of this model daily. Its extremely simple shape and limited number of components reduced its production costs to a minimum and resulted in the first genuine "consumer chair".

The name of Michael Thonet is so closely associated with bentwood furniture that the existence of other makers remains virtually unknown. Michael Thonet and his sons are credited not only with the invention of this totally novel form of furniture, but with an astute awareness of the social, political and economic climate in which they were working. Thonet's realisation of the potential of mass production and his ability thereby to present a well designed and constructed piece of furniture at extremely low cost to a universal public have gained him the reputation of being the first truly industrial designer in the field of furniture production.

Michael Thonet was born in Boppard, a small town on the Rhine, in 1796. In 1819, at the age of twenty-three, having completed his apprenticeship and achieved the status of Master Carpenter, he set up in business as a joiner and furniture maker, supplying household items to the local community. It was not until the 1830s that he began experimenting with the possibilities of bending and glueing woods in an attempt to minimise labour and material costs. In 1841 he was able to take out patents for new methods of utilising woods in France, Belgium and England, but more importantly in that year samples of his work shown in an exhibition in Coblenz caught the eye of the Chancellor of Austria, Prince Metternich. The Chancellor's introduction of Thonet's designs to the Austrian Court led on to the award of a patent from the

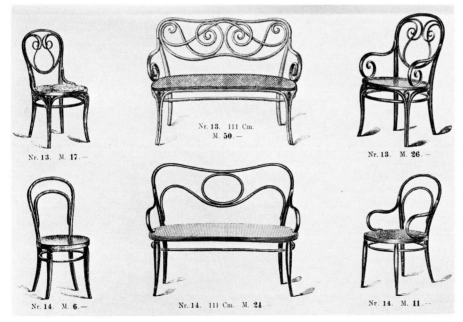

Figure 3. Design from a Thonet Bros. catalogue of 1888. The now famous chair no.14 is shown in the lower left-hand corner and its armchair equivalent to the right.

Figure 4. Thonet production no.13 as shown in the 1888 catalogue illustrated here. Courtesy the Victoria & Albert Museum.

Chancellery of Vienna in 1842 for "the supply of the best quality of wood in selected shapes and curves by chemico-mechanical means". For the following four years Thonet was employed in Vienna by the firm of Carl Leistler and was able to execute his ideas in the furnishing of the Liechtenstein Palace.

Not content to work solely on high quality and still hand-produced furniture, he continued to pursue his interest in the possibilities of mass production through mechanisation. In 1849 his association with Carl Leistler came to an end and together with his five sons he established his own business in Vienna. His first major commission came in that

year from the Café Daum in Vienna and from then on the business flourished. In 1851 he was awarded a Medal of Merit in the "Luxury Furniture" range at the Great Exhibition in London. In 1854, one year after the firm was handed over to his five sons and renamed Thonet Bros., the company won a First Class Prize Medal at the exhibition in Munich. A similar award was gained at the Paris International Exhibition in 1855.

When Thonet first began his experiments his prime intention was to minimise costs of a simple, but time-consuming, process, that of producing a continuous curved wooden shape from a straight piece of timber. The problem had traditionally been met by cabinet makers by either joining two or more sections of wood together or by carving the shape from one solid piece. In Thonet's view both methods were unsatisfactory — joints could easily come apart and a carved piece was liable to split along the fibres as it lost moisture. The problem appeared two-fold. On the one hand, although the process of bending wood through the application of heat or immersion in water was already known, a thick piece of wood could not be bent individually to a sufficient degree; the fibres on the outer edge of the curve snapped under strain. On the other hand, it could not be bent satisfactorily in more than one direction. Thonet first overcame the problems by bending several thin sections of veneer separately to the same shape and then glueing the pieces together to form a thicker and stronger section. Soaked in glue, these larger sections could then be pressed and dried in a wooden or metal mould to produce a second curve. This method enabled cheaper woods to be used for the inner sections and more expensive veneers to be applied to the outer surfaces. The process, however, was still time-consuming and had to be done largely by hand.

Determined to find a solution Thonet finally abandoned his experiments with

Figure 6. Armchair example of Thonet production no.20 Courtesy Sotheby's Belgravia.

strips of veneer and concentrated on bending solid pieces of timber. His perseverance was finally rewarded. By firmly attaching an unbent metal strip to a length of timber the two materials could be bent simultaneously. The wood was then held entirely in compression and, unable to expand, the fibres on the outer edge were prevented from breaking. On 10th July 1856 Thonet Bros. were granted their major patent for "the finishing of chairs and tables out of bentwood, the bending of which is achieved by the introduction of steam or boiling liquids". Until it lapsed in 1869 the patent guaranteed Thonet Bros. sole rights for the production of bent-

Figure 5. An illustration from the Cabinet Maker & Art Furnisher, July 1st 1887 *showing a wide variety of Thonet articles exhibited in an Exhibition in New York in that year.*

Figure 7. Unusual bentwood table with beechwood frame and mahogany top. Courtesy Sotheby's Belgravia.

wood furniture and by that date the company had already achieved international fame.

The considerable demand for Thonet's bentwood furniture during the early 1850s enabled the firm to build their first major factory in 1856. Michael Thonet designed the buildings and most of the machinery himself and when choosing a location took proximity to the source of raw materials as his primary consideration. The expansion of the railway system provided easy access to commercial centres from where the goods could be distributed. The furniture was sent from the factories in pieces and screwed together and polished on arrival at its destination. The first factory was built near the copper-beech forests of Koritschan in Moravia where the supply of wood was plentiful and the unskilled labour required to operate the machinery relatively cheap. Further factories were built at Bystritz-am-Holstein in 1861, Grosz-Ugrocz in Hungary in 1865 and Hallenkau in 1867. At the time of Michael Thonet's death in 1871, these four factories were producing cheap consumer furniture for sale throughout the world with wholesale establishments in major cities in eight different countries.

Although large numbers of competitors appeared after 1869 and by 1901 there were fifty-two registered companies in Austria, Hungary and Poland producing bentwood furniture based on Thonet's designs and patents, Thonet Bros. consistently upheld their position as the leading manufacturer and continued to expand. In 1880 a factory was built at Nowo-Radomsk in Russian Poland and in 1890 another at Frankenberg, Hesse. By 1900 the company had over 6,000 employees producing a daily average of 4,000 pieces of furniture.

The Thonet company were essentially chair makers although they always included a small number of table designs amongst their repertoire. During the last quarter of the 19th century they also produced hat and coat stands, screens, cradles, canterburies and other items, but in a limited range of designs. The majority of chairs had canework seats, but later a variety of pressed wood seats was introduced. Upholstery was uncommon except on some settees and rocking chairs. Every Thonet design was given a production number and each individual piece was either labelled or stamped with their name.

It is generally thought that Thonet Bros. did not establish a wholesale outlet in London until after Michael Thonet's death in 1871 although an article in *The Cabinet Maker & Art Furnisher July 1st 1887* suggests the date 1861. "The London branch was opened in 1861 in Ludgate Hill and after a time moved to High Holborn. It is now at 47 Oxford Street, where may be seen a fine assortment of these bentwood articles; indeed, a permanent exhibition complete of finished drawing, dining and bedroom chairs. Messrs. Thonet have extensive warehouses at Bucknell Street, where a stock of over 12,000 chairs is stored. The goods arrive in pieces, in bales, and are mounted and repolished on the premises, thus ensuring a perfect finish".

The same article also gives a detailed account of the Thonet factories. "Only the wood of the beech tree is used, and the enormous forests in Moravia, Galizia and Hungary supply the immense quantities required for manufacturing the furniture. The trees are from 120 to 150 years old, and replanted at once. About 2,600 acres are cleared annually, producing but 1,300,000 cubic feet of useable wood, as 60 per cent. of the trees are only good for charcoal and firewood. One chair takes about a cubic foot of material. The factories are in or

Figure 8. Hat, coat and umbrella stand from a Thonet Bros. catalogue for 1888.

Figure 9. Late 19th century example of a bentwood armchair with straight turned and reeded legs. Courtesy Sotheby's Belgravia.

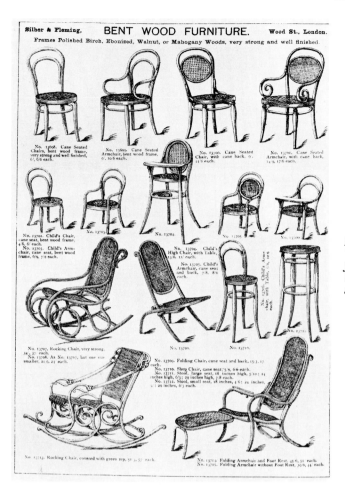

Figure 10. "Bent Wood Furniture" from an 1890s Silber & Fleming sales catalogue.

modern design have been recognised by designers and furniture producers throughout the 20th century. In 1899 the architect Adolf Loos included chairs first produced in 1859 in his designs for the interior of the Viennese coffee house, Café Museum. Joseph Hoffman designed bentwood chairs to be made at the Thonet factory for the now famous Purkersdorf Sanatorium in Vienna between 1903 and 1906. A Thonet armchair produced since 1870 was included amongst the furnishings of Le Corbusier's Pavillon de L'Esprit Nouveau in 1925. During the 1920s Thonet Bros. worked in collaboration with many of the Bauhaus designers and some of the first cantilevered tubular steel chairs were produced at the Thonet factory.

The large quantity of 19th and early 20th century bentwood chairs still remaining in this country is unremarkable when considering the high levels of production. The scarcity of other types of bentwood furniture is also easy to understand for not only were they produced in smaller quantities and generally over a shorter period of time, but they never equalled the popularity of large numbers of chairs for use in hotels, restaurants and other public establishments. In addition bentwood is reputed to have found less favour in this than in other countries and no attempts appear to have been made by British manufacturers to oppose the monopoly of the Austrian producers. Bentwood furniture was strictly an imported phenomenon.

near the forest. The wood is sawn according to the required size, steamed till soft, bent over iron shapes like the form of the article, put in the dry room until quite dry, taken out of the moulds, planed, rasped, polished and put together. Then it is taken to pieces again, and stored until wanted for export, when it is packed in cases of one cubic yard containing three dozen chairs, and sent to the next station, proceeding from thence to the place of destination. The work is piecework, and the people have to buy their own tools and materials. Every care is taken of the lives of the hands, for the factories are provided with fire brigades, model dwellings, schools for the children, and reading and club rooms".

Comparisons have been made between the aims of Thonet and those of the Arts & Crafts movement. While Thonet's chairs show certain Arts & Crafts characteristics — simplicity of form and construction and availability to a universal public due to its low price — they were essentially machine-made and therefore directly opposed to the principles of craft tradition advocated by William Morris and his associates. Thonet was primarily an industrialist and his success was the result of his business ability, not a desire to reform.

The close relationship between Thonet's furniture and principles of

Figure 11. One of a set of eight dining chairs stamped and labelled "Thonet Wien". The actual bent wood of these unusual chairs is limited to the seat frame and the horizontal bars of the back. Courtesy Sotheby's Belgravia.

Figure 12. Chair designed by Joseph Hoffmann for the Purkersdorf Sanatorium in Vienna between 1903 and 1906. Courtesy the Victoria & Albert Museum.

A Mennecy Box

by Diane O'Neil

My choice of a Christmas present is a luxury item, far beyond the dreams of most porcelain collectors, not due to its monetary value but because of the sheer extravagance of possessing a beautiful object which is not directly related to my own collecting.

I have a small, somewhat imperfect and as yet unrepresentative collection of the 18th century French porcelain manufactured at St. Cloud. All of the pieces are white with either artichoke moulding or raised prunus sprigging. Thus, my choice of a coloured, silver mounted, rectangular box from the Mennecy factory is true self-indulgence!

I first saw this delightful little object on one of our rare, idyllic summer days and perhaps it was the effect of the sunlight enhancing the innate delicacy of the soft porcelain with its silver mounts that was so completely captivating.

The available literature in English on French porcelain boxes is limited. Apart from scattered sentences and rather poor illustrations in a few books, the main source of any helpful information is to be found in the sale catalogues. Here one can acquire some idea of the range of shapes, types of decoration, variety of metal mounts and possible uses. Rectangular porcelain boxes tend to be called snuff boxes, whereas those in the form of animals, people and other miscellaneous objects appear as "bonbonnières" in American catalogues and as "snuff boxes" in English ones!

In early English porcelain small rectangular boxes are unknown, their place being exquisitely filled by the finest enamel boxes with silver or gilt metal mounts. At Chelsea during the late red anchor and early gold anchor periods a few bonbonnières were produced mounted in gilt metal often with enamel lids. They were, however, a relatively limited element of the output of the Chelsea manufactory by comparison with their Continental counterparts.

Of all the French soft-paste porcelain manufactories Mennecy probably produced the greatest range of shapes in boxes and bonbonnières. They were modelled as pug dogs (on or off cushions), spaniels, cats (with or without kittens), hens, rabbits and even a dromedary! Other shapes included slippers, fruits and a very unlikely assortment of personages — nuns, shepherds and Chinamen!

And so to the object itself! It is quite small when compared with the snuff boxes illustrated in recent catalogues, the great majority of which are almost double its length. The dimensions of "my box" are 4.5cm x 3cm x 2.5cm and I would prefer to imagine that it was for cachoux rather than snuff; however, to me this is immaterial.

The silver mounts are contemporary and although the discharge marks are rubbed they appear to be for Paris, 1754. This would date the box's manufacture fairly accurately since it would not be functional until hinged and silver mounted and it is difficult to imagine the decorated porcelain components of such a fragile object lying in the manufactory for any length of time after its initial production. Contemporary silver mounts, not found on early English porcelain, enhance the superb rich soft paste in a way that no amount of flamboyant gilding could

achieve, in its gaudy attempt to simulate the metal without any thought to the material of which the piece is made.

The paste is soft, rich and milky-white, yet blemished by minute black spots and covered in a brilliant clear glaze. The overall effect is of a very feminine porcelain, far more so than Chantilly or St. Cloud. The exterior is moulded with chevrons, adding a three-dimensional effect to the surfaces and also serving to protect the decoration from the wear which would inevitably result from constant use. Beneath the silver thumb-piece are small raised rectangular areas simply painted in rose-pink monochrome — they have lost much of their glaze and decoration from continual handling but as they were obviously intended for this purpose this in no way detracts from the beauty of the box. Both the palette and the style of decoration are restrained, consisting entirely of small floral sprays in cool, fresh tones of rose-pink, pale yellow, blue and green, sometimes outlined in sepia. The painting is attractive rather than "fine" but it fully contributes to the wonderful blend of elegance and simplicity. The palette and style of painting could be compared to Derby of the late 1750s and the palette was imitated at Bow in the 1760s, though not always successfully.

In conclusion, this simple yet sophisticated little box crystallises all that I like best in French porcelain. It may not have the novelty of the animal bonbonnières, which seem inelegant by comparison; however, its "line" and "feel" satisfy the senses and it emanates a radiance which is to me uniquely French.

Figure 1. Ebonised bracket clock by Sam. Watson, London, c.1700.

Figure 2. Ebonised bracket clock by Constantine, London, c.1700.

Figure 3. Fruitwood bracket clock by John Fladgate, London, c.1770.

BRACKET CLOCKS

by V.S. Camerer Cuss

Christie's

Anyone who invested in a bracket clock a year ago may well have to face the disappointing fact that his or her nest egg is at the moment rather hard boiled.

The prices being realised today are for the most part stagnant at the level of last year and this discounts inflation at whatever rate you choose. It is of course mainly the monetary situation, home and abroad, that has caused many categories of the antique market to lull as traders and collectors feel the pinch. Only the elite have been buying and they, as always, are engaged in the star pieces.

Figure 1 has all the qualifications for success: an early piece c.1700 with an elegant case, warm brass dial and a movement which, although restored, has a signed and engraved backplate. It realised £2,500 in June 1980. Figure 2 realised £2,000 in June 1981 and to all intents and purposes is the same clock. This surely emphasises that although figure 2 is "worth" as much as figure 1 the price realised reflects what people are prepared to pay today and unfortunately the people involved in this case are not ready to part with as much as they did the previous year.

There are reasons why this example is not alone and why other types are suffering less. Figures 1 and 2 are ebonised, and black is not the most befitting colour for electric lighting. Their design, although elegant, is utterly usual and the movement is horologically standard. They are both one of a kind which at the moment is numerous. Col-

lectors seem to have had their fill while with fewer funds the trade buyers have changed to items more readily saleable.

Therefore condition comes to the fore and with it a large portion of the auction market has a question mark placed against it to the extent that some very presentable clocks by known makers are simply ignored when eighteen months ago they would have been bought and restored. Clocks in good condition, however, are fought over and their value climbs away from the distressed examples making in many ways a healthy market.

Size as well as condition is the watchword today. Clocks that are over 18ins. high and/or 6ins. deep suffer from a handicap that is really very straightforward. The reason is that they are difficult to house; originally designed to sit on a bracket, the combined height of bracket and clock today proves too much for most decors and thus the clock moves to the mantel or bureau where it is confronted by the confining limits of depth.

Figure 3 is small, 12ins. high. Its condition is good, the fruitwood case is well moulded and the gentle outline is complemented very well by the brass beading. It does not have date indication and the escapement is antiquated for its date, c.1770 (late compared with figures 1 and 2), yet it realised £4,400 in July 1980 and would be likely to fetch £4,800 today.

To take market comparison further, look at two extreme examples of early 19th century production. English four

glass striking clocks have the "in vogue" size. Their price last year would have ranged between £1,600 and £2,200 depending on the maker and/or the escapement employed; today the estimate one could confidently quote would be £1,800 to £2,600; not a large increase but a rise all the same. A three-train quarter chiming mahogany clock of the same period (costing as much if not more when produced) would last year have realised £1,800 to £2,400 but today £1,400-£1,600 is the estimate.

There are, of course, exceptions to every rule. Unusual features, whether they be case wood, calendar indications or duration, all push the item into the rarity slot, thus attracting the seemingly bottomless pockets of collectors. A good maker's name overrides all other factors and a signed backplate can multiply the value by two; this, however, is hardly a reflection of the last twelve months since it has been the case for some years.

In the coming year I should imagine that the widening of prices between good and bad examples will continue. More money plus will be spent for a perfect clock while its twin that has been altered will be ignored. A clock of later date and by a lesser maker but in some way special will in all probability attract greater demand still.

For pure investment (which is deplorable) in the short term go for the better end of the market, never mind the category; for the long term perhaps the lower/middle bracket will show the best percentage profit.

Conversations of a Vetting Committee (5)

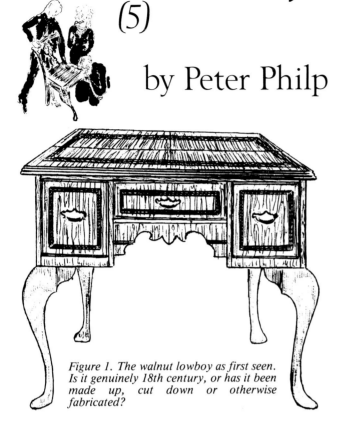

by Peter Philp

Figure 1. The walnut lowboy as first seen. Is it genuinely 18th century, or has it been made up, cut down or otherwise fabricated?

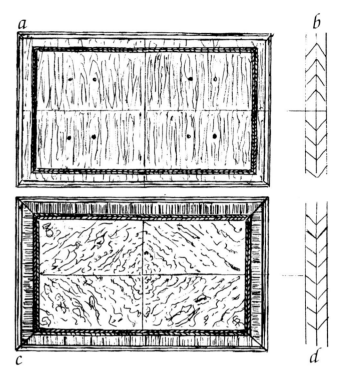

Figure 2. (a) Top of the lowboy viewed from above. It appears to have the usual quartered veneers, but the grain is "straight" — lacking in "figure". It has "herringbone" banding but this shows an eccentricity. At each end, half the chevrons point in one direction and half in the other (b). In each quarter, there is a pair of suspicious-looking circles of veneer. The moulding on the front edge and the two ends is original but that on the back has been "replaced" — not in itself condemnatory but, taken with the other evidence, not a recommendation either. The same principle applies to the absence of crossbanding.
(c) Top of a lowboy as the vetting committee would prefer to see it, with figured walnut veneers, crossbanding, all original moulding and herringbone banding following a consistent "one way traffic" system all around the perimeter as in the detail (d).

For new readers

This, the fifth in our series of dialogues translated from the sagas of the Anteeksandart people, demonstrates once again that, as has recently been said of the Vikings, they were not only raiders but traders. Their festivals, which were very numerous, varied greatly in significance, but all were dedicated, however improbably, to the profit motive. This was to some extent disguised by the splendour of the fetishes displayed at the more important festivals, which were raised to the level of quasi-state occasions by opening ceremonies performed by royal or aristocratic persons. Owing to an ever increasing preponderance of faked fetishes on the open market, it was deemed necessary for all those on display to be examined by a committee of saintly men and women whose wisdom, virtue and sheer bloody-mindedness were beyond dispute. These little groups of gurus were known as *Rot Ten Bast Ards*, which is best translated as Vetting Committees. In all the sagas so far deciphered, the committee is composed of a High Priest, a Second Priest and a Priestess, but this may well have been a literary device on the part of the chronicler; the composition of the committee probably varied considerably in practice.

Now read on...

"I don't want to appear alarmist," said the Second Priest, "but I think we ought to take a good look at this low daddy."

"Low *what*?" cried the Priestess.

"Low daddy. American term for lowboy," explained the Second Priest.

"When I was a boy —" the High Priest began, only to be interrupted.

"Were you low, daddy?" asked the Priestess. No one laughed.

"When I was a young man," the High Priest continued patiently, "we didn't call that sort of walnut-veneered side-table a lowboy. That term is, in itself, an Americanism — but a respectable one, I grant you, known to have been current in New York as early as 1785. They made lowboys to match

tallboys — or highboys, as they more often call them."

"I had a quick peep at this little chap before you two turned up," admitted the Second Priest, "and in my opinion, this lowboy was probably made from the bottom half of a tallboy — and by a wideboy."

"I must say, I find all these boys very confusing," said the Priestess. "You'd better explain."

"We'll start with the top, and work downwards," the Second Priest announced. "Perhaps I should mention that I am assuming the piece to be English, or at least British — not American. Perhaps lowboys were made quite differently in America, thus accounting for some of the things that worry me..."

"Do get on with it," muttered the Priestess. The Second Priest took a deep breath and got on with it.

"The top," he began, "has what purport to be quartered veneers, but the grain is much straighter than is usual for that kind of finish. I would expect there to be much more figure, with the veneers reversed and arranged to form a symmetrical pattern. This relatively straight-grained veneer is the sort we find on the less elaborate chests of drawers and tallboys of the early 18th century. So is the herringbone banding, used without crossbanding. Personally, I like to see some crossbanding on a table-top of this period."

"So do I," agreed the High Priest, "but I've seen perfectly genuine examples without it. Next point?"

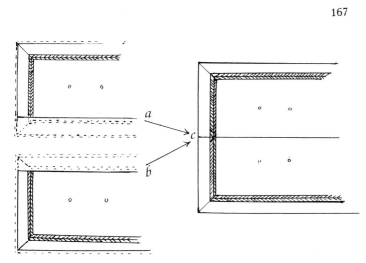

Figure 3. Diagram illustrating a way in which two drawer-fronts could have been used to construct the top of the lowboy. They have been cut along their top edges to remove superfluous herringbone banding and tell-tale cut-outs for locks. The dotted lines indicate what has been removed. They have then been brought together so that points A and B meet at C. The surplus herringbone banding has been used to make good what is needed for the drawers of the lowboy — see figure 4(a).

"There are small pieces of veneer let into the top which I feel sure are there to mask the holes made by drawer-handles. And I think I can prove that to your satisfaction. Let us take out the drawers — we'll return to them later — and turn the whole thing upside down...You see? Holes stopped up on the underside of the top — the pine foundation — corresponding exactly with those bits of veneer on the upper surface. My argument is that this top has been made from two drawer-fronts, trimmed to eliminate unwanted herringbone banding which would otherwise have appeared grotesquely as two lines across the table-top. The trimming has likewise got rid of the old cut-outs for the locks on the drawers."

"Point taken," said the High Priest sagely. He was very good at giving the impression that he knew about these things all the time, but was waiting for the youngsters to show off their paces. "These legs," he said, "have been quite well done, using seasoned timber, but they are almost new. In spite of industrious waxing, there is no depth to the patina, and the feet show precious little signs of wear."

"What about the way they join the carcass?" asked the High Priestess. "They're just screwed on — with modern screws doctored with acid to make them look old. Surely the leg should continue upwards as a square corner-post, into which the front and ends should be tenoned?"

"That, again, is how I like to see it done," said the High Priest, "but not everyone would agree with me. Some good judges accept this method of construction, with the cabriole legs screwed and blocked on to the under-frame of the carcass. Personally, I don't, but I hesitate to reject a piece on those grounds, as opinion is somewhat divided. Let's take a look at the drawers."

"They demonstrate a splendid combination of old and new dovetails," said the Second Priest. "The two deep drawers have old dovetails on their outer sides, new ones on the inner. The dovetails on the shallow centre drawer are all new. And if you look carefully at the fronts, you will see that the herringbone is original on one side and the top and bottom of the deep drawers, but has been made good — using the spare bits we spoke of just now — on the remaining side of each. Also, if you look at the under edge of that prettily shaped apron, I'm sure you will agree that it was cut on a bandsaw, probably last Tuesday. Also, there are tell-tale bits of herringbone where they ought not to be."

"We could go on and on with this one," said the High Priest, "but the evidence against it already is more than sufficient. I think you're right — it has been made up from parts of what you choose to call a 'tallboy'. Personally, I prefer to avoid that misleading term and refer to a chest-on-chest or, if it has legs, a chest-on-stand. No doubt the top was totally missing, and someone — the wideboy you mentioned — used the bottom to produce a fashionable article. But it won't be offered for sale here."

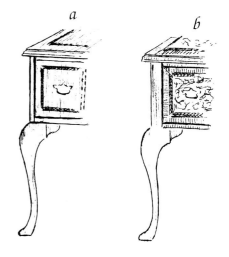

Figure 4. (a) Detail of lowboy showing the way in which the carcass has been constructed and the clear line of demarcation where the cabriole leg joins it. The dotted lines on the drawer-front indicate the making good of herringbone banding with surplus left over after making up the top.
(b) Detail of a walnut lowboy as the vetting committee would prefer to see it. The square shaft of the leg continues upwards to form a stile, or corner-post, for the construction of the carcass. This feature is more obvious in oak and other examples made in the solid, but the line of the shaft is usually discernible even on veneered pieces. The difference can easily be seen when the piece is "turned up". Not everyone would agree with the committee on this point, as there was more than one way to make a lowboy.

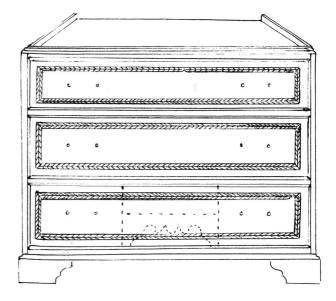

Figure 5. The lower half of a "tallboy" or chest-on-chest — the probable source of the material from which the lowboy has been made up. The two upper drawer-fronts have provided the top, and the bottom one has been skilfully cut to make the three drawer-fronts and the shaped apron in the kneehole. There would be no shortage of linings for the drawers, and only one length of moulding needs to be made for the top. The ends and back are all provided with something to spare, and there is ample cockbeading for the reconstructed drawers.

CHRISTOPHER SAXTON –

Father of English Cartography

by

Yasha Beresiner

Figure 1. Frontispiece to the first atlas of the counties of England and Wales. Saxton's atlas was the first ever to be devoted to one country and its cartographic impact world-wide was considerable. £250.

*This humble earth bears Saxton's body
Who while he was living England scarcely recognised.
Now snatched away the earth bears his corpse
But neither England nor sky can muffle his fame
For although he is dead, he lives countrywide. **

Figure 3. The south-west section of the Wiltshire map (figure 2) shows in detail the coat of arms of Thomas Seckford, mentor and financier of Christopher Saxton. At the base of the compasses the names of Christopher Saxton and Remigus Hogenberg can be clearly identified.

Figure 2. Saxton's Wiltshire engraved in 1576 by Hogenberg. The relative clarity of the map is due to the absence of roads and other symbols on the map. £1,500.

An epitaph of a worthy man who was to British cartography what Shakespeare was to English literature. There is more to the two men than the mere fact that they were contemporaries. Giants in their own fields, each obtained royal recognition and the patronage of an aristocrat who enabled them to devote much of their lives to serve their communities.

They probably never met. The concept of travel was such at the time that to venture out of one's own immediate surroundings was considered a major, even dangerous, undertaking. There were, of course, roads frequented by travelling merchants, ruling gentry attending the Queen's court, military troops and others going about their business, but the trip from Dunningley,

near Leeds in Yorkshire, where Christopher Saxton was born, to Stratford upon Avon would have been an arduous one indeed!

Saxton did make his way to London, having spent some time in Cambridge and met a well-known Suffolk gentleman and lawyer named Thomas Seckford. The encounter was timely. A complete survey of England and Wales had never before been made and Christopher Saxton — albeit still under thirty — was capable of undertaking such a task. Thomas Seckford was prepared to finance it.

Saxton became attached to the Seckford household. Seckford, being such a prominent man and a Master of Requests to the Court, enabled Saxton to obtain several facilities, not least a grant of land and his appointment, in 1574, by Elizabeth I to undertake a cartographic survey of England and Wales. He was also well recommended by the Privy Council.

Figure 4. The lower half of Saxton's map of Dorsetshire shows some of the decorations used by Saxton in adorning the borders of his maps. Seckford's motto "Pestis Patriae Pigrities", changed in 1576 to "Industria Naturam Ornat", is clearly visible. Also Saxton's introduction of the south "meridies" on the border indicating the south.

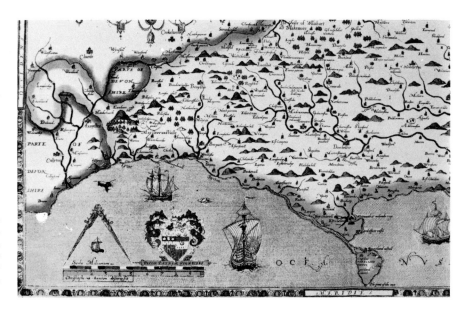

Figure 5. Lincolnshire, being a relatively hilly county, appears slightly more crowded, with the hills all duly represented and also a considerable number of drawings of trees. Elizabeth I's coat of arms and the royal motto are identifiable on the top left-hand side. £1,500.

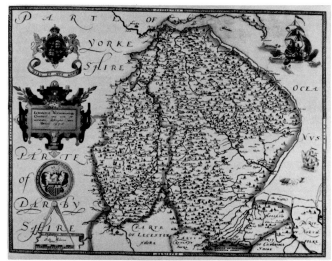

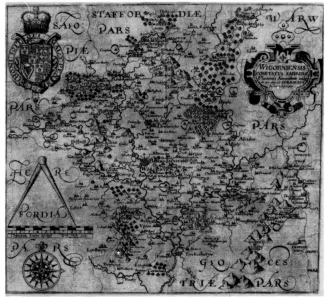

Figure 6. The map popularly referred to as the Saxton-Hole appeared for the first time in Camden's Britannia published in 1607. These were based on Saxton's surveys but reproduced on a smaller scale. The map of Worcestershire was engraved by William Hole. The other engraver involved in the publication of Camden's Britannia was William Kip. £110.

In the case of Wales, special injunctions were forwarded to the local authorities in 1576, requesting the justices of the peace and mayors to assist Saxton in the most practical manner; to have him "...conducted unto any towre, castle, high place or hill...". He was to be accompanied by men who knew the terrain well and on leaving any town or city "the said towne do set forth a horseman that can speke both Welshe and Englishe..." and who was to ensure that Saxton reached his next destination safely. More honours were to follow. In July 1577 Saxton obtained a ten-year privilege — what we would now refer to as a sole right — to make and market the maps of the counties of England and Wales. On 1st July 1589 he was granted a personal coat of arms by Elizabeth I, an honour not conferred on any cartographer since.

It shows a great deal of the character of the man, his courage and perseverance, that he physically undertook on foot and horseback the study of the land he was to map. The fulfilment of his duties took half a decade, having begun in 1574, and although the complete atlas

of thirty-five maps was not finally published until 1579, the first map had already been produced and probably sold for 4 pence per sheet in 1575.

The maps in the atlas are all dated, except that for Northumberland, which was probably engraved in 1576. It is easy to trace a chronological order to the maps. Norfolk and Oxfordshire are dated 1574 and six other maps are dated 1575. Eight are dated 1576, twelve bear the date 1577 and the five maps dated 1578 are all Welsh. (The map of England, dated 1579, will be considered later.)

Much information has been made available to us by the fact that William Cecil, Lord Burghley, contemporaneously followed closely Saxton's progress and was able to obtain the first maps from the first plates engraved for Saxton. The original copy of the "Burghley-Saxton Atlas" is in the British Museum and scholars have been using this to compare and study additions and changes in later editions.

Six engravers were employed in London to execute Saxton's work on copper plates. Their names appear on the maps. They were all craftsmen, well-established and respected in their own right. Remigus Hogenberg, the famed Fleming, had been working in England for some years and engraved nine of Saxton's maps. Three more engravers of Flemish origin worked for Saxton: Lenaert-Terwoort engraved five maps and Cornelis de Hooghe and Johannes Rutlinger executed one each. The other three engravers were English. Four maps were engraved by Augustine Ryther (who added the word "Anglus" to his name, to indicate some pride in his

were quite substantial. Although the new atlas entitled *The Shires of England and Wales* by Christopher Saxton was thought to be a reprint of the 1645 Webb edition, the changes and additions are so prominent that they could make this a new work in its own right.

John Speed's popularity has already been mentioned, and the Lea maps used Speed's insets of town plans and had them engraved on the old plates. Decorations were added, titles changed from Latin into English and roads, taken from Ogilby's surveys, were also inserted. Finally, Speed's divisions into Hundreds were incorporated. There were two editions of Lea's atlas, the first published in 1689, the second in either 1693 or 1694. In all thirty-nine maps appear; thirty-three of these were from the original Saxton plates and the additional six maps were from other plates engraved for and belonging to Philip Lea. Collectors refer to these as the Saxton-Lea edition of maps.

R.A. Skelton in his *County Atlases of the British Isles*, published in 1970, suggests the possibility that some of Saxton's original plates may have been lost in the Great Fire of London. Thus Devonshire and Northumberland are Philip Lea's own work. The former does indeed state that it was engraved by Francis Lamb and the latter is clearly based on the maps of John Speed and Joannes Blaeu. Another original map of Lea's is that of Middlesex which is based on John Ogilby's map of the county. The other three are those of Essex, Surrey and a new map of England and Wales.

The remaining maps all state that they were by Christopher Saxton — sometimes just the initials "C.S." are given — and that they have been "corrected" or "newly revised and amended" or "...with...additions of Roads" etc., by P. Lea.

These, then, form the most important editions of Saxton. The plates did pass on and were used again in the 1720s by George Willdey, as well as Thomas Jefferys in 1749 and C. Dicey and Company in 1770, a fact which merely emphasises how really important and influential Saxton had been to British cartography.

One often wonders why Saxton ceased his activities at a time when he appeared to be at the peak of his career. After his surveys and publication of his atlas, the only contribution he made to the science was the engraving of a great wall map of England and Wales on twenty copper plates. Two examples of the original work survive, one in the British Museum and the other at the Birmingham Public Library. Re-issues of this wall map by enterprising publishers were being sold as late as 1795 but are hardly a match to the originals.

The possibility of obtaining an

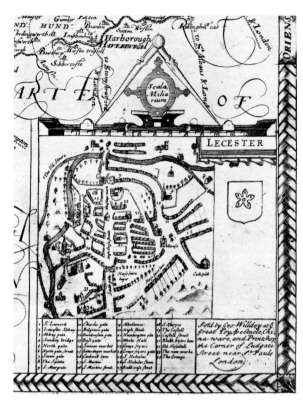

Figure 9. George Willdey was among the last of the mapsellers to make use of Saxton's plates and he offered the atlas for sale in 1720. The photograph shows the town plan of Leicester as an inset in the south-east part of the map of Leicestershire. George Willdey's name and his place of work can be clearly identified in the bottom right-hand corner.

original Saxton atlas today is quite remote, but if one ever came on to the market it could possibly fetch a six figure sum. Individual maps, however, can still be encountered. At the time of writing, Saxton's map of Cornwall was purchased at auction by a dealer for £1,800, suggesting that the retail price would be somewhat above that. The cheapest of the maps, subject to being in good and clean condition, would not be less than £1,000. The Saxton-Kip and Hole maps mentioned from Camden's *Britannia* fetch between £75 and £150, depending on the county and edition in question.

The maps of the Home Counties are invariably more popular. The Saxton-Lea maps fetch between £250 and £1,000. Kent, Sussex, Surrey and Middlesex, which were engraved on one plate, would fetch about £1,000 — again, subject to the condition of the map being good and clean.

Several reproductions of Saxton's complete atlas have been produced in the past few decades. The most famous is the British Museum publication of 1936 with a revised edition which was published in 1939. These had an introduction by Edward Lynam, the well-known scholar and Keeper of Maps at the British Museum. A more recent publication of the atlas is by The Collectors' Library of Fine Art and has been published in a limited edition of five hundred copies at £390 each.

Finally, the British Museum continues to offer individual maps reproduced from the 1579 edition of Saxton's atlas for £1.90 each. For those whose interest is only academic, the price difference must be tempting!

Christopher Saxton died about 1610 aged approximately sixty-six. He is probably buried with the rest of his family in Woodkirk, Yorkshire, although, amazingly, there appear to be no records to show any details of his death.

The relatively short period of his life which he devoted to cartography will allow him to remain immortal in the hearts of map enthusiasts.

*These are the first five lines of the two stanza verse found in the diaries of Dr. John Favour, vicar of Halifax from 1593. The diary is now in the Bodleian Library, Oxford.

Acknowledgements and Bibliography
My gratitude is extended to Bruce Marsden, Head of the Map Department of Stanley Gibbons Antiquarian, for his guidance and advice in the preparation of this article, and to Brian James who is responsible for the high quality photography.

The following sources have been used. Credit is duly acknowledged.

Thomas Chubb: The Printed Maps in the Atlases of Great Britain and Ireland, *London, 1927.*
R.A. Skelton: County Atlases of the British Isles, *London, 1970.*
Raymond Lister: Old Maps and Globes, *London, 1965.*
Ifor M. Evans and Heather Lawrence: Christopher Saxton Elizabethan Mapmaker, *Wakefield, 1979.*
J.B. Harley: Christopher Saxton and the First Atlas of England and Wales, *The Map Collector, September 1979, No. 8.*

Figure 7. Philip Lea used Ogilby's road surveys and John Speed's insets on Saxton's original plates before reprinting a new atlas in 1689. The map of Dorsetshire has Lea's name appearing where Seckford's coat of arms was previously and a plan of Dorchester where the coat of arms of the Queen was previously. £500.

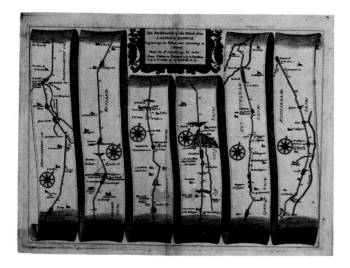

Figure 8. Ogilby's strip map showing the roads from London to Barwick (Berwick). These maps were the basis of the roads included in Philip Lea's utilisation of Saxton's original plates. £75.

The compiled work proved to be a great success and was immediately in demand. Six editions are recorded by Thomas Chubb in his *Printed Maps in the Atlases of Great Britain and Ireland*. These were published in the original form between 1579 and 1600. Thereafter changes began to occur.

The first "irregular" atlas to appear is not a true Saxton item. It would more correctly be classified under the works and titles published by its author, William Camden. The maps appeared in his *Britannia* in 1607 and consisted of fifty-seven maps based on Saxton's and Norden's original surveys, but reduced in size. They were engraved by William Kip and William Hole and are popularly referred to by collectors as the Saxton-Kip or Saxton-Hole maps. Although this was the sixth edition of the *Britannia* it was the first with maps and later editions, published in 1610 and 1637, would indicate considerable success.

Saxton's original plates, meanwhile, found their way into the possession of a certain William Webb.

The publication of John Speed's *Theatre of the Empire of Great Britaine* in 1611 had no doubt put a stop to Saxton's "monopoly"; it is not entirely surprising, therefore, to see new revised editions of his atlas being published. In 1645 Webb was offering for sale, from the Globe in the Cornhill, an atlas entitled *The Maps of all the Shires in England and Wales*. The description of the volume continued thus: "Exactly taken and truly described by Christopher Saxton...newly revised, amended and reprinted".

The revisions and amendments related to the titles and dates on the maps. They were now dated 1642. The royal coat of arms was that of Charles I instead of Elizabeth. Some changes on the faces of the maps also appeared. The map of Yorkshire, for instance, although still produced in double format from the 1579 plates, had the Seckford coat of arms replaced by the city plan of York. Some more decorative additions are also in evidence. These are popularly known as the Saxton-Webb maps. There was only one edition of Webb's atlas.

The next we hear of Saxton's original plates is when they appear in the hands of a well-known London instrument maker and mapseller, Philip Lea. The plates must have been in the hands of Lea for some years before being used as, by the time his revised atlas was published, the changes to the original plates

ancestry!), two by Francis Scatter and one by Nicholas Reynolds. The remaining maps, without the names shown, were presumably also engraved by the same men. There is a possibility that the maps of Wales were engraved by Saxton himself.

There is a diverse range of watermarks in the paper on which the maps were produced; furthermore, the considerable inconsistency in the individual maps (e.g. relating to sizes and the variance in the scales used) suggests that, when initially undertaken, the survey was not necessarily intended to produce a final bound atlas. It is logical to suppose that it was only after the last of the maps had been engraved that Saxton — possibly influenced by the production of Ortelius's *Theatrum Orbis Terrarum* in 1570 — felt it to be a good idea to produce the first ever atlas of the counties of England and Wales.

Thus a frontispiece was engraved, probably by R. Hogenberg, dedicating the whole atlas to Elizabeth I whose coat of arms had already appeared on all the maps. An index was prepared and a map of the whole of England and Wales, engraved by Augustine Ryther, was added. These three are all dated 1579, the date of the publication of the atlas.

Thomas Seckford, Saxton's mentor, patron and financier, had not been forgotten. Each map bears his coat of arms and his motto "Pestis Patriae Pigrities"; this was changed by Seckford after 1576 to "Industria Naturam Ornat" — "Industry Adorns Nature". Christopher Saxton's name also appears on every map, often ornately as a scroll, in latinised form "Christophorus Saxton Descripsit". There are no page or plate markings nor is there any text on the back of the maps. With the exception of Yorkshire, which appears as a fold-out map, each county was engraved on a single copper plate. The atlas was entered to Christopher Saxton at Stationers' Hall in 1579.

Left. Figure 1. A pair of Minton polychrome pâte sur pâte *vases, 41.8cm, 1878. £8,000.*

Right. Figure 2. A pair of Minton "Dresden scroll" vases and covers, 31.5cm, c.1835. £750.

19th Century English Porcelain

by Paul J. Mack

Sotheby Beresford Adams

The market in later porcelain has in the past been a fluctuating one to which it was difficult to apply trends. This probably stemmed from a lack of consistent sales devoted to later date items, a gap which has been filled with the advent of specialised sales by the major auction houses. This has effectively increased interest as well as knowledge. Consequently the mid-'70s has shown a rationalisation of prices which has been reflected again over the past year. The mainstream factories still provide the "safest bets" investment-wise with the usual provisos with regard to condition and attractiveness. Damage is increasingly important, the lower priced items attracting little interest and it being taken very much into account with higher priced pieces.

Recently an unusual amount of Minton *pâte sur pâte* decorated plaques and wares were sold with strong competition for all pieces. The highest price was for a superb pair of polychrome vases which realised £8,000, a price which reflected the cataloguer's research in discovering an engraving of one of the vases in the 1878 Paris International Exhibition Catalogue (figure 1). Not of the same quality but still attractive were the pair of Minton vases (figure 2) which made £750. These are typical of the neo-rococo style for which Coalport is probably the most famous exponent. Collectors here should take special notice of condition — this flower encrusted ware is rather susceptible to damage, and modern copies, especially of Coalport, do exist.

Royal Worcester has again proved very consistent with anything signed making good prices. The pair of vases typically painted with highland cattle and sheep by John Stinton made £620 (figure 3). In the same sale a large pot

Figure 3. A pair of Royal Worcester vases, 21cm, 1904. £620.

pourri vase and cover, also by John Stinton, made £1,300. Royal Worcester figures have sold well and the attractive figure of a sailor boy (figure 4) made £650. Generally speaking the price range for this size of figure is between £200-£400.

Royal Crown Derby has also stood the test of time and even comparatively recent Imari wares sell well. Of the Imari-type pattern the miniature wares are worth keeping an eye out for as they always attract strong competition. Appealing subjects such as coal scuttles and flat irons were made which realise between £70-£200 each, depending upon rarity. Royal Crown Derby wares painted and signed by artists such as Desire Leroy, A. Gregory and others are expensive. A single plate by the former (figure 5) fetched £1,250 and a pair of vases by the same artist made £1,650. A Royal Doulton plate with painting of a similar quality, painted and signed by G. White, made £450 (figure 6), a very high price for a single Doulton plate but still reasonable in comparison.

Services have also been selling well with figures 7 and 8 as typical examples. Before buying, care should be taken to go through every piece to look for damage and for replacement pieces of a later date. Despite having increased in value, 19th and early 20th century services are still reasonable, especially in comparison with their modern counterparts. The latter can be very expensive to buy and can be worth as little as half when trying to re-sell. Better to buy an old service to use which stands a chance of retaining its value.

Figure 4. Royal Worcester figure of a sailor boy, 18cm, 1898. £650.

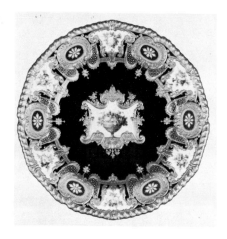

Left. Figure 5. A Royal Crown Derby plate painted by Desire Leroy, 22.8cm, 1906. £1,250.

Figure 7. A Staffordshire green ground dessert service (twenty-five pieces), c.1840. £620.

Left. Figure 6. A Royal Doulton plate painted and signed by G. White, 22.2cm, 1903. £450.

Figure 8. A John Ridgway dessert service (nine pieces), c.1850. £600.

Approximate Price Guide (in £) to English Dial Clocks

by Ronald Rose

	Pre-1800		1800-1850		1850-1900		After 1900	
	Timepiece	Strike	Timepiece	Strike	Timepiece	Strike	Timepiece	Strike
Approx. 12ins. Dial Diameter								
Brass dial, verge	1,400	1,800	1,200	1,600				
Brass dial, anchor	1,100	1,550	950	1,300				
Wooden dial, verge			950	1,100				
Wooden dial, anchor			600	875				
Wooden dial, trunk case			750	1,000				
Iron dial, flat			400	575	325	500	160	350
Iron dial, convex			450	625	400	525	200	375
Iron dial, trunk case			475	650	425	550	250	400
Drum dial clock			475	650	450	600		
Octagonal dial clock			500	750	475	700		
Approx. 8ins Dial Diameter								
Brass dial, verge	1,500	1,900	1,300	1,600				
Brass dial, anchor	1,200	1,600	1,100	1,350				
Wooden dial, anchor			750	950				
Wooden dial, trunk case			800	1,000				
Iron dial, flat			425	575	375	550	280	400
Iron dial, convex			450	600	400	575	300	425
Iron dial, trunk case			475	625	450	600	350	475
Octagonal dial clock			475	700	425	600		
Approx. 16ins. Dial Diameter								
Brass dial, anchor	1,450	1,800	1,250	1,600				
Wooden dial, anchor			750	1,000				
Wooden dial, trunk case			800	1,000				
Iron dial, flat			475	575	450	550	325	425
Iron dial, convex			500	600	475	575	350	450
Iron dial, trunk case			525	625	500	600	375	475
Drum dial clock			525	650	500	625		

It must be appreciated that this is only a very rough price guide to the amount that would have to be paid for a clock where both case and movement are in the very best condition and absolutely genuine. Also the saleability of any clock, and therefore its price, depends finally on its appearance and proportions. It would be a mistake to think that an ill proportioned clock could fall into any of the categories on this chart.

Conversations of a Vetting Committee (8)
by Peter Philp

A curious fact emerging from a study of both the archives and artifacts of the Anteeksandart people is that many of them must have had very small knees. The mysterious knee cult is traditionally believed to have been initiated by the legendary matriarch Mother Brown, whose name is immortalised in tribal song and dance. Attempts to identify her with the Priestess who plays an important rôle in many of the sagas have so far proved inconclusive. The near-magical significance attaching to knees is indicated by the large number of pieces of furniture featuring the so-called "kneehole" — a minute space into which it is difficult to insert a pair of standard modern knees. A recent experiment conducted by a well-known, rugger-playing anthropologist resulted in his having to be cut free with a fret-saw. A proper appreciation of the reverence accorded the kneehole is essential to an understanding of the following saga. Without it, the reader might well be left wondering what on earth all the fuss was about.

Figure 1. The mahogany kneehole desk in question, described as c.1760, with replaced handles and bracket feet.

"That's a nice little kneehole desk," said the Second Priest.

"Dressing table," the Priestess corrected him.

"It's a moot point," interposed the High Priest, diplomatically. "Chippendale called it a 'buroe dressing-table', leaving himself free to flog it as either one or the other, depending on what the customer wanted, and I don't see why the same flexibility shouldn't be utilised by the dealer of today. Chippendale used the term in the 1762 edition of the *Director,* when the basic type had been around for about fifty years — first in walnut, then in mahogany. If the people who made the things hadn't been able to make up their minds as to what they were for by that time, I don't see the point in arguing about it now."

"Agreed," said the Second Priest.

Figure 2. One of the small drawers from the left-hand side of the desk. The drawer-side on the right has been replaced with wood having a more open grain than the rest. At the right-hand end of the drawer-front is a plugged hole which originally received the bolt of an earlier handle.

"Let's get on with the job of vetting it, shall we? What does the exhibitor have to say about it on the ticket?"

"He's even more vague than Chippendale was," said the Priestess, glancing at the ticket. "Mahogany kneehole c.1760. Not a desk nor yet a dressing table. Just a kneehole. How can you sell a hole as an antique?"

"He also says the handles and the bracket feet are replaced," remarked the High Priest. "I wonder if that's all that's happened to it?"

"Shall we turn it up?" asked the Second Priest, who habitually spent so much time peering at the bottoms of pieces of furniture that he frequently forgot to take a good look at them the right way up.

"By all means," said the High Priest, "but I doubt if we'll be very much the wiser. However . . ."

With a sigh he helped the others to remove the drawers and turn the article upside down. "As I thought," he murmured. "New glue blocks everywhere, but that is only to be expected when, as stated and as permitted by the rules of the game, the feet have been renewed. The bottom board is old. The mouldings around the edges and the batten rail at the back are new but if one accepts that the feet had to be re-made, then the related replacements have to be tolerated too. The assumption is that the thing got badly knocked about at its lower extremities."

"Then you think it's all right?" asked the Priestess.

"Not so fast," cautioned the High Priest. "What I said was that we wouldn't learn very much from looking at the bottom. I'm rather more interested in the drawers. Not the long one at the

top. That's probably as made. But take a good look at any of the six small ones. Notice anything?"

The Priestess and the Second Priest each took a small drawer and examined it. "Mine has one drawer-side replaced," the Priestess pronounced, firmly. "That's odd," exclaimed the Second Priest, "so has mine. They've used old wood, but the grain is different — more open."

"I'm sorry to say," said the High Priest, "that all six drawers exhibit the same peculiarity. And in every case, if you put the drawer back into its correct

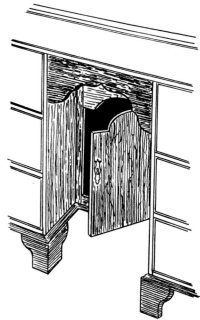

Figure 3. Detail showing the kneehole. All shaded areas have been reconstructed, using wood not original to the chest from which the desk has been converted.

position in the carcase, you will find that it is the inner drawer-side that has been renewed. Now, while I am willing to believe that even oak drawer-sides can become so infected with woodworm that they sometimes have to be renewed, I feel that credibility is strained when I am asked to accept that any brigade of woodworms is as tidy-minded as that.''

"Drawers reduced in size,'' snapped the Priestess, who occasionally became impatient of the High Priest's tendency to embroider his themes to the point where no one knew, any longer, what he had been talking about in the first place.

"And just look at the drawer-*fronts*!'' chirruped the Second Priest. "There's a mark on every one of them, near the inner edge, where the hole drilled for the bolt of an earlier handle has been plugged. It's very small and it's been done very neatly, but it's there just the same. It's obvious what has happened. Each pair of small drawers has been made from one long one. The outer drawer-side has been retained but a new inner one had to be provided throughout. The handles on what was no doubt a chest of drawers were originally nearer the centre, and it is the inner bolt-hole that has had to be plugged and camouflaged.''

"So what about the kneehole?'' demanded the Priestess. "If this was originally a four-drawer chest, there was no kneehole at all, and no little cupboard set into it.''

"If you look at the whole of that area carefully,'' said the High Priest, "you will find it has been entirely reconstructed. The difference in the wood is not immediately apparent, partly because it is in shadow, and partly because, as was quite usual, the arched door of the cupboard is veneered in figured mahogany that would be different from the rest, even in a genuine article.''

"But the plain mahogany used in the returns of the kneehole is, when you come to examine it, rather different from that used on the ends; and surely it ought to be much the same?''

"That,'' said the High Priest, "is what I would expect myself — although provincial makers did sometimes use up odd pieces of timber where they would not be too prominent. But you will find the frame around the door is of yet another kind of mahogany, and the shaped rail above the kneehole another one again.''

"Surely,'' asked the Second Priest, "that ought not to be a fixed rail? Wasn't it always a shallow drawer?''

"I would agree with you,'' said the High Priest, "but again, it is always possible that, for the sake of economy and to please a mean customer, a saving was made in this way. So I wouldn't condemn the piece on that alone. But the under edge of the rail shows the

marks of a band saw — a machine not invented in the 18th century. In general, the craftsmanship of this kneehole section is just not up to the standard of the rest, and it becomes increasingly obvious, as one looks at it, that it has been introduced as a feature to raise a good, honest, four-drawer chest out of its comfortable rut to the level of the much rarer kneehole desk or dressing table.''

"Hang on!'' cried the Second Priest. "Surely, if this started life as a Georgian chest of drawers, the drawers would have been graduated, whereas these are of equal depth — as they should be in a kneehole desk.''

"It's a good point,'' agreed the High Priest, "— or it would be but for the fact that the thing has been manufactured out of one of those rather nice, low George II chests in which the graduation is not very marked, only the bottom drawer being a little deeper than the rest. You will find, if you measure them, that the dimensions here conform to that principle.''

"So it's still a fake,'' concluded the Priestess, "and we chuck it out.''

"Spoken like a man,'' said the Second Priest. "But I do wish you didn't reject things with such *relish*. People are simply *terrified* of us.''

"Good thing, too,'' said the Priestess. "Discourages some of them from getting up to quite so many tricks like this one.''

Saleroom Report

Right: George III mahogany and kingwood-banded oval-shaped work table, with pleated silk well, and associated base, c.1790, 2ft.6ins. high x 1ft.6ins. wide. £600. Sotheby, King & Chasemore.

Part of a collection of 160 horse brasses including a bust of Queen Victoria, a crown, sailing vessels, a horse-drawn cart, letters, various animals, a church, windmill and one as a hammer and dividers. £990 (total). Phillips.

George II mahogany library armchair, stuffed serpentine back, shaped stuffed arms on moulded supports, stuffed seat, cabriole legs, front two richly carved with cabochon and leaves, hairy paw feet, c.1755 (re-railed). £680. Sotheby's.

Victorian walnut-framed settee. £1,050. Sotheby Bearne.

BOOKPLATES

by
James Wilson

Figure 1. An Early Armorial bookplate.

Right: Figure 2. A scarce Jacobean bookplate. The owner's name (Thomas Townsend) is handwritten.

Below: Figure 3. A pair of similar stock pattern bookplates in the Chippendale style.

Bookplates or ex libris are those printed or engraved labels often found pasted inside the front covers of books to denote ownership. Their prime purpose is to remind borrowers whence the book came, and to whom it must be returned; but these labels also indicate the owner's pride in his books and his wish permanently to mark his link with each cherished volume.

Bookplates were first used in Germany, but they have been employed in Britain for about four hundred years, during which time many tens of thousands of individual bookplates have been designed. This provides collectors with a vast treasure-store in which to seek the styles, themes, particular artists or families of owners which most appeal to them.

Collections are usually arranged in chronological styles. The first users of bookplates were nobles and gentry who had their armorial bearings printed from copper engravings. There are three or four sub-divisions, but generally these bookplates are known as Early Armorials and are desirably handsome with their flowing decorative mantling (figure 1). Naturally, many of these old bookplates and the books which housed them have been destroyed over the years, but despite their comparative rarity they are still to be discovered in those ancient odd volumes which some second-hand booksellers offer for a pound or two.

From early in the 18th century the pattern of bookplates developed into the so-called Jacobean style (figure 2). The main identifying feature of this dignified style is the fish-scale decoration on the solid-looking designs which are reminiscent of the carved wood furniture and house ornamentation of the period.

The most frequently met ex libris, except for the Victorian and modern die-sunk engravings, then followed from about 1740. These were in the Chippendale style (figure 3), and it is a revelation to note the variations achieved by the engravers around this graceful and usually charming rococo theme.

Incorporated in some of the Chippendale designs are dragon heads, cherubs and trophies of arms, the latter of course for the books of military gentlemen.

Engravers have always used favourite designs as stock patterns, and in all styles it is interesting to find identical or very similar designs used by different owners, with suitable alteration to the armorial content of the 'plate.

Following the Chippendale style (with some overlap as indeed there was between all stylistic periods) came the Festoon and Wreath and Ribbon 'plates based upon the simple spade shield graced with a surround of floral sprays and ribbons (figure 4). Though there is less scope for variety, nevertheless some very pleasing bookplates are found in these late 18th/early 19th century associated styles.

A quite different kind of bookplate which also became popular at about this period was the landscape pictorial (figure 5) featuring, usually, a wood-engraved view with the owner's name shown on a rock, or perhaps with his shield of arms leaning against a tree. Thomas Bewick and his pupils certainly created a number of these pleasing little pictures which are amongst the most popular items in our collections.

In the 19th century the much wider use of bookplates encouraged stationers to supply steel-engraved armorial ex libris which were technically accomplished but monotonously plain and unembellished. These "die-sinkers"

Figure 4. A Festoon/Wreath and Ribbon 'plate for the Revd. Dr. Barrow who ran an Academy in Soho Square. Amongst his pupils was James Boswell's second son. Johnson's biographer wrote of Barrow that he was "a coarse north-countryman, but a very good scholar"! There are three varieties of this bookplate.

(figure 6) are abundant and not sought after except by those collectors who are interested in family genealogy and heraldry.

Die-sinkers have been in vogue for over 150 years, and are still being supplied by "society" stationers in London's West End. Thankfully, there has been co-existent with these dull efforts an almost continuous output of much worthier work by artists of merit and imagination — William Blake, Edward Burne-Jones, Walter Crane, Aubrey Beardsley (figure 7), William Strang, Edward Gordon Craig (who wrote an important essay with fifty of his bookplate designs tipped-in), Eric Gill, Reynolds Stone, Joan Hassall: the list would include a majority of the best known artist-engravers of the last two hundred years.

The beginner today could still form a collection representative of all the styles, including some less important but interesting fashions not mentioned above, and could do it at much less cost than might be expected.

My own collecting began about seven years ago. I suppose in this time I have spent between £2,000-£3,000, but for this I have acquired some 40,000 book-plates. Many of these will be discarded as and when I find leisure to sift through them; but to be retained will be my 'plates by Hogarth, Vertue, Pyne, Bewick, Blake, Lucien Pissarro, Kate Greenaway, Robert Anning Bell, Eric Gill, Stephen Gooden, Paul Nash, Oscar Kokoschka and so on into the scores of names of distinguished artists, examples

Henry Sandall.

Figure 6. A steel-engraved "die-sinker".

Figure 7. A bookplate designed by Aubrey Beardsley.

of whose work in other fields could certainly not be obtained so reasonably.

You will wish to know something of current prices: undoubtedly these are rising for in recent years the founding of the Bookplate Society (currently two hundred members) and the publications and exhibitions organised by that body have stimulated interest. However, quite attractive early plates can still be bought for upwards of 50p, die-sinkers and Continental modern plates can be had from 5p each, and in my own stock at present are bookplates by Beardsley for £3, by Stephen Gooden for £2, by Rex Whistler for £3.

For those who would be more interested in collecting thematically or want to concentrate on acquiring the 'plates of famous owners such as distinguished authors, statesmen, actors, the scope is wide and prices usually reasonable. For example, the copper engraved bookplate of David Garrick (figure 8) with bust of Shakespeare above his name upon a car-touche is £8; the rather less pictorially attractive 'plates of Charles Dickens, Neville Chamberlain, and other "modern" personalities are found for £1 — or less, if you examine carefully some of the tattier books at jumble sales!

Royal bookplates are popular, and I have copies of the personal ex libris of William IV, Queen Victoria (several varieties one of which is shown in figure 9), Edward VII, George V, Queen Mary, The Prince of Wales (later Duke of Windsor), and several of the Royal Princes and Princesses including our present Queen when she was Princess Elizabeth.

My foreign 'plates include those of Hitler, Mussolini, F.D. Roosevelt and a number of leading dancers, musicians and bibliophiles.

Collecting thematically is not much practised in Britain but why not if you want to!

The first bookplates I sold were to a young lady who selected a dozen or so armorials. When I asked if she was a

Figure 8. Chippendale
pictorial bookplate of
the famous actor.

*La premiere chose qu'on doit faire quand on a
emprunté un livre, c'est de le lire afin de pou-
voir le rendre plutôt.*

Menagiana. Vol IV

Figure 9. One of Queen
Victoria's bookplates.

Case   Shelf

HER MAJESTY'S PRIVATE LIBRARY.
BUCKINGHAM PALACE.

Figure 10. A design by Leo Wyatt, well-
known calligrapher and engraver, 1976.

Figure 11. Designed and wood-engraved
by Richard Shirley Smith for the
author's books about the countryside.

collector of bookplates she showed surprise and asked what they were. When I
remarked that she had just bought some,
she said that she collected pictures of
pussycats, and liked those on the
selected 'plates. She had chosen
armorials which featured heraldic lions
and other brave felines. Pussycats
indeed!

A Continental collector known to me
collects 'plates depicting owls; another
collects ex libris featuring Don Quixote
and has many hundreds. Other collected
themes are musical 'plates, military,
architectural, ladies 'plates (there is a
book on the subject), art deco designs
and so on to infinity!

Should you wish to commission a
bookplate for your own books, then it is
advisable to have it designed by an artist
experienced in working in miniature, for
a larger design which is then reduced
photographically is not often as pleasing
as an engraving or line drawing done to
size. The Hon. Sec. of the Bookplate
Society can suggest some artists.

Concerning the removal of ex libris
from books: this is best effected by
cutting a piece of blotting paper to
overlap fractionally the bookplate,
wetting the blotting paper and placing it
firmly upon the bookplate. After a
minute or two (and perhaps another
wetting) the 'plate can usually be lifted
away. The removal of particularly
important bookplates should not be
attempted. The book itself must be kept,
and this applies also if the bookplate has
an interesting association with the book;
an author's own copy, for example.

By the way, condition is of
importance. Should an exceptionally
rare ex libris turn up in torn or stained
condition then it ought to be kept; but,
as in all forms of collecting, a sound,
clean copy is much more precious than
one which is torn or dirty.

Collections of bookplates are now
appearing at book auction sales to meet

the increasing demand. Not many booksellers or dealers are handling them yet,
but there are indications of interest in
dealing now that collectors are asking
for bookplates.

Be wary, for one or two dealers who
know little about the subject are asking
high prices for worthless die-sinkers;
though, conversely, they may be under-
charging for better things I've not yet
had the luck to experience this!

For further reading about this
absorbing field for collectors I would
explain that a series of important books
was published at the turn of the century
and remain of importance today. Since
then little of note had been published
until this decade during which several
interesting books and lengthy articles
have been published, the most valuable
being the extensively illustrated and
most authoritatively written *British
Bookplates — A Pictorial History* by
Brian North Lee, published this year by
David and Charles at £12.50. This is
most highly recommended both for
beginner and expert collector. It can be
obtained from the Bookplate Society.
The other most useful titles are:

Warren. *A Guide to the study of
Bookplates,* 1880 (as Lord de Tabley, a
second edition was published in 1900).
Journal of the Ex Libris Society, 18
volumes, 1891-1908.
Castle, E. *English Bookplates,* 1892,
enlarged edition 1893.
Hardy, W.J. *Bookplates,* 1893, second
edition 1897.
Hamilton, W. *Dated Bookplates,* 1895.
Fincham, H.W. *Artists and Engravers
of British and American Bookplates,*
1897.

The Hon. Sec of the Bookplate Society
will provide details of modern
publications and of membership of the
Society. He is Professor W. Butler, 9
Lyndale Avenue, London NW2 2DQ.

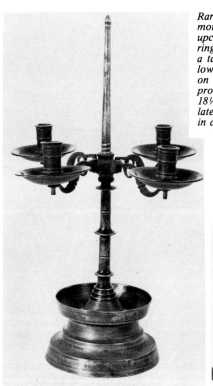

Rare Gothic candleholder, moulded base and integral upcurved drip-catch rising to ringed spindle stem supporting a tall ornamental pricket with lower section to accept a screw-on lug for candle branches, probably Flemish, c.1500, 18⅛ins., now fitted with four later candle arms terminating in dished drip pans and ringed cylindrical sockets. £1,561.

Left to right. One of a pair, early George III, separate sconces, c.1760-70, 10⅞ins. (one with base repaired). £128.22. One of a pair, George III, last quarter 18th century, 8⅜ins. £78.05. One of a pair, last quarter 18th century, 10¹⁵/₁₆ins. £35.68. One of a pair, last quarter 18th century, 8¼ins. £61.32.

Left to right. One of a pair of German bell-based candlesticks by the maker? LW, maker's mark on foot rim, mid-17th century, 9¼ins. £1,170.75. Single of a more coppery alloy, perhaps Dutch or English, late 16th century, 4⅛ins. £379.10. Single, perhaps Dutch or Scandinavian, 17th century, 5¾ins. £367.95.

AUCTION FEATURE continued

Left to right. Small Charles II candlestick, second half 17th century, 5½ins. £892. Another similar, 6¼ins. £669. Another, larger and plainer, base with a more pronounced "step" to the foot, mid-17th century, 7⅝ins. £423.70. Early Tudor candlestick, early 16th century, 9⅛ins. (upper stem repaired). £613.25.

Left to right. Single candlestick with bracket feet cast on the underside with maker's mark of a shell, 5⅛ins., sold with another with inverted baluster stem on octagonal base with circular grease depression, 4½ins., and another on square base 5⅛ins., last quarter 17th century. £128.22. Single, 6¼ins., sold with another with knopped cylindrical stem on octagonal base, 6ins., 17th century. £144.95. Single, 7¼ins., sold with another 6¼ins., and another later, 8½ins., 17th/18th century. £195.12. Single, 11ins., sold with another with baluster stem on similar base, 9ins., perhaps Indo-Portuguese. £22.30.

Left to right. One of a pair, late 17th century, N.W. Europe c.1675-1700. 6½ins. £312.20. Single William III, c.1690-1700, 6½ins. £267.60. One of a group of three early Georgian, c.1720-30, 6⅞ins. to 7ins. (one with lip replaced). £122.65. Single Queen Anne or George I, c.1710-15, 6⅞ins.£72.47.

Left to right. Dutch or Scandinavian sheet brass candlestick, last quarter 17th century (sconce and drip pan probably from a contemporary octagonal-based candlestick), 9½ins. £133.80. One of a pair, probably French or Spanish, first quarter 18th century, 6¼ins. £66.90.

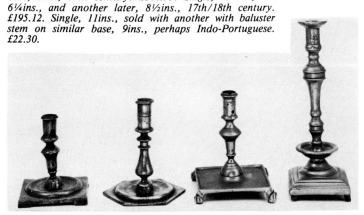

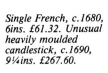

Single French, c.1680, 6ins. £61.32. Unusual heavily moulded candlestick, c.1690, 9¼ins. £267.60.

Left to right. French, second half 16th century, 8½ins. £267.60. Another similar but slightly later, c.1600, 8⅛ins. £172.82. Single, probably Netherlands, 17th century, 8⅜ins, £183.97. One of a pair, 5⅜ins. £139.37.

Rare ancient lamp base of Coptic Roman type, dished and waisted drip-catch raised on stem with bladed knops divided by baluster moulding, all on shaped tripod base with concave panels and three hoof feet, relief-cast markings on underside of base, 5th/6th century, 10¼ins. £1,728.25.

Right: Left to right. One of a pair, George II, twist-type candlestump ejector mechanism, c.1750, 6¾ins. £245.30. One of a taller pair, similar ejector mechanism, c.1750, 8ins. £323.35. One of a pair, push-rod ejectors, c.1750-60, 8½ins. £289.90. One of four similar, all c.1750-60, two 8ins., one 9⅝ins. (brim of socket wanting), one 9⅞ins. £161.67.

Left: Large Cromwellian candlestick, c.1650, 9⅝ins. £1,393.75.

Right: Left to right. Candlestick with both rectangular and circular ejection holes, c.1600, 5½ins. £334.50. Another with large "gothic window" ejection hole, most probably Spanish, 16th century, 5¼ins. £490.60. Another with shaped octagonal border to the drip pan, 16th century, 4¼ins. £579.80. Another with wavy edged border to the drip pan and ovolo-moulded gadrooned foot rim, probably Spanish, 16th century, 4⅝ins. £579.80.

Left to right. One of a pair, 9⅞ins., sold with similar but smaller pair, 8⅞ins., both 19th century. £53.52. One of a pair, 8⅜ins., sold with pair with knopped conical stems on domed base with octagonal foot, 9¾ins., both 19th century. £89.20. One of a pair, 8⅝ins., sold with another pair with multi-knopped stems on square moulded foot, 9⅛ins., both 19th century. £83.62.

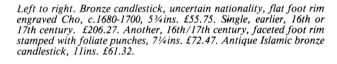

Left to right. Bronze candlestick, uncertain nationality, flat foot rim engraved Cho, c.1680-1700, 5¾ins. £55.75. Single, earlier, 16th or 17th century. £206.27. Another, 16th/17th century, faceted foot rim stamped with foliate punches, 7¼ins. £72.47. Antique Islamic bronze candlestick, 11ins. £61.32.

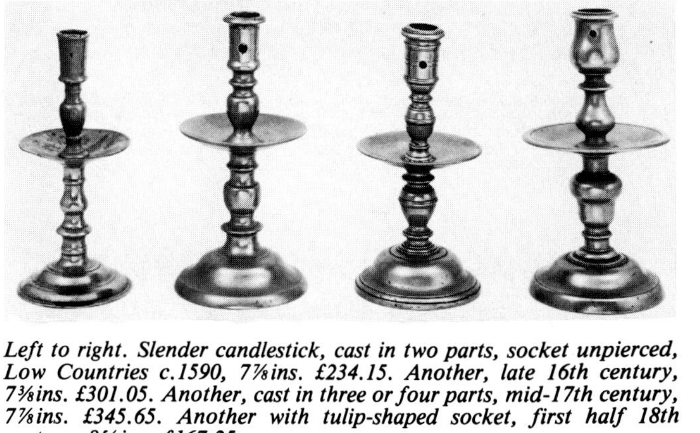

Left to right. Slender candlestick, cast in two parts, socket unpierced, Low Countries c.1590, 7⅞ins. £234.15. Another, late 16th century, 7⅜ins. £301.05. Another, cast in three or four parts, mid-17th century, 7⅞ins. £345.65. Another with tulip-shaped socket, first half 18th century, 8⅝ins. £167.25.

Left to right. One of two square-based Spanish or Portuguese, 17th century, 5½ins. and 5¾ins. £94.77. One of a group of three candlesticks on peg feet, 17th century, 5ins. to 6ins. £234.15. Single, 17th century, 5½ins. £189.55.

Left to right. One of a pair, maker's mark E¹K cast inside base, push-rod ejectors, 9½ins., sold with similar smaller single stick, 6⅛ins., last quarter 18th century. £61.32. One of a pair, 8¾ins., sold with smaller pair, similar but raised on octagonal foot rim, 7¼ins., both with push-rod ejectors, first half 19th century. £78.05. One of another pair, 9⅞ins., sold with pair with inverted conical stems and circular bases, 9¾ins., both first half 19th century. £78.05. One of another pair, 7¼ins., sold with a single with baluster stem, 8⅞ins., another with hexagonal foot, 7¾ins., and another on rectangular foot with rounded corners, 7¼ins., all 19th century. £72.47.

AUCTION FEATURE

A study collection of Old Brass Candlesticks formed by the late Ronald F. Michaelis,

Sotheby's 1st November

Left to right. Single candlestick, 9⅝ins., sold with another similar, with square knop to the stem and sconce en suite, 8⅝ins., both second half 18th century, and another, taller, on circular base, 12¼ins. £94.77. One of a pair, George III, slide ejector, c.1760-80, 7½ins. £89.20.

One of a rare pair of tall George III candleholders, slide ejector, last quarter 18th century, 16¼ins. £301.05. One of a pair of candleholders stamped on bases J. Crampton's patent, sprung slides to push the candle against the screw-on sconce with unusual cover concealing all but the candle wick, mid-19th century, 10⅛ins. £31.22.

Left to right. Squat N. European candlestick cast in two parts with ribbed cylindrical socket fixed directly on to the drip pan with its hollow incurving base, socket with filed rectangular ejection apertures, 4⅞ins., perhaps English, first half 16th century. £245.30. Another, circular ejection holes, first half 16th century, 4⅞ins. £172.82. Another, rectangular ejection holes and incised ornamental reedings on drip catch and foot rim, 16th/17th century, 5¼ins. £446. Candlestick of similar general outline but with heavier socket ornamented by three bladed mouldings, circular ejection holes, raised on short cylindrical stem springing from ring knop, perhaps French, early 17th century, 5¾ins. £334.50.

continued over page

Charles I tent stitch picture c.1640, 15¾ins. x 17¼ins., £260. Sotheby's.

Saleroom Report

A Paul Storr cup, thought to be one of a set of eight or twelve punch cups which perhaps hung round the edge of a punch bowl, 6¼oz, £480. Manchester Auction Mart.

Set of four enamelled game bird menu holders, S. Mordan & Co., Chester 1911, £150. Christie's South Kensington.

Figure 1. Dish made by the Herculaneum Pottery, Liverpool. Indian scene with foliage border.

Blue-printed Earthenware

by A.W. Coysh

Figure 2. Dish made by the Herculaneum Pottery, Liverpool. Printed mark "French Scenery". Floral border and gadrooned edge.

If I were promised a piece of blue-printed earthenware for Christmas I should hope that the pattern might show a landscape of some kind, crisply engraved, and preferably on a meat dish. It would please me if I could find a maker's mark or "backstamp" as it is sometimes called, for many potters did not identify their wares. I should hope that it might have been made in the reign of George III or George IV, and it should have a story to tell. I like marked pieces made by the potteries noted for "quality" such as Adams, Clews or Spode in Staffordshire, the Leeds and Don potteries in Yorkshire, or the Herculaneum pottery in Liverpool. I also admire the fine jugs with views of Edinburgh made by Watson's pottery at Prestonpans in Scotland. Even among these quality can vary and many of the wares made by potteries which did not mark their wares can reach an equally high standard. The most beautifully engraved and printed piece in my own collection was made by an unknown potter.

As I live in the south I should choose a piece made in one of the northern potteries because their wares are not very often seen in my part of the world. After all, those were the days of the stage coach. It was quite an operation to transport a dinner service of 120 to 200 pieces; if they could be sold locally, so much the better. Indeed, the potteries made miniature pieces as "traveller's samples" for their journeymen to carry round to show potential customers. They were not unlike the children's toy services of Victorian times. If I had to narrow the choice to a single pottery I should choose Herculaneum, and for a particular type of pattern I would choose one of the Indian patterns used on dinner services around 1815 (figure 1). I can imagine the excitement there must have been in those days when one

of these services arrived and the family gathered round to examine it — every shape with a different scene. After all, few people in Britain had ever seen an elephant. A few wild animals were kept in sordid menageries but real zoos were almost unknown. The London Zoo opened in 1831. Distant places with strange animals and strange buildings had a romantic aura.

The Herculaneum dish is full of eastern promise. I should immediately ask — "Where is it?" and "Where did the potter find the picture?" It stimulates question after question and I should have hours of pleasure trying to answer them. I should search for a copy of the original print on which the pattern was based. India was little known in the early 19th century so it could well have been taken from one of the watercolour drawings by that enterprising 18th century traveller, Thomas Daniell, who journeyed through India with his nephew, William, in order that he might "transport to Europe the picturesque beauties of these favoured regions". Some of his watercolours were translated into aquatints for a monumental work called *Oriental Scenery* issued in six parts between 1795 and 1808, costing £210 a set, a very large sum in those days. Daniell was an archaeologist and an artist and his work combines the scientific accuracy of a Fellow of the Royal Society with the artistic merits of a Royal Academician for he had the rare distinction of holding both these honours.

Looking closely at the Indian view on the dish, I suspect that it will not be an exact copy of the original which in any case will have been rectangular. In the

early 19th century potters were wary of leaving large areas unprinted lest impurities in the clay might be seen. So the trees were probably added by the engraver and the hill fort which forms the background was probably taken from another Daniell print. I should hope to find out.

It is possible that I might be given a less desirable piece and I have chosen a second meat dish (figure 2) from the same pottery made some fifteen years later which I would gladly accept as an example of Herculaneum wares. It is a fine piece of its kind with a smoother glaze and a body free from impurities. It is well engraved and printed. However, it does not stimulate my imagination. The moulded gadrooned border is in imitation of contemporary silver, and the view — despite the fact that the printed mark calls it "French Scenery" — is surely just a romantic invention of the artist or engraver? The "cult of the picturesque" had gone too far.

I chose meat dishes to illustrate because they can be hung on the wall like a picture. They are, of course, much rarer than plates which are the commonest items in any dinner service. Well printed early dishes with a landscape cost well over £100 today. Plates are generally less expensive. They are equally acceptable for they are all co-operative works of art produced by skilled artists, engravers, printers, transferrers and potters. One may never find the original print but the hunt for it will give immense pleasure. I have a plate on the living room wall by the Staffordshire potters John Rogers & Son of an eastern scene. Beside it is the corresponding Daniell print — "Remains of an Ancient Building near Firoz Shah's Cotilla, Delhi". Nearby are some travellers' samples with the same pattern. The odds are one hundred to one against a repeat performance but it would be fun to try!

THE MARKET FOR MINTON

by Paul Atterbury

Figure 1. A rare Minton pierced plate painted by A. Boullemier, signed, 26.6cm, printed globe mark, impressed mark and date code for 1883. £320 (Sotheby's Belgravia, 14th May 1981).

Figure 2. A large Minton "majolica" jardinière, 60cm, impressed Minton's, shape number 1359 and date code for 1872. £700 (Sotheby's Belgravia, 14th May 1981).

Although the name is well known, the products of the Minton factory have never achieved the same status or collector appeal as those made at Wedgwood, Derby or Worcester. This is irrational because the wares made at Minton during its long life have often been more varied, more interesting and of better quality than those associated with the more popular rivals. However collectors are often notably eccentric in their enthusiasms; there must have been twenty or thirty books published about Derby, a factory of limited interest and predictable production after the 18th century, while there has only been one about Minton, the greatest of all Victorian potteries (and that one hardly touches the Victorian period).

Prejudices against post-1840 ceramics are still rife among collectors and specialists, particularly in academic circles. Many national museums now collect the wares of the 18th century and before, and the studio pottery of the 20th century, but are still afraid of the century that lies between. There is no museum in Britain with a good general display of Victorian ceramics. At the same time, prices in the salerooms for Victorian ceramics are often higher than their 18th century equivalents, the prices determined by the few percipient collectors who compete for the masterpieces that are still available. While museums and academics haggle over the trivia of the 18th century, the major productions and exhibition pieces of the Victorian period are quietly disappearing into private collections, many of which are abroad.

Now is therefore a good time to reassess the products of the Minton factory, for many splendid examples are still to be found. The extraordinary diversity and range of Minton's output makes it impossible to consider the factory as a whole, but many areas of production are now showing considerable investment potential.

Among collectors, the factory is particularly known for its ornamental porcelains, richly painted and gilded, often in 18th century taste. These were first produced in any quantity during the 1830s and 1840s and then, after Minton's success in the Great Exhibition of 1851, they became a staple part of the factory's output. Elaborate table centres in Sèvres style were still being made as late as the 1920s. Many artists were employed as painters and decorators for these wares, including a number who came to work at Minton from France, Austria and other European countries. Some developed highly skilled but quite conventional styles, while others, such as Anton Boullemier (figure 1) and Edouard Rischgitz, introduced styles and techniques drawn from contemporary fine art painting. Unless pieces are signed, it is very hard to identify artists with any certainty, although both dealers and collectors are inclined to attribute in a very casual manner.

Although conventionally popular and thus expensive, ornamental porcelains are often sold regardless of date or historical interest. Little distinction in price exists between a piece made in the 1840s or 1850s and one dating from the end of the century. Percipient collectors can therefore find early pieces, or even examples that were actually shown at the various international exhibitions without paying any premium if they are prepared to undertake a little homework.

Another area ripe for development is that of Oriental influence. Minton was one of the first factories in Britain to reflect the craze for Japanese styles that swept across Europe during the 1860s, and some extremely adventurous and decorative wares were produced during

this period. Splendid imitations and versions of Japanese decorative techniques such as cloisonné, lacquer, carved ivory and metalwork can still be found quite cheaply, some reflecting the influence of avant garde designers such as Dr. Christopher Dresser. Others echo more conventional Chinese styles, for example the forms and decoration of jades, archaic bronzes and colourful monochrome glazes.

In the field of pottery, Minton's major claim to fame is the range of coloured glazes developed by their French art director, Leon Arnoux, that they marketed under the confusing title of "majolica" (figure 2). Between 1850 and the 1890s a range of exuberantly modelled and brightly coloured wares was produced, often of considerable size and frequently designed by contemporary sculptors. Majolica is the most original and the most exotic of the various Victorian ceramic forms, and it was an ideal medium to express the stylistic confusion and decorative extravagance of the period.

After being disregarded for years, majolica is now becoming both expensive and desirable, and a number of exhibitions featuring the ware are being planned for 1982 by dealers and museums. However, interesting and unusual pieces can still be found. The last fling of Victorian majolica took the form of a range of casually decorated but richly coloured wares in European

Figure 3. A good and large Minton pâte sur pâte plaque decorated by L. Solon, signed and dated, 19.5cm x 36.5cm, 1906, framed. £1,600 (Sotheby's Belgravia, 14th May 1981).

art nouveau style, with abstract and stylised floral patterns raised in relief. Minton launched their Secessionist range in 1902 and discontinued it in about 1914. It was not particularly successful at the time, but the pieces are now becoming popular again, reflecting as they do the most decorative aspects of art nouveau.

There are some Minton products that may well not show any dramatic rise over the next year or so, for example the pâte sur pâte wares decorated by Solon (figure 3), and the painted plaques made at the short-lived Art Pottery Studio in South Kensington, the latter because relatively few are of top quality. However, there are many other areas that could well show an increase, for example some of the more interesting tiles and tile panels, the historical wares based on the Renaissance or Classical styles, including the St. Porchaire-style inlaid faience made by Toft and the imitations of Limoges enamels, even the early tablewares of the period 1773 to 1830 and the most dramatic of the parian figures (figure 4). In all cases, the guide should be quality. The best Minton products are always remarkable, both technically and aesthetically, and so the collector should always try to find the best, regardless of style or period.

Despite the lack of published material, those wishing to expand their knowledge and appreciation of Minton

Figure 4. A pair of unusual Minton tinted and part-glazed parian figures of Dorothea and Clorinda, after John Bell, 33.5cm and 34.5cm, impressed mark, one with applied sculptor's name and registration mark, the other with moulded sculptor's name, impressed date codes for 1869. £240 (Sotheby's Belgravia, 18th September 1980).

can satisfy their needs at the Minton Museum, which is open to the public during weekdays at the Minton factory in London Road, Stoke-on-Trent.

Prices attained by Minton pottery and porcelain over the last few years underline the theme of this article. In all areas a premium is paid for first class work by named artists. Splendid and elaborate examples of majolica often fetch £250 and £500, while the really exceptional items, particularly those on a grand

scale, can fetch four figures. Similarly, the best and grandest examples of parian command high prices, especially if they are in the complex tinted or multicolour styles. Both these wares reflect the changed attitudes to Victorian design; pieces that previously were regarded as curiosities can now fetch more than their 18th century equivalents. At the same time, common or relatively uninteresting pieces in these categories can still be bought for well under £100.

In the porcelain area, prices vary greatly. As mentioned above, the market does not often distinguish between early and late ornamental porcelains. Thus rare and interesting pieces in the Meissen or Sèvres style, dating from the period 1830-50, may fetch from £150-£750, while single plates of the 1870s or 1880s, painted by Anton Boullemier in his typical whimsical style, can cost £300. The increase in this area has been in the porcelain by named artists, making the early wares seem to be increasingly good value.

Pâte sur pâte has always been expensive. However, prices have fluctuated over the last few years. A good vase which sold for £5,000 in the mid-1970s might not fetch much more today. Except in exceptional cases there has been no dramatic increase, although the recent American discovery of this material has resulted in some high prices in New York.

19th and 20th Century Scientific Instruments
by Hilary Kay   Sotheby's Belgravia

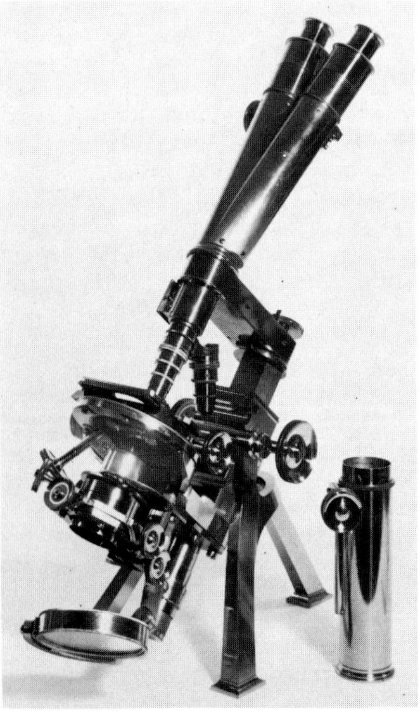

The market for 19th and 20th century scientific instruments has been a popular one for a number of years with, unsurprisingly, instruments of excellent quality or of outstanding historical importance fetching thousands of pounds. There have, however, been subtle changes in some collecting trends, with instruments of comparatively recent manufacture date or of comparatively poor quality beginning to be sought after, particularly by European collectors.

Monocular microscopes (those with only one eyepiece) from the early part of the last century have been widely collected for a number of years with prices for good quality instruments by manufacturers such as Powell & Lealand, Dancer or Cary fetching between £300 and £1,000 at auction. Over the last twelve months some European buyers have become interested

in the comparatively modern and less mechanically complex microscopes produced by Leitz and Zeiss towards the end of the last century and during this century. Prices for this type of microscope which two years ago were as low as £30 or £40 are now raised to between £60 and £100; the rapidity of this rise can be partially explained by the parallel interest of these European collectors in Leitz and Zeiss cameras and accessories of the same period which have enjoyed a similar price increase.

Binocular microscopes (those instruments with two eyepieces) from the mid-19th century have continued slowly to rise in value, with fine examples reaching £2,000 and above (see figure 1).

There has been a sharp rise in interest in 19th century medical and dental instruments recently with a large number of practising or retired surgeons, doctors and veterinary surgeons interested in ob-

Figure 1. A Powell & Lealand No. 1 binocular microscope, c.1903. £1,100 on 29th May 1981.

taining equipment closely related to their own profession. This interest has been encouraged by a number of books recently published on this subject and, in England, the important collection of medical instruments owned by the Wellcome Institute has now been donated to the Science Museum where it will be on permanent display. Many of the major collectors live either on the Continent or in the United States where salaries for physicians and surgeons are high enough for them to invest fairly large sums in medical instruments. Items of particular interest to this group of collectors include surgical and post mortem instruments, scarificators, medicine bottles and chests, sectioned models of wax illustrating muscle and bone structure and pieces of furniture such as dental chairs and cabinets (see figure 2).

In contrast to this very buoyant trend there has been a recent steadying in the market for apothecaries' chests. These are usually in the form of rosewood or mahogany chests approximately 8ins. to 12ins. wide with hinged lid and a drawer in the base. Prices rose steeply three years ago and chests, if complete with their original bottles, balance, mortar and pestle, were reaching between £400 and £700; as with almost every market which rises quickly, apothecaries' chests have now plateaud with similar items today fetching between £250 and £500 (see figure 3).

Nautical and navigational instruments are becoming increasingly attractive to boat or shipping line owners and, as with medical instruments, there have been a number of books produced in the last two years to encourage the new

Figure 4. A Troughton & Simms "Y" brass theodolite, late 19th century. £340 on 6th February 1981.

collector in this field. Octants from the early part of the 19th century have continued to hold steady at between £250 and £350, and sextants follow close behind at between £180 to £250. Some of the rapid rises in this field, as with microscopes, have been in the comparatively modern instruments; compasses from between the wars, for example, which were seldom seen to reach above £25 a year or two ago, have now doubled in price. The more recent sextants have not yet experienced such a growth of interest, and it is possible that the next two years will witness a comparable increase in value to compasses.

As with other fields of scientific

instruments of the 19th century, it is now the more modern surveying instruments which have shown a greater percentage increase in value compared with those of the last century. Whilst theodolites of the 19th century have remained fairly steady at the comparatively low figures of between £250 and £450, theodolites of this century rose from approximately £100-£150 to £200-£250. A parallel can be drawn between the prices of 19th century levels at £150-£250 and 20th century examples which now are valued at between £70 and £100. Other surveying instruments such as miners' dials have retained their unexciting 1980 values at between £150 and £200 (see figure 4).

As with any other field of collecting it is important that scientific instruments are as complete as possible in order to retain and increase in value. This not only means having nothing missing from the main body of the instrument, but also the investor should only seriously consider those items which have additional accessories such as lenses, tripods, telescopes and, wherever possible, the original cabinet-made fitted wooden case. From this, with its fitted interior to hold accessories, it is simple to tell at a glance if there is anything missing from the apparatus. Some manufacturers are more sought after than others and, whenever possible, instruments should bear the name of the maker. It is also vital that care is taken to investigate the area chosen for investment so that the collector is able to determine the value of a particular name and to ensure that the instrument is complete with the accessories with which it was originally sold.

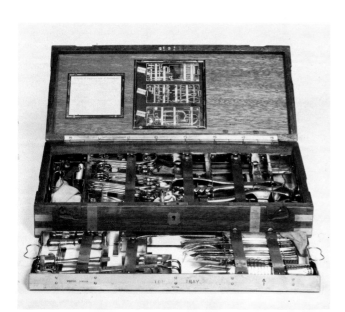

Figure 2. A J. Weiss army surgeon's instrument case, English, c.1917. £420 on 22nd February 1980.

Figure 3. An apothecary's chest, English, c.1850. £420 on 6th February 1981.

George V and Mary Coronation 1911. Colour transfer on porcelain mug, 2⅞ ins. high. Green-printed mark: SHELLEY / LATE FOLEY / ENGLAND.

George V and Mary Coronation 1911. Earthenware mug transfer-printed in brown or crimson, 3⅛ ins. high. Unmarked. Price: £9 to £15.

Commemoratives
by Ian Smythe

We had three major royal cele-brations in the space of fourteen years, and by the Coronation of George V and Queen Mary in 1911 the design of commemoratives, which had been free and varied for the 1887 Jubilee, had for the greater part crystallised into a formal presentation of portraits-in-ovals surrounded by the accoutrements of royalty; and in the same period we find the develop-ment of the colour lithograph transfer for use on ceramics brought to a remarkable degree of refinement.

There are three quite different variations of this Shelley mug, the difference being in the portraits (this and one other show the King's hair parted on the wrong side, which gives him a slightly unfamiliar appearance). But all three versions are superb examples of the species, like the setting of fruit after a gorgeous flowering; a fine, delicate and imaginative arrangement of crown and sceptre, with palm fronds and sprays of rose, thistle and shamrock, and a dainty ribbon carrying a patriotic wish of long life to the King and Queen. A secondary transfer showing a crown above a trumpet with the King's name on a banner appears on the inside of the mug, leaving the back free for a local name of town or school (here the Urban District of Chadderton).

All this is colour-transferred on to fine china with gilt embellishment to the rim and handle.

This represents the highest point of the art of full-colour lithograph transfer-making, strength and delicacy combined in beautifully judged proportions. From here on the only direction was down, and this robust vigour with its echoes of funny old Victorian ornateness was to go right out of fashion. Twenty-four years later, for the Silver Jubilee, Shelley themselves were to use the same basic design, the pair of ovals, the central crown and Union Jack shield, and the ribbon below — and that's all, everything else shorn away and discarded in the name of "clean" design and in fear of prettiness; bath-water and baby thrown out together.

But the 1911 piece says it all, everything is there, the acme of artistic and technical accomplish-ment.

But ... the best Christmas present? There is a rude clamouring for attention by something lying right at the bottom of Saint Nicholas's sack. From the nether world of the same event comes this awful, crude, coarse, primitive mug from an anonymous pottery. The astonished collector is confronted with mono-chrome instead of colour, with earthenware instead of porcelain and a curiously woolly line which looks as though the original were drawn on blotting-paper. But what a surprising impact it has! The bold design fills the shape; the back has two big flags, another crown and a large swag of flowers; and tying it all together with sure and simple touch is a strange stripey band round the top with four tiny shields representing South Africa, India, Australia and Canada. From beaded ovals the glassy-eyed portraits in Early Identikit style stare hypnotically among a riotous assembly of royal trappings, crown, flags, roses, thistles and shamrocks. The King's beard and uniform are inversely balanced by the Queen's coiffure and crown, so that one has the dizzy impression that turning the mug upside-down would reveal two more faces like a puzzle-picture in a children's book. Tucked in at the bottom is a mad, marvellous, tiny lion, paws stretched out in front, wearing a serene expression and a huge crown.

How strange that such a hilarious piece of nonsense should have such a power to move us; yet move us it does. We feel intuitively the sense of joy in a particular event, the pleasure taken by an untutored but far from inarticulate artisan in an unknown pottery, reaching across seventy years to convey that pleasure to us; and that, of course, is what com-memoratives are all about.

Commemoratives, one of the few fields where extremes of taste may be indulged. Choose between a Stafford-shire figure and a Worcester figurine; choose between a piece of Fabergé and a West African carving; between Meissen and Clarice Cliff, Wemyss and Paragon. Choose between the precise beauty and classic sophisti-cation of the Shelley mug and the primitive directness and romantic naïveté of the anonymous one. Choose one for a Christmas present? The choice is simple ... isn't it?

NAPIER'S BONES

by Richard Garnier

Figure 1. Loose bones displayed on lid of box.

Frame of calculating tray with units marked on left.

Occasionally in auction catalogues of scientific instruments you will see a strange item included under the name of *a set of Napier's Bones* (see figure 1). Normally dating from the late 17th or early 18th centuries, they are rare — indeed I know of only about four sets sold in London in the last five or six years. The inclusion of a set in a recent sale at Christie's (£1,400) prompted me to find out how they are supposed to be used, and a long search it has proved to be.

Living in an age fascinated by the "natural sciences" and things mathematical, Samuel Pepys recorded in his diary during 1667 that he was very impressed by "the mighty use of Napier's bones" and declared his intention of buying a set. Despite Pepys' fascination on seeing them for the first time, calculating bones had been invented some time before: in 1617 by John Napier (1550-1617), of Merchiston in Scotland, who is perhaps better known for the invention of logarithms in 1614.

Once the technique of using Napier's bones has been mastered, they provide a remarkably quick way of multiplying and dividing large awkward numbers. His bones consist of a number of rods or plates (lamellae) made of wood, metal, horn, pasteboard or suchlike. The surfaces of each lamella are divided into nine squares, each square in turn divided into two triangles by a diagonal line. Each surface is inscribed with a multiplication table disposed so that within each square, downwards from 1 to 9 times, the "units" are in the right-hand (lower) triangle and the "tens" in the left-hand (upper) triangle. In addition a calculating tray is provided with the units 1-9 marked down the left-hand side.

Multiplication. Enough rods or lamellae are placed on the calculating tray so that the numbers at their top form the number to be multiplied (the multiplicand). Figure 2 shows the bones set up for the multiplicand 675469409. The calculation now follows as in the long multiplication one was taught at school, but with no knowledge of multiplication tables necessary.

To multiply the given multiplicand by 84352, find the right-hand digit (2) of the multiplicator in the "units" column of the calculating tray. The product of each figure of the multiplicand when multiplied by 2 will then be found in the row extending to the right from this. Since the tens (left-hand triangle) on any one rod represent the units of the next rod left (right-hand triangle), the addition of any digits in such contiguous triangles (together forming a rhomb)

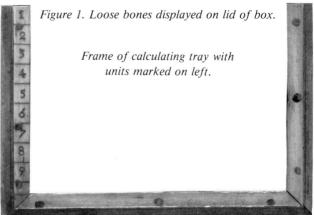

Figure 2. Bones arranged for the multiplicand 675469409.

gives the appropriate total product.
Thus

	6	7	5	4	6	9	4	0	9
2	1/2	1/4	1/0	/8	1/2	1/8	/8	/0	1/8

adding from the right, can be read as follows:

	6	7	5	4	6	9	4	0	9
2	13	5	0	9	3	8	8	1	8

Figure 3. Bones arranged for the divisor 6474.

The next digit (5) of the multiplicator is treated similarly, taking care to start writing down the product one space to the left, and then successively for the other digits of the multiplicator. The sum of all these gives the final answer (if I am correct!), thus:

```
              6 7 5 4 6 9 4 0 9
            1 3 5 0 9 3 8 8 1 8
          3 3 7 7 3 4 7 0 4 5
        2 0 2 6 4 0 8 2 2 7
      2 7 0 1 8 7 7 6 3 6
    5 4 0 3 7 5 5 2 7 2
  4 7 2 8 2 8 5 8 6 3
6 0 7 9 2 2 4 6 8 1
─────────────────────
6 6 0 9 0 3 0 4 6 2 8 8 7 9 6 8
```

Division. As with long division, the use of Napier's bones involves a certain amount of trial and error, but again obviates the need for multiplication tables. Instead of the number to be divided (the dividend), the divisor is arranged to read across the top line of the rods. A simple example will show how to do a division 12948 ÷ 6474 (figure 3):

By trial and error see how many times the divisor can be multiplied in order to equal or be as near as possible below the dividend. In other words, as before, add the figures appearing together in each rhomb across from one of the units in the column on the left. In this case

6474 × 2 reads 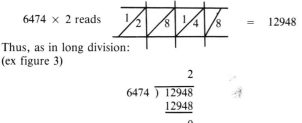 = 12948

Thus, as in long division:
(ex figure 3)

```
              2
6474 ) 12948
       12948
       ─────
           0
```

For dividends of more places, continue as in long division, working in stages and after each subtraction bringing down enough additional digits from the dividend for the next stage, thus:
(ex figure 2)

```
            1032
675 ) 6970654
      675
      ───
      2206
      2025
      ────
       1815
       1350
       ────
       4654  etc.
```

using:

675 × 2 reads 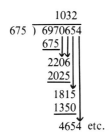 = 1350

675 × 3 reads 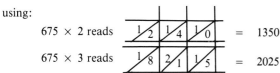 = 2025

I said it was a long search to discover the secret of Napier's bones; eventually an early 19th century encyclopaedia turned up an explanation, but in such obscure language as needed some time to work out what was meant. I hope my explanation enables you to understand the use of these bones, for to those of us who can never remember our times tables and do not have a pocket calculator to hand, they would provide an invaluable aid.

Acknowledgement
The illustrations in this article are reproduced by courtesy of Christie's.

(Unless otherwise stated, books measure 11ins. x 8½ins.)

FURNITURE

English Furniture from Charles II to George II by R.W. Symonds. *12ins. x 8¼ins. 269 pages. 259 b. & w. illus. Limited edition reprint of 1,500 copies. £35.*

The Price Guide to Victorian, Edwardian and 1920s Furniture by John Andrews. *218 pages. 650 b. & w. illus. £14.50.*

The Price Guide to Antique Furniture, 2nd Edition, by John Andrews. *290 pages. 1,043 b. & w. illus. £14.95.*

Oak Furniture, The British Tradition by Victor Chinnery. *580 pages. 1,100 b. & w. illus. and 22 in col. £27.50.*

Pictorial Dictionary of British 19th Century Furniture Design, an Antique Collectors' Club Research Project. *583 pages. 6,200 b. & w. illus. £27.50.*

HOROLOGY

Old English Clocks — The Wetherfield Collection with an introduction by F.J. Britten. *12ins. x 8½ins. 114 pages. 133 b. & w. illus. Limited edition of 1,000 copies. £25.*

Thomas Cole and Victorian Clockmaking by J.B. Hawkins. *253 pages. 190 b. & w. illus. and 3 in col. £14.50.*

The Marine Chronometer — Its History and Development by Lt. Com. Rupert T. Gould, R.N. *8½ins. x 5½ins. 287 pages. Over 80 plates and diagrams. £14.95.*

Carriage Clocks, Their History and Development by Charles Allix, illus. by P. Bonnert. *484 pages. 500 b. & w. illus. 16 in col. £22.50.*

Camerer Cuss Book of Antique Watches by T.P. Camerer cuss. *322 pages. 380 b. & w. illus. 8 in col. £19.50.*

English Dial Clocks by Ronald E. Rose. *198 pages. 190 b. & w. illus. 27 in col. 430 line drawings. £17.50.*

Horological Hints & Helps by F.W. Britten. *8½ins. x 5½ins. 375 pages. 158 engravings. £7.95.*

Watch and Clock Makers' Handbook, Dictionary and Guide by F.J. Britten *8½ins. x 5½ins. 499 pages. 460 engravings. £12.*

The Price Guide to Clocks 1840-1940 by A. and R. Shenton. *8½ins. x 5½ins. 540 pages. 428 b. & w. illus. £12.50.*

English Domestic Clocks by Cescinsky & Webster. *12ins. x 9½ins. 535 pages. 407 b. & w. illus. £19.50.*

The Antique Collectors' Club Edition of **Britten's Old Clocks and Watches and Their Makers — 3rd Edition.** *517 pages. 1,050 b. & w. illus. £19.50.*

English Barometers 1680-1860 by N. Goodison. *388 pages. 194 b. & w. illus. 4 in col. £19.50.*

ARCHITECTURE

Suffolk Houses by Eric Sandon. *12ins. x 8¼ins. 344 pages. 389 b. & w. illus. 10 col. plates. 94 figures. £19.50.*

Houses and Gardens by E.L. Lutyens described and criticised by Lawrence Weaver. *340 pages. 580 b. & w. illus. £19.50.*

SCULPTURE & METALWORK

Bronze Sculpture of 'Les Animaliers' — Reference and Price Guide by Jane Horswell. *339 pages. 316 b. & w. illus. £19.50.*

Old Domestic Base-Metal Candlesticks by Ronald F. Michaelis. *140 pages. 202 b. & w. illus. £14.50.*

Books published by the *Antique Collectors' Club* on Furniture and Horology together with some other leading titles

SCULPTURE AND METALWORK continued

Dictionary of Western Sculptors in Bronze by J. Mackay. *414 pages. £19.50.*

Art Deco and Other Figures by B. Catley. *344 pages. 1,100 b. & w. illus. 43 in col. £25.*

The Price Guide to Metal Toys by G. Gardiner and A. Morris. *8½ ins. x 5½ ins. 214 pages. 610 b. & w. illus. 41 col. plates. £14.50.*

The Price Guide to Victorian Silver by Ian Harris. *8½ ins. x 5½ ins. 276 pages. 270 b. & w. illus. £9.95.*

The Barye Bronzes — a catalogue raisonné by Stuart Pivar. *280 pages. 280 b. & w. illus. £22.50.*

SOME OF OUR OTHER TITLES

The Price Guide to More Collectable Antiques by James Mackay. *8½ ins. x 5½ ins. 390 pages. 381 b. & w. illus. £9.50.*

The Price Guide to Dolls by C.E. King. *8½ ins. x 5½ ins. 483 pages. 420 b. & w. 17 col. illus. £12.50.*

The Price Guide to Jewellery 3000 B.C. — 1950 A.D. by Michael Poynder. *385 pages. 340 b. & w. illus. 44 in col. £19.50.*

Guide to the Antique Shops of Britain 1982 edited by Rosemary Ferguson and Stella King. *8¾ ins. x 5½ ins. 1,116 pages. £5.95.*

VICTORIAN AND EDWARDIAN FURNITURE—
The Winners and the Losers

by John Andrews

Author of The Price Guide to Antique Furniture *and* The Price Guide to Victorian, Edwardian and 1920s Furniture

The writer of a detailed Price Guide is liable to be pursued with relentless fury by two types of person:

1. Dealers who see one of their most highly prized pieces of stock portrayed at some modest, if not derisory, value — fortunately, a rare occurrence.

2. Collectors who search for an illustration of one of their most cherished possessions and find that it is not portrayed at all or, worse, laughingly dismissed as a stylistic aberration.

In an investment article, therefore, it is something of a relief to discuss general highlights and shadows in recent market movements whilst at the same time taking the opportunity to correct a misprint in the former category. From the second category there can be no escape; beauty is in the eye of the beholder.

The market for Victorian and Edwardian furniture has continued to develop during the last year although there have been some notable disappointments. After the battering which the market has taken in terms of reduced demand at retail level and in certain categories of exports, or "shipping" goods, it will be a relief to many collectors to see the comparison with 1973 levels portrayed in the tables, even if the 1980 comparison may not always be such a comfort.

Why 1973? Because the *Price Guide to Victorian Furniture* was first published in that year, and the arrival of the Victorian, Edwardian and 1920s Guide which replaces it provides a good moment for looking back and taking stock. Investment in antiques should *never* be made on a short term basis.

It is for this reason that the terms "Winners" and "Losers" in the tables opposite are purely relative when compared with the 1973 figures. There are no real "losses", only "gains" for the longer term collector of shrewd judgement over the period. What has happened, though, is that over the last twelve to eighteen months certain types of piece have continued to forge ahead in price — the "Winners" — whereas others have stagnated or even dropped back — the "Losers".

It is well to remember that in the five years between 1973 and 1978 Victorian furniture as a whole increased by about 250% to 300% in value, as the graphs at the back of the *Price Guide to Antique Furniture* show. Interested readers will, therefore, get a mental note of the progress of the various pieces in relative terms since 1978 by keeping index figures of 1973 = 100 and 1978 = 250/300 in mind.

Now to business. In general terms it is fair to say that any piece of high quality with a "known" designer or maker has commanded a high premium and prices for such pieces have continued to surge upwards. Whether the piece be by Eastlake, Talbert, Godwin, Gimson or even the better known manufacturers like Edwards and Roberts, the name is the game. Anything ordinary, plain, unattributed, run-of-the-mill, unexceptional, has stagnated. A few comments on the major categories follow.

Winners

1. The William Morris settle sold by Sotheby's Belgravia at £8,000 plus premium was a considerable advance on the £4,000 paid some four months previously in Yorkshire (NOT £900-£1,200 as misprinted in the *Guide* — the author is a poor proof-reader) for a similar piece. This has been chosen to illustrate the significance of a "name" — but not always William Morris, as Losers item one shows. Pieces by the big names of the period are fetching five figures now.

2. "Long" sets of chairs — from sets of ten or more. The illustration is of quite a good Victorian reproduction type, but even quite unattractive chairs have rocketed up in price when in quantities of ten or more.

3. Wootton Patent desks — or "Wells Fargo" to the romantically cowboy-minded. London auction rooms have been short of them in the last six months. Spectacular increases for the mid-70s purchaser.

4. Inlaid Edwardian Sheraton furniture of high quality is still going well, especially if by a "good" manufacturer.

5. There is a small, if dedicated, band of art nouveau enthusiasts and another similar band keen on Arts and Crafts. Prices for Arts and Crafts pieces are still modest but the appreciation has been very rapid.

Losers

1. Since "Winners" was started with William Morris it seems only fair to do the same in this section. The "Sussex" chair was produced in large numbers and was much copied — many identical copies abound. After a period of enthusiasm, interest seems to have waned, mainly because we are not all trendy aesthetes and require something comfortable to sit on. "Not an Englishman's dining chair."

2. Smoker's bows — the roaring success story of the '70s — have run into a problem. I came back from a trip to the U.S. and Canada this month with a set of their 1981 Price Guides. Smoker's bows are the same price there as they are here. After over-accelerating to three figures in some London area shops they are dropping back. After all, you can buy really excellent robust baluster-turned reproductions that look quite old for £48 each now.

3. Ordinary davenports, not to be confused with high quality, burr walnut, piano-top or otherwise high quality versions, are not so desirable any more. The market has learned to discriminate. There was a time when almost any davenport started at £300. Recently at Sotheby's Belgravia they have been knocking down the ordinary ones at £240 or so.

4. Aesthetic movement furniture by no known designer has yet to convince the market. There have been some markedly unsuccessful sales of such pieces. When the sideboard illustrated here appeared in the Price Guide at the end of 1980, an irate East Anglian dealer 'phoned me to say he had an almost identical one in stock plus its matching corner cupboard, both just bought at auction. For £350 he would deliver them to me anywhere and what was I waiting for? He could tell me — for a customer, like him.

5. and 6. After more than a decade of leading the Victorian furniture market and of providing a living for an army of button-oriented upholsterers, these rococo chairs have finally flattened out in price. The U.S.A. is no longer willing to pay as much and there are now some first class reproducers pinning down what was once a unique product to a commodity market price.

7. Whether because the relationship between the pound and the Italian lira is so out of kilter or whether because the market is tired of these highly decorative but fragile pieces, it is hard to say, but this sector is also stagnating.

The Future

The same message as so often before — high quality, exceptional features and sound provenance always pay off. In this period, the cachet of a celebrated designer pushed prices beyond any logical progression.

WINNERS

Illustration Ref.					
Type of Piece	William Morris painted settle	Reproduction Chippendale chair, 19th century "Long" sets	Wootton Patent Office Desks "Wells Fargo" desks	Inlaid Edwardian Sheraton high quality	"Art Nouveau" — actually Arts and Crafts — sideboard
1973 Price		£30-£40 each in sets of six	£60-£100	£80-£120	£14
1980 Price	£4,000 (provincial auction)	£100-£150 each in sets of six	£900-£1,500	£700-£900	£120-£200
1981 Price and Comments	£8,000 (London auction)	£100-£150 each for set of six £250-£300 each for set of ten	£1,500-£1,700 £2,500-£3,000 for a "two-door" version of quality £5,000+ for exceptional quality	£750-£1,000 Add 50% if by, say, Edwards and Roberts	£150-£200 £250-£350 if by "known" designer

Remember: If 1973 price is 100, then on an index basis 1978 is 250-300, so the change from 1978 to 1980/81 is one that can also be considered.

LOSERS

Illustration Ref.						
Type of Piece	William Morris "Sussex" chairs	Smoker's bow chair	Davenport desk — ordinary quality	Aesthetic Movement sideboard — ebonised. Unknown designer	Victorian rococo "spoonback" chair	Victorian rococo chaise longue	"Credenza" side cabinet — medium quality
1973 Price	£15-£25	£5-£15	£150-£200	Probably £10	£60-£80	£120-£180	£300-£350
1980 Price	£55-£70	£60-£120	£350-£500	£500-£750	£200-£300	£450-£750	£800-£1,200
1981 Price and Comments	£50-£70. Many versions not by Morris. Uncomfortable.	£60-£90 and falling. Excellent "old" looking repros. now available at £48 each. U.S. prices same as U.K.	£300-£400. Consistently sold at auction for £260-£340.	Undesirable. Many auction lots withdrawn. Provincial price about £350-£450.	No progress — still £200-£300. U.S. prices same as U.K.	£450-£600. Auction pricing around £450 mark.	£800-£1,000. Little progress — high quality also similarly becalmed.

The Price Guide to British County Maps by *Yasha Beresiner.*
11ins. x 8½ins. Approx. 400 pages. 500 black and white and 24
colour plates approx. The British county map is a common
adornment to be found on the walls of homes all over the country.
Often the apparent names of the cartographers can be found but
this leaves aside the vital question of who actually made the map?
When was it published? How much is it worth? It is these
questions that this book answers. The clear, lucid style and the
wealth of information make this an extremely valuable source of
reference as well as an interesting account of the cartographers'
art in Britain over the centuries.

Publication March '82

New and Forthcoming Publications
from the *Antique Collectors' Club*

*Further details and prices available from the
Antique Collectors' Club, 5 Church Street,
Woodbridge, Suffolk.*

Oriental Rugs: Vol. 1 — Caucasian by *Ian Bennett.* 8¼ins. x
10ins. 376 pages, illustrating 340 examples in colour. An
important book for the rug collector for, besides containing the
most colour illustrations ever produced in a book devoted to this
subject, the selection has been based on a typical cross-section of
the rugs available to collectors. The author has provided an
extremely detailed — and at times critical — text. This is an
important book that will be welcomed by collectors, dealers and
museum staff alike.

To be followed in the Spring by volume two of this new series
which will be **Persian Rugs.** By sharing the printing cost with a
distinguished German publisher, we are able to offer some 300
colour plates together with a good basic text on this popular
subject. Other subjects in this series are now being planned.

Publication Dec '81

The Longcase Clock by *Thomas Robinson.* 11ins. x 8½ins.
Approx. 350 pages. 500 black and white and 22 colour plates
approx. Considering the popularity of the longcase clock,
relatively little has been written on this subject, so that this
excellent book fills a much needed gap. The book is written by a
leading expert on the subject who understands both the cabinet
and clockwork aspects of the subject. *Publication Dec '81*

**Some Outstanding Clocks over Seven Hundred Years
1250-1950** by *H. Alan Lloyd (not illustrated).* 11ins. x 8½ins. 350
pages, 247 black and white illustrations, 24 line drawings. This
great work, first published in 1958, marked a departure in
horological literature. The author concentrates on clockmakers in
England and on the Continent who hitherto had not been widely
known, and yet who, as the reader will see, are deserving of the
highest recognition. This edition is limited to 1,000 numbered
copies. *Now available*

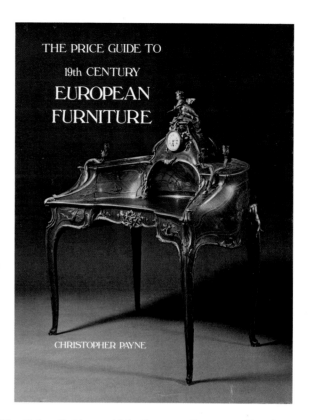

The Price Guide to Antique Silver *by Peter Waldron.* 11ins. x 8½ ins. Approx. 250 pages and 1,100 black and white illustrations. This is the second edition of a title first published in 1969. Peter Waldron heads the Silver Department of Sotheby's. A larger format has been used which has enabled over 1,000 photographs to be discussed — double the number possible in the original edition. *Publication Feb '82*

The Price Guide to 19th Century European Furniture *by Christopher Payne* 11ins. x 8½ ins. Approx. 500 pages. 1,540 black and white illustrations and 20 pages of colour. Following the highly successful price guides to Antique Furniture and Victorian, Edwardian and 1920s Furniture, comes this copiously illustrated price guide on the vast creative output of furniture manufactured on the Continent of Europe from 1830-1910. *Publication Nov '81*

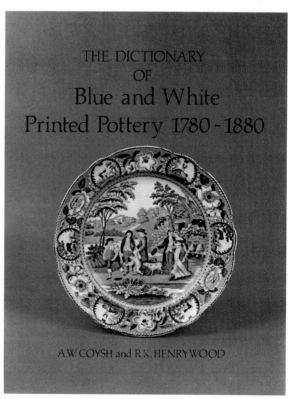

The Price Guide to Antique Edged Weapons *by Leslie Southwick.* 11ins. x 8½ ins. Approx. 350 pages, 800 black and white and 10 colour plates. This book is intended to be a guide to the pricing of swords, daggers and staff weapons, and to provide a useful illustrational reference to the many types of edged weapons in use from the medieval period to the early twentieth century. *Publication Feb '82*

The Dictionary of Blue and White Printed Pottery 1780-1880 *by A.W. Coysh and R.K. Henrywood.* 11ins. x 8½ ins. Approx. 400 pages. 680 black and white and 20 colour plates. This illustrated Dictionary brings together in one volume as many facts as possible about blue and white printed pottery at the height of its popularity and production. *Publication Feb '82*

KEYLESS WATCHES

by

Malcolm Fairley

Figure 1. Charles Frodsham No. 09692. A good heavy gold cased tourbillon watch, with keyless half plate movement and fusee, 58mm. Sold by Sotheby's Bond Street on 10th May 1979 for £18,000.

One finds references to keyless or self winding watches as early as 1651, but it was not until the middle of the 19th century that they were being produced in any quantity.

Around 1750 Pierre Caron (later famous as the dramatist Beaumarchais) made a watch for Madame de Pompadour in the form of a finger ring, wound by a lever projecting from the case.

The pedometer type of self winding was patented in 1780 by Louis Recordon of London. The motion of the body in walking moves a weight attached to a pivoted lever which engages a ratchet wheel connected to the mainspring.

Another successful early form was the "pump wind" mechanism, patented in 1793 by Robert Leslie. The mainspring is wound by moving the pendant in and out.

In 1820 Thomas Prest patented a mechanism that actually used a winding button but still the hands needed to be adjusted with a key. It was not until the late 1830s that setting the hands by turning the button was possible. These early keyless watches, particularly those by Breguet or the better Swiss makers, for example Antoine Lecoultre, Audemars Frères or Adrien Philippe, are both rare and expensive.

Throughout the rest of the century the watch was developed to a very high degree so that one could combine a movement of great accuracy with repeating or musical mechanisms and calendar work. The finest of these can fetch up to £50,000.

The precision movements made in the second half of the century provide one of the most interesting aspects of horology. It is inadvisable to buy these unless one already has a relatively good knowledge of watch mechanics. Probably the easiest way to learn about these and also their values is to attend the pre-sale viewing at the major auction

Figure 2. An 18 carat gold centre seconds keyless lever watch, 50.5mm. Sold by Sotheby's Belgravia on 29th March 1978 for £170.

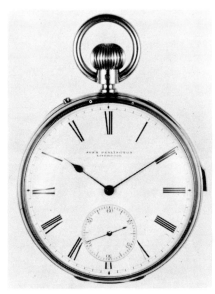

Figure 3. 18 carat gold minute repeating keyless lever watch No. 14176 by Jos'h Penlington, Liverpool, 52.5mm. Sold by Sothebys Belgravia on 29th November 1978 for £1,650.

rooms. This, combined with his own reading, should soon enable the collector to buy wisely.

At the top end of the range is the tourbillon. Invented by A.L. Breguet in 1781, it was designed to eradicate some of the errors in time keeping due to the change in position of the watch (figure 1). The entire escapement is fitted into a cage or carriage which revolves, in most instances once per minute. A good example will cost in excess of £15,000. The karrusel, another revolving escapement, is easier to produce than the tourbillon and is easier to produce. These range in price from £1,500-£2,500. In the same sale as the illustrated tourbillon, a good gold keyless level karrusel fetched £2,100. Considering the quality of the watch, this price seems quite low.

The chronometer movement was developed primarily for the purpose of determining longitude at sea. There are various types of chronometer, all of which are fitted with a "detent" escapement. The Swiss, however, use the term chronometer to describe a watch of high accuracy but not necessarily fitted with a detent. Thus, one should not be fooled by the frequent appearance of the word "chronometer" inscribed on the cuvette of Swiss watches. These vary in price greatly, depending on nationality and quality, but one must be prepared to pay at least £1,000 for an average example.

To obtain a watch with a fine quality movement, one need not pay anything like the price of a tourbillon or chronometer. An English lever watch can be bought for £200, although the price rises rapidly with quality. An example with a free sprung compensation balance, chain fusee and up-and-down dial fetched £800 at Sotheby's Belgravia on 6th June 1979. Further down the range an ordinary 18 carat gold half hunter will fetch £150-£300 (figure 2).

An interesting silver lever watch with a waterproof case, half plate movement, free sprung balance, up-and-down dial and Class "A" Kew Observatory rating is to be sold at Sotheby's Belgravia on

17th October 1979. It is estimated at £350-£500, but could exceed this.

Repeating watches have always been very popular. Prices of these have not really altered over the past year and for between £1,200 and £2,000 a clean English minute repeater would seem a good buy. A thinner cased Swiss example would be less expensive at £400-£1,000. Quarter and five minute repeaters are proportionately less and, of course, a far better quality watch could be bought for the same price as a second rate minute repeater (figure 3).

A repeating mechanism combined with a calendar or chronograph movement will enhance the value. A Swiss minute repeating chronograph will fetch £600 plus, while its English equivalent will be more than double this. Naturally there are many very fine examples of Continental watches which would also fetch higher prices.

Calendar watches vary in price so much that it would be misleading to quote any figure. It is very important to ascertain whether or not it is a perpetual calendar, i.e. one that accounts for leap years. These are frequently combined with repeating mechanisms and can command very high prices.

If one wanted a purely functional watch for everyday use, a gold half or full hunter would be a sound choice. A standard 18 carat gold example, such as figure 4, would cost £150-£200. This is also a very good investment, since the gold content alone is very nearly this price. Examples in silver are very much less and one can buy a perfectly serviceable watch for £25-£40.

It is worth remembering that repairs can be very costly and could even cost more than the original watch. The dial should be carefully checked for any hairline cracks and any damage to the case should be taken into consideration. The movement and escapement are rather more difficult and it is often very hard to tell if they have been repaired.

In the lower price range one frequently finds those with gold plated cases. These are often American made by the Waltham Watch Co. and in perfect condition would seem to be a good choice for the first time buyer with limited funds. In fact American mass produced watches are an unexplored and very cheap area of the market and one can still form an interesting collection without spending a great deal (figure 5). This is not to say that they did not produce some fine quality watches. The Riverside Maximus made by Waltham is an example.

Finally, one must take into consideration the style and quality of the case. Figure 6, a lever watch by Appleton, Tracy & Co. of Waltham, Massachusetts, cast in overlaid multi-coloured gold, fetched £500 at Sotheby's Belgravia on 29th November 1978. This

Figure 4. An 18 carat gold hunting cased keyless lever watch No. 55261 by Jas. Chalmers, Glasgow, 54mm. Sold Sotheby's Belgravia on 6th June 1979 for £160.

Figure 6. A hunting cased keyless lever watch by Appleton, Tracy & Co., with multi-coloured gold overlay, 54mm. Sold by Sotheby's Belgravia on 29th November 1978 for £500.

Figure 7. A gold and enamel hunting cased keyless lever watch by Omega, 51.5mm. The reverse had been poorly re-enamelled and in good condition it would have fetched double the £600 it realised at Sotheby's Belgravia on 29th March 1978.

Figure 5. Brass lever watch "The Dollar Watch", 52mm, which sold for £5 on 1st August at Sotheby's Belgravia. The button is false, and the watch is wound by the folding "key" on the backplate.

style has seen a noticeable increase in price during the last two years.

Enamelled cases have always been popular and, combined with a very ordinary movement, will still fetch high prices. They are often inset with diamonds or pearls and engraved under the enamel (*basse taille*). Many still retain the original enamelled pendant. It is vital to ensure the enamel is not damaged. It is a costly repair that is seldom satisfactory (see figure 7). The quality of engraving varies greatly, but even the mass produced Swiss fob watches of the last quarter of the century are very attractive. These range in price from £50-£100.

The case can be made in virtually any shape or form. Square, triangular or spherical ones are not unusual. There are even those in the form of insects, the wings hinged to reveal the dial (figure 8).

The wrist watch is another very important style and appeared around 1900. Thereafter it gained popularity and contributed to the decline in popularity of the pocket watch.

Figure 8. A diamond, gold and enamel scarab watch with keyless lever movement, 40.5mm long overall, c.1900. Sold by Sotheby's Bond Street on 15th December 1978 for £1,850.

Books Published by the *Antique Collectors' Club* on Painting and Porcelain

(Unless otherwise stated, books measure 11ins. x 8½ins.)

PAINTING

Dictionary of British Watercolour Artists up to 1920 Vol. I — The Text by H.L. Mallalieu. *298 pages. £17.50.*

Dictionary of British Watercolour Artists up to 1920 Vol. II — The Plates by H.L. Mallalieu. *268 pages. 795 b. & w. illus. £17.50.*

Dictionary of British Artists 1880-1940. *567 pages. £22.50.*

Dictionary of British 18th Century Painters *by Ellis Waterhouse. 444 pages. 580 b. & w. illus. 12 col. £29.50.*

Dictionary of Sea Painters by E.H.H. Arichibald. *700 b. & w. illus. 32 col. plates. 169 line drawings. £29.50.*

Dictionary of Victorian Painters, 2nd edition by C. Wood. *11,000 artists. 764 pages. 540 b. & w. illus. £29.50.*

Dictionary of British Book Illustrators and Caricaturists 1800-1914 by Simon Houfe. *520 pages. 330 b. & w. illus. 16 in col. £25.*

Dutch Painters of the 19th Century by Marius. *307 pages. 330 b. & w. illus. 12 in col. Reprinting Spring '82.*

A Dictionary of Contemporary British Artists, 1929 edited by Bernard Dolman. *8¼ ins. x 5½ ins. 561 pages. £14.50.*

20th Century British Marine Painting by Denys Brook-Hart. *381 pages. 254 b. & w. illus. 37 col. £25.*

British 19th Century Marine Painting by Denys Brook-Hart. *370 pages. 206 b. & w. illus. 32 col. Reprinting Spring '82.*

The Williams Family of Painters by Jan Reynolds. *331 pages. 175 b. & w. illus. 5 col. £17.50.*

Collecting Miniatures by Daphne Foskett. *500 pages. 850 b. & w. examples and 150 in col. £25.*

PORCELAIN and CERAMICS

The Price Guide to the Models of W.H. Goss by Roland Ward. *182 pages. 486 b. & w. illus. 4 col. £12.50.*

Flight and Barr Worcester Porcelain by H. Sandon. *245 pages. 190 b. & w. illus. 16 in col. £14.50.*

The Price Guide to Pot-lids and other Underglaze Multicolour Prints on Ware, 2nd edition, by A. Ball. *320 pages. 1,000 b. & w. illus. 16 in col. £17.50.*

Godden's Guide to Mason's China and the Ironstone Wares by Geoffrey A. Godden, F.R.S.A. *316 pages. 362 b. & w. plates. 14 col. plates. £17.50.*

The Price Guide to 19th and 20th Century British Pottery by David Battie and Michael Turner. *244 pages. 600 b. & w. illus. 16 col. pages. £14.50.*

18th Century English Porcelain Figures 1745-1795 by Peter Bradshaw. *328 pages. 200 b. & w. illus. 26 col. £25.*

Collecting Victorian Tiles by Terence A. Lockett. *9¼ ins. x 5½ ins. 235 pages. 468 tiles illus. in b. & w. 10 in col. £9.95.*

The Price Guide to 19th and 20th Century British Porcelain by David Battie and Michael Turner. *8½ ins. x 5½ ins. 486 pages. 480 b. & w. illus. £9.95.*

The Price Guide to 18th Century Pottery by Sally Mount. *8½ ins. x 5½ ins. 425 pages. 398 b. & w. illus. £9.95.*

Caughley and Worcester Porcelains 1775-1800 by Geoffrey Godden. *10¼ ins. x 7¾ ins. 336 pages. 350 b. & w. illus. 10 col. plates. Limited edition reprint of 1,500 copies. £27.50.*

Coalport and Coalbrookdale Porcelains by Geoffrey Godden. *10¼ ins. x 7¾ ins. 310 pages. 257 b. & w. illus. 10 col. plates. Limited edition of 1,500 copies. £27.50*

The Dictionary of Wedgwood by Robin Reilly and George Savage. *414 pages. 580 b. & w. illus. 24 col. pages. £25.*

Figure 1. A novelty inkwell in the form of a tortoise with hinged tortoiseshell back, 8.2cm long, maker's mark of Sampson Mordan of S. Mordan & Co., London, 1881. £320.

A pill or snuff box in the form of a tortoise, 8.8cm long, maker's mark of Jane Brownett of Harris & Brownett, London, 1887. £290.

Gossip on Victorian Silver Knick Knacks

by John Culme

Figure 2. A mussel shell vinaigrette, 4.7cm long, maker's mark of Sampson Mordan of S. Mordan & Co., London, struck with the Patent Office Design Registry mark for 29th February 1876, parcel number 12. £220.

Figure 3. A novelty ash tray, cast, 14.5cm long, maker's mark of Thomas Johnson, London, 1882. £130.

Year after year in the 1870s and '80s the shop of Walter Thornhill & Co., a fancy goods and stationery store in New Bond Street, was filled at Christmas-time with a remarkable variety of gifts, "novelties and specialities". It was an age of silver and silver-mounted trinkets and Thornhill's, an old established firm of retail cutlers and silversmiths, were perhaps the most successful in this line of business. Rivals included Asprey & Co., the only survivor from those days, Jenner & Knewstub and Alfred Clark, all of whom were supplied by the gold and silver workers of Soho and Clerkenwell in London and of Birmingham.

Soho and Birmingham were the traditional centres in England for the manufacture of small goods in the precious metals and where the roles of the jeweller and the goldsmith were often very close. In Birmingham, especially after the introduction of mechanisation and steam power at the end of the 18th century, work was more usually of the mass-produced kind such as we see in the output of the workshops of Samuel Pemberton or Nathaniel Mills, both significant box makers. To collectors and the small-time dealer nowadays the name of Mills is too well known to need introduction, and no wonder since his factory was by far the largest producer of vinaigrettes, snuff boxes and card cases during the middle years of the last century. George Unite, a past apprentice of another Birmingham box maker by the name of Joseph Willmore, eventually succeeded to the Mills workshop and continued to produce wine labels, boxes, chatelaines and other smallwork until well after 1900. Among other Birmingham workers in this field must be mentioned Edward Smith, whose snuff boxes and vinaigrettes were occasionally made in gold, David Pettifer and, at the end of the century, Lawrence Emanuel who diversified into every branch of decorated silver-mounted goods.

While much of the work from Birmingham found a national and an international market, the London workshops, where finer items were made, concentrated on supplying shops such as Thornhill's in the metropolis. The names of these firms of smallworkers were usually unknown to the public of the day because they had no retail outlets of their own. Besides, the retailers who patronised them found it necessary to guard with much secrecy the names of their suppliers for fear of piracy. Eventually this led to the practice of firms like Thornhill's, or Leuchars of Piccadilly, without workshops of their own, registering so-called makers' marks, or indeed actually buying out their suppliers entirely. Thus the present day Asprey's incorporates a number of firms such as Leuchars, who in turn engulfed several other businesses including that of H.W. & L. Dee, one of the finest firms of small gold and silver workers of the 1860s and '70s.

In their day the brothers Dee and their staff of jewellers, silversmiths and designer, Thomas Reeves, could be called upon to make up to order anything from match boxes to elaborate silver-mounted and jewelled scent flasks. In the 1870s the latter were especially popular, usually in the form of a tube with a hinged or screw-on cap at either end for scent and smelling salts. In the more elaborate examples the whole body would be hinged at the centre revealing a hidden vinaigrette. Turquoises and coral or pearl beads were the preferred jewels, and the clear or coloured glass of the body was often etched with anthemions or festoons of flowers for extra richness. Posy holders, too, appeared in a large variety of designs at this time and some of those from Dee were ingeniously fashioned so

Right: Figure 5. A novelty pepper mill in the form of a barrel with two millhorses, 8.5cm high, maker's mark of Louis Dee of H.W. & L. Dee, London, 1880. £190.

Left: Figure 6. The base of a finely engraved snuff box, 8.3cm long, makers' mark of Charles Rawlings & William Summers, London, 1836. £360.

Figure 7. A silver-gilt posy holder, 10.5cm high, maker's mark of Thomas William Dee of T.W. Dee & Son, London, 1866. £140.

that the stem was hinged in three sections to provide folding legs. Again these were often gilt, engraved, enamelled or even set with jewels.

A properly run business supplying these expensive trinkets to the trade could be highly lucrative, much of the profits going to the owners as well as to the middleman like Walter Thornhill. A case in point is that of the Dee family, the eldest of whom, Thomas William Dee, died in 1869 leaving a comfortable estate of nearly £20,000. His younger son, Louis, latterly the most active

member of the family in the firm, died at his house in Hammersmith leaving over £35,000. This was in 1884 shortly before the firm was assigned to Leuchars; their patterns and tools relating to "collar and badge" work, gold and enamelled chains of office and other decorations, had been offered at a nominal fee to J.M. Garrard of R. & S. Garrard & Co. This already well established and prestigious connection with the royal goldsmiths no doubt did much to help the Dee brothers in their success.

The Dees' work, in some respects, may be compared with that of Rawlings & Summers, another firm of goldsmiths who were established in Soho. Here again, the senior partner, Charles Rawlings, carried on a very successful business which enabled him to retire to a house in Cheyne Walk, Chelsea, where he died in 1863 having amassed a fortune of some £40,000. Working from premises in Marlborough Street, Rawlings & Summers specialised in gold and silver snuff boxes, vinaigrettes and wine labels. Much of their work is decorated with finely engraved scrolling foliage incorporating vignettes or exotic birds and there is at least one vesta case, an early example of 1843, engraved with a foolish monkey igniting a cheroot from the light of a smouldering bomb. Rawlings & Summers were among the first of the silversmiths during the middle of the 19th century to produce "novelties", some of which were related to the pleasures of smoking, and several of their designs were protected by the law under the provisions of the Patent Office Design Registry. One of these is a pipe and vesta stand in the form of a

long-haired hound in a begging position holding a top hat between its forepaws.

This type of object in silver, and sometimes silver-mounted glass, increased in popularity throughout the 1860s and '70s until by the 1880s the need for pig-shaped mustard pots or budgerigar-shaped oil and vinegar bottles had developed into a craze. Walter Thornhill & Co. of course were not slow in encouraging this peculiar taste and one could buy silver screw or nail-shaped propelling pencils for a modest price of between 7s.6d. and 21s. On the other hand "Thornhill's potatoe (sic) bowls with & without silver mounts", "an elegant present", could be had for between 15s. and 10gns.

Many of these small items were made for Thornhill's, sometimes under licence, by Sampson Mordan & Co. whose factory was just north of Hatton Garden. This large firm was established around 1813 for the manufacture of pencils. Later they expanded to make inkstands and other items for the desk and later still, in the 1860s and '70s, their range was enlarged to include scent flasks, some gold-mounted, enamelled vesta cases, which today have become a popular collectors' item, wine labels, and mounts for large objects such as claret jugs made in a variety of materials including horn, ivory or glass.

For Thornhill's Mordan's made large numbers of bugle-shaped vinaigrette/scent flasks with or without chased decoration, others in the form of miniature barrels, or vesta and pin boxes shaped as tortoises with real tortoiseshell backs. But Mordan's had a very large market to supply besides Thornhill's, and their work went all over the country and abroad. After the craze for little trifles for the desk and dinner table had subsided in the 1890s, they concentrated on the manufacture of engine-turned cigarette boxes and the like until their closure just before World War II.

Right: Figure 8. A large table snuff box with engraved and applied die-stamped and chased decoration, 13.5cm long, maker's mark of Nathaniel Mills of N. Mills & Son, Birmingham, 1845. £750.

Below: Figure 9. A greyhound scent flask, 7cm high, maker's mark of E.H. Stockwell, London, 1877, struck with the Patent Office Design Registry Mark for 28th November 1877, parcel number 9. £240.

A squirrel pepperette, 7cm high, maker's mark of Thomas Stapleton, London, 1885. £320.

A fish posy vase, 10.8cm long, maker's mark of Jane Brownett of Harris & Brownett, London, 1884. £65.

A pug-dog pepperette, 7cm high, maker's mark of E.H. Stockwell, London, 1877. £260.

The Queen, the lady's newspaper, and various other periodicals did as much to promote the popularity of smallwork in silver as did Thornhill's themselves by continuing reports on visits by their reporters to the shops. Thus in 1876 they were able to declare that "as the trains even of outdoor dresses get longer and longer, a serviceable dress holder becomes more and more indispensable". This neat device, made of engraved silver, was able to grasp the material of the dress without ruining the fabric. Here a note of usefulness was introduced in a trade which dealt almost exclusively in unnecessary trifles. The buying public, for a time at least, needed little persuasion to find owl pepperettes and grizzly bear cigar lighters amusing, especially when they were made with the care and excellent modelling typified by the workmanship of J.B. Hennell's workshop. Later, however, with rising costs and fierce competition from Birmingham, the London specialists relinquished their lead. Imports from Holland and Germany, too, helped to undermine this lead with machine-made toys milled with pretty scenes of naked cherubs and girls in panniers reminiscent of mid-18th century watch cases. Shops like Thornhill's closed or, like Jenner & Knewstub, sold their interest to other companies and a flood of cheaply made nonsense came from Birmingham and Chester, Groningen and Bad Kissingen to be sold throughout the Edwardian period in shops all over London and the provinces.

The present day collector in this field, like any other, should look for the best in workmanship and design. As stressed

in this article, most of the finest work emanated from the now defunct workshops of London, most of whom were operating in the period 1830-1900. Without doubt the best were Rawlings & Summers and H.W. & L. Dee, for general mounted and unmounted smallwork; Thomas Johnson, J.B. Hennell and E.H. Stockwell for special items including animal figures and unusual scent flasks; Edward Beazer for curling tong boxes; and Sampson Mordan & Co. for propelling pencils, mounted and unmounted scent bottles, and vesta cases.

Figure 10. An enamelled silver vesta case, 6cm high, maker's mark of S. Mordan of S. Mordan & Co., London, 1886, Patent Office Design Registry number 28283. £200.

Figure 11. A shaped rectangular card case with a die-stamped and chased view of Warwick Castle, 10.1cm long, maker's mark of Nathaniel Mills of N. Mills & Son, Birmingham, 1843. £250.